RUSSIAN CROSSROADS

YEVGENY PRIMAKOV

Translated by Felix Rosenthal

Russian Crossroads

TOWARD THE NEW MILLENNIUM

YALE UNIVERSITY PRESS   NEW HAVEN & LONDON

Yale University Press gratefully acknowledges the financial support given for this publication by Carlos Bulgheroni. Also published with assistance from the Mary Cady Tew Memorial Fund.

Designed by Rebecca Gibb. Set in FontShop Scala and Scala Sans by Duke & Company.
Printed in the United States of America.

Library of Congress Cataloging-in-Publication Data
Primakov, E. M. (Evgenii Maksimovich)
   Russian crossroads : toward the new millennium / Yevgeny Primakov ; translated by Felix Rosenthal.
      p.   cm.
   Includes bibliographical references and index.
   ISBN 0-300-09792-1 (hardcover : alk. paper)
1. Russia (Federation)—Politics and government—1991–92. 2. Post-communism—Russia (Federation). 3. Primakov, E. M. (Evgenii Maksimovich). I. Title.
   DK510.763.P744 2004
   947.086—dc22

2004008354

A catalogue record for this book is available from the British Library.

The paper in this book meets the guidelines for permanence and durability of the Committee on Production Guidelines for Book Longevity of the Council on Library Resources.

10 9 8 7 6 5 4 3 2 1

CONTENTS

THE MOST mind-numbing terrorist acts in human history were carried out on September 11, 2001. In the aftermath of the attacks in New York and Washington, most of the world responded with an outpouring of sorrow and compassion for the American people and rage for the terrorists who had committed such atrocities. But a shock must be followed by a period of reckoning. Without exaggeration, this period is indispensable for the future of humankind.

The world is facing a new situation in which a self-sustaining autonomous terrorist organization can declare itself a new player in the international arena by committing a great crime. If this danger to all the world's people is to be neutralized, the world's countries must cooperate in reinforcing mechanisms of defense and deterrence.

In the situation in which we now find ourselves, it has become imperative to settle international conflicts without delay, particularly those in the Middle East, which are preparing the ground for the growth of international terrorism. The future development of other regions of the world should be viewed from a new angle as well. Globalization must not continue to widen the gap between the wealthy West and the rest of the world. Preservation of this gap is encouraging the forces that seek not to join the developed countries but to destroy them.

The world community must recognize that under the conditions that now prevail, many of the means and methods of building security that served in the past must be reconsidered. None of us can continue to focus exclusively on our own security and that of our allies, and on establishing regional and global stability. Our main goal must be to develop and adopt reliable methods to oppose international terrorism. To do so effectively, it is imperative that the world's constructive forces unite.

The struggle against terrorism will be ineffective without Russia's participation. A strong Russia, that is. A weak country torn apart by internal conflicts and in possession of a huge nuclear arsenal is unstable and unpredictable. Such a Russia threatens the interests not only of its own people but of the rest of the world.

A strong Russia should not be seen as a threat to world stability. The idea that Russia represents a threat can result only from inertia, from survival of the Cold War mentality, and from underestimation of the changes that have taken place in Russia and are taking place now. Russia must be seen as it actually is if the international community is to seize every opportunity to resolve the issues common to all of us in our turbulent world.

In this book I want to show Russian political and social life as I have known it in my many capacities, from *Pravda* correspondent to head of the government. If it helps to rid American readers of a simplistic or prejudiced perception of Russia, I shall consider my task fulfilled.

It is not a biographical book. But it is not a memoir either, although I took part in many of the events I describe.

It is gratifying to me that the book is being published in the United States. It is very important that we know each other well.

RUSSIAN CROSSROADS

CHAPTER ONE

From Yeltsin to Putin

OPERATION HEIR APPARENT

On December 31, 1999, Boris Yeltsin announced his resignation as president of Russia and named Vladimir Putin as his preferred successor.

The New Year's Eve announcement caught most of us by surprise; certainly it surprised me. Not that Russians in general were unaware of the president's inability to govern: that had been clear since 1996. And not that anyone could seriously believe that Yeltsin's closest allies were withdrawing their support from him, even less that they had come to realize they needed to relinquish their hold on power. Everybody was well aware of Yeltsin's insatiable thirst for power. His lack of concern for his physical condition, weakened by illness and bad habits, had always stood in sharp contrast to his urge to manage, to rule, and to hire and fire top government officials with a stroke of the pen. Yeltsin's self-indulgence was one of the man's primary characteristics; that had been clear long before he became seriously ill. It is unlikely that Yeltsin's inner circle, the so-called Family,[1] realized the hopelessness of his staying in power.

So what was it that encouraged those who arranged Yeltsin's resignation to prompt that surprising move on New Year's Eve? Yeltsin's memoirs, ghost-written by members of that inner circle, stressed that the president himself had conceived the plan in secret and had let nobody know about his intentions for fear of a premature leak. It is possible that the authors of Yeltsin's resignation announcement diverted his attention from the heart of the matter by playing a game of hide-and-seek, fearing Yeltsin might back down at the last moment. The suddenness of the announcement suited the Family, but not because they feared that some forces of any social significance would try to preserve Yeltsin's presidency. The fact that the president's approval rating had fallen close to zero made that scenario out of the question. There were other reasons for the rush.

It was the question of continuity of power that lay behind the New Year's Eve bombshell. Under the current constitution, if Yeltsin resigned before the end of his term, new presidential elections were to be held within three months. To those who hoped to retain their power, it must have seemed too risky to wait until the end of Yeltsin's term. At the same time, moving the elections up gave them an opportunity to build on the success they had underhandedly achieved in the December parliamentary elections, only a few weeks before Yeltsin's resignation. They had managed then to consolidate the administration's leverage in the State Duma, principally by using the so-called administrative factor: they were able to apply pressure to the mass media and to political figures in the constituent states of the Federation to support their candidates, and they applied it heavily.

There was no doubt that the architects of Yeltsin's early resignation wanted to make sure that his successor did not deviate from the course pursued by Yeltsin—that he would continue the policies that had already resulted in their fabulous enrichment and in their increasing influence on state policy, including the appointment of top executives. And of course the successor was expected to ensure reliable security for Yeltsin and the Family, not only his relatives but his cronies as well. Make no mistake: his successor was nominated by a specific group of people with clear-cut objectives.

Who is Vladimir Putin? What role was he to play, the man who occupies the nation's top position not only under the Constitution but also in Russian political reality? Why was he chosen as Yeltsin's successor? These questions overshadowed the emotions aroused by Boris Yeltsin's departure. There was no doubt that by making Putin the country's president the Family intended to co-opt the chief of the Federal Security Service (FSB, successor to the KGB), who was one of the most well informed people in the country. And surely no one would be better able to guarantee the Family's security.

Many people, I among them, were looking for an answer to another question, one that was perhaps even more important for Russia and the rest of the world: whether Putin, if indeed he were elected, would be guided by the same motives that led to his choice as Yeltsin's successor. After all, a president who has achieved his office by popular vote is then free either to follow or to disregard the blueprint provided him when he was nominated.

Vladimir Vladimirovich Putin has held several state and municipal posts, including relatively minor positions in foreign intelligence. As for me, during my tenure as director of the Foreign Intelligence Service I never met him or heard a thing about him. Before his appointment as prime minister (which took many people by surprise), a couple of months before his nomination as Yeltsin's successor, Putin worked in the office of the mayor of St. Petersburg for several years, in the Kremlin administration, and then as director of the Federal Security Service. This career hardly qualified him as a politician.

At least, that was my opinion, and I was not alone. But when we were members of the same cabinet—I was first foreign minister and then prime minister and Putin was FSB director—I found him to be a smart and determined man who kept his word. My conversations with him allowed me to sketch Putin's ideological and political profile. His patriotism was not tainted by chauvinism, he avoided swaying either left or right, and his political sympathies and antipathies were determined by Russia's national interests, as he saw them, naturally. Undoubtedly, that was very encouraging.

I like Putin as an individual. I was very pleased when, after my removal from the position of prime minister, he called me and offered to arrange a meeting for me with the FSB board. When I replied that I would be pleased to go to FSB headquarters, he said no, no, the board members would be pleased to visit me. Indeed, this informal meeting, during which they spoke warmly of me, took place at my dacha. This was a serious matter, and I very much doubt that Putin had cleared his and especially the board's visit to my dacha with anyone.

When he was appointed prime minister, Putin came to help me celebrate my seventieth birthday with a few friends in a rather modest Moscow restaurant. Putin knew I had not invited any of President Yeltsin's closest advisers. (Yeltsin had not yet announced his resignation.) Putin not only attended the party but had some very kind words for me.

All that undoubtedly aroused my sympathy for Putin. I think he appreciated my decision not to run against him in the presidential race. I informed him personally that I would not run. Not that I had any chance of winning;

I had none, because strings were pulled by those who controlled the mass media. Besides, Putin was gaining in popularity, especially after he shouldered the responsibility for resolute action against the Chechen terrorists and separatists. But my participation in the presidential race might have necessitated a run-off election. As it was, Putin won in the first round.

In short, we have developed stable and good relations, which enabled me to meet with Putin and speak to him on the phone after he was elected president. Naturally, I wanted to know what course he intended to pursue. I have to admit that the dialogue was not always lively. I probably did most of the talking, especially at the beginning, but his remarks, sparse though they were, led me to conclude that Putin desired changes and undoubtedly realized the necessity for them.

The main issue, however, remained: could Putin distance himself from those who had originally promoted him? I rejected media speculations about Putin's bondage to the "oligarchs."[2] I have no doubt Putin is an honest and decent man. But would his very decency make him keep promises he may have made to the people who nominated him? As far as I can tell, with the passage of time those concerns have lost their relevance.

In typical fashion, the Russian media speculated as to whether Putin would be relying on his old St. Petersburg colleagues or the former KGB community. Analysis of Putin's appointments suggested he favored both groups. A joke popular at the time is about a passenger on an overcrowded bus who asks the man pressing against him, "Excuse me, are you from Petersburg?" The man says no. "Are you from the FSB, then?" When the man again says no, the passenger barks at him, "Get off my foot, you bastard!"

My own interpretation of Putin's appointments is that the new president, not having a team of his own and intending from the beginning to push the Family aside gradually, decided to rely on people he knew personally. In my opinion, however, the predominance of St. Petersburg politicians and intelligence officers among his new appointees is a temporary expedient. In any case, nobody, not even his opponents, dared to use his meetings with Yeltsin on national holidays to accuse him of continuing to rely on the Family.

BREAKING THE GENETIC LINK

My attitude toward Putin began to take firmer shape when I analyzed his practical course, which differed markedly from that of his predecessor. First, he strengthened the executive power from top to bottom. Quite obviously, this idea took strong hold of the new president's mind because in his earlier official positions he had become convinced that the authoritarian rule of many governors and leaders of the national republics that make up the Russian Federation posed a real threat to Russia's territorial integrity. Events in Chechnya must have added fuel to the fire. As prime minister Putin was closely associated with a determined struggle in 1999 against militant Chechen separatists, who by that time had spread the "Chechen experience" over Dagestan and Ingushetia and had launched terrorist attacks on Russian territory.

The means to build the vertical line of executive power to bind together all of Russia's territorial units into a single federal state were open to debate. But it was evident that Putin was not just thinking about this issue but taking steps to resolve it by limiting the governors' field of action, so that they would no longer be so free to engage in unconstitutional and illegitimate activities. It was no secret to most people that the objective of the law "On the Reform of the Federation Council," introduced by Putin in the Duma and passed with few amendments, was to replace the governors with representatives in the upper chamber of the Russian Parliament. Thus the governors lost the immunity that had been guaranteed them earlier.

Although this course of action took Putin far from the path followed by Yeltsin, by itself it could hardly be considered a direct threat to the Family's interests and status. But another of Putin's moves did directly affect its immediate interests. Realizing the importance of the mass media, especially the electronic media, Putin took steps to limit the influence of the oligarchs, who under Yeltsin had managed to establish control over many television channels and newspapers.

Readers in the West probably have very incomplete understanding of the situation in Russia at that time. For instance, a person who owned only a negligible number of shares in a television station, newspaper, or magazine but had a great deal of money would pay large sums to the managers, editors, and reporters and would then be in a position to call them on his cell phone and tell them what to say during a talk show or what to write in a story; he decided who would be smeared and who promoted. This practice was common under Yeltsin. Family members were involved in it. Putin came out openly against it.

He was not deterred by the campaign in defense of "freedom of the press" and against "dictator Putin" launched by the oligarchs when they found themselves losing their stranglehold on the mass media. This campaign, which unfortunately found support in the West, was deliberately misleading; freedom of the press was never under attack in Russia. One has only to consider the program content of channel NTV since it ceased to belong to Vladimir Gusinsky. It is clear that NTV's programs contain even more direct and indirect criticism of the Russian leadership now than they did when Gusinsky was calling the shots.

One can argue about the legal nicety of the methods used to cleanse the electronic media of the oligarchs' control, but eliminating freedom of the press was by no means the ultimate goal. Putin was simply determined to free the Russian mass media, especially the electronic media, from their unrestrained pursuit of the oligarchs' private ends, which went against both Russian social tradition and ethics. And unlikely as some people may find it, he wanted Russian broadcasters to follow the best examples of Western television. Putin knew how closely the oligarchs were connected to the Family and how they were using the powerful media machine to manipulate public opinion during the political struggles of the second half of the 1990s.

Putin's views on many of Russia's developmental problems, especially after the economy was freed from tight central control and integrated with the world economy, as well as his views on other issues, emerged during long conversations in Sochi with a group of leading scientists of the Russian Academy of Sciences in the summer of 2000. When I proposed such a meeting to Putin, I urged him to let the suggestion come from him, but in his note to Yury Osipov, president of the Russian Academy of Sciences, Vladimir Vladimirovich said the idea was mine. His only contribution, he said, was to pick Sochi as the meeting place, because a vacation resort would permit uninterrupted time for frank discussions. Unlike his predecessor—and this is very important—Putin is not eager to take credit for somebody else's ideas, even in the interests of public relations. I had observed this characteristic of Putin as a politician on earlier occasions; in his relations with other people he is a decent man.

Here are some of the ideas that the president either voiced or unconditionally approved: Russia is through with isolationism forever. Not only is it part of the world economy but it feels itself increasingly at home there. But what are the prospects for our country in this respect? It must be admitted that if the tendencies that came to the fore at the end of the twentieth century were to carry over into the next century, the rift between Russia and the economically developed countries could widen. And the point is not to turn Russia into a supplier of natural resources for the West. Inadequate attention to exploration for natural resources and to modernization of extraction processes may sharply reduce Russia's competitiveness in this area very quickly. Without new approaches in economic policy, Russia's industry, with its obsolete framework, both moral and physical, will also fall into hard times.

Putin listened attentively to the scientists who took part in the meeting and fully agreed with their conclusion that Russia's future depended heavily on scientific and technological breakthroughs and on its ability to participate actively in the international project of adopting innovative technologies. Putin's realism and his lack of adventurism were made clear when he agreed that Russia was not yet ready for a breakthrough across the board. Therefore, the scientists outlined seven or eight so-called critical technologies in which Russia could succeed because it had some reserves there, scientific staff (despite a catastrophic brain drain), and the potential for innovation. The president also agreed that this objective could be reached only if the state supervised and financed the appropriate programs.

In the course of the meeting Putin spoke once again of the need for tougher measures against those who broke the law and used their positions for purposes that had nothing in common with the interests of the general population; he also spoke about the need to keep corruption in check. Corruption comes up often in the president's speeches and he is taking practical steps to reduce it.

Putin's comments and statements have outlined his political course, but it must be admitted that many of his proposals have been implemented inefficiently and inconsistently. Apparently one of the main reasons is that the people who surround Putin lack professionalism, even those who sincerely wish to advance the course he has chosen.

Another reason is that a group of people who are trying to discredit Putin often manage to make good ideas ineffective and practical steps counterproductive. For instance, when the positions of presidential representatives were introduced in the regions and the country was divided into seven territories, the move was correctly perceived as strengthening the influence of the Center. But the functions of the "supergovernors" were never clearly defined. As it turned out, some of Putin's inherited staff applied a brake to the process. Meanwhile some of Putin's regional representatives were surrounding themselves with layers of bureaucrats and setting themselves up as provincial rulers. Their pretensions antagonized the governors, not only the dishonest ones but also those who were known to be doing a good job.

Or take the government's proposals for the state budgets for 2001, 2002, and 2003. The government tended to concentrate financial resources in the Center and then distribute them among the regions in the form of transfers and subsidies, which were used mostly for consumption. This practice contradicted the idea of consolidating Russia's economy as a whole. Putin brought it up at one of his meetings with the leaders of parliamentary blocs. These and other provisions of the proposed budgets were somewhat corrected during the Duma hearings. But such trends in budgetary policy testified to the fact that during his first year in office the president was not in a position to exercise full control over the government, which often concentrated on short-term gains.

When Putin proposed new Russian state symbols—they had not yet been formally adopted—and restoration of the old Soviet national anthem, of course with a few changes in the words, a big campaign was launched against his proposal. Prominent figures were drawn into it—even Yeltsin! —and the Russian patriarch's position was grossly distorted. They ignored the fact that it was Putin who proposed to replace the red Soviet flag with the prerevolutionary tricolor, and the hammer and sickle with the Russian two-headed eagle.

In my opinion, these events reflect deliberate attempts by certain individuals to tell Putin in effect: "Rely on us, as Yeltsin did, because we're the only ones you can count on." Theirs is a mixed team but they have a common goal—to stop Putin.

Some apparatchiks in Putin's administration are trying to please the new leader and at the same time to serve the interests of various oligarchs. At times the two aims have collided. On October 14, 2000, an open letter to the president signed by 102 State Duma deputies was published in the press. Headed "Curb the Oil Predators," it said, among other things, that the oil barons were exploiting the oil fields in ways that harmed the environment and were evading taxes, raising fuel prices excessively in the domestic market, and taking their profits out of the country. Even deputies considered pro-Kremlin were among the signatories. The bureaucrats knocked themselves out trying to counter the negative impact of the "thoughtless" letter. A week after it was published, their efforts seemed to have succeeded. The Interfax news agency reported that sixty members of the pro-Kremlin Unity group were withdrawing their signatures. But suddenly the situation took a new turn, and government officials had a bigger headache. The Duma received Putin's answer to the open letter: "The problem raised by the deputies is quite correct." Furthermore, addressing the tax minister and the head of the Federal Tax Police, the president added, "Your inactivity is surprising."

This episode is indicative of two things: it exposes both the nature of the apparatchiks working with Putin and the problems the president himself is facing. But it is impossible to replace the whole staff all at once.

I am confident that the genetic links between Putin and Yeltsin and his people will inevitably be broken, and the process is under way. A new balance of power in the country's leadership has also become evident. The oligarch Berezovsky, who under Yeltsin attempted to play the part of gray eminence, and not unsuccessfully, has left the country and declared his strong opposition to Putin. I am not at all convinced that Putin is supported, especially actively, by other members of the Family who did not openly follow Berezovsky's example. For the time being they are lying low.

I am impressed by many of the things that Putin is doing. He is undoubtedly a capable and sharp individual who can address any audience; he is composed and at the same time strong-willed. Will these qualities be in evidence when he begins to form a team of his own and in the process starts to force some oligarchs out of their cushy positions, and their corrupt henchmen with them? This question was worrying Russians as this book was being written.

WHAT CHOICE IS RUSSIA FACING?

Many people in Western countries are asking themselves: Will the new course, so different from the one the country followed under Putin's predecessor, lead Russia backward, away from the market economy and from democratic reforms as well as from its positive role in the international arena? I think these concerns are caused by the difficulty of understanding the events that have been taking place in our country.

Russia's development in the 1990s has had one result that can't be denied: such a vast and varied potential for change has been accumulated that it precludes a return to the Soviet model of governing the economy, the state, and the society as well as a return to Soviet-style foreign policy.

At the same time, the road covered by Russia in the 1990s has proved to be too contradictory, the dynamics of change poorly thought out and impetuous, and the consequences inadequately analyzed. As a result, having entered the twenty-first century, Russia is facing a choice once again. What is this choice? Is it:

- Between civilized market relations and the domination of omnipotent monopolies using those relations to the detriment not only of the government but also of small and mid-sized businesses?
- Between a socially oriented mixed economy and a system with a growing number of citizens living below the poverty line?
- Between laws binding on all and pervasive lawlessness and corruption?
- Between public order that ensures the people's security and leniency in suppressing organized crime with tentacles that reach into some law enforcement agencies?
- Between a strengthened federalism and the separatist aspirations that have emerged in some regions?
- Between democracy and chaos?
- Between strengthening the state's role under society's effective control and dictatorship?
- Between protecting the nation's interests without confrontation with foreign states and seeking membership in the "club of civilized nations" at any cost, totally submitting to the United States in policy matters?

It is perfectly clear to me that Putin is not just pondering all those issues, he is making his choices in favor of the civilized market, of enforcement of law binding on all, and of a resolute policy to preserve Russia's territorial integrity, stability, and security. And all of that without introducing dictatorial rule.

Of course, it is difficult to follow this road in Russia with its painful history, especially when the bad mistakes of the 1990s are taken into account. Putin is not immune to mistakes, either. Sometimes he will have to be firm, but I do not believe he will resort to dictatorial methods. Putin's opponents and ill-wishers in Russia are beginning to accuse him of authoritarian rule. These accusations are picked up in the West, often without factual evidence. And I cannot help marveling at the choice of the Russian "experts" referred to in the U.S. media when conclusions are drawn about various events in Russia. As a rule these are highly biased individuals widely known to be anti-Putin or incompetent upstarts who are completely unknown in Russia.

It is obvious that Western politicians and the Western public have no way of judging Putin without knowledge of his world outlook, which underlies the basic principles of his foreign policy and which will inevitably determine Russia's place and role in the modern world.

When Putin was named Yeltsin's successor, Yeltsin's admirers in the West probably believed Putin would follow in his footsteps and were happy to think so. But they were wrong. They were concerned about his first visits abroad as president, when he not only toured Europe but also went to China, North Korea, India, Mongolia, and Cuba. His independence became clear in his discussions with Western leaders. However, it was not the posture of a man trying to dominate the others or, still worse, to provoke a confrontation. Some foreigners who spoke with Putin and whom I also had a chance to meet told me they were surprised to discover a newly elected president who approached complex international issues professionally and was open-minded and predictable.

But is Putin's desire to protect Russia's national interests in conflict with this image? Not at all. I am positive that the toughness he shows in defending Russia's interests does not imply confrontation. Moreover, my discussions with Putin have convinced me that he does not want the steps he has taken to consolidate the Russian state and diversify Russia's foreign policy or his statements about the need to defend Russia's national interest to be interpreted as hostile to the United States.

He fully appreciates the special role of the United States in the modern world and is keeping a close eye on the development of Russian-American relations. At the same time, Putin is doing a great deal to advance Russia's relations with the E.C., China, India, the Arab world, and Latin America. I don't think he can be expected to sacrifice Russia's ties with those countries to advance its relationship with the United States or vice versa.

I would like to single out other features of the president's thinking on foreign policy. Without doubt he considers his top priority to be the preservation and strengthening of the Commonwealth of Independent States, those states that emerged in the territory of the former Soviet Union; but at the same time it is highly unlikely that Putin would overlook Russia's interests in order to resolve CIS problems at any cost. Putin's prudence, realism, and pragmatism are most clearly demonstrated here.

And not only here. For instance, his openly negative reaction to the statement of the Russian finance minister, supported by many Russians, regarding unilateral "postponement" of Soviet debt payments to the Paris Club is well known. At Putin's urgent request, this extremely unsound statement was immediately retracted.

Putin took a firm position on the barbaric acts of terrorists in New York and Washington on September 11, 2001. He was the first of the world leaders not only to express his sympathy to the American people but to declare Russia's readiness to assist the United States in its fight against terrorism. He followed that statement by concrete steps to support the American operation in Afghanistan, including approval of the decision by the former Central Asian republics of the USSR to offer their territories to the American military, even though this measure was criticized in Russia. Putin demonstrated that he is not afraid to go against the current when he knows he is right. Putin's firm stance on the matter turned the tide.

Putin's approach to the settlement of the Middle East crisis is further evidence of his character as a politician, demonstrating balance and restraint. Here is one example: In October 2000 I visited Penza with other members of the parliamentary alliance Fatherland–All Russia. The president called me there to say he intended to do his best to stop the bloody Arab–Israeli clashes and therefore was going to take part in the conference in Sharm al-Sheikh, in Egypt. At his initiative the Russian Ministry of Foreign Affairs issued a statement announcing our country's readiness to be represented at Sharm al-Sheikh on the same basis as the other countries. In addition to the leaders of Palestine and Israel, the conference was to be attended by Presidents Bill Clinton of the United States and Hosni Mubarak of Egypt, U.N. General Secretary Kofi Annan, and Javier Solana, executive secretary of the European Union. No invitation arrived for Putin.

Later the Americans privately blamed the Israelis, the Israelis blamed the Americans, and the foreign minister of Egypt apologized and said that his country only provided the site for the meeting. Despite all that, Putin gave instructions not to overdramatize the situation or to use it to stir up passions. He stressed Russia's continued readiness to use its influence and experience in the effort to get the peace process going again.

Also typical is Putin's reaction to the election of Vojislav Kostunica as president of Yugoslavia. A firm statement recognizing him as president was accompanied by a meeting between the Russian foreign minister, Igor Ivanov, with Slobodan Milosevic in Belgrade in the hope of preventing bloodshed. Putin urged Milosevic to accept the popular choice, and he did.

Putin's appreciation of the problems, his aversion to posturing, and his avoidance of overfamiliarity with his foreign colleagues make it clear that he is by no means an extension of Yeltsin. To my mind, Russia's current president is a much better and more predictable partner for foreign politicians.

CHAPTER TWO

Looking Back

DISSIDENTS WITHIN THE SYSTEM

GETTING RID OF IDEOLOGICAL SHACKLES

So now it's not Yeltsin, it's Putin. And we're discussing issues that not so long ago we couldn't even think about. It's hard to believe history could have shaken Russia apart so quickly. I'd like to look back and tell about developments that few people are aware of but that are important for understanding the evolution of Russian life. Besides, I witnessed some of these events and took part in others.

Much has been written, here and abroad, about the dissidents who shook the Soviet system apart. Their names are widely known: Andrei Sakharov, Aleksandr Solzhenitsyn, Mstislav Rostropovich. . . . But they had never been part of the system. They criticized the system, struggled with it, and sought to destroy it. But they were doing so from outside it, even when they were still living in the USSR. Although these people certainly did a lot, their movement would not have succeeded if awareness of the need for radical social reform had been maturing only outside rather than also inside the system.

Although they are seldom mentioned, there were other people, some top officials among them, and scientific institutions and certain newspapers and journals that stood up not only against the criminal practice of mass repressions but also against the prevailing ideological dogmas and the ridiculous and anachronistic official theories. Their activities helped bring about radical and profound changes in Soviet society.

As a rule, these changes are associated primarily with Gorbachev's perestroika in the second half of the 1980s. But these people and institutions had tried to change the situation in the USSR and to overhaul its official ideology much earlier; they laid the groundwork for the changes that eventually came.

The activities of the so-called inside dissidents took two paths, one branching off from the other. The first, which followed the Twentieth Congress of the Communist Party of the Soviet Union (CPSU), tried to convince the Soviet people that Stalin had distorted Lenin, that the system Stalin created contradicted Lenin's ideals, thoughts, and directives. The main emphasis was on Stalin's repressions, which cost millions of innocent lives, and on his barbaric methods of collectivization, which destroyed the peasantry. But the critics did not stop there. They began to question the very principles that underlay the Soviet government and the Communist Party.

Back in the early 1960s, long before perestroika, Academician Aleksei Matveevich Rumyantsev, the editor in chief of *Pravda,* where I was working at the time, wrote an article on the need to return to Leninist principles, intending to publish it on May 5, Soviet Press Day. When Party factions had been banned, he wrote, debates had ceased. So Lenin proposed to fill the vacuum by forming two special political centers: a committee of the Communist Party—the Central Committee—and that committee's newspapers and journals. In this situation, the Party's principal newspaper was called upon to criticize not only the lower-level party organizations but also the Party committee that published it. Since *Pravda* was the organ of the Central Committee of the CPSU, Rumyantsev held, the paper had the right to criticize the Central Committee and even the Politburo. It was a dangerous heresy in those days.

A deputy chief of the Propaganda Department of the Central Committee called on Rumyantsev and suggested on behalf of Mikhail Suslov, the chief Party ideologist at the time, that the essential part of the article be deleted. Rumyantsev refused point-blank and simply withdrew the article from publication. I was on duty at the printing plant that night, and I remember how frantically we tried to find other material to fill the resulting void.

But Rumyantsev was not just an ordinary Party member. That was why he could challenge the omnipotent Suslov.

Gradually the ideology underlying the existing system was being eroded from another direction. This criticism was not aimed at "Stalin's apostasy" alone, but recognized in various ways that the dogmas of Marxism-Leninism were in contradiction with reality.

Once again Rumyantsev stirred the hornet's nest when he ran two long essays on the intelligentsia. He rejected the central role assigned to the proletariat by Marxism and showed that the true leading role was played by the intelligentsia. The usual practice at the time was for the proofs of such stories to be sent to the Politburo members for their comments. Comments came from one of the general secretary's assistants. In a memo to the Central Committee Aleksei Matveevich replied that since he was a member of an elected committee, he was not going to be corrected by a Party bureaucrat. The essays were published, but he was not absolved. Sometime later Rumyantsev was transferred to the Academy of Sciences and a new editor came to *Pravda*.

At that time we lived in the same apartment house and often took long walks together in the evening. I spent many hours talking to this most honest, frank, and somewhat conservative person, whom I respected and liked.

Rumyantsev became an inside dissident when he was editing the journal *Problems of Peace and Socialism*, established by the Central Committee of the CPSU in Prague. Its editorial board included representatives of several Communist parties. In time the journal developed into the Party's own center of dissent.

A group of talented people who worked at the journal later advanced to top positions in the Foreign Relations Department and the Department of Socialist Countries of the CPSU Central Committee in the 1970s and 1980s. Their activity, slow, irresolute, and rather inconsistent though it was (it could not have been otherwise at the time), was helping the Party gain a realistic appreciation of the international situation, as opposed to its bookish and dogmatic Marxist interpretation. Their role in that process cannot be overestimated.

It is indicative that Yury Andropov, general secretary of the Central Committee, evolved in the same direction after his move from the post of ambassador to Hungary. He surrounded himself with gifted people, most of whom came from the journal *Problems of Peace and Socialism* and worked as his consultants. One of them, Nikolai Shishlin, told me that at first Andropov was often irritated by the tenor of their conversations, but later he couldn't get enough of those frank and relatively intense insider discussions. Among the party intellectuals who worked for Andropov at that time were Georgy Arbatov, Fyodor Burlatsky, and Aleksandr Bovin.

The Institute of World Economy and International Relations (IMEMO), where I worked on three occasions, played an important role in the attempts to overcome the dogmatic thinking imposed by the official ideology. My first encounter with IMEMO took place in 1962, when I was transferred from the Foreign Department of the State TV and Radio Committee (Gosteleradio) to *Pravda*. This transfer wasn't my own idea. Nikita S. Khrushchev promised the newly appointed head of Gosteleradio that he would support him by sending him new journalists. I had a fairly good record then. In 1956, when I turned 26, I was put in charge of broadcasting to the Arab countries, and after structural reorganization I became the deputy editor of the entire Foreign Department. But I felt in my bones that the head of the Central Committee division in charge of radio disliked me. Perhaps he didn't like the way I spoke at Party meetings. Whatever the reason, after I accompanied Khrushchev on his trip to Albania in 1958, I was denied the right to travel abroad for several years. I wasn't even allowed out of the country as a tourist. It was at that time that rumors of my "secret Jewish origin" began to spread. According to that story, my real name was Kirshenblat. Actually Kirshenblat was the name of my aunt's husband, a well-known doctor whom I loved very much. Later I learned that in other files I was called Finkelshtein. In this case I was completely at a loss—where did that come from?

Anti-Semitism has always been an instrument of persecution for dim-witted Party officials. I never knew my father and have always borne my mother's name, Primakov. A romantic story is connected with my maternal grandmother, who was Jewish. A headstrong girl, she defied her father, a mill owner, and married a common worker, who was Russian. The Primakov name comes from him. Later they moved to Tiflis, and her husband, my grandfather, who worked as a road-building contractor in Turkey, died in a fight with some Kurdish lowlifes. My sister is the only other survivor in our large family. Some died of disease, others were killed in the Russo-Japanese war, and my mother's last brother was executed in 1937.

Neither chauvinism nor nationalism has ever been part of my makeup. I still don't think God chose one particular nation over the others. He chose all of us and created us in his own image and likeness. . . .

At that time I was introduced to the deputy editor of *Pravda*, Nikolai Inozemtsev, who was responsible for the paper's international coverage. It was he that invited me to join *Pravda* as a correspondent in the Asia and Africa Department. I told Inozemtsev I was in some sort of trouble because I was not being allowed to travel abroad. Nikolai Nikolaevich summoned the head of the Personnel Department and told him in my presence: "Apply to the appropriate organs for permission to use Primakov as *Pravda*'s special correspondent in one of the capitalist countries." I realized that I would be subjected to a most thorough check, and that was fine by me.

It took some time to complete the security check. Assuming that the Gosteleradio management might be displeased to hear I was leaving, as indeed it was, Inozemtsev suggested that meanwhile I apply for a senior fellowship at IMEMO (by that time I had acquired a master's degree in economics).

My first four-month tenure at IMEMO ended after a nighttime phone call from *Pravda*'s editor in chief, Pavel Satyukov. I was told he was waiting for me and that a car had been sent for me.

"When can you start?" asked Satyukov. After we left the Chief's office (to subordinates, the top editor was the Chief), Inozemtsev told me the "appropriate organs" had advised him there were no objections to my traveling abroad as a *Pravda* correspondent.

"As for that character from the Central Committee, *Pravda* is beyond his reach," added Nikolai Nikolaevich with a smile.

My second stint at IMEMO occurred when I managed to defend my doctoral dissertation while I was working as *Pravda*'s Middle East correspondent. I received an invitation from Inozemtsev, who had been appointed director of IMEMO, to join the institute as his first deputy. A similar offer came from Georgy Arbatov, who became the head of the new Institute of the U.S.A. and Canada (ISKAN), which branched off from IMEMO. I decided to join IMEMO.

At that time Inozemtsev and Arbatov worked closely with the general secretary of the Central Committee, Leonid I. Brezhnev, and took part in the meetings of a group that usually gathered at a dacha near Moscow to prepare materials for the plenums, the Party congresses, and Brezhnev's speeches. There was no unity among the authors of these documents. The "progressives," who were promoting the idea of departing from the most blatantly lifeless dogmas and coming closer to grasping the real state of domestic and foreign affairs, were opposed by an equally strong group. Typically, each group developed contacts among the Party's top leadership. Inozemtsev, for instance, was enthusiastically telling me even then how Mikhail Gorbachev, then a secretary of the Central Committee, reacted when some Politburo members wanted to drop a reference to the need to give collective farms more economic independence from a speech that was being prepared for the general secretary.

"'If they don't accept it,'" Inozemtsev quoted Gorbachev with delight, "'people will solve this problem themselves.'"

I realized that the discussions in these work groups were quite serious and that they provided much room for fresh ideas. But Brezhnev, who had intended to carry out significant Party and social reforms, according to Inozemtsev, changed radically after 1968. He was very frightened by the Prague Spring, and then Brezhnev's illness and senility took their toll.

In 1977 I was appointed director of the Institute of Oriental Studies, an important academic institution as large as IMEMO. My third tenure at IMEMO began in 1985, when I replaced its director, Aleksandr Yakovlev, whom Gorbachev appointed to head the Central Committee's propaganda department.

IMEMO was a place that generated new ideas, new approaches, and new attitudes toward world developments. Besides, it held a special place among academic social-scientific institutions because of its practical orientation and its closeness to the organizations that charted the country's political course. Yakovlev was the one who lobbied for my appointment to head IMEMO. At first Gorbachev hesitated, but when Yakovlev persisted, he finally agreed.

IMEMO was established after the 20th Party Congress, during the "Khrushchev thaw." Its first director, Academician A. A. Arzumanyan, deserves credit for opening IMEMO's doors to a number of brilliant scientists, including some with "blemished" biographies. More important, he was responsible for the atmosphere of creative inquiry there. The fact that he and Anastas Mikoyan were married to sisters helped him considerably in the 1950s and 1960s and prevented the Party reactionaries from interfering with the institute's development as an innovative and creative organization.

Arzumanyan hated Stalin and made no bones about it. But not many people went along with this attitude. One should not underestimate the depth and breadth of pro-Stalin sentiment throughout the society, especially after the war. Only a few disagreed. My mother, Ana Yakovlevna, was one of them. After all her relatives and friends had fallen victim to the purges of 1937, she lived in seclusion and worked as a doctor at a textile mill in Tbilisi for the last thirty-five years of her life.

I remember a vacation from school when I went to Tbilisi in the early

1950s. I began talking with my mother about Stalin. I admit I was shocked to hear her call Stalin a "bastard and a primitive murderer." I exploded. "How dare you say that? Have you read anything written by this 'primitive' man?" I was stunned by my mother's calm reply: "And I won't. Go and inform on me, he likes that." I felt cold sweat break out all over me and I never brought up the subject with my mother again.

After the 20th Party Congress, attitudes toward Stalin began to change radically. And I can assure you that the thoughts he arouses in most Russians today are far from worshipful.

IMEMO truly blossomed when Academician Nikolai Nikolaevich Inozemtsev headed it. Apart from our working relationship, we were friends, and more important, we trusted each other. Undeniably he was an outstanding man, educated, profound, intelligent, and brave; he served as an artillery officer during World War II and was awarded several military medals. At the same time he was very vulnerable, especially when he had to counter vicious attacks by jealous enemies.

From today's vantage point you almost have to laugh when you think about the kinds of ideas we had to fight for against the resistance of (to put it mildly) "conservative elements." But it wasn't at all funny at the time. Take this ridiculous case: In the 1970s IMEMO was deeply involved in long-term projections of the world economy, and our journal was publishing various scenarios. One of our readers, a retired NKVD general, complained to the Central Committee that all those scenarios, with their projections to the year 2000, showed the capitalist world as "not yet sent to the dustbin of history." We were accused of revisionism and had to write an explanatory note for the Central Committee's science department.

And the energy that was wasted to establish that, contrary to the conclusions of the Marxist-Leninist classics, certain principles of production were common to both socialist and capitalist societies! But the opponents of this obvious proposition were shutting the door firmly against the use of any Western experience in our country.

This useful experience was described in many memos addressed to the country's leadership. Under Brezhnev, IMEMO supplied these memos generously to various work groups, and when Gorbachev came to power they managed to make their way up to the top. During the perestroika years Nikolai Ivanovich Ryzhkov, then chairman of the Council of Ministers, convened a large conference of industrial managers and scientists to discuss the key issues of Russian machine building. At IMEMO we prepared for this meeting by thoroughly studying the experience of Sweden and West Germany in this respect. We came to the Kremlin meeting fully armed with a plan for establishing four scientific and production companies and described their structure in detail. Back then we could talk about reforms only within the framework of state ownership. And to everybody's surprise, we explained that all four companies would produce the same product; that would lead to competition. After our presentation, the minister in charge of the automotive industry addressed the chairman: "I guarantee a breakthrough in ball-bearing production by different means. I need another deputy minister."

Smart man that he was, Nikolai Ivanovich called a break and told the minister he was "totally unprepared for the meeting." After that we were never invited to the Kremlin to discuss the subject. . . .

At dinner at Inozemtsev's home one evening during Brezhnev's time he appeared very excited: for the first time, he said, he was to address a plenary meeting of the Central Committee, of which he was a candidate (associate) member. From the plenum's podium Inozemtsev objected to the monopoly on foreign trade, not even by the state but rather, as he rightly put it, by the Ministry of Foreign Trade of the USSR. The second subject of his speech was the need for concentrated effort to guarantee the best results in the key areas of science and technology. Everything was going well until Academician Inozemtsev cited capitalist Japan as an example. Nikolai Nikolaevich was very upset when he learned about a remark made by one of the leaders after his speech: "Don't you see, he's trying to teach us!" A permanent assistant to several general secretaries, A. M. Aleksandrov-Agentov, who was known for his sarcasm and sharp tongue, told Inozemtsev: "After your speech it's clear that we're facing a dilemma—we must either expel the intelligentsia from the Central Committee or make the committee intelligent."

IMEMO got into a lot of trouble trying to prove that capitalism was subject to change. The conservatives, who lorded it over such CPSU Central Committee departments as those for science and propaganda, were hostile to the perfectly obvious arguments advanced by representatives of IMEMO and other institutions, such as the ability of modern capitalism to achieve significant successes in economic regulation at the micro and macro levels.

Now it seems rather funny, but IMEMO was proud of being the first to openly assert the "irreversible and objective nature" of the economic integration of Western Europe.

And how about IMEMO's criticism of the postulate, good for all time, that the working class would inevitably be reduced to dire poverty under capitalism? But from that postulate followed the inevitability of the revolution that was to overthrow the capitalist system everywhere.

Perhaps the main obstacle that prevented us from seeing the true nature of the life around us was the rejection of the theory of convergence, or the impact that socialism and capitalism have on each other. But a number of papers, some written by members of the IMEMO staff, upheld the idea that socialism was compatible with the market and market relations. Life itself led to this conclusion.

Vivid examples confirmed the convergence idea. In the mid-1970s I met Wassily Leontief, one of the top American economists, who received world-wide recognition for his development of linear programming and its introduction into the U.S. economy. In the 1920s Leontief had worked for Gosplan in Moscow. When he was sent to Berlin as a Soviet trade representative, he defected and then settled in the United States. There he developed his theory, in which he ingeniously and cleverly integrated some of his Gosplan skills and ideas.

In the 1970s Leontief visited IMEMO, and Inozemtsev invited him to have dinner at his home. Nikolai Nikolaevich had recently moved into a splendid apartment in the building that had originally been intended for the Politburo members; at the last moment they refused to move in because they didn't want to live in the same building, so this special apartment house was given to the Academy of Sciences, which distributed the apartments among its members. Leontief examined the numerous nooks and crannies —the library, the winter garden, the cloakroom, the service room, the halls— and squinting at his host he asked, "Nikolai Nikolaevich, come to think of it, maybe I shouldn't have left here?"

It was hard to imagine that the old guard would step aside to make way for those who were ready to change the system from within. IMEMO's opponents began attacking Inozemtsev. By that time I had moved to the Institute of Oriental Studies, but of course I was concerned about my friends. IMEMO's enemies prepared to take advantage of the arrest of two young institute staffers on charges that they were working for Western intelligence; later the charges were dropped and they were released with apologies. Then followed reports on Inozemtsev himself. Nikolai Grishin, secretary of the Moscow Party Committee, and the Central Committee's science department were actively involved in this campaign. Nikolai Nikolaevich gave me the details when I visited him at the hospital on Michurinsky Prospekt.[1] He was in very bad shape.

Everyone close to him suggested he should see Brezhnev, but he flatly refused. Then Arbatov and Bovin did it for him. In their presence Brezhnev summoned Grishin, who headed the commission formed to investigate the "IMEMO affair." When he asked Grishin what was going on with Inozemtsev and his institute, Grishin, frightened, blurted, "I don't know anything about it, Leonid Ilich, I'll look into it right away." That put an end to the open attacks. The enemies of change lay low. . . .

I should point out that when the "period of stagnation" was at its peak, the USSR Academy of Sciences was a real island of freethinking. The paradox was that most of the physical scientists, who were in the majority at the academy, were directly or indirectly connected to the defense industry. One would think that this environment would be the least auspicious for political protest, that it would encourage compliance with the orders from above. But the reality proved otherwise. I was elected an associate member of the Academy of Sciences in 1974 and acquired full membership in 1979. Of course I attended all the general meetings and witnessed many events that were not typical of those times. I remember the great lengths to which the academy hierarchs went to overcome the resistance to their efforts to elect to full membership Sergei Trapesnikov, head of the Central Committee's science department, who was close to Brezhnev. But the general meeting of the academy turned thumbs down.

The scientists' negative attitude toward the Party and state bureaucrats had its effect. They could allow some of them to become associate members but seldom let them attain full membership. I recall the general meeting where Vyacheslav Yelutin, an associate member who served as minister of higher education, was to be elected to full membership—to become an academician. A well-known physicist, Academician Mikhail Leontovich, asked a question: "What has Yelutin done in the four years since he became an associate member?" In response the candidate produced a long list of works, written either by himself alone or with a co-author or by a group of scientists he had headed. Academician Leontovich then took the floor and said, "If Yelutin has managed to do so much in the field of science, it means he was a poor minister, because he simply wouldn't have had time for that job. Or vice versa." A secret ballot was taken and he was rejected.

There were other reasons for such a reaction. When the nomination of a respectable and fairly well known lawyer was discussed, Valentin Glyshko, one of the major rocket designers, took the floor and quoted a few passages from the candidate's works, in which he had supported the so-called presumption of guilt—the doctrine that confession alone was sufficient for an indictment. Academician Glyshko asked the candidate where he had been working in 1937. His answer, that he had worked in the general prosecutor's office, sealed his fate. In this case, dislike of and even open hatred for anyone in any way associated with the mass repressions came to the fore. The repressions had not spared many of those scientists and designers, now decorated with medals, who were casting their ballots at the meeting.

The saga of Andrei Sakharov is typical. Although some of his colleagues had put their signatures to a letter to *Pravda* condemning him, the question of expelling him from the academy was never put on the agenda, despite strong pressure from above. There was no doubt that a secret vote on this issue would have failed utterly.

The president of the academy, Mstislav V. Keldysh, asked several members, including myself, to draft a reply to a group of American scientists who had protested Sakharov's persecution. Keldysh told us, "Please don't be overzealous. Sakharov is a great scientist who has done a lot for his country." Academician Keldysh, who could permit himself this liberty, was to say indignantly that the leaders of the Party and the state had never met with Sakharov.

When under Gorbachev Sakharov returned to Moscow from his forced exile in Nizhni Novgorod (then Gorky), everyone in the academy sighed with relief.

INTERNATIONAL RELATIONS: BEHIND THE SCENES

We realized the need to abandon the dogmatic approach in both foreign policy and the military-political area.

In this connection a theoretical interpretation of the peaceful coexistence of the socialist and capitalist systems became a priority issue. Traditionally it was regarded as a "respite" in the relations between socialism and capitalism in the international arena. But with the development of nuclear weapons by both sides, weapons capable of destroying not only the two superpowers but the rest of the world with them, peaceful coexistence between the two systems came to be treated as a more or less permanent condition. But we never failed to add that it by no means took the edge off the ideological struggle.

This interpretation of current relations with the West, coupled with the aspirations of some powerful and influential circles in the United States and other Western countries to do away with the Soviet Union, brought about permanent instability and disequilibrium in the world arena.[2] Thus was created the vicious circle of the arms race.

At that time IMEMO and some other scientific centers it had spawned, especially the Institute of the U.S.A. and Canada and later the Institute of Europe, headed by Academician Vitaly Vladimirovich Zhurkin, were busy preparing new foreign policy approaches that they hoped would overcome tendencies that could lead to a thermonuclear war and at the same time to bring adequate defense spending into balance with the resources required to expand civilian production and develop the social sphere in the USSR. The term "reasonable sufficiency" was introduced, which implied a departure from the disproportionate role the military-industrial complex played in the Soviet economy.

The point is that we were not only building up our weaponry but responding to the United States in lockstep fashion. But our disregard of the principle of sufficiency as a restraining factor combined with the possibility of dealing critical damage to the other side was very costly to us. The USSR's economy could not withstand the arms race under the rules we had accepted.

IMEMO and a number of other institutes under the Academy of Sciences were scrupulously analyzing the activity of the United Nations, which in our opinion was to play an extremely active role in establishing a new world order. We were already considering various options for reforming the U.N. so that it could adapt to future realities.

A leading figure in the research was my friend Professor Grigory Morozov. He had a difficult life, made more so by his marriage to Stalin's daughter, Svetlana. Their marriage ended in tragedy. They were in love, but Stalin separated them. Morozov's father was arrested and he was denied the right to see his son. He had to earn his living by writing articles under assumed names.

When Svetlana, having emigrated to the United States, returned to Moscow with her American-born daughter, Grigory Morozov did his best to help them find a place in our life. Perhaps Svetlana was hoping to resume their old relations, but by that time they both had changed too much. . . .

In the 1970s and the first half of the 1980s our contacts with the governments of the United States and other Western countries were sporadic (compare that pattern with today's regular summits and high-level meetings, the leaders' routine telephone conversations, the conferences of ministers and regular discussions at intergovernmental commissions). Of special importance were discussions of the most burning foreign policy issues conducted by public organizations of various countries. In the past we had tried to explain our policies, make friends, and meet like-minded people among scientists, artists, and intelligentsia through the Soviet Peace Committee, of which I was a deputy chairman. But now other channels of cooperation were opening up as well.

In the beginning we worked toward our objectives in parallel with the Peace Committee. But little by little more emphasis was being placed on probing the possibilities of reaching agreement on vital problems. Of special significance in this respect were IMEMO's relations with the Strategic Center of the Stanford Research Institute (SRI), one of the leading scientific research centers in the United States.

Sometimes amusing incidents occurred. During a meeting in Washington, for instance (other meetings took place in Moscow and Stanford), almost all the Pentagon representatives applauded Professor Revolt Entov, who had given a detailed analysis and proved that the way the SRI experts calculated the Soviet defense budget was faulty and altogether inadequate. Later Professor Entov was elected to full membership in the USSR Academy of Sciences. It turned out that the U.S. Defense Department had paid the SRI a large sum of money for that research. The military must have rejoiced at the rout of the civilian eggheads who got the money and had doubtless been very proud of themselves.

But we chose not to make an issue of this "inside incident." IMEMO had had to expend a great deal of effort to get approval for Revolt Entov's trip to the United States. The Central Committee, whose word on whether or not a person could leave the country was final, opposed Entov's trip—it would be his first trip to the West and they probably were not sure they could trust him. In those days that was normal procedure.

Comparing the ways defense budgets were calculated brought us closer to the beginning of arms reduction. Two political movements played especially significant roles in this regard: the international Pugwash movement[3] and the Soviet-American Dartmouth meetings. The Pugwash movement brought together scientists from various countries, with emphasis on the natural sciences. Physicists, some of them outstanding, played a leading role there.

General ideas on the mortal danger of nuclear weapons for all humankind originated with the Pugwash movement. Having built a theoretical model of a nuclear war, members of the movement proved that it would be followed by "nuclear winter," with temperatures declining so sharply that no life could survive on Earth. They had also made a sizable contribution to the banning of nuclear tests in the atmosphere and brought us closer to a moratorium on all nuclear testing.

As for the Dartmouth meetings, they were held regularly to discuss and narrow the differences in the ways the two superpowers approached the disarmament issue, find ways out of various international conflicts, and create conditions for economic cooperation. IMEMO and ISKAN played special roles in organizing these meetings. The American side was represented by a group of political analysts, for the most part retired executives from the State Department, the Pentagon, the White House, and the CIA, as well as active bankers and businessmen. David Rockefeller headed this group for a long time and he and I had very warm relations. With an American colleague, Harold Saunders, a former assistant secretary of state, I was co-chairman of the work group dealing with conflict situations. I believe we made significant progress in developing coordinated measures for normalizing the situation in the Middle East. Naturally, both sides were sending their progress reports to the very top.

The meetings were held both in Russia and in the States. Vital personal relationships, so difficult to establish at the time, were developed there. During a meeting in Tbilisi in 1975, for instance, somebody suggested inviting the American and Soviet participants to visit a Georgian family. I offered to invite them to dinner at the home of Nadezhda Kharadze, my wife's aunt, who was a professor at the Tbilisi Conservatory and formerly a star of the Tbilisi Opera. Like other members of the true intelligentsia of Georgia, she lived quite modestly—so modestly that she had to borrow a dinner set from her neighbors. Soon rumor spread all over the house that "Rockefeller himself" was going to visit her. Among the other guests were Senator Frank Kelly Scott of Florida and his wife; Charles Yost, former U.S. representative at the U.N.; and Hedley Donovan, editor in chief of Time Inc. We had approached Eduard Shevardnadze, first secretary of the Central Committee of the Communist Party of Georgia at the time, for his permission and got it. It was by no means merely a polite gesture at the time.

Nadezhda Kharadze lived on the fourth floor of a building without an elevator. The city fathers, having neglected to paint the walls of the stairway before our arrival, solved the problem by taking out all the light bulbs. So we walked up in complete darkness, broken only by dim light spilling from the apartments on every floor. It was like a scene in an Italian movie—every apartment door on each floor came open and all the inhabitants, young and old, stared at us in silence as we passed.

The party was a success. The Georgian food was wonderful, and we sang Russian, Georgian, and American songs. David Rockefeller delayed his departure and left when we all did, at three in the morning. He told me on many occasions later that he would keep the memory of that wonderful evening for a long time, though at the beginning he had doubted the sincerity of our hosts and even wondered if it was another Potemkin village. He even went up to a picture of Ernest Hemingway that hung above my nephew's desk and moved it slightly aside to see whether the wallpaper behind it was faded. It was, so the picture had not been pinned to the wall for his visit.

In general, Rockefeller enjoyed special popularity in Tbilisi. Ted Kennedy, who was visiting the capital of Georgia at the same time as our group, complained that as soon as people saw him in the street, they shouted, "Hello, Rockefeller!"

David Rockefeller tried hard to improve relations between our countries. During one of our trips to the United States, this outstanding and charming man invited our group to his family home. The informal and warm atmosphere there helped all of us to make progress on complex international issues. In some areas we succeeded. A kind of laboratory was established to analyze a whole series of questions, some of which were later resolved on the official level.

Meetings organized by IMEMO and the Japanese Security Council (Anpoken) acquired great importance. In the first half of the 1970s, following a proposal by Ichiro Suetsugu, a permanent initiator of such meetings, Zhurkin and I visited Tokyo and agreed on a schedule, the composition of the groups, and the issues to be discussed. Apart from Suetsugu, the Japanese side was represented by Professors Inoki and Saeki and many other individuals who were highly respected in their country; perhaps even more important, they, like the entire Anpoken, were influential members of the ruling Liberal-Democratic Party.

At first such annual roundtable discussions looked like a dialogue of the deaf. Each side kept stating the importance of developing relations between the USSR and Japan. Our Japanese colleagues kept repeating that no relations were possible until the "northern territories" issues were resolved, and we responded just as persistently that the problem did not exist.

But slowly the ice began to melt. With each meeting a feeling of mutual respect was growing. I will never forget that when Suetsugu learned about my son's death in 1981, he spent all night meticulously rendering the characters of an old Japanese saying that in essence called for enduring all hardships humbly while thinking about the Eternal. He gave this writing to me. Of course, the Japanese wisdom could not muffle the terrible pain caused by the sudden death of my 27-year-old son, who died of a heart attack during the May Day parade in Moscow. But to this day I greatly appreciate the sincere impulse of my Japanese colleague. I was saddened to learn of his death in 2001.

I believe it was our meetings that laid the foundation for progress in relations between the two countries. After all, neither side stopped with a formal presentation. Suetsugu did his best to introduce me and the others to the top political leaders of Japan. Prime Minister Yasuhiro Nakasone was one of them. The first of our many meetings took place in an ancient Japanese restaurant.

"Mr. Prime Minister, let's be realistic," I said. "Public opinion in your country doesn't allow you to give up the idea of gaining sovereignty over the islands. We can't give up our sovereignty over them either, because nobody in our country would appreciate that. What shall we do under the circumstances? We're facing a dilemma: we can either freeze relations between our two countries for a long, long time, which runs against our common interests, or turn our backs on the extreme positions. We'll stop insisting there is no territorial issue—how come there's no issue when you're claiming possession of the islands and we're rejecting your claims?—while the Japanese will give up their requirement that the islands must be handed over as a nonnegotiable condition for the development of bilateral relations. Let's begin to cooperate step by step, especially in the economic sphere. That will gradually strengthen confidence and create a basis for the solution of the toughest issues."

To my great surprise, Nakasone immediately agreed with this logic. Later he came to share an idea we had been nurturing, that the islands' economy come under joint management.

Looking through the notes I took during the meetings with my Japanese colleagues at that time, I come to the same conclusion, that joint economic activity on the islands is the only solution, that eventually it will make the sovereignty issue less acute. The signing of a treaty between the two countries is long overdue.

Our conversations and talks with the Japanese arranged by Anpoken were translated by Rju Chaku—or Yury Mikhailovich, as we called him—who was an excellent professional, fluent in Russian, Japanese, and Korean. I made friends with him. At his request I took him from IMEMO to the Institute of Oriental Studies and then back to IMEMO. Rju Chaku had had an amazing life. As a Japanese soldier he was taken prisoner by us. He decided to stay in the Soviet Union. He married a Russian woman. He got his Ph.D. During one of our first trips to Japan he came up to me with a staggering request: he wanted permission to call his mother in South Korea, who for thirty years hadn't even known he was alive. I can imagine how happy his mother was when she heard the voice of the son she had considered dead for so long. Naturally, we did not talk much about that phone call back in Moscow. After all, it was still the mid-1970s.

Having lost his wife, Rju left for Seoul, where he remarried. His new wife, too, was Russian, a woman who taught Russian at a local university on an exchange program. In the 1990s, after becoming a citizen of South Korea, he translated my talks with the South Korean president. But he has remained our friend forever.

IMEMO's involvement in practical policies was enhanced by the fact that we began to develop an entirely new line of research, situation analysis, which had direct bearing on politics. I was in charge of developing brainstorming techniques and presided over most of the sessions. I will cite only a few of our conclusions. We predicted that the United States would bomb Cambodia during the Vietnam War four months in advance; we predicted that Anwar Sadat would turn to the West at the expense of close relations with the USSR after Nasser's death; and after the victory of the Islamic revolution in Iran we predicted that war between Iran and Iraq was inevitable (it broke out ten months later). The list could go on. Of no less importance were our realistic predictions of the economic consequences of the energy crisis caused by the sharp increase in oil prices that followed the 1973 war in the Middle East.

In 1980 a group of scientists, which I headed, received the USSR State Prize for our development and preparation of situation analysis. Our group and representatives of the defense industry were on the "closed"—that is, secret—list of nominations; the nature of our achievement was so sensitive that it was not to be discussed openly. During the award ceremony, when each of us was given his prizewinner's badge and certificate, we were surprised to see that as many prizes went to people on the closed list as to those on the open list. The secretary of the Central Committee, the deputy chairman of the Council of Ministers, and the head of the Central Committee's defense department bestowed the awards. When I asked whether, like members of a secret society, we should wear our badges on the back side of our lapels, they responded without a trace of humor, "You can wear them openly."

The "new political thinking" in the USSR is generally associated with the Gorbachev era. Indeed, much was done then. These new approaches were developed and put together into a system at a state dacha in Lidzava, in Abkhazia, in 1987. Their principal author was A. N. Yakovlev.

It was at that time that it dawned on us that with so many weapons of mass destruction stockpiled, there could be no winner in a thermonuclear war; and that understanding was reflected in political decisions.

We came to yet another conclusion: the military approach to containment—the "balance of terror"—could not be relied on if outer space became the battlefield between missiles and Star Wars defenses. It is conceivable that in those circumstances, military decisions could be made by machines. It was this conclusion that led us to the idea of preserving parity, but at the lowest possible level.

It should also be noted that for the first time our foreign policy initiatives began to take account of Western public opinion—not only the opinions of sectors ideologically close to us but also mainstream attitudes, even those repugnant to us.

It is common knowledge that there had been no Soviet-American summit since 1979, whereas Mikhail S. Gorbachev met with Ronald Reagan five times. I happened to be a member of the group of experts at the Geneva, Reykjavik, Washington, and Moscow summits. I saw close-up how difficult it was to get a dialogue going and how much effort it took to move the world away from the flash point.

President Reagan arrived in Geneva with the message that we should first establish trust by resolving the human rights issue and settling regional conflicts; after that we could begin to talk about arms reduction. In the end, after intense disputes, we agreed to work on all issues simultaneously. In essence that had been our preliminary plan.

Unfortunately, the Americans did not appreciate the homework the

Soviet delegation had done for Geneva. Gorbachev tried to steer mutual re-
lations in a new direction by proposing several fundamentally new approaches.
First, we would give up the all-or-nothing formula we had used in the past.
In other words, for the first time we began to take into consideration the
Western belief that it was impossible for the Soviet Union and the United
States to do without maintaining a certain number of nuclear warheads for
the foreseeable future, especially because of the mistrust that had built up
between the two countries and the lack of guarantees of nonproliferation of
nuclear weapons. The former defense secretary Robert McNamara, whom
I knew personally and valued not only as a professional but also as an individual, cited 400 as a "warhead guarantee," far fewer than each country
possessed.

Second, we defined our new position on the control issue. Earlier we
had agreed that each country would control its own arms reduction process.
If Gorbachev discussed a change in our position on this issue with anybody,
it must have been with only a few insiders. In Geneva the experts were unexpectedly invited into a "safe room,"[4] where Gorbachev, Shevardnadze, First
Deputy Foreign Minister Georgy Kornienko, and others were gathered. I
have to admit that although we were professionally engaged in foreign affairs,
we were nonetheless children of our time and we were quite surprised by
what we heard: "Perhaps there is no sense in clinging to the old philosophy
on the control issue." It was not only that national means of control could
not be depended on in all cases, as the West believed; by rejecting other
methods of control we were playing into the hands of those who said that
ours was a closed society where agreements could not be verified, so it was
not worthwhile dealing with us. We should declare our readiness for the
stiffest controls, including international ones; we were prepared for on-site
inspections, even ready to open up our laboratories.

Upon hearing Gorbachev's words, Academician Yevgeny Velikhov immediately asked whether that applied to our opponents as well. We were unanimous in believing we should not open up unilaterally.

Unfortunately, time has shown that neither side was genuinely ready to
open up its labs. I cannot speak for the Americans, but I am confident that
for the scientists I had been dealing with, such "secretiveness" always resulted
from their foreign colleagues' wish to apply a double standard: "We want to
know what you're preparing for and what you're doing, but that doesn't mean
we're about to let you into our own kitchen."

We did not rule out the possibility of discussing human rights issues, to the great surprise of the Western politicians.

They failed to hear us in Geneva. Perhaps it happened because, among other things, the American leadership had underestimated the dissidents, who were gaining significant strength. So that was how we approached the summit in Reykjavik, the capital of Iceland, in October 1986. I can testify that the atmosphere was entirely different this time, with a wide range of questions raised and intensive talks, with compromise not ruled out. For the first time Gorbachev decided to dilute the concentration of Foreign Ministry officials in the negotiating work groups. Shevardnadze raised no objection, at least openly, perhaps because he was not yet in full control of his staff, although later the Foreign Ministry's prestige was sometimes his top priority.

I headed the Soviet subgroup on conflict situations. My American partner was Assistant Secretary of State Rozanne Ridgway, a woman of strong character and an outstanding professional. It was important that we reach an understanding on a whole range of issues and agree on the wording of a joint document. It took us thirty-six hours of uninterrupted work. But in the end everything depended on whether agreement could be reached in the main disarmament group. They failed to agree, though they came close, so our document was not signed.

Gorbachev had been determined to have successful talks. I could see that Reagan, too, was disappointed that the summit produced nothing. When Gorbachev was seeing Reagan off, as the door of Reagan's limousine was opened for him Gorbachev suggested they could go back and sign the arms reduction treaty. But Reagan shook his head.

Still, the rapprochement continued. To a large extent that was the result of our readiness at least to acknowledge our mistakes and try to correct them. One of them was clearly the deployment of medium-range missiles (known as SS-20's in America) in Europe. In retaliation the United States decided to deploy Pershing 2's, which could reach Moscow from Western Europe in six to eight minutes. The United States could not consider SS-20's strategic weapons, since U.S. territory was beyond their range, but that's precisely what Pershing 2's were for the USSR.

But not everyone on our side saw the need to resort to what seemed like an asymmetrical solution in order to avoid making our own mistakes. Experts among the scientists—some of my own generation, such as Oleg Bykov, and younger scientists such as Aleksei Arbatov and Sergei Karaganov—sharply

criticized those who complained that on a one-to-one basis, we were destroying more warheads than the Americans, in accordance with the treaty on the
reduction of medium- to short-range missiles signed in Washington in 1987.

Of special importance was acknowledgment of our mistake in invading
Afghanistan. It wasn't the inside dissidents who were most strongly against
sending our troops to Afghanistan but rather those who had broken with
the Soviet system. But reactions to the events in Afghanistan began to change
even among the apparatchiks when the "temporary deployment of a limited
contingent" expanded over the years and had such dire consequences. The
vast majority of the USSR's population welcomed the withdrawal of our soldiers from Afghanistan with relief.

At the same time, it would have been another grave mistake to close our
eyes to policies the United States and its allies were pursuing to isolate the
USSR and make difficulties for us in various parts of the world. Later, when
I worked in foreign intelligence, I came across materials indicating that the
Americans had supplied the Afghan mujahedin with some of the most sophisticated weapons in their arsenal, such as Stinger anti-aircraft missiles,
with the aim of doing as much damage to the Soviet troops as possible. Such
were the "rules of conduct" during the Cold War. Incidentally, according to
our information, the idea of deploying the Stingers was supplied by Osama
bin Laden, who had been cooperating closely with the CIA at the time.

The Americans continued to support certain groups in Afghanistan after
our troops were withdrawn. When the Taliban captured Kabul and established
control over most of Afghan's territory, I told Secretary of State Madeleine
Albright, "Don't repeat our mistakes. If you want peace and stability in
Afghanistan, it has to be done only on the basis of a coalition. A single force,
ethnic or political—the Taliban represent only the Pashtuns—won't be able
to control the situation in the country." We knew full well that the Taliban
movement had been formed by the Pakistani military and their intelligence
service, with the Americans' concurrence, especially in the beginning. I
think Washington has come to realize that mistake, among others, inasmuch
as Afghanistan turned into a training ground for terrorist groups that have
spread their tentacles over many other countries throughout the world.

I don't think all Pakistanis found inspiration in the Taliban's practices.
In any event, in the mid-1990s Prime Minister Benazir Bhutto complained
to me that it was difficult to push the genie back into the bottle, if it could
be done at all.

But let's go back to the end of the 1980s. When the new president came to the White House, our hopes that Bush was less ideological and more pragmatic than Reagan were for the most part justified. It was of some importance, too, that Bush could make use of the potential created by joint Soviet-American effort to stabilize the international situation. Bush the pragmatist seemed more open than Reagan to the idea of leaving ideology out of bilateral relations. He diverged slightly, though not completely, from the stereotype of an American politician. For instance, if the USSR focused on improving its relations with Western Europe or China, it was assumed we were doing so to split NATO or were playing some other card against the United States.

Incidentally, before President Bush came to power, Gorbachev had visited India and later China. Both these visits were of major importance. Gorbachev regularly consulted with experts, even during negotiations. He would even send some of us to a country he was going to visit before he went there himself.

We were very impressed by India. Naturally my imagination was captured by the ancient cultural and architectural wonders, as well as by the sheer size of the country. But it was the high level of scientific and technological progress that amazed members of the Soviet delegation who had had no previous experience of India. In many areas India was approaching a position of leadership. Conditions were so openly favorable to political rapprochement, to expansion of economic ties, and to joint development of military technologies that we were gaining an entirely new perspective on cooperation between the two countries. We exchanged our views with Gorbachev at his residence in New Delhi.

As our embassy counselor drove me to the meeting, he made a vulgar remark about Indians—not the sort of thing I believe most of our embassy personnel would say. I immediately interrupted him: "How can you work here if you show such little respect for the people of this country?" He mumbled something apologetically. After all, we came from Moscow. So when Gorbachev, Shevardnadze, and the rest of us began to discuss the encouraging prospects for relations with India, I said that if those prospects were to materialize, some of our representatives here should be replaced.

The conversation that followed nearly changed my career. But more about that later.

The visit to China was no less important. Gorbachev and the people accompanying him went there at a time when the People's Republic of China was at a crossroads. On the one hand, Deng Xiaoping was introducing fundamental economic reforms that could unleash the human potential of this great people. On the other hand, the Chinese leadership was determined to maintain the political superstructure, including the Party, to preserve stability and keep control of the economic changes. As a result, democratization in the economic sphere was not accompanied by democratization in the political sphere.

A double standard was applied to Gorbachev's visit, too. He was received as the leader of a reformed socialism that was moving toward free market relations under new rules, which we as well as the Chinese then believed would demonstrate once and for all the superiority of the socialist system of production. At the same time, the Chinese leadership feared this visit might excite the imagination of the intelligentsia and particularly the students, who obviously were stirred by the introduction of glasnost in the Soviet Union.

As it turned out, their fears were well founded. Passions flared in Beijing during Gorbachev's visit. Students demonstrated in Tienanmen Square and virtually blocked the "government island," where the homes of Chinese leaders and guesthouses were scattered around a picturesque area of many hectares.

Students asked Gorbachev to speak at their meeting. We were adamantly against that. And we were probably right. Had Gorbachev addressed the students, his meeting with Deng Xiaoping, which I attended, would not have been so fruitful as it was. This meeting can be considered a turning point in the relations of the two countries. In fact, the conversation with Deng opened the door to broad-ranging cooperation between the USSR and the People's Republic of China.

Deng, sitting in a large armchair next to Gorbachev in a similar chair, addressed Gorbachev in a friendly manner and seemed to make a special effort to show his respect. Gorbachev was also extremely friendly. He had found a formula that, in his words, showed the difference between the USSR and China but did not divide them: "We began with political reforms and you with economic ones, but we'll come to the same results." Deng nodded his head in silence.

Deng pointedly demonstrated his respect for the USSR, underlining the huge importance for China of past Soviet assistance and support. He spoke about the extreme importance of Soviet-Chinese cooperation, not only for our two countries but for the world at large.

In the course of this conversation, which lasted more than an hour, one could see how bright this old man was and how very respectfully he was treated by everyone present.

During one of the breaks in the talks, Gorbachev invited me for a walk on the grounds of the residence. We talked about everything, including international affairs, of course. I remarked that the strength of our foreign policy lay in cooperating not with an isolated group of states but with a broad range of states, especially in Asia. With this configuration it would be easier for us to deal also with the West. Gorbachev agreed, and suddenly he said he had plans for me. I didn't think it appropriate to ask him to be more specific, and he didn't elaborate.

Our visits to India and China produced another result—we no longer viewed Soviet-American relations in isolation. But did that mean we were playing the so-called Chinese and Indian cards? That is a simplistic view, since it rests on the idea that "American egocentrism"—the view that the United States is the center of the universe—cannot be challenged. Such perceptions are doubly crude because they don't take into consideration the interest of the USSR and then of Russia in actively developing its relations with these two fast-growing Asian giants, which together encompass half the world's population. At the same time, we could not and cannot forget that the diversification of our international ties must not damage our relations with the United States.

REVERSALS OF FORTUNE

After the trip to New Delhi, the Central Committee invited me to deliver a report to the members of its department that oversaw staff stationed abroad. After my speech, the head of the department, Stepan Chervonenko, paid special attention to me. He even escorted me to the elevator, quite an uncommon thing to do at the time. His deputy, with whom I was on friendly terms, called me at the institute and said, "Don't tell where you heard this, but it's been decided in principle that you're going to India as ambassador, and Gorbachev has approved it."

I was seriously worried. By that time my wife's health had sharply deteriorated and I realized that India's climate was far from ideal for her. I went to Shevardnadze and he said, "Don't worry. Of course we won't press you, although this position is very important and you should've taken it."

So I did not become ambassador to India. Soon I was elected a candidate to the Central Committee and then a full member. But I did lose my wife.

She passed away in 1987, and who knows, maybe the Indian climate would not have been too bad for her weak heart.

I felt her loss very keenly. Laura Vasilievna Kharadze was a large part of my life. We had lived together for thirty-six years. I catch myself thinking she sacrificed her varied and special talents for me and her children. She was well educated, well versed in the arts and a brilliant pianist, although by training she was an electrochemical engineer. She was unshakably direct, never went against her conscience, and couldn't stand lies and hypocrisy, including those in official politics. She was a convinced internationalist but at the same time she sincerely admired the best that both Russia and Georgia could offer. She was a charming woman and was perceived to be so both by me and by those around us.

The publication of Aleksandr Solzhenitsyn's "One Day in the Life of Ivan Denisovich" and then "Matryona's Home" in the monthly journal *Novy Mir* was a big event for our whole family. My wife, Laura, admired these outstanding works in her own forceful way and could neither tolerate nor miss any of the critical comments that were beginning to circulate.

At the death of Aleksandr Tvardovsky, *Novy Mir*'s liberal editor, one of my KGB acquaintances told me his funeral would undoubtedly turn into a political event and everyone who attended it would draw the KGB's attention. I didn't mention this to Laura, knowing that nothing would keep her from that funeral—not because she knew Tvardovsky personally (she didn't) but because she would consider it her duty to pay her last respects to that outstanding man. I am sure that nothing could have stopped her. Her public spirit and sense of justice could not be extinguished, and more important, they were her natural guides, not virtues trotted out for public show.

Laura was not ambitious for me. When I was moved to *Pravda* from Gosteleradio, she asked me, "Why, don't you like your work in foreign broadcasting?" When I defended my dissertation and was ready to move on to the Academy of Sciences, she said, "You enjoy journalism so much, why change?" The only time she referred to my status, she was in the hospital: "Say, why don't you wear your Supreme Soviet Member's lapel pin? I'd like you to have it on."

Seven years after Laura's death I married for the second time. After my losses, life was good to me again. Irina is a wonderful woman, a friend, a brilliant specialist—a practicing therapist. She is loved and respected by all my relatives. Many of her traits remind me of Laura, whom she did not know but whose memory she reveres with special warmth.

After Laura's death I buried myself in work at IMEMO, which satisfied me in every respect. And not only at IMEMO, but also at the recently created Soviet National Committee of Asia-Pacific Economic Cooperation, of which I became the first chairman. Formally the committee was established as a national group required for admission to APEC, the Asia-Pacific Economic Council. In addition, the committee was supposed to accelerate development of our Far East and Eastern Siberia. If that goal was to be achieved, those areas had to fit naturally into the global economic relations of the Asia-Pacific region, though certainly not at the expense of our country's territorial integrity. The country's immense size, however, makes direct economic ties with the neighboring Asia-Pacific region most beneficial to those rapidly developing countries. Another objective pursued at that time, which is also relevant today, was to reorient the financial and economic resources of the USSR toward the Far East and Eastern Siberia. There was no doubt then and there is none now that Russia's future depends in many ways on whether we manage to develop this vast territory, extremely rich but sparsely populated.

As head of the group of experts on the Soviet committee I covered most of this area. My impressions were simply staggering. I met with and spoke to hundreds of people, smart, energetic, and ready to do their best for their regions. I remember the words of one of them, an engineer who believed in the boundless potential of the Far East. He said, "The United States became a great power only after they developed their Pacific West. And it didn't take them too long to do it. Doesn't it teach us anything? You see, we're just passing decrees without implementing them."

I was working on very promising and interesting projects at the time, but my life was about to change once again. One day in May 1989 I was sitting at my desk on the sixteenth floor of IMEMO, editing a memo prepared by my staff on small and mid-sized businesses in the United States, when the Kremlin telephone rang. When I answered, I was surprised to hear Gorbachev's voice. He had never called me before.

"Do you remember our conversation in Beijing?" he asked. "Do you remember I said I had plans for you? Now it's time to carry them out. What I mean is your work at the Supreme Soviet of the USSR."

"Well, Mikhail Sergeevich, whatever you say," I replied, thinking that as a member of the Supreme Soviet I was most likely to be placed at the head of its foreign affairs committee.

"Well said," he answered. "What do you think about heading one of the chambers of the Supreme Soviet?"

I was taken aback by this unexpected offer.

"But I'm a scientist," I said.

"So what?" said Gorbachev. "We need you to take care of other things."

"What about the institute?" I asked.

"I promise you'll have a voice in selecting your successor."

I was succeeded by Vladlen Martynov, my first deputy, who later became an academician. He did a good job as head of the institute. As for me, when I was introduced to the sitting members of the Supreme Soviet, someone asked Gorbachev how I was going to combine my position as chairman of the Council of the Union (the lower house of Parliament) with my work at the Academy of Sciences. Besides heading IMEMO, I managed the Academy of Sciences' Department of World Economy and International Relations, whose members included all the academy's scientific research institutes that dealt with international affairs; I was also a member of the academy's presidium. Gorbachev declared, "He's leaving all his positions at the academy." He had never said a word to me about it.

At that time the whole country was engrossed in the life of the Supreme Soviet. Everything was new. Speeches full of criticism and hot debates turned into abrasive arguments, and it was all broadcast live, without editing. Then when it became evident that people had simply stopped working to gather in front of their TVs, it was decided to run prerecorded Supreme Soviet sessions in the evening or late at night, still without editing, "in response to popular demand."

The camera was always aimed at the podium, so the house chairman was always in the picture. Sitting from morning to evening almost every day knowing that many millions of TV viewers are watching you is quite an unpleasant experience.

Of course, my work as head of the Council of the Union of the USSR Supreme Soviet was not limited to sitting in front of the cameras. It included preparing the contents of the laws under which we believed the country should begin to live. Undoubtedly my position in the Supreme Soviet was reinforced by the fact that in September 1989 I was elected candidate member of the Politburo of the CPSU Central Committee. That position brought me beyond the parliamentary framework to the level of the executive power, where important state issues were decided. Despite all that, the job of Speaker of the Supreme Soviet chamber was decidedly contrary to my nature. In the end I begged Gorbachev to give me another job—any other job.

That was how I became a member of the Presidential Council.

CHAPTER THREE

The War That Might Not Have Been

KUWAIT UNDER IRAQ

The most memorable and significant event during my tenure at the Presidential Council, in general a rather amorphous body, was the crisis that exploded in the Persian Gulf in 1990–91.

The crisis began when Iraq invaded and annexed Kuwait. The overwhelming majority of the world community were unanimous in demanding Iraq's unconditional withdrawal and restoration of Kuwait's sovereignty. The U.N. Security Council adopted the appropriate resolutions without a hitch and without the long negotiations and diplomatic convulsions common in such cases. But although the Security Council's stance was becoming more unyielding with every resolution, it did not produce the expected results. Saddam Hussein, with his peculiar psychology, probably thought his own tough stance bought him plenty of time for maneuver.

But the series of resolutions became a reality. And most important, with the U.N.'s unswerving approval the United States and some other countries, including Arab states, poured troops into Saudi Arabia, which, fearing it might become the Iraqi military's next victim, had turned to Washington for help.

Paradoxical as it may seem, the tough sanctions and the demonstration of military might provided considerable room to search for a political way out of the dead end created by Saddam Hussein. The idea of sending an envoy from the USSR's president to Baghdad came up for the first time that August. The idea was not implemented immediately because another channel opened up instead. At Hussein's request, Iraq's foreign minister, Tariq Aziz, was received in Moscow. The shortcomings of this method of negotiating, however, became apparent immediately. Aziz, like everyone else under Hussein, could make no independent decisions. He was just an interpreter with strictly limited prerogatives and a messenger delivering Hussein's statements.

And there was something else: our Foreign Ministry was opposed in principle to sending a Soviet envoy to Baghdad.

On September 9, at the instigation of President George H. W. Bush, a Soviet-American summit was held in Helsinki. It was important for Bush to receive the USSR's public support and to demonstrate that the two powers were united in their desire to secure the withdrawal of Iraqi troops from Kuwait. It was decided to agree with Bush's proposal without delay.

I have to admit that the prevailing opinion in Moscow was that war could be prevented and that the combined effect of political, economic, and military pressure on Saddam Hussein would produce the desired result. At the same time, the view was growing that a just world order was achievable and that the USSR and the United States were to play special roles in establishing it.

Gorbachev was under the impression, which he shared with his advisers, that the president of the United States was also leaning toward resolving the Kuwait issue by political means.

After talks between members of both delegations and a face-to-face meeting of Gorbachev and Bush, dinner was served. I was sitting between Barbara Bush and General Brent Scowcroft, the president's national security adviser. Doubtless knowing that I had specialized in the Middle East for many years and knew many Arab leaders personally, Scowcroft asked me when I had last met with Saddam Hussein. I assumed the general wanted to know whether I had visited Baghdad since the crisis began. "No, I haven't been there yet," I told him with a smile.

My long acquaintance with Saddam Hussein was no secret. As a Middle East correspondent for *Pravda* in the 1960s, I wrote about my trips to northern Iraq and my meetings with Mustafa al-Barzani, a well-known leader of the Kurdish rebels who were waging war against Baghdad at the time. The Soviet Union opposed that war, mainly for humanitarian reasons and also because it was against our political interests. We were broadening our relations with Baghdad and we also valued our ties with the Kurds. Both sides reacted well

to the Soviet position. The Kurds appreciated our support for their broad national rights and Baghdad welcomed our opposition to the separatists, who
were intent on tearing the Kurdish areas away from Iraq. This fundamental
approach enabled us to establish good contacts in Baghdad.

I met Saddam Hussein for the first time in 1969, although I had heard
about him before. As a very young man he had taken part in an attempt to
assassinate Prime Minister Abdul Karim Kassem, was wounded, but managed
to escape and went into hiding. At first the Iraqis called him Saddam Hussein
Al-Tikriti, but he dropped the last part of his name, probably to conceal his
relationship with President Ahmad Hassan Bakr, who also came from Tikrit.

When I met Saddam for the first time, he was already an influential
member of the Iraqi leadership; soon he was the second most powerful man
in Iraq and many of his rivals had lost either their influence or their lives.
A significant role in Saddam's career was played by his involvement in the
creation of the special intelligence service within the Ba'ath Party structure,
an omnipotent organization that helped him gradually to take full power
into his own hands.

At that time my interest in Saddam was sparked by a job assignment.
As a correspondent of *Pravda*—published by the CPSU Central Committee
—I was assigned to try to bring Baghdad and the Kurds to the negotiating
table. The Council of the Revolutionary Command of Iraq appointed Saddam
to head the delegation that was to negotiate with the Kurds. That same year,
1969, I became quite closely acquainted with Tariq Aziz, who edited the
newspaper *As-Saura* and was among Hussein's closest advisers. It was a time
of instability. The wing of the Ba'ath Party to which both Saddam and Aziz
belonged had just come to power. Fighting was escalating among those at
the helm of power, the country's leadership. Both Saddam and Aziz had machine guns in their offices.

Many of the personal characteristics for which Saddam is known were
already visible at that time: toughness often spilling over into cruelty, a re-
markably strong will verging on recalcitrant stubbornness, readiness to stop
at nothing to achieve his goal at any cost, unpredictability in decisions and
actions. But at the same time he shows a streak of realism, especially when
he senses danger. He is also capable of taking advice, though not always
immediately.

Two examples will show Saddam's character. Early in 1970 a moment
came when the peace agreement with the Kurds seemed about to become

a reality. Suddenly Saddam said, in effect, "I can't sign it. What's to guarantee the Kurds won't start fighting again?" "There's no guarantee," I answered. "But if the Kurds do violate the agreement while Baghdad adheres to it, they'll have to fight without the support of the Soviet Union or many of the other forces that were backing them before. Doesn't that mean anything to you?"

Having thought a bit, Saddam agreed.

On March 11, 1970, the agreement was signed. But the tension remained and slowly developed into tough confrontation. During a new escalation of tension in northern Iraq I met again with Mr. Barzani. At the time I was deputy director of the Institute of World Economy and International Relations of the USSR Academy of Sciences. He told me about the assassination attempt against him. Some sheikhs came to visit, and a bomb was planted in the tape recorder one of them carried to record the conversation with the Kurdish leader. The driver, outside the house, used a remote control to activate the bomb. Barzani escaped unharmed only because a man who was serving tea bent over Barzani just as the bomb went off and shielded him from the blast.

This is Saddam's doing, Barzani thought. He was sure of it.

Exceptional suspiciousness is another feature of Saddam's psychological makeup. Those who surrounded him could take advantage of it by presenting events and facts to him in a way that would arouse associations, prejudices, and animosity.

I met with Saddam many times during his visits to Moscow and on my visits to Baghdad in the 1970s and 1980s. I thought we had developed a relationship that allowed me to speak with this very complicated man without diplomatic finesse. And yet I should point out that in dealing with political figures of the Arab world and of Eastern origin in general, one should never forget how keenly sensitive they can be to any perceived slight to their honor and dignity.

FLYING TO BAGHDAD

Apparently my acquaintance with Saddam Hussein was taken into consideration when President Gorbachev sent me to Baghdad as his personal envoy. He set me two tasks: to secure a guarantee that our specialists in Iraq could freely leave the country and to convince Saddam Hussein that it was useless to refuse to comply with the requirements of the U.N. Security Council.

Our plane set down first at the airport in Amman, Jordan. That was not a refueling stop. We had saved that day to exchange views with King Hussein and other Jordanian leaders. We were also to meet with the leaders of the Palestine Liberation Organization; Yasir Arafat flew to Amman when he learned I was going to be there.

The Jordanian leaders clearly understood the threat posed by the unfolding events but they seemed to feel powerless to escape from the torrent that was sweeping them inexorably toward a whirlpool. In any event, it was clear that King Hussein, whom I had known for a long time and truly respected, had very little room for maneuver. A large portion of the Jordanian population is Palestinian; the country borders on Israel and had fought two wars with the Israelis in the last forty-five years; finally, Jordan's economy is closely entwined with that of Iraq. At the same time, Jordan's king has always valued his relations with the United States, Britain, and other Western powers; without them he could not keep his balance from day to day on the razor's edge between the Israeli–Palestinian conflagration and his volatile Arab neighbors. That was why the king condemned Iraq's annexation of Kuwait and promised to support the U.N. sanctions by closing the port of Aqaba but left open Jordan's border with Iraq, permitting free passage for food, medicine, and other vital supplies. In short, King Hussein found himself between a rock and a hard place. To a large extent that was why he was eager to do anything he could to encourage any degree of political flexibility on the part of the Iraqi leader.

The meeting with the Palestinians was another matter. As always, it began with rhetoric that in the circumstances could be justified. The Palestinians were more eager than anybody else to make sure a double standard did not prevail in the Middle East, one with respect to Kuwait and another in respect to their own destiny. But occasionally the rhetoric had alarming overtones: if war broke out, it could create new conditions "favorable to the struggle for a just solution of the Palestinian problem."

Of course I did not agree with this approach. I spoke of my discussion with Palestinian leaders in Damascus back in 1970, shortly before "Black September," a large-scale clash between Jordan and Palestine, which threatened to draw in Syria on the side of Palestine, to be followed by Israel as soon as Syrian tanks moved in. When those Palestinians voiced similarly optimistic forecasts, I warned them that a clash with the Jordanian army would sharply complicate their situation and would so far weaken their position in the country that a solution of the Palestinian question would hardly be possible. And that in fact was what happened.

To do justice to Arafat and his colleagues, I should point out that after that digression into the past, the tenor of our conversation changed. Not only Arafat but many other Palestinian leaders (Abu Mazem, Abd Rabbo) openly expressed concern over a military solution of the Kuwait crisis.

At the end of the day Arafat ordered his plane prepared for departure because he wanted to arrive in Baghdad before us so that he could, as he put it, "do his best to make our meeting with Saddam Hussein fruitful." I have no doubt he did do his best.

In Amman I received a coded message from Shevardnadze, who was attending the U.N. General Assembly in New York. Under the circumstances, it said, any contacts with Saddam Hussein were "immoral." I answered with my own coded cable that it was immoral not to contact Saddam, at least in an effort to ensure the return of thousands of Soviet citizens and other foreigners to their homelands.

On October 4 we flew from Amman to Baghdad. Tariq Aziz met us at the airport. We talked for several hours, and it was perhaps the most difficult conversation I ever had with him. Aziz was determined to prove that historically, politically, and economically Kuwait was part of Iraq. He cited dates, figures, events, and names. He insisted that no regime, including the monarchy, had ever recognized Kuwait as an independent state.

Dissatisfaction with the Soviet position came through very distinctly in Aziz's monologue. In his words, the USSR "must behave differently, in accordance with its appropriate treaty with Iraq." But when I asked Aziz why Saddam Hussein had failed to notify Moscow about his plans to invade Kuwait and then about the actual invasion, he evaded an answer.

I made a strong point of insisting that all Soviet citizens should be given an opportunity to leave Iraq and return home. About five thousand Soviet specialists were working in Iraq at the time. Some still had their families with them, although most dependents had already been flown back to the Soviet Union. Nearly 150 Soviet military experts were also in Iraq to maintain military equipment we had sold to Iraq before the Kuwait crisis. By the time we arrived in Baghdad, quite a few demands had been made for the free exit not only of the military specialists, whose contracts were about to expire, but also of all the other Soviet citizens who were working there on construction projects undertaken with our technical assistance. Iraq did not openly reject the idea but did nothing to implement it either.

My conversation with Saddam Hussein took place on October 5. Viktor

Posuvalyuk, the Soviet ambassador to Iraq, joined me on the Soviet side. The Iraqi side was represented by Tariq Aziz and the first deputy prime minister, Taha Yassin Ramadan. The meeting was held in the presidential palace, where Hussein usually received foreigners. One of the Iraqis pointed out that we were the first foreigners Saddam had received at the old palace since August 2.

Having carefully read President Gorbachev's message (it had been translated into Arabic at the Soviet Foreign Ministry in advance), Saddam Hussein showed no visible sign of concern over its firm demands for immediate withdrawal from Kuwait and restoration of that state's sovereignty. But the atmosphere at the beginning of the talks was tense.

After Saddam Hussein repeated everything about Kuwait that we had heard before from Tariq Aziz, I raised the issue of our specialists. Hussein seemed to be ready for that, because he responded immediately that everyone who wished to leave could do so, but no more than a thousand in the next two months, so that work could go on and the projects not be delayed. Knowing that our embassy had received about fifteen hundred applications for departure, I proposed a schedule of fifteen hundred people a month. In the end Hussein said, "Have it your way."

Saddam gave a detailed account of the economic pressure to which Iraq had been subjected. According to him, Saudi Arabia, Kuwait, and the United Arab Emirates had violated oil export quotas set by OPEC. As a result, oil prices fell from $21 to $11 a barrel, a decline that could "lead to the economic collapse of Iraq."

Some of his accusations were true, others paranoid fictions. Yet as far as I can judge, he believed what he was saying.

"Don't you think the Iraqis are beginning to develop a Masada complex like the Israelis?" I asked Saddam, referring to the fortress where the Jews made their last stand against the Romans after the fall of Jerusalem in A.D. 70. Its defenders, realizing the hopelessness of their situation, vowed to die rather than surrender.

Saddam nodded.

"But then, to a large extent, your actions will be determined by the logic of the doomed?"

It looked as though Saddam agreed with that, too; at least he didn't answer.

We then discussed possible implications of refusal to withdraw Iraqi troops from Kuwait and the world's reaction to the crisis. I intentionally brought these subjects up because I suspected Saddam was not well informed. Doubtless he was told about developments that would please him—support for Iraq in the Arab world, antiwar demonstrations in the West, any sign of discord in the anti-Iraq coalition.

We spelled out the kind of war he would have to wage if he did not leave Kuwait. During its war with Iran, as all the world knows, Iraq had air superiority and a big advantage in military hardware on the ground. Now, in the event of a military conflict with an international coalition whose chief component was the United States, Iraq's position would be reversed. The advantage of the U.S.-led coalition in the air was quite obvious, as was its military and technological superiority over Iraq.

We also stressed to Saddam the degree of Iraq's isolation from the world community as a result of its invasion of Kuwait. The atmosphere at the U.N. General Assembly, which was in session at the time, made that quite clear.

I suggested that we conclude our meeting by talking face to face. Saddam asked if I'd mind if Tariq Aziz joined us. I had no objection. Our side was also represented by Sergei Kirpechenko, who was one of our best Arab experts and fluent in Arabic. Later he became Russia's ambassador to the United Arab Emirates and then to Libya. He translated the conversation.

"If you don't pull your troops out of Kuwait," I began, "a strike against you will be inevitable. You should feel responsible for the war. You certainly understand I didn't come here to intimidate you. But perhaps withdrawal of the Iraqi troops is the only way out of the situation."

Saddam Hussein replied, "If my only options are to fall on my knees and surrender or fight, I'll choose the latter." I am trying to quote him as closely as possible. "As a realist I can imagine that under certain conditions a withdrawal of troops is possible. But I cannot agree to that unless the withdrawal is preceded by a resolution of the Palestinian problem. I want to make sure it implies the beginning of talks covering the substance and the methods of resolving the Palestinian issue. The Kuwait problem cannot be solved unless these points are clarified.

"You see," he went on, "now that I have given up all the results of the eight-year war with Iran and returned everything to prewar conditions, the Iraqi people will not forgive me for unconditional withdrawal of our troops from Kuwait. 'What about our access to the sea?' they will ask me."

I argued, "If the Iraqi people have accepted without reservation the fact that all the results of the bloody war with Iran were given up for nothing, then they will also agree with your decision on Kuwait."

Saddam kept laying down conditions for withdrawal of his troops from Kuwait, but there was some shift in his position. Even at this first meeting the line that had seemed to be set in reinforced concrete on August 12 softened slightly. Then he had insisted that the Kuwaiti and Palestinian issues had to be settled simultaneously; now the links between Kuwait and Palestine became more flexible. Of course, all that was said privately. In public Saddam kept declaring his "uncompromising principles."

I told Hussein directly that the "living shield" of foreign hostages who were forcibly kept at military and other strategic sites would not prevent a U.S. military strike if the Iraqi troops failed to withdraw from Kuwait. I pointed out that by such actions Saddam had turned the whole world against him.

Saddam said nothing and sat in silence, deep in thought. . . .

Policy with regard to some groups of foreign hostages shifted in October. This subject came up at our second meeting, on October 28. Now, however, the Russian delegation had to send a cable to Moscow reporting on our talks in Baghdad, and we gathered that night in the office of the Soviet ambassador to discuss what we should say. Of course, we were delighted that the evacuation of the Soviet specialists was taken care of. By that time the next month's schedule of additional Aeroflot flights to Baghdad had been approved, and, as events were to prove, the Iraqis strictly adhered to it.

No one failed to point out that we had managed to make Saddam grasp a number of facts and arguments and developments of which he might not have been informed before. We were also unanimous in glimpsing some light at the end of the tunnel, which gave hope for a political settlement.

As Tariq Aziz was driving me to the airport in the morning he said, "Saddam Hussein is expecting to see concrete proposals. We expect the contacts to continue."

"Tariq, can you say that again in front of our ambassador at the airport?" I asked.

"What for?"

"Because after all, we'll be on the plane, and your message is important. We'd better put it in a coded message to Moscow. It will sound more reliable."

Tariq agreed and did as I asked.

THE MISSION WILL BE CONTINUED

As soon as I returned to Moscow on the evening of October 6, I gave Gorbachev a detailed account of my Baghdad meetings. In the course of my briefing the idea came up to send my observations to Presidents Bush, François Mitterrand of France, Hosni Mubarak of Egypt, and Hafez al-Assad of Syria and to King Fahd of Saudi Arabia, and then to meet again with Hussein. Shevardnadze and I were to prepare instructions for those trips.

The foreign minister was upset by the idea of my mission. Our relations became especially strained after we exchanged "niceties" in front of Vladimir Kryuchkov, head of the KGB, and Prime Minister Ryzhkov. When Shevardnadze called my proposals a recipe for disaster in the Middle East and predicted they would lead to "the collapse of our whole foreign policy," I blew up: "How dare you, a graduate of a correspondence course from a teachers' college in Kutaisi, lecture me on the Middle East, the region I've studied since my student days!"

Gorbachev raised his voice: "Yevgeny, stop right now!"

The Foreign Ministry had never sent any proposals regarding my mission. I decided to call Shevardnadze. "Why have our relations turned so sour?" I asked him. "They were so good before. You were the one who were going to make me an honorary citizen of Tbilisi. Do you really think I want to replace you as foreign minister?"

"But that rumor is all over the ministry," answered Shevardnadze.

And apparently he believed it. Later, according to a book by two Washington insiders, the Soviet foreign minister made an unprecedented move: before my meeting with the U.S. president he "had informed President Bush" that he could ignore "Primakov's ideas." He disavowed the mission that his own president had ordered! "That marked the beginning of a new stage in the relations between the two countries—the Soviet foreign minister and the U.S. Department of State had conspired against the Kremlin's special envoy."[1]

I was preparing for my meeting with the heads of states with whom I was to share my ideas about the "invisible package." To begin with, Iraq had to declare that it was withdrawing its troops from Kuwait and then do so without delay. Under that plan, however, Saddam Hussein was to be assured in advance that withdrawal of his troops would be followed by serious work leading to settlement of the Arab–Israeli conflict and that the U.N. Security Council members would take an active part in the process.

Another important part of the so-called invisible package to be laid before Hussein before the full and unconditional withdrawal of his troops was the security system the world community wanted to see in the region after the crisis was over. That system must respond to the concerns of Iraq's neighbors, who were justifiably alarmed by Iraq's aggressive behavior based on its burgeoning military potential, and Saddam Hussein himself, who complained to me that he would still be within shooting range even if he withdrew his troops from Kuwait.

When I was preparing for my trip to Paris I received a message from our ambassador in Italy, who said that Prime Minister Giulio Andreotti, who was chairman of the European Community at the time, would like to see me in Rome. Quite a few of the ambassadors accredited to Moscow were requesting a meeting. It was one more indication that the political activity of the Soviet Union in the Middle East was at the center of the world's attention.

We landed at Fiumicino airport about 2 P.M. on October 16. The appointment with Andreotti was set for 3:30 and we had to cover a fairly long distance. I saw for myself what the Italian police motorcyclists were capable of. At high speed they skillfully maneuvered the other cars aside to clear the road for us. One of them fell on a sharp curve, but fortunately he sprang to his feet and was quickly on his way again. We reached the prime minister's palace on time. Andreotti asked me to repeat some details of my conversation with Hussein, and he expressed concern that even before all the political options were exhausted some "objective circumstances" could induce the United States and others to begin military action. These circumstances included, among other things, weather conditions (in March, sand driven by strong winds makes military operations in the Arabian Desert extremely difficult) and the season of pilgrimage to Mecca and Medina, which begins in June. About a million and a half Muslims come from all over the world to make their hajj every year. Andreotti predicted that the war could become a reality in the very near future.

Most important, Andreotti said, "If Washington agrees with your approach to a political settlement, we will undoubtedly support that." I got the feeling that he regarded the USSR's activity as one of the real alternatives to slipping into the abyss of war.

On the morning of October 17 we left Rome for Paris. Our meeting with President François Mitterrand took place at his palace on the Champs-Elysées that afternoon. He, too, agreed that no extreme measures were to be used until all other possibilities had been exhausted. But like Andreotti, the French president did not doubt that war was imminent. Supporting the USSR's efforts to avoid a military confrontation, Mitterrand told us what France itself was doing in that regard. At the same time he stressed the importance of coordinating the efforts of our two states, both permanent members of the U.N. Security Council.

Perhaps more than any other Western leader President Mitterrand felt the necessity of pushing for a solution to the Palestinian problem as a means to resolve the Kuwait crisis. But he doubted that Washington would go along with it.

So on to the United States. Our meetings with American leaders began upon our arrival in Washington on October 18. The first meeting was with D. Ross, head of the State Department's planning department, actually State's chief Middle East expert. Ross came to the Soviet embassy to clarify our position in advance. Delving into the details, Ross listened to my explanations with reservations, even disapproval. Rejection was written on his face. He openly disapproved of the idea of advising Iraq that after its troops were withdrawn from Kuwait, more steps would be taken to resolve the Palestinian issue.

"Israel won't accept that," declared Ross flatly.

Little new was achieved in subsequent meetings with Secretary James Baker and the president's national security adviser, Brent Scowcroft. Baker was surely waiting for the meeting with Bush, while Scowcroft was more interested in our perception of the situation in Iraq than in our proposals for resolving the crisis. Only the president's special adviser on the Persian Gulf crisis, Condoleezza Rice, seemed to realize that there was some rationale to our proposals.

The meeting in Scowcroft's office was enlivened by the unexpected arrival of President Bush, who had run through the pouring rain from the White House and walked in soaking wet, just, he said, to shake my hand. "I couldn't help doing it, knowing you were at Scowcroft's." It was a gesture I highly appreciated.

"I'm looking forward to our meeting tomorrow morning," we heard President Bush say as he was leaving.

Bush received us in the White House on the morning of October 19, 1990. Baker, Scowcroft, and the White House chief of staff, John Sununu, were already there. The president emphasized his great appreciation of the fact that Gorbachev had sent his personal envoy to Washington to inform them of our efforts in the Middle East. He repeated this on several occasions.

Bush was extremely interested in my impressions of our negotiations with Saddam; he asked about the specifics of his psychology and the history of my relations with him. Bush kept asking me to clarify points and took notes. It was obvious that some of our observations differed from the president's view. In general, I received the impression that George Bush still had not made a final decision on whether to strike Iraq. He not only did not rule out another meeting with Hussein but supported the idea, stressing that its only purpose would be "to inform Hussein of the uncompromising position by the United States." But still he added, "If a positive signal comes from Hussein, it will be heard."

At the end of the two-hour discussion President Bush said, "You've told us a lot of interesting things. There's something new for me in a number of your ideas. But I have to consult with my assistants. Are you going to stay in Washington a bit longer?"

I said I was ready to do so if necessary.

"I'll give you an answer in two or three hours," Bush replied before saying good-bye to us warmly.

The answer came more quickly. It seemed that many of Bush's advisers became much more vocal after our departure than they had been at the meeting. In any case, it did not take them two or three hours. At lunch, hosted by Sununu forty-five minutes later, I was told: "The president asked me to tell you you can schedule your departure to suit yourself." So our discussion was not to continue.

After we sent a detailed account of our meetings with the American officials to Moscow, I exchanged general impressions with Ambassador Aleksandr Bessmertnykh and Permanent Representative to the U.N. Yuly Vorontsov, who came in from New York. We all agreed that the efforts of our independent mission in no way conflicted with Soviet-American cooperation in achieving the main goal: Iraq's withdrawal from Kuwait.

To my great satisfaction, the same idea was voiced at a White House press conference. On March 2, 1991, after the Gulf War was over, President George Bush stated that he "had never had any complaints" about Gorbachev's attempts to find a peaceful solution to the Kuwait crisis. "I would like to support the Soviet Union in its desire to continue its multilateral diplomatic efforts, which have already made a significant contribution to the solution of Middle East issues," declared Bush.

A few hours before our departure for Moscow we had to change our route. We received Gorbachev's instructions to stop over in London first to meet with Prime Minister Margaret Thatcher at her request. Similar requests came from the governments of Japan and Canada. But because we assumed that we would be making a second visit to the Middle East, we had to forgo flights to Canada and Japan.

Our ambassador in London, Leonid Zamyatin, pointed out that the prime minister rarely received visitors at Chequers, the prime minister's country residence. I think the reason I was given that honor was simply that it was Saturday, and Mrs. Thatcher preferred to spend weekends in the country. After an hour-long car ride, Mrs. Thatcher met us on an impeccably flat gravel driveway at the heavy gate of an ancient English country house.

The prime minister received us informally. We sat in antique armchairs by the fireplace. I first met the prime minister at a session of the Inter-Parliamentary Union in London in September 1989. A few days later I had a chance to meet her at the Moscow airport when her plane made a scheduled stop there on her way to and from Tokyo. Thatcher recalled that I had said she had a magic touch. In the few days between her two stops at the Moscow airport, I was elected an alternate member of the CPSU Politburo.

Everything seemed to promise a relaxed conversation. There was nothing to be concerned about. The prime minister carefully listened to all the information we gave her without interrupting. But then she spoke nonstop for almost an hour, openly advocating an approach that was steadily gaining strength: we should not stop with securing the withdrawal of Iraqi troops from Kuwait but should deliver a crushing blow to Iraq, "break Saddam Hussein's spine," and destroy the country's whole military and possibly industrial potential. "Nobody should prevent us from solving this problem," said Thatcher. "Saddam Hussein must not have even a shadow of a doubt that the world community will not retreat and will achieve its goals. Nobody should even try to save his regime from attack."

"So you see no alternative to military action?" I managed to interject.

"I don't," Thatcher replied.

"In that case, when will the military action begin?"

"I can't say, because it should start unexpectedly for Iraq."

The conversation with Thatcher had gone on for more than two hours now. Feeling it was getting increasingly harsh, I said: "Perhaps we should stop at that, Mrs. Prime Minister? It was useful speaking with you. Your position has become clearer to me. I hope the conversation was of some use to you as well."

At that point the "Iron Lady" instantly turned into a kind and gracious hostess. She said, "Let's change the atmosphere and go to the library. Let's forget about our business for a while." I think Thatcher was pleased that, like herself, I preferred whiskey to other drinks.

She saw us off at the entrance to the ancient Chequers. But this ending didn't change my opinion in the least. The conversation with Thatcher had been designed to be a cold shower for us.

HOPE STILL LINGERS

After our trips across the ocean and to Europe, the main conclusion boiled down to this: everything was pointing toward a military solution. This conclusion certainly did not gibe with the statement that the anti-Saddam coalition was unanimous in its approach to the Kuwait crisis. The positions of French President Mitterrand and Italian Prime Minister Andreotti were in sharp contrast to that of British Prime Minister Thatcher. But the peculiarity of this situation was that France and Italy and probably many other West Europeans who favored a cautious approach did realize that if a political solution was not found, they would be drawn into the war.

President Bush was probably still holding back. But he must have been under growing pressure. At the same time the leaders of the countries I had visited were expressly interested in continuing our contacts regarding the Persian Gulf situation.

After listening to my report, Gorbachev told us to continue the mission and to fly to Cairo, Damascus, Riyadh, and Baghdad. In the capitals of Egypt, Syria, and Saudi Arabia I was to discuss various possibilities of "invigorating the Arab factor" in an effort to make Iraq withdraw its troops without the use of military force and without "remuneration." And during my second meeting with Saddam I was to give him a vivid picture of the situation he would have to face if he rejected the demands of the world community. The mission was of special significance because it represented practically the only channel of direct communication with Saddam Hussein.

On October 24 we once again flew out of Moscow. Our destination was Cairo.

On the way from the airport I talked with Foreign Minister Boutros Boutros-Ghali, who had met me there. He was gravely concerned about the consequences of the war, which he predicted with great certainty. I sensed a feeling of anxiety about the future during my long conversation with my old friend Usama al-Baza, who headed the political office of President Mubarak. Baza was troubled not only by the fact that Egyptian soldiers were part of the multinational forces and that hundreds of thousands of Egyptian workers were in the Persian Gulf countries, which could turn into a war theater; he worried also about the postcrisis situation. The prospect of a growing Islamic fundamentalism seemed a serious possibility.

He agreed that without the "invisible package" designed to ensure the withdrawal of Iraqi troops from Kuwait, the war was practically inevitable.

But two unexpected problems stood in our way. The first was technical. President Mubarak was visiting the Gulf countries and was ready to cut his trip short and meet with us in Cairo, according to Baza, but only on October 26. The second problem was essentially political. Baza, who was in direct contact with the foreign minister of Saudi Arabia, Saud al-Faisal, said that Faisal asked me to go first to Baghdad and then to Riyadh. But a phone call from the Iraqi ambassador to Cairo indicated that Baghdad wanted us to reverse the order of our visits. We decided to accept the Saudi option, because if events developed favorably, we would be able to go to King Fahd not entirely empty-handed.

October 25 remained open, and since we were pressed for time, I asked to reschedule my meeting with President Hafiz al-Assad of Syria for that date. A positive response came quickly.

I have known Assad for many years and have met him on many occasions, so our conversation was informal from the start. Assad had a way of listening intently and weaving his ideas into the fabric of the conversation. As a very experienced politician, Assad put forward an interesting formula. What if we held an Arab summit to call on Saddam Hussein to withdraw his troops from Kuwait "in the interests of the entire Arab world"? We could also declare that the Arab leaders hoped the withdrawal would open the way to a resolution of the Palestinian issue.

Would it be possible to convene such a summit? I asked.

He was not certain, but he thought the chances were good because anti-war feeling in the Arab world was very strong, even in the countries that categorically demanded Iraq's withdrawal from Kuwait. "If we don't hold a summit," continued Assad, "there are other kinds of Arab initiative, such as a message to Saddam Hussein signed by Arab leaders, even if not by all of them."

Assad emphasized that the USSR was "perhaps the only country in contact with Saddam Hussein capable of preparing an Arab solution."

On October 26 we returned to Cairo, where we met with President Mubarak, whom I had also known for many years.

Here too the desire to avoid war was accentuated. Mubarak also spoke in favor of the Soviet initiative and enriched it with the following proposal: If Hussein agreed to withdraw from Kuwait completely and unconditionally, guarantees could be given that conditions favorable for his future negotiations with Kuwait would be created for him. Asked about it directly, Mubarak answered without hesitation: "Egypt can give such guarantees in advance."

"What about Saudi Arabia?"

"I can promise firmly that Saudi Arabia will join such guarantees."

At the same time, Mubarak was more skeptical than Assad regarding the possibility of holding an Arab summit. He did not conceal his personal dislike of the Iraqi leader and even hostility toward him.

President Mubarak was in close contact with the American administration on the Kuwait crisis. Neither he nor Baza nor Foreign Minister Essmat Abdel-Magid, whom we also met, concealed that fact. That is why it was even more important that we have similar views on such questions as the difference between "rewarding" Iraq and offering a package of proposals aimed at Iraq's complete withdrawal from Kuwait.

After the meetings in Damascus and Cairo, more grounds for optimism seemed to be forming. But the key to the success of this mission was certainly in Baghdad, and my trip there suddenly became questionable. Tariq Aziz had summoned our Ambassador Posuvalyuk and told him that the Iraqi leadership was extremely unhappy about a new resolution of the U.N. Security Council, which demanded compensation from Iraq for the damage it had inflicted on Kuwait. According to Aziz, the Soviet union was "actively supporting the resolution." In the circumstances, he believed a visit to Baghdad by the Soviet president's envoy could hardly be fruitful.

I decided to contact our embassy in Baghdad and dictated a message for Tariq Aziz that read something like this: "At the very least, we are perplexed that at this crucial moment, when Moscow is doing everything in its power to find a political solution to the situation, the Iraqi side is putting obstacles in our way." I told Tariq Aziz that in the circumstances my arrival in Baghdad would be possible only upon receipt of another invitation. "If we don't hear from Baghdad by tomorrow afternoon, the visit will be canceled."

Our ambassador to Baghdad passed the message immediately and just as quickly came Tariq Aziz's response: The representative of the president of the USSR would be received at the highest level in Iraq. The answer that came from Baghdad also settled the order of my visits to Baghdad and Riyadh.

We landed at the Baghdad airport the next day. The second meeting with Saddam Hussein was as lengthy as the first and also consisted of two sessions, first with the advisers and then in private.

I was interested to see that Saddam brought practically the country's entire leadership to the meeting. Everyone was dressed the same, in military uniform. Saddam opened the talk by saying, "I have invited my colleagues in the government deliberately. Let them hear our conversation, because there are both hawks and doves among them."

"I would prefer to have only doves here," I told Saddam.

"In that case, only our beloved president will remain here," responded Taha Ramadan.

It is conceivable that by dividing the leaders of Iraq into two groups, Hussein intended to show that there was some room for maneuver. But I doubt that the words about differences of opinion in the Iraqi leadership described the real picture. One man decided everything. Those who disagreed with him in the past were, as they say, "far away." And those who remained expressed their full support of all the decisions made.

Their subordination showed in their behavior. When I once again asked to speak with him in private, every Iraqi came up to Saddam, clicked his heels, and bowed to him before leaving the room. Perhaps their "independent thinking" was expressed mainly by how zealously those present at the meeting with their leader nodded their heads to demonstrate their full agreement with his statements; some nodded with lesser enthusiasm, but they still nodded.

This meeting with Saddam Hussein was interesting by comparison with my first encounter with him. In my opinion, shared by my colleagues, certain changes had taken place in the three weeks between the meetings. On October 5, as I mentioned earlier, Hussein's main point was that Kuwait belonged to Iraq "historically"; on October 28 he did not mention the subject.

On October 28 Saddam Hussein did not react negatively, as he had done three weeks before, when I said that withdrawal of troops from Kuwait "had to precede any other action." Furthermore, he expressed a desire to talk about the specific terms of the withdrawal, albeit in allegorical form. At our face-to-face meeting (in the presence of Sergei Kirpechenko, who translated for us) he remarked, "How can I declare the withdrawal of my troops if I don't know the terms of the U.S. withdrawal from Saudi Arabia? Will the U.N. Security Council's sanctions against Iraq remain in effect or will they be canceled? Will there be any linkage between the withdrawal of our troops from Kuwait and the resolution of the Palestinian issue?"

I would not want to simplify matters. Certainly Hussein kept linking his withdrawal from Kuwait with a number of other issues. But the questions he posed do suggest that his position was not set in stone, although it was still far from satisfactory.

Another positive development was that Hussein no longer kept silent, as he had done during our first meeting, but was now ready to discuss the issue of foreign hostages in Iraq in sufficiently concrete terms. He even found it possible to publicize the fact that we had discussed the subject. When he was interviewed on the American TV channel CNN, Hussein said that "it was yesterday that I gave Primakov a number of specific ideas regarding those people who are not given an opportunity to leave the country."

His ideas boiled down to this: He wanted the presidents of the USSR and France to call upon him to free the hostages and to confirm their adherence to a "political solution of the Persian Gulf crisis and other regional problems"; and they should denounce any use of force against Iraq.

I told Hussein that that wording was not realistic, but I promised I would immediately inform Gorbachev, who was in France at the time, about Hussein's proposal. It's interesting to note that when I said the wording was unacceptable, Tariq Aziz said they were ready to discuss other proposals by the Soviet and French presidents on this issue.

Hussein also demonstrated his interest in the idea of Arab participation in the settlement process. I noticed that Hussein singled out Saudi Arabia as the main and possibly the only Arab partner for negotiations; he stressed that he was ready to meet with Saudi representatives in person or to send his envoy to meet with them "at any time and any place."

But Saddam did not say yes to the main question. When we talked face to face I began by saying, "You've known me for a long time and you must have been convinced that I always try to tell you the truth. So a strike against Iraq, and a very powerful one, is inevitable unless you declare your withdrawal from Kuwait and carry it out."

In response, Saddam repeated that without knowing the answers to the questions he had posed, he could do nothing. "That is why I expect our contacts to continue," he stressed.

Thus a mechanism for a political settlement could be set in motion, slow and difficult as it was. I emphasize the words "slow" and "difficult." Of course, there was no reason to overestimate the chances of the process. But at the same time—and I say it with confidence—there was no reason to disparage them, either.

As we were flying from Baghdad to Riyadh, the presidents of the USSR and France were holding a press conference in Paris. News agencies announced that Gorbachev and Mitterrand were discussing all the nuances of our meeting with Saddam Hussein in detail. (We learned more about it later, when we returned to Moscow.) Gorbachev also referred to a political solution at his press conference when he mentioned that he received my cable from Baghdad at five in the morning.

So now we are in Saudi Arabia. The main meeting was held in Jidda. The leading members of the Saudi ruling family, headed by King Fahd, sat behind a long rectangular table similar to those in the offices of Soviet executives. Present were Crown Prince Abdullah, Defense Minister Prince Sultan, and Foreign Minister Prince Saud al-Faisal.

I thought it necessary to outline our position on the Kuwait crisis. I said that the Soviet Union's unyielding position was based on the undeniable necessity of the withdrawal of the Iraqi troops and the restoration of the situation that existed in Kuwait before August 2, and that the USSR hoped to achieve those goals by political means. King Fahd applauded. In general the Saudis are very likable people because of their frankness and sincerity. It may be traced to the Bedouins, who are known for their friendliness and kindness.

The king and his advisers did not reject the idea of the "invisible package" for negotiations with Saddam Hussein. At the same time they, like the Americans, were seriously concerned that Saddam could use it as a pretext to gain time to strengthen his position in Kuwait. Apparently some members of the royal family favored the immediate use of force. However, I think King Fahd took a more balanced position. The nature of our conversation—pronouncedly open and friendly—was not just evidence of the Saudis' traditional hospitality. King Fahd, I daresay, sincerely hoped to finally force Iraq out of Kuwait by political means.

Their relations with Iraq were their sore thumb. We heard complaints that the Iraqi leadership had failed to appreciate the plentiful assistance and support, especially financial, that Iraq had received from Saudi Arabia, Kuwait, and the Emirates during its war with Iran. There were reasons for those complaints. But Riyadh's attitude toward Baghdad was by no means motivated solely by resentment. One could not overlook King Fahd's reflection on whether a day would ever come when Iraq would be unable to threaten its neighbors again even if the Kuwait crisis was resolved peacefully. "If that doesn't happen, we'll have to arm ourselves to the teeth," said the king.

I certainly relayed to the king Saddam's remark that Fahd would play a greater role than any other Arab leader in resolving the Kuwaiti crisis. I also told him about the proposal of a meeting between Iraq and Saudi Arabia. I sensed that the king was reluctant to make an immediate decision. Close coordination between the Saudis and the American leadership had its effect (it could not be otherwise, especially with American troops stationed in Saudi Arabia). But Fahd spoke unequivocally in favor of the continuation of our mission and said he would send a message to the Soviet president with his thoughts about the situation, giving due consideration to our wide-ranging discussion.

Foreign Minister Saud al-Faisal told us that the emir of Kuwait wished to meet with the Soviet president's representative. During the Iraqi invasion the emir had managed to escape from the palace under attack and leave for Saudi Arabia. The Saudis told us that the royal jet could take us to Taif, close to the Sheraton hotel that was the emir's temporary residence.

The Saudis' interest in our meeting with the leader of Kuwait was obvious. This meeting was important for us as well, because it gave us an opportunity to learn directly from the Kuwaiti leader what he felt about the USSR's political activity. For quite obvious reasons, Kuwait took the toughest line of all and wanted force to be used against Iraq.

The Kuwaiti foreign minister met us at the airport. In the car he told us about the tragic fate of his country's people under occupation. Some of his relatives had died; the fates of others were unknown.

The emir of Kuwait greeted us warmly and expressed not the slightest doubt that we were doing the right thing in seeking a political way out of the labyrinth. Thus our conversation at the Sheraton Hotel served as one more corroboration of the rightness of our approach.

In my mind I was going through my talks with the leaders of the Arab states that formed the anti-Iraq coalition. Naturally these discussions varied. But I had a strong feeling that although they all felt very strongly about Saddam and wanted to keep him in check or even do away with him, they could not get rid of the thought that, after all, Iraq was an Arab country. That was why they seemed willing to talk about a peaceful political solution.

We left for Moscow on October 30. We stopped at the Larnaka airport in Cyprus, where we were met by Cyprus's foreign minister. A small helicopter was parked nearby, its engines running. The minister told us that President Georghios Vassiliou asked us to "hop over" for a brief visit.

"Cyprus," said Vassiliou, "is ready to provide its territory for possible meetings, including confidential ones, if they are needed to push back the threat of war."

After we returned to Moscow and reported to Gorbachev, the Soviet president called George Bush and told him he was ready to send his envoy to Baghdad once again. Bush's radio address contained a positive response to Gorbachev's proposal. But several hours later the Soviet ambassador to the United States reported that Bush did not oppose the Soviet representative's trip to Baghdad provided he again told Saddam Hussein: "Get out of Kuwait."

IT'S WAR AFTER ALL

In the meantime, war was chosen as the way to resolve the conflict in the Persian Gulf. A telephone call woke me up at 2:45 A.M. on January 17, 1991. Gorbachev was on the line. He said Defense Minister Dmitry T. Yazov, Foreign Minister Bessmertnykh, and KGB chief Kryuchkov were already on their way to the Kremlin, and he wanted me to come over. He explained that the U.S. secretary of state had called Bessmertnykh, who had assumed his office only the day before, and informed him that military action would begin within minutes.

As expected, the war began with powerful air strikes. First Iraq's airports and radar installations were hit by missiles launched from U.S. warships in the Persian Gulf. Then followed several waves of bombers, Stealth among them.

It seems that until the last moment Hussein did not believe the multinational coalition would initiate military action. That was another of his errors, perhaps a fatal one. During my third trip to Baghdad (I shall describe it later) I was told that after Hussein received President Bush's proposal of a meeting between the U.S. secretary of state and the Iraqi foreign minister, he told his advisers, "I did tell you the Soviet Union was trying to intimidate us when it said a strike was inevitable. Events are following a different scenario."

Despite the obvious losses for Baghdad, it became apparent that a large number of its mobile missile systems survived, including those that targeted Israel and Saudi Arabia. A few words about those missiles. The media often referred to them as "Scuds," which implied their Soviet origin. Indeed, the USSR had supplied its R-300 tactical missiles, known in the West as Scuds, to Iraq and some other Arab countries. But the missiles that were used against Israel and Saudi Arabia were not the so-called Scuds but other missiles called al-Hussein and al-Abbas, which had been manufactured in Iraq with the help of a number of Western European companies. The range of these missiles was two to three times that of the R-300's.

Iraq attached special significance to missile strikes against Israel. Iraq undoubtedly gambled that Israel would retaliate, in which case Iraq expected to get support even from Arab countries that until then had remained neutral, some leaning slightly against Iraq, and possibly from Muslim states in general. Indeed, a wave of public outrage rose in Israel and the government felt considerable pressure to retaliate against the Iraqi provocations. It required a lot of effort to hold the Israeli leadership back. That effort came primarily from the United States.

The Soviet Union strongly condemned missile strikes against Israel and Saudi Arabia. At the same time, Moscow advised the Israeli leadership of the need to show restraint at such a critical moment.

Meanwhile the war was rapidly escalating. The air raids and missile attacks against Iraq and the Iraqi forces in Kuwait were growing more intense. Their main targets were the military sites and installations and industrial enterprises producing matériel for the Iraqi army. The United States attached special importance to hitting nuclear reactors, chemical factories, and the laboratories where biological weapons could be developed. Naturally, we needed information on whether the destruction of these sites would affect neighboring countries close to Iraq, the Soviet Union being one of them. Gorbachev issued instructions for our scientific and technical facilities to maintain round-the-clock surveillance over the country's southern areas, only 250–300 kilometers from Iraq.

At this time a crisis work group was formed in Moscow, consisting of the foreign and defense ministers and the minister of internal affairs; the chairman of the KGB; the president's adviser on foreign affairs, Anatoly Chernyaev; and myself. On the third day of the war, January 19, Gorbachev called us in and told us he had decided to advance another political initiative in the hope of stopping the war in the Persian Gulf. The Soviet ambassador to Baghdad received instructions to contact Hussein immediately or to deliver the following message to him through Foreign Minister Aziz: If we receive his assurance that Iraq is ready to withdraw its troops from Kuwait without reservations or conditions, we shall propose a cease-fire to the United States. Gorbachev gave the American leadership advance notice of the USSR's efforts. I emphasize that because people who either did not know the truth or chose to ignore it accused us of going behind the United States' back.

Baghdad remained silent for two days and then in a radio broadcast declared that such proposals "should be addressed to President Bush."

In the meantime, increasing numbers of civilians in Baghdad and other cities were being subjected to air and missile attacks. All the country's power stations were destroyed. As a result, water treatment facilities and sewage pumps stopped working, threatening epidemics. Soon targets that could hardly be considered military were under attack.

The war in the Persian Gulf acquired ecological dimensions as well. Huge amounts of oil were spilled in the Gulf waters. The oil spill posed a serious threat to the environment. Danger was mounting that Iraq might use all the weapons of mass destruction at its disposal.

Many specialists believed Iraq did not possess nuclear weapons, but they did not rule out the possibility that it could spray radioactive agents over the troops and possibly over civilians in Israel and the Arab states that were fighting against Iraq. That was a grave concern.

So were statements from American quarters suggesting the possibility of using tactical nuclear weapons in the ground war against the Iraqi army.

Foreign Minister Aleksandr Bessmertnykh visited Washington between January 26 and January 29. A joint Soviet-American statement was issued. Secretary of State Baker pointed out that the United States and its partners in the coalition were seeking to liberate Kuwait, not to destroy Iraq. In view of the American position, Bessmertnykh agreed that withdrawal of Iraqi troops from Kuwait should remain the objective of the international community.

According to the statement, the foreign minister and the secretary still believed that a cease-fire was possible "if Iraq gave its unambiguous commitment to pull out of Kuwait." They also agreed that this commitment should immediately be backed up by concrete steps leading to full implementation of the U.N. Security Council resolutions.

This statement was extremely important, since it declared explicitly that the main objective was to make Iraq withdraw its troops from Kuwait unconditionally. And it was precisely this part of the statement that was sharply criticized in the United States. Another criticism of the Soviet-American statement was that it said that elimination of the sources of conflicts and instability in the region was impossible without a vigorous peace process that involved reconciliation of Israel, the Arab states, and the Palestinians. There was a feeling that the hardening of the U.S. position was backed by influential forces in that country.

At the February 9 meeting of the crisis group we suggested that Gorbachev invite Tariq Aziz to Moscow.

"No," said the president, "we should send our representative directly to Hussein. We don't have time for intermediaries." Turning to me, Gorbachev told me to leave as soon as possible.

BAGHDAD UNDER FIRE

This time it was incomparably more difficult to get to Baghdad. We decided it would be best to go by way of Iran. Iranian authorities allowed us to fly from Teheran to Bakhtaran (formerly Kermanshah), and from there we drove four hours to the Iraqi border.

Our motorcade took a mountainous road, and our accompanying guards and local escorts changed as we passed from region to region. We felt like the baton in a relay race. Some escort vehicles were police cars; other vehicles probably belonged to the Islamic Revolutionary Guards. One of them followed us for about fifty kilometers. A boy, almost a teenager, stood in the wind on the open deck of that truck, his finger curled around the trigger of an anti-aircraft machine gun. It made us feel cold just to look at him, but he was doing his duty unperturbed.

As we went on, I was amazed to see bombed-out towns and villages the length of the 100 kilometers along the border, where fighting had been heavy during the war between Iraq and Iran. Villages and towns literally lay in ruins, razed to the ground, with here and there the remains of burned-out tanks. I have to admit that I never thought the war between Iran and Iraq had been so devastating as to leave behind such a ghastly landscape.

Incidentally, when we reached Baghdad and Tariq Aziz began to fume about the air raids against Iraq, I remarked that war was always terrible and told him what I had seen on Iranian territory invaded by Iraq.

It was dark by the time we reached the border. The Iranian Islamic Revolutionary Guards were now performing all security functions in their territory, including border formalities. As they began to process our papers, we left the "guest tent" and immediately found ourselves amid a crowd of refugees. Suitcases, bags, bales, crying children, women with somber faces . . . It was cold and there was no shelter. We talked with some of them. At that time most of the people who crossed the Iranian border were foreigners from Southeast Asia and Sudan who had worked in Iraq.

On the Iraqi side of the border we were met by Deputy Foreign Minister al-Faisal and Soviet Ambassador Viktor Posuvalyuk. It was late and we drove to Baghdad at high speed. The headlights of our cars, blinking on and off from time to time, snatched sections of the road from the pitch-darkness. When we reached the suburbs of Baghdad two and a half hours later, our motorcade instantly fell apart. The cars we had been riding in were covered with mud for camouflage, as all cars used by the Iraqi leaders were. It occurred to me that the mud served to differentiate these cars from all others and thus could betray their official passengers.

We arrived at al-Rashid Hotel at eleven o'clock. We were told that was the safest place in the Iraqi capital because foreign journalists stayed there, Peter Arnett of CNN among them. There was no light; the elevators did not work; my grand suite was lit by a kerosene lamp (I alone was accorded this privilege; my colleagues had no lamps); there were buckets of water in the bathroom.

It was quiet. Air raids usually started at this time; tonight they were late, and American journalists who kept dropping by, attracted by the light, joked, "Stay awhile longer, they may cancel the raids." But, as they say, we brought disaster on ourselves: an hour later air raid sirens howled. As many people attested later, the city came under devastating air attacks the two nights we were there.

We met with Saddam Hussein the same evening. We expected to go down into the bunker or perhaps someplace far from Baghdad, but everything was much simpler: we were taken to one of the guesthouses in downtown Baghdad. We thought it was a temporary stop, that our descent to the underground would begin from there. But the guesthouse lights, powered by a generator, suddenly came on and in walked Saddam Hussein with his lieutenants. He sat down near one of the small stoves, took off his trench coat, unbuckled his gun belt, as he usually did, and put it down on the floor. At that moment I noticed how much weight he had lost. He must have lost fifteen or twenty kilos since we last met. But he looked composed.

Hussein began with a few phrases that could be interpreted as an attempt to show the firmness of Iraq's position. The tone of the conversation and the nature of his statements were probably dictated by the presence of his entourage. We got the impression that he was addressing them rather than us.

When we were alone, I stressed that the Americans firmly intended to begin a large-scale ground operation, which would result in the total defeat of the Iraqi troops in Kuwait. I reminded him that politics is the art of the possible, and I proposed that he announce the withdrawal of troops from Kuwait on the shortest possible timetable. The withdrawal must be complete and unconditional.

Saddam Hussein said he was ready to pull his troops out of Kuwait and asked if I could stay in Iraq a little longer because he had to consult with his colleagues. Fearing a delay in his answer, I said I could not, I had to leave for the Iranian border at six in the morning. Saddam agreed to call a meeting of the Iraqi leadership that night and said Tariq Aziz would deliver a brief answer to the Soviet embassy in a few hours. (Telephone lines had been destroyed by air raids.)

I immediately left for the embassy. Most of the thirteen Soviet citizens who were still in Baghdad were gathered in one room. These brave men endured all the hardships of life in Baghdad without grandstanding or complaining. They had no fresh water or electricity and lived in unheated buildings. (That was the cold season in Baghdad; if it rained at night, the puddles were frozen by morning.) To make things worse, the gasoline shortage was becoming acute. Every liter that might have been used to heat the building or provide light was saved to power the generator in order to maintain contact with Moscow. The embassy staff who had volunteered to stay on and perform their duties spent considerable time in a metal tube two meters wide, covered with soil and reinforced by beams. The tube could hardly be called a bomb shelter, but, as our friends assured us, it provided protection from the splinters that showered Baghdad during air raids.

Tariq Aziz arrived at two in the morning on February 13, bearing a written statement to the effect that the Iraqi leadership was seriously considering the ideas that had been set forth by the representative of the president of the USSR and would give their answer as soon as possible. Tariq Aziz said he was leaving for Moscow on Sunday. I was completely bewildered. Didn't Hussein understand that time was short? Was he still hoping for something?

Aziz arrived in Moscow the evening of February 17 aboard a Soviet plane

that had been sent to Teheran for him. I was invited to participate in negotiations both with the minister of foreign affairs at 9:00 A.M. and with the
president at 10:45. Gorbachev proposed that the Iraqi leadership announce
full withdrawal of its troops from Kuwait without delay and within the shortest
possible time. Gorbachev immediately got in touch with the U.S. president
and with the leaders of a number of Western European countries. Tariq Aziz
left for home by way of Iran.

On the evening of February 20 we received a message from Baghdad
that Tariq Aziz was coming to Moscow again and wanted us to send a plane
to Bakhtaran to pick him up at 5:00 P.M. the next day.

Gorbachev phoned several times for information on Aziz's arrival. There
was none. The only thing we learned was that he was delayed in Teheran,
where he was negotiating with the Iranian leadership. A message that he
had boarded the plane finally arrived at 8:15 P.M. Moscow time on February
21. It would be so late when he arrived that we discussed postponing the
meeting with the president until morning. Gorbachev said no, the situation
was critical and the talks should begin without an hour's delay.

Tariq Aziz came to the Kremlin straight from the airport a little after
midnight. The talks lasted till three in the morning. The Iraqis repeated Saddam's readiness to withdraw all his troops from Kuwait but insisted they
could not do so on short notice, since they had to pull a huge army out of
territory where bridges and roads were destroyed. At first they said they
needed three to four months for the operation, then under pressure agreed
to withdraw in no more than six weeks.

We were to continue negotiations in the morning.

When Tariq Aziz was about to leave the president's office, he was informed that we required the quick release of a group of CBS reporters and
other journalists whom the Iraqis were holding in Kuwait. Gorbachev had
received a message from Henry Kissinger, the former U.S. secretary of state,
asking him to exert his influence on Iraq in this matter. The top CBS executives thanked us for our efforts, which proved to be decisive in freeing the
journalists.

After 3:00 A.M. Gorbachev received a call from President Bush. They talked
for an hour and a half. I remained in the president's office during the conversation. Bush said he appreciated the efforts undertaken by the Soviet Union.
At the same time, he stressed that he was especially concerned for the lives
of the Kuwaiti POWs, who were being held in extremely rough conditions.

The U.S. president was also dissatisfied with the timetable for the withdrawal of the Iraqi troops. As soon as Gorbachev put down the phone he told us, "During your negotiations with the Iraqis in a few hours, pay special attention to Bush's comments."

As a result of our morning talks, several points were agreed upon; the first and main one read: "Iraq agrees to fulfill Resolution 660 and without delay and unconditionally to withdraw all of its troops from Kuwait to the positions they occupied on August 1, 1990." The Iraqis agreed to complete the withdrawal of troops within twenty-one days and to pull out of the city of Kuwait (which is almost the entire country) in the first four days. All POWs would be freed and repatriated within three days after the cease-fire and the end of military operations. Control and supervision of the cease-fire and the withdrawal of troops were supposed to be conducted by either U.N. observers or U.N. peacekeepers.

"Can we assume that Iraq accepts the entire package?" we asked Tariq Aziz. He said he needed Saddam Hussein's approval, but he did not doubt the answer would be positive. But despite his apparent confidence, Aziz suggested I fly to Baghdad with him to "inform Hussein." Realizing that time was almost up, we rejected this option in the belief that we could reach the Iraqi leadership from Moscow.

"But how can we do it?" asked Aziz. After the radio station of Iraq's foreign ministry was destroyed, the Iraqi embassy in Moscow had no connection with Baghdad. We offered Aziz the use of our radios to send their message through the Soviet embassy in Baghdad, even if Iraqi codes were used. But the decoder at the Iraqi foreign ministry could not be used for lack of power. So with Aziz's approval, we had to translate the message into Russian in Moscow, send the coded message to our embassy in Baghdad, and then have it translated into Arabic there.

On February 22 at 7:00 P.M. Moscow time President Bush presented Iraq with an ultimatum: its troops must be withdrawn from the territory of Kuwait within one week and from the city of Kuwait within forty-eight hours, the withdrawal to begin before noon New York time on February 23.

At two in the morning on February 23 (in Washington it was still February 22) we received Saddam Hussein's acceptance of the points agreed upon in Moscow.

At noon on February 23 in Moscow, Tariq Aziz met with journalists at the Foreign Ministry Press Center and announced the Iraqi leadership's decision to pull the troops out of Kuwait unconditionally and without delay, in response to President Bush's demand.

Tariq Aziz immediately left Moscow. Seeing him off, I took him aside and said, "Isn't it clear that the Iraqi leadership always delays? If, for example, you had came to Moscow on February 17 with the same proposals you brought on your second trip on February 21, or better yet, if Saddam Hussein had approved those proposals when I met with him in Baghdad, the situation might have been different. Can't you understand there is no room for bargaining or maneuvering at this point?"

After the large-scale ground military operation was over, after the Iraqi forces in Kuwait were routed and the invaders quickly left, many people kept asking: Had it even been worthwhile to try to reach a political settlement? Maybe the military solution was the best one.

I cannot agree with this conclusion, principally because the death of any human being is a tragedy. The coalition suffered few losses, but the real picture of destruction and death on the Iraqi side became apparent after the dust of Operation Desert Storm settled. And that picture was terrible. In the course of military operations all information about the victims and destruction was heavily censored in the United States.

Of course, it's impossible to change events that have already taken place. In retrospect it's easy to put everything in its place. But if Iraq had not invaded Kuwait, had not tried to annex that country, had not been catastrophically late in grasping reality, if the Iraqi leadership had more sense of responsibility, and if somebody in the West had not pushed the military solution and had not regarded the USSR's mission as a self-serving political move, the war itself and its escalation would not have been.

CHAPTER FOUR

Paradoxes of Perestroika

OPPOSITION: GORBACHEV—YELTSIN

After my unsuccessful attempt to steer the Persian Gulf situation to a political solution, I focused primarily on foreign trade issues at the Presidential Council. Sometimes I was also involved in other matters.

What caused me the most concern and even indignation at that time was the lack of progress in strengthening the power of law. With public discontent rising over the inertia of the state bodies and the lack of order and discipline, voices were increasingly clamoring for an end to "playing the democracy game" and for a return to a "strong hand" at the helm. The danger was seriously aggravated by the fact that those voices were not solely those of nostalgic conservatives; they came also from those who were disappointed by the inability of the powers that be to organize things and achieve results during the transition to democracy.

I told Gorbachev all that on the telephone. "You don't fit into the mechanism," he said.

The next day I sent Gorbachev a personal letter that said: "After our conversation yesterday I have made up my mind to resign. It's not a momentary reaction and certainly not the action of a capricious or nervous man. I trust you know I've never been either. But in the last month or so I've had the distinct feeling that you've begun to treat me differently; or perhaps it's simply that you have little need for me now. Both things make it impossible for me even to think of continuing my current duties." Attached to the note was a formal request for permission to transfer to the Soviet Academy of Sciences.

Gorbachev firmly rejected my resignation. His desire to keep me on his active team was confirmed in early March, when members of the Security Council were chosen. I don't know exactly who was working against me in the Supreme Soviet, but someone was, and the outcome of the voting was surprising and even discouraging: I did not pass. I think it was surprising to many others as well. Gorbachev spoke sincerely and passionately. He stressed that my membership in the Security Council would be useful, and he moved for a second round of votes. I took the floor and said it was not necessary. A debate followed. At that moment I felt especially thankful to all the deputies who, irrespective of their political convictions, took the floor to speak in my support. I passed after a second vote.

During the 28th Congress of the Communist Party, in early July 1990, I declined to run for the CPSU Central Committee, as did some other Politburo members who held government positions.

Doubtless the configuration of the Security Council created an opportunity to shift the axis of federal power toward the government. In any case, such an idea was entertained, but at that stage it did not materialize. If that situation continued, only one way out was possible—to split up the Party. Its smaller part (but it totaled two to three million well-organized people) would choose the path of perestroika (restructuring). Gorbachev flatly rejected all such proposals. Apparently he was afraid, instinctively or consciously, of being called a splitter.

At the beginning of the 1990s a lot of people focused on moving to a presidential republic, believing that in that way they could get rid of the Party bosses who opposed perestroika. But the presidential republic model did not envision an end to the leading role of the CPSU. That is why Gorbachev, as general secretary of the CPSU, did not seek the office of president of the USSR. It was all about one person holding two offices. No emphasis was put on political pluralism or democratization within the CPSU itself. The process was limited to the extremely important but by no means compensating development of glasnost (openness). At that stage glasnost opened the way to pluralism of opinions but not of parties.

Naturally, from the vantage of hindsight it's easier to see both the drawbacks and the mistakes that flowed from the leadership's inertia and the alignment of forces that were seeking a new way. But the fact remains that the first contradiction, which they failed to overcome and which led to further failures of the restructuring process, lay in the fact that no economic and democratic reforms could be achieved as long as the "leading role" in the country belonged to the Central Committee of the CPSU, with its practically unchanged functions, and to the Communist Party in general.

Party bosses, especially in the regions, were very much against any diminution of their importance. They voiced their opposition at all-Union forums in speeches that strongly criticized the "antisocialist" idea of perestroika. In most cases their criticism was based on a purely dogmatic understanding of socialism or was camouflage adopted to hide their personal motives. But some speakers expressed sincere distress that the direction of perestroika, especially its economic component, had not been made clear, and that the Party had made no effort to curb either the crime that had become rampant or the separatist movements that were rocking the country.

I heard quite a few such speeches at the plenary sessions of the Central Committee, the Congress of People's Deputies, and the Supreme Soviet of the USSR. Gorbachev and a number of people in his circle felt hurt by them. I was one of those who believed that only the most rational ideas expressed in such speeches should be taken into account, and then only if it was clear that the speakers were in favor of radical changes in our social and economic life.

At that time Yeltsin's popularity was rising and he was moving quickly to a position of leadership in the country. Without the so-called Yeltsin factor, it was impossible to make sense of the situation or predict where it was going.

As far as the role and place of the Party were concerned, Yeltsin's initial position did not differ radically from Gorbachev's. As the first secretary of the Moscow City CPSU Committee and an alternate member of the Politburo, Yeltsin had never spoken against the leading role of the Communist Party, but he did speak out against the practices of the Party's governing body. I was present at the plenary session of the CPSU Central Committee when Boris Nikolaevich announced his resignation from the Politburo, to the surprise of most of those present. With this move he was promoting the idea of democratizing the Communist Party. Yeltsin was very nervous. It was obvious that it took a lot of nerve to make such an unprecedented announcement. But notice that he did not resign from the office of first secretary of the Moscow City Party organization. In fact, after the plenary session he phoned Gorbachev and said he wanted to keep that office.

The reaction was predictable. Everyone condemned Yeltsin's "blunder," some strongly, others mildly. No one present at the plenary session supported Yeltsin. Yeltsin's resignation was approved, and a few days later he was also relieved of his duties as first secretary of the Moscow City Committee. That was the work of a well-organized anti-Yeltsin campaign launched by the Central Committee's Party work department.

In my opinion, at that time Gorbachev did not take an extreme position; he even tried to keep the door open. The anti-Yeltsin mood was set by other Politburo members.

And even then Yeltsin was not ready to deny the Party's leading role. At the 19th Party Conference he defended the policy of democratizing the Central Committee, at the same time admitting his mistakes. It was only after the Party failed to respond to his speech as he had hoped that Yeltsin began to drift toward the position that the Party leadership model had to go before the society could be democratized. Then after the aborted coup organized by the State Emergency Committee, he switched his position again: now the Party itself had to go.

Once a friend of mine, a political scientist, told me, "You know, if Yeltsin had been elected the Party's general secretary, it would have kept its important position in society." I think that was true at the first stage, which ended after the 19th Party Conference. After that the situation followed its own logic. Its two main elements were, first, the growing hostility, competition, and struggle between Gorbachev and Yeltsin, and second, the increasing influence of the Interregional Group. That well-organized group, which possessed considerable brainpower, was openly pushing Yeltsin to become the country's leader. Yeltsin was more of a hostage of those two processes than the author of the turn against communism.

If the Party had split up into pro-perestroika and anti-perestroika factions, the Interregional Group's field of action would have been sharply narrowed. But that never happened, and those former Party members who no longer associated themselves with the CPSU and were drifting in the direction of the old order were joining the Interregional Group. Part of the group consisted of outside dissidents, those who no longer lived within the system, led by Academician Sakharov. But he was more like a tsar than a leader. He was backed by many of those who earlier would have been classified as inside dissidents. Now they, too, finally broke with the system. They needed Yeltsin as a ram to break it apart. His character made him good for that role, and the ordinary people considered him one of them.

But a considerable number of inside dissidents remained with Gorbachev.

In 1990 and the first half of 1991, relations among the Union republics became dramatically exacerbated, and that had a direct impact on the relationship between Gorbachev and Yeltsin. That was when the Soviet Union started down the road to disintegration.

There were many reasons for the breakup, some with deep roots in the past. In the last years before his final illness Lenin spoke in favor of federalism. Later the idea transmogrified into the make-believe federalism seen in every version of the Soviet constitution, strictly for show. In fact, a unitary state was formed. Union republics were sovereign and self-governing only on paper. In reality, everything of any importance was prescribed by Moscow.

It is true that national literature, arts, cinematography, and theater were encouraged and nurtured. These developments were supported by the close cooperation of the intelligentsias of the various republics. Science and industry made progress in the regions as well. But everything was managed from the Center. Decisions on the construction of some enterprises in the republics were often made not on the basis of their economic feasibility but for political reasons. Steelworks built in Rustavi, not far from Tbilisi in Georgia, for instance, had to import their ore and coking coal from a great distance. But the steelworks were intended to forge a true working class in a republic considered dismayingly petty bourgeois.

The Center imposed its personnel policy, which had to be strictly followed. They even contrived to appoint the governors as second secretaries of the central committees of the republican Communist parties; since the second secretaries were sent from Moscow, the governors were sent from Moscow. Since to all intents and purposes the Party authorities were in charge of everyone and everything, sometimes first secretaries of the central committees of the Union republics were also sent from Moscow. Lazar Kaganovich and then Leonid Melnikov were sent to Ukraine, Brezhnev to Moldova and then to Kazakhstan, and so on. Persons of the "title" nationalities, as they are now called, usually did not head the republican KGBs; the Party and the KGB authorities were the actual rulers of the republics.

How was the "federal vertical axis" implemented in the Supreme Soviet, the USSR's version of a parliament? The CPSU Central Committee's Party work department would supply each republic with a list of the republican candidates for membership in the Supreme Soviet, to be appointed by Moscow. For instance, when the Central Committee decided that the director of

IMEMO had to be a deputy in the Supreme Soviet, I was elected to represent the Kirghiz Republic (of course I ran unopposed). I had a number of meetings with my constituents, at which they proved to be interested mainly in whether I could help this or that region get construction materials or build a school or get long-awaited combine harvesters and trucks for a collective farm.

In the mid-1990s the situation began to change. Groups that stood for independence and sovereignty were coming to power in the republics, swept into office by growing hostility to the Russian Center. The belief that the Center had been pumping resources out of the "rich Union republics" and siphoning them into Russia was widespread.

The direction in which siphoned resources had actually been flowing became apparent after the disintegration of the common economic area, when living standards became substantially lower in the former Soviet republics than in Russia. Exhausting ethnic conflicts in some of the former republics had also had their effect. The allegations that Russia had been taking more money and resources from the other republics than the republics were getting from Russia were proved utterly false.

Public sentiment in support of Russia's own sovereignty was spreading rapidly in Russia, too. Russians yearned to stand united on their own territory and to be done once and for all with submersion in the USSR, however commanding Russia's position in it. The situation was aggravated by popular dissatisfaction that Russia was still a donor of resources at a time of economic decline and degradation of its largest territories, such as the non–black earth zone, the Trans-Ural region, and the Far East.

That was the time when the Russian center headed by Yeltsin was formed, and by then Yeltsin had completely cast aside the idea of the Communist Party's vanguard role. Yeltsin also won the struggle for the Supreme Soviet of the Russian Federation and then became Russia's first president.

From that moment on, in view of Russia's position in the USSR's economy and politics, the real clout and power gradually shifted from Gorbachev to Yeltsin. Of course, it was not an easy process. The Soviet leaders still kept vital control mechanisms in their own hands. The problem was that they were using those controls less and less efficiently and more and more irrationally if the goal was to develop the country's economy, maintain the integrity of the Soviet Union, and overcome the existing and often imaginary contradictions with Yeltsin's center. They would not give an inch.

The line was drawn by the attempted coup. No matter what was said later, Gorbachev did recognize Yeltsin's decisive role in the suppression of the coup. In Foros, where I went with the others to pick up Gorbachev (more about that later), he abruptly asked Anatoly Lukyanov, chairman of the USSR Supreme Soviet, "If you couldn't convene the Supreme Soviet right away to put down the putsch, why didn't you join Yeltsin then?"

But Yeltsin had already made his choice. It was evident in the humiliating scene after Gorbachev's return from Foros, when he was summoned before the Russian Supreme Soviet and spoken to in insulting tones. All the same, I think we could have avoided such an ending if the Soviet authorities had managed to resolve the main problems facing the country at the time.

I believe the main problem was the difficulty of achieving three objectives simultaneously: giving sovereignty to the republics, preserving a common economic space within the boundaries of the former Soviet Union, and co-ordinating the transition to a market economy. Success could be achieved only if decisions were coordinated and agreed upon by the Union government and the government of the Russian Federation, or by Gorbachev and Yeltsin. But no such decisions were made. Gorbachev did not persist in his initiative, either, even though he appreciated the enormousness of the task much better than Yeltsin and at the time could do much more to accomplish it.

In my archive I still keep the notes I made at a meeting Gorbachev held with economists on March 16, 1991. One of those economists was M. L. Bronstein, an Estonian professor who was highly respected by the Baltic deputies. "The main reason for the difficulties," he said, "is a dramatically growing confrontation between the Center and the republics. Signing of the economic and political union treaties should be separated in time."

This was not the first time that idea had been voiced. I was one of those who had suggested to M. S. Gorbachev that he sign the economic treaty first. I was confident everybody, including the Baltic states representatives, would sign it because I had discussed the issue with the heads of many union re-publics. I can't say that Gorbachev was very enthusiastic about that suggestion at first, but he didn't reject it out of hand, either. But the next day he said, "It won't work."

"Why not?" I asked. "You know it's doable because all the republics have tentatively agreed that if the economic treaty is signed, they'll take on certain obligations indispensable for the functioning of the common economic market."

"If we sign the economic treaty," Gorbachev responded, "many of them will stop right there and won't sign the union treaty, which is ready and which all of them are willing to join."

"Yes, but the economic treaty also implies setting up national structures. We should begin with the economy and then start building the political structures of the union."

Gorbachev rejected this idea. I think he was obsessed by the idea of the union treaty and believed its signing was a realistic goal. In any case, it proved to be impossible to separate the economic treaty, acceptable to all, from the political treaty.

We were coming closer to the disintegration not only of the Union but also of a common economic area. Some people said, "Let's follow Western Europe, where independent states with their independent economies have entered a common integrated flow." There were no grounds for such a comparison. The Soviet Union was a single whole. (I am not speaking here about its deficiencies, but rather underline the fact that the country was indivisible, with all the ensuing consequences.) Therefore, the slogan "First split up, then integrate" meant tearing apart thousands of well-established industrial ties. The knife of disintegration could not help cutting the living organism. And that is exactly what happened.

THE WEST DOES NOT RUSH TO HELP

Generally speaking, we could not expect to get much help from abroad to dull the pain or at least reduce the problems of the transition period. The main issue boiled down to our own ability to overcome our difficulties in the process of rejecting the deeply rooted administrative system of the command economy. We could not expect another Marshall Plan, but still . . .

I was sitting in my Kremlin office (which used to belong to Vyacheslav Molotov, then to Geidar A. Aliev) discussing something with Academician Stepan Sitaryan, an old and reliable friend since our days as graduate students in the Economics Department of Moscow State University. My secretary told me that Grigory Yavlinsky was there to see me. I asked him to come in. That was our first meeting.

He told me he had received an invitation to take part in a seminar at Harvard University. It was supposed to deal with specific measures of economic aid to the Soviet Union. The aid would amount to at least $30 billion. But the most important thing was that it was target (special-purpose) aid: each increment would come in response to our appropriate steps down the road to reform. Deregulation of prices in the USSR, for instance, would be followed by a massive supply of Western consumer goods; when we made our ruble convertible, the West would set up a stabilization fund for us.

"Can you cosign the letter saying we agree to this plan?" Yavlinsky asked me. "And another request—could you arrange a meeting for me with Gorbachev?"

I said I would. The next day we edited the letter at my apartment, and Grigory Yavlinsky was genuinely surprised that I signed it without asking for anyone's approval. Then he was received by Gorbachev.

This was not long before a delegation of Soviet economists that I headed visited the United States. A lot of false rumors were circulated about our stay there. This is what really happened. Vladimir Sherbakov, then deputy chairman of the USSR Council of Ministers, and I arrived in Washington to explain Soviet economic policy in a nutshell to the U.S. government. Gorbachev had asked Yavlinsky, who was in Boston at the time, to join our delegation as well, and he did. The Americans expressed great interest in his ideas and insisted that he join us when we met not only with Secretary of State James Baker but also with President Bush. It looked as though they wanted to demonstrate that there was opposition in the USSR to its current economic policy and to find reasons to justify their reservations about that "half-baked" policy.

Despite our differences, I have to admit that on the whole Yavlinsky was part of our team, though at the meetings he attempted to demonstrate his intellectual superiority over the rest of the delegation. We were quite tolerant about it.

After the official meetings were over, President Bush invited me to a business lunch on May 31. He was there with Brent Scowcroft, his national security adviser, and an interpreter, Pyotr Afanasenko. The atmosphere was truly friendly. I told President Bush that he was looking very well. It was appreciated, especially since Bush had fainted at a reception in Tokyo not long before. Afanasenko later told me that one of our generals had started a conversation with Bush by saying, "Mr. President, for some reason you don't look too well today," and the meeting, scheduled to last half an hour, was over in five minutes.

Bush asked many questions, spoke about everything, and said nothing specific about anything. After lunch he took me to his private office, where he showed me his new computer; he was very proud of it. He typed a letter to Gorbachev on the computer. When I asked if I might have a copy, he summoned his secretary and asked her to make a copy of the letter for me. The woman grumbled, "Mr. President should know that he has to press this button and the computer will make as many copies as he needs."

So our meeting was very impressive, but there was no serious conversation about economic support for our reforms.

The work of the Soviet-American group at Harvard, so promising at the beginning, also produced no results. Nobody offered us $30 billion under any conditions. Allison, Yavlinsky, and others had their own explanations for the failure, but there it was.

At that time I became a "Sherpa"—named after the guides who help foreigners climb Himalayan peaks. One such aide was assigned to the head of each state that was a member of G-7, later G-8. We got our own Sherpa, even though at that time we were not members of the club. The list of my responsibilities included holding preliminary meetings with my colleagues to prepare for our participation in the G-7 summit in London. The heads of the G-7 states were scheduled to meet with Gorbachev on July 17, 1991.

I arrived in London before the scheduled meeting. I had to discuss certain details with the British Sherpa, and we agreed to meet with him after the G-7 meeting was over. A policeman held me back to let the heads of state get into their cars. Bush, Baker, and others were standing at the entrance. The square was empty. A group of journalists, most with TV cameras, were standing about fifty meters away. They were not allowed to get closer. Suddenly Bush gave me a friendly wave and said, "Primakov!" Naturally, I went up to him. Nobody stopped me. Handshakes, greetings, questions—when is Gorbachev arriving? Baker lowered his voice and asked if I had brought any herb-flavored vodka with me. He remembered the drinks we had had in Moscow at the apartment of the famous sculptor Zurab Tseritelli. I jokingly answered that if it would get us any closer to success at tomorrow's talks with Gorbachev, I would get some herb-flavored vodka even there in London.

TV people and photographers did not hear what we were talking about but were filming and taking pictures of us from a distance. In a couple of minutes the news was spreading that American top government officials were discussing something lively with the Soviet Sherpa.

"What were you talking about?"—it was the first question that Gorbachev asked me at the airport where I met him in a couple of hours.

The next day the long-awaited discussion between the leaders of the seven countries and the president of the USSR took place. Gorbachev and I represented the Soviet team. The rest, including Vladimir Sherbakov, Stepan Sitaryan, Foreign Minister Aleksandr Bessmertnykh, the president's assistant Anatoly Chernyaev, and his adviser Vadim Zagladin, were in another room. I could reach them only by fax, which I used only once, to tell them the talks had begun—after all, I had to use this machine somehow, especially since it took them so long to explain to me how to work it.

I was taking very detailed notes of what was said but I heard nothing specific about economic aid to the USSR. Some speakers expressed enthusiasm about the "first historic meeting of the G-7 with the head of the Soviet Union," but it was obvious that the West was not going to provide any full-scale support to the USSR. Or perhaps the speakers had heard that the State Emergency Committee was cooking something up in Moscow. Indeed, the London meeting took place not long before the coup. But most likely the Western nations were simply unprepared and unwilling to help the Soviet Union join the world community as their equal. That was their big mistake.

The coup was launched on August 19, 1991. At that time I was with my grandson, Yevgeny Junior, at Yuzhny, a spa about ten kilometers from the dacha in Foros where Gorbachev and his family were vacationing. Also on vacation there were Rafik Nishanov, chairman of the Nationalities Council of the USSR Supreme Soviet; Pyotr Luchinsky, secretary of the Central Committee; and Minister for Internal Affairs Boris Pugo and his wife. The president's assistants Anatoly Chernyaev and Georgy Shakhnazarov were staying there as well and visited Gorbachev every day.

Something disturbing was in the air. On August 17 Shakhnazarov and I were taking a walk around the resort, talking about the union treaty, which was to be signed in a Moscow suburb two days later. We were afraid that the most active participants might be arrested to disrupt the signing of the treaty, which offered extensive rights to the Union republics.

In the two weeks I spent near Foros Gorbachev never phoned me. When he had been at Foros and I at Yuzhny a year ago, everything was different. What went wrong? Tolya Chernyaev, feeling a little ill at ease, especially because Gorbachev spoke with Nishanov, Luchinsky, and Pugo several times a day, kept assuring me his boss was going to invite me to his dacha before he left. Truth to tell, such a hiatus in our relations did not spoil my vacation, although I still haven't been able to find an explanation for it. On August 16 Mykola Bagrov, who chaired the Crimean regional executive committee, invited the Pugos, to whom I was quite close, my old friend Luchinsky, and me up into the mountains (Nishanov, more closely involved in preparations for the union treaty than the others, went back to Moscow earlier). We all got food poisoning on the mountain, I think because we ate a watermelon stuffed with nitrates. When on August 18 Pugo and his wife, not yet fully recovered, were about to fly back to Moscow, I said, "Boris, why such a rush? Why can't you stay another couple of days?" He smiled and replied, "I can't, I have to be in Moscow." That was the last time I saw him. Pugo, involved in the State Emergency Committee, turned out to be more honest than the others: when they came to arrest him after the coup failed, he and his wife shot themselves to death.

But that was after the failure of the State Emergency Committee on August 21. On the afternoon of August 18 my direct line to the Kremlin, the local phone, and the phones of other high-ranking officials vacationing at the resort were cut off. At seven o'clock in the morning on August 19 I was awakened by Pyotr Luchinsky, who looked extremely anxious: "Turn on the TV!" The address of the State Emergency Committee was on. Gorbachev, we heard, was forced to resign for reasons of health. He would be replaced temporarily by Gennady Yanaev, the vice president. I immediately put in a request for air tickets and flew back to Moscow.

At eight o'clock the next morning I went to the Kremlin. They let me in as usual, without delay. In half an hour I walked into Yanaev's office, some thirty meters from mine. "Are you out of your mind?"

Yanaev looked confused. "If I refused like in April," he said cryptically, "then . . ." and he eloquently knocked his index finger on his forehead. "What shall I do now?"

"Go on television and say you're through with the State Emergency Committee."

"Yevgeny, believe me, everything is going to be all right. Mikhail Sergeevich will come back and we'll be working together."

"That seems hard to believe. Tanks should be removed from the Moscow streets immediately," I said.

It appeared—and it really was so—that Yanaev, appointed acting president by the State Emergency Committee—the first person in the country— was by no means the first fiddle in the conspiracy, and sincerely wished that everything that had happened were only a bad dream. He was never far from a bottle at that time, and it seemed to help him feel better.

Two members of the Security Council, Vadim Bakatin and I, spoke against the coup organized by the State Emergency Committee. At 11:30 on August 20, 1991, the following announcement, signed by both of us, was carried by the Interfax News Agency and repeated several times on the radio station Echo of Moscow:

> We consider the declaration of a state of emergency and the handing over of all power in the country to a group of individuals to be unconstitutional. According to the information available to us, USSR President Gorbachev is not sick.
>
> Our responsibility as members of the Security Council requires us to demand the immediate withdrawal of armored vehicles from the streets of the cities and that everything be done to avoid bloodshed. We also demand that the personal safety of M. S. Gorbachev be guaranteed and that he be given an opportunity to make a public announcement.

On August 21, at a press conference held on the premises of the Industrial Union, Ivan Silaev, who chaired the Council of Ministers of the Russian Federation, called and asked if Bakatin and I would agree to fly to Foros with a group of state representatives. We agreed but still decided to phone Yeltsin and ask his opinion. He approved Silaev's proposal without hesitation.

We had to hurry. A group representing the State Emergency Committee had already left for the Crimea and some of us were afraid they would pick Gorbachev up and put him away. We rushed to the Vnukovo I airport. On the way we passed by the tanks leaving Moscow. They were following the orders of the Defense Ministry. In practical terms, that put an end to the conspirators' attempts to solve the problem by force.

The road was damaged, covered with dirt, and cars were skidding on it. Our plane, a TU-134, was ready to take off. Army officers formed a circle around us as the plane was all but stormed by reporters eager to accompany us. But the plane was so overcrowded that several guards had to get off. Ivan Silaev, Aleksandr Rutskoy, Nikolai Fyodorov, the Russian minister of justice, and a group of police special forces dressed in civilian clothes and carrying machine guns were aboard the plane. Several foreign journalists, some newspaper and TV reporters, and a French diplomat were there too.

We took off without knowing where we were going to land. We were told we couldn't land at the Balbek military base, not far from Gorbachev's dacha in Foros, because a plane was parked on the runway. Later we learned that the commander of the Black Sea Fleet had ordered us shot down during our approach, and after they cleared the runway for us and allowed us to land at Balbek, he gave orders to shoot to kill. But we found out about all that later.

At the Balbek base, where we landed about eight o'clock at night, it was suspiciously quiet. Not a single person in sight. By that time Gorbachev's telephone lines were switched on (we found out later) and he ordered that we be allowed to land without delay. We went directly to Foros. Gorbachev and his family were happy to see us there. We returned to Moscow together.

Of course the main events surrounding the liquidation of the State Emergency Committee took place in Moscow. The conspiracy failed only because the country had changed. Yeltsin's personal courage mattered a lot, too. And fortunately, the putsch leaders proved to be totally inept.

CHAPTER FIVE

In the Intelligence Service

THE PRESIDENT AT YASENEVO

Some time after the coup was suppressed, my career took another turn—I was placed at the head of the Foreign Intelligence Service, first of the Soviet Union and then, after its collapse, of Russia. Could this have happened by accident? Yes and no.

My transfer to intelligence came at the suggestion of Vadim Bakatin, who became chairman of the KGB after the failed coup. By the time he proposed me to head the Foreign Intelligence Service, it had been decided that it would become an independent entity.

Bakatin had been having a hard time ever since it was discovered that he had given the Americans blueprints showing the locations of listening devices planted in the concrete walls of the new U.S. embassy in Moscow. His action was widely debated among Russians; many deplored it. He had naively believed the Americans would give him similar blueprints in return, and the exchange would help to establish friendly relations. But our American partners offered nothing but their gratitude.

The Americans could have afforded to make a goodwill gesture in return. When I joined the Intelligence Service I learned that five eavesdropping systems with dozens of microphones had been planted in the living quarters and reception area of our new embassy complex in Washington during the first stage of its construction. Investigation by the Center's teams at the second stage of construction, which included the administration and mission building and the superintendent's area, revealed about 150 microphones and sensors. Numerous listening devices were also discovered in the nineteen-story, 256-apartment building for the Russian permanent mission to the U.N. For strategic reasons, we announced the discovery of only a portion of the devices we had detected. So the Americans did have something to give us in return if they had wished to do so.

I have always thought well of Vadim Bakatin, and I do now. He is an honest and decent person. But his proposal that I head the Intelligence Service was so staggering that I confess I didn't take it seriously at first. I completely forgot about it when I went to the Middle East in September with representatives of the Soviet executive power in the hope of getting the credits the country so badly needed. We managed very well there—unsecured loans alone totaled $3 billion. I had made the most of my personal contacts when we visited Saudi Arabia, Kuwait, the United Arab Emirates, Egypt, Iran, and Turkey. But my contacts mattered less than the high esteem in which the Arab world held our country.

I returned to Moscow on the wings of success, but Gorbachev did not call me in to deliver my report. Gorbachev phoned me and without a word about the results of our trip said he wanted me to become his foreign trade counselor now that the Security Council was abolished. I realized that although Gorbachev treated me well, they were looking for a new job for me. I may have felt somewhat offended because the offer was made hastily and by phone. Whatever the reason, I answered, "Mikhail Sergeevich, I'm rather tired of counseling."

"Then take the office of intelligence head. Bakatin told me about it."

"I agree," I answered instantly. I surprised even myself.

Several days passed and nobody brought up the subject. Later Bakatin told me why. Already no appointment to any important government post could be made without Yeltsin's approval, and he was vacationing in the south at the moment. Bakatin called him. At first Yeltsin hesitated, but according to Bakatin, he persuaded him.

By that time Yeltsin knew me quite well. In my capacity as chairman of the Union Council, the lower house of the Supreme Soviet (the Soviet parliament), I was responsible for the international activity of the entire Supreme Soviet. When Yeltsin was a member of the Supreme Soviet he used to contact me before his trips abroad. On one occasion I told him a trip he planned to Bonn would be used to work against Gorbachev.

"Where did you get that from?" he asked.

"Our ambassador mentioned it in his cable. I can show it to you."

"Never mind, I won't go," Yeltsin said.

I was honestly against a confrontation between Gorbachev and Yeltsin, or more precisely, I wanted to avoid a head-on collision. But many people were involved on both sides and I don't think they were taking sides for ideological reasons at the time. I had no reason whatever to believe Yeltsin took a negative view of me, but I realized why he hesitated when the question of my appointment to head the Foreign Intelligence Service came up. I was on Gorbachev's team. I didn't belong to Yeltsin's entourage, and the top jobs were going only to people who had worked for him before.

Since intelligence work was still under the KGB, I was appointed deputy chairman of the KGB as well. I turned down the rank of general and was never sorry. My decision was appreciated by the staff, who had to work many years as operatives to become senior officers. Besides, had I become a general, nobody would have remembered I was an academician.

A month after my appointment, intelligence was separated from the KGB and became the Central Intelligence Service (CIS). So I held the title of deputy chairman of the KGB for only one month. But that does not prevent people who publish my biographical details, both in Russia and elsewhere, from emphasizing my "roots" in the KGB.

After the collapse of the Soviet Union, Yeltsin signed a decree establishing the Foreign Intelligence Service (FIS) of the Russian Federation on the model of the CIS. I immediately called him to ask a question that was not at all trivial to me: Who would implement the decree?

"That's not for a telephone conversation. Come over and we'll talk," answered Yeltsin.

I went to see Yeltsin at the appointed time.

"I trust you, have no doubt about that, but the staff doesn't seem to."

"Well," I replied, "if you told me you didn't trust me, that would be the end of it, of course. But I was hurt when you said you'd heard that people didn't like me in the Service itself. I admit I don't believe that's so, but maybe I'm wrong."

"Well, I'll meet with your deputies."

"I've already appointed some of them. You'll get an objective picture if you meet with the entire administration—it's about forty or fifty people."

All the FIS department heads gathered in my office at 10:40. It was the first time in the country's history that the head of state had visited the intelligence community. They learned the reason for Yeltsin's visit from Yeltsin himself. After repeating that he had no grounds for distrusting me and saying that "Primakov is one of the few Politburo members who haven't screwed me up," Yeltsin said, "You spies are courageous people, so I expect you to be frank about your chief." Twelve people spoke up, and without exception all spoke in favor of my appointment as director of the FIS. Yeltsin took the decree out of his leather folder and signed it then and there. "I have another decree with somebody else's name on it, but now I won't tell you the name."

As I rode down in the elevator with the president, I told him, "You've lifted a heavy load from my shoulders."

"I've learned something, too," answered Yeltsin.

During our many meetings later we never referred to either the sources of his information about me or the name of the alternative appointee.

So now I am director of the FIS. This change in my destiny did not, after all, happen by accident. It was predetermined by all my previous work, which in one way or another was connected with international relations and their analysis. There was something else: when I worked for *Pravda* as well as for the academic institutions, I carried out some assignments for the country's leadership, such as my mission to seek a peaceful settlement between Baghdad and the Kurds. I met with General Gaafar Mohamed el-Nimeiri right after he had come to power in Sudan. I was the first foreigner to visit the leftist leaders of the Ba'ath Party after their coup d'état in Damascus in February 1966. Hafez al-Assad was one of them. In 1971, after Nasser's death, I went to Egypt in my capacity as deputy director of IMEMO to report on the changing situation there. I took the private plane of the sultan of Oman from Jordan to Masqat, where a confidential agreement was reached on the establishment of diplomatic relations between the USSR and Oman. On several occasions I had closed meetings with the Israeli leaders to probe the possibility of a peaceful settlement with the Arabs.

All those missions were carried out at the direction of the Politburo or the Central Committee Secretariat. As a rule, the KGB was instructed to provide the security measures and communication procedures. Yet rumors to the effect that I had been with the KGB practically since infancy were repeatedly spread in the West and eagerly picked up by some Russian papers.

I did know many Russian intelligence officers personally. I had long enjoyed friendly relations with many who had stamped their names indelibly on the service. But it was common sense and not those connections that led me to believe that replacing personnel in the Intelligence Service was not and could not be an end in itself. Some chiefs and deputy chiefs of departments and then some directorate chiefs were replaced, but most of those changes were routine. The appointment of a new first deputy director, however, was out of the ordinary. I realized that this position should be held by a top professional who enjoyed wide support among the staff, a person whom I trusted completely and who, under the circumstances (after all, I was a newcomer there), must be "one of them" in the intelligence community.

After I was transferred to the Intelligence Service I had to deal with Vyacheslav Trubnikov on many occasions. He headed Department 1, the principal political intelligence department, which dealt with the United States. He was noted for his erudition and broad outlook: an expert on India by training, he became an outstanding specialist on America. He was a very cultured person, respectable and highly professional. Trubnikov had risen from an ordinary operative to resident in one of the large countries and had an impeccable record. His promotion from department head to first deputy director of the FIS—a big jump—aroused no grumbling among my deputies and was welcomed by the FIS as a whole. I worked closely with him, and when I was about to leave the FIS I was certain he was the best candidate for the directorship. The president agreed with my recommendation.

The cream of the officer corps is concentrated in the FIS. For the most part its members are intelligent and well educated; many speak several foreign languages. By vocation and training they are state-minded people. At the same time, some officers who had served in the Committee for State Security (the KGB) for many years—many decades in some cases—were thrown into confusion when it was broken into separate parts. Even worse, officers, especially young ones, kept leaving the FIS. Their future there was uncertain, and businesses were eager to offer big salaries to well-trained people.

The CIA and the British Secret Intelligence Service (better known as MI6) had instructed their residents to take full advantage of the hard times in Russia's special services and establish contact with some of its representatives. To aggravate the situation, the CIA and MI6 began to change their tactics with regard to officers they had recruited earlier. As a rule, the turncoats, whether they were "applicants" (that is, had volunteered to collaborate)[1] or had been recruited by a foreign service, were kept as "moles" as long as possible; they were taken out of the country to the United States, England, or another country only when their exposure seemed imminent. Now that some unexposed moles could get good jobs in business, their handlers sometimes ignored standard procedure and encouraged them to escape during their business trips.

MOLES IN THE FIS

Before I joined the Intelligence Service, Lieutenant Colonel Mikhail Butkov, who worked under cover as a journalist in Norway, escaped to England in May 1991 with the help of the British special services. Butkov's moral qualities can be judged by his later adventures in England. At the end of 1997, he and his mistress, who had joined him in England, were arrested by the British authorities and sentenced to prison for financial manipulations in their business activities. His mistress, whom he later married, was the wife of a Russian embassy employee in Oslo. (Butkov had left his wife, who now lives in Russia.) Yet the Russian press and airwaves were filled with inspiring stories about the "ideological fighter" Butkov, who had been forced to cooperate with British Intelligence!

Early in 1991 two officers from the Scientific and Technological Intelligence Service failed to return home from trips abroad. Lieutenant Colonel Illarionov had operated in Italy under the guise of vice consul in Genoa and left for the United States with the assistance of American special services; Major Haiduk was a senior engineer with our trade mission in Ottawa.

After I joined the FIS, one of our officers fled to the United States from Belgium and another from Finland. But perhaps the biggest traitor was Colonel Viktor Oshchenko, who was recruited by the British while he was in Paris on assignment and was secretly taken to Great Britain. Those three also belonged to the Scientific and Technological Intelligence Service. Oshchenko had been slated to be promoted as soon as he returned from his assignment abroad. What was the reason for his hasty escape? After reading the report of an investigation by a special commission, I suspected that he was afraid to return because he would have had to pass a routine test at the Center before he undertook a new assignment, and in all probability it would have revealed that he was "dirty." As it turned out, Oshchenko had pocketed some money from the funds to be paid to informants. There was reliable evidence to the effect that along with the list of agents Oshchenko gave his MI6 bosses, he provided an entirely different version of the reason for his hasty escape from Paris.

I am writing here about the traitors. But many unsuccessful attempts were made to recruit our officers during that time, especially when their term in office was coming to an end and they were about to return to Russia.

After I became head of the FIS I studied a CIA paper on recruitment methods. The CIA had created a peculiar "recruitability model" that stresses such characteristics as "dual loyalty," narcissism, vanity, envy, ambition, mercenary nature, unprincipled sexual activity, and propensity to drink. Special attention was to be paid to dissatisfaction with the prospect's official status and family relations and to everyday problems that caused stress. No ideological or political reason for susceptibility to recruitment was to be found in the CIA model. According to Richard Helms and William Colby, former directors of Central Intelligence, they knew of no Soviet or Russian deserter who had defected for ideological reasons.

Oleg Gordievsky was not an ideologue either. He was a former Foreign Intelligence deputy station chief in London who had been recruited many years before, when he was stationed in Denmark. I have learned a lot about the Gordievsky case from one of the former chiefs of foreign counterintelligence of the First Main Directorate (PGU). Gordievsky, who had been under suspicion, was instructed to return to Moscow under the pretext that he was to be appointed to the post of station chief. During a prolonged debriefing conducted by the general (now retired) who told me about it, Gordievsky was close to confessing when he began to probe the possibility of actively operating against the British, and even offered various guarantees that he could work successfully as a double agent. The KGB leadership was informed that day.

Foreign Intelligence officers were confident he would admit everything the next day. But suddenly an order came from above to stop the debriefing, remove outside surveillance, and send Gordievsky to a health center near Moscow for rest. From there he fled across the Finnish border, with help from British Intelligence.

I have also looked through the Gordievsky dossier and read the commission's conclusions on this case. The story is widely circulated that the information on Gordievsky's spying activity was provided by Aldrich Ames. Gordievsky himself holds to this version. It turns out that Gordievsky's exposure was by no means a one-time affair. Soviet Intelligence had at one time received information that the Danes had given the British special services information on him as a Soviet intelligence agent "potentially suitable for recruiting." In 1974 they helped establish his contact with the British station chief in Copenhagen, Robert Francis Browning. (Gordievsky stayed in Denmark on two occasions.)

At first this information was greeted with skepticism. But then came an indirect but alarming signal from Britain—not from a source in their special services who could be aware of Gordievsky but from an agent in an entirely different British organization. It blurred the picture but encouraged a serious analysis, which revealed that Russian Intelligence officers operating in London who were above Gordievsky had suspiciously been put out of action. The deputy station chief, Gordievsky's immediate superior, was expelled in 1983. In April 1984 the station chief, Arkady Guk, was declared persona non grata. Wasn't that an attempt to clear the way to the station chief's post for Gordievsky?

It was then that the decision was made to bring him back to Moscow and work with him directly.

The Gordievsky case proved once again the need to intensify and improve the operation of foreign counterintelligence. In doing so we had to avoid several pitfalls. This intensification must by no means create an atmosphere of suspiciousness at the FIS or undermine trust in its personnel, directly or indirectly. At the same time, carelessness had to be eliminated once and for all. Intelligence clearly had to have its own security service, but it should work closely with the Federal Security Service (FSS). It was instructed to do so.

And finally we faced the by no means easy question of the use to be made of the information we received from our sources. Sometimes it was quite difficult to reconcile the need to protect our most valuable sources with the need to take urgent action against the traitors they had exposed. Not infrequently we happened to be sluggish or negligent ourselves. Consider the treachery of Lev Resun, known in the West as Suvorov, a brilliant author of several books on Soviet Military Intelligence (GRU).

At the end of May 1978 Soviet Foreign Intelligence got a report from its source in the British special services (it can now be revealed) that MI6, through its station chief in Switzerland, had been working with Resun, an officer in the GRU post in Geneva, whom they had recruited a year earlier. Our Foreign Intelligence obtained a complete list of the MI6 officers involved with Resun.[2] But since this information came from a very carefully protected source, only a highly restricted number of officers could be allowed to work with it. The problem was complicated by the fact that Resun belonged to the GRU, a different intelligence service, so the FIS had to coordinate all the necessary operations with them. I don't rule out the possibility that rivalry between our two special services may have interfered with the coordination effort.

On June 8, 1978, Resun got in touch with his bosses at British Intelligence and claimed that he was about to be exposed. He and his family were flown from Basel to Great Britain. Our source reported that Resun's departure did not upset MI6. For the whole time he had worked for the British, Resun had always been afraid of exposure and feared he would be recalled to Moscow prematurely for lack of action. He even proved unable to take advantage of a British offer to help him recruit a foreigner in order to raise his prestige in the GRU residency.

It is curious that despite his talk about his disapproval of the Soviet regime and his claims that his father and mother were subjected to repression, British Intelligence was firmly convinced that the material benefits he received were Resun's main motivation for working for MI6.

Meanwhile he is currently presented in the West as an "ideological fighter" for freedom whose works have told the world about "the incredible crimes of the GRU."

WHY WAS BELGARD'S RECRUITMENT STOPPED?

What line should the FIS pursue? It was not an easy question. There was no doubt whatever that intelligence should continue as one of the state's most important mechanisms, especially since that mechanism had never been exposed in another country. That being the case, I decided to take my time, make no aggressive moves in such sensitive matters as the recruitment of foreign nationals, and respond positively to any promising signal from the intelligence service of the United States or any other NATO country.

The case of the CIA officer Leonard Herman Belgard was typical. Belgard was fluent in Russian and had been actively establishing contacts with members of the Soviet embassy and attracting the attention of our foreign intelligence as far back as his first stay in Mexico. From July 1981 to August 1983 Belgard had been employed at the U.S. consulate in Leningrad, and the KGB knew everything about his activities there. As a result, one of his valuable agents was exposed. Apparently Langley had no idea why, for in October 1983 Belgard was sent to Geneva under the cover of a member of the United States' permanent mission to the U.N. European office. Having a considerable amount of information on him, the PGU carefully followed his activities in Geneva as well. Under the eyes of our foreign intelligence Belgard was trying to recruit two Soviet citizens and nine people from East Germany, Czechoslovakia, Poland, Bulgaria, and Hungary.

In October 1988 he was promoted and sent to Sweden as the CIA's deputy station chief in the guise of the first secretary of the U.S. embassy. But in July 1991, after his work with a Soviet citizen came to nothing, he was transferred to Paris.

Following the protocol of the game played for many years, the FIS elaborated a detailed operation for inviting this CIA officer to cooperate with us intentionally. We planned to reveal the real state of affairs to him, that for many years he had been operating practically under our supervision, and to propose that we organize a new "success" for him in order to strengthen his professional reputation. Everyone involved in the operation thought it had every chance of succeeding. Then it was decided to abort the operation. Was that the right decision? I can't give an unequivocal answer today.

Soon after we stopped working on Belgard, we received a well-documented file from our most reliable source. According to that file, the CIA was interested not only in securing information about the power alignment in the Russian leadership, its possible actions inside and outside the country, the implementation of agreements on redeployment of nuclear weapons from Ukraine and Kazakhstan to Russia, and the security of nuclear materials; it was working to cause the collapse of those state bodies that could help Russia retain its status of a great power and to prevent the CIS countries from rallying around Moscow.

Everything finally fell into place after CIA Director Robert M. Gates, addressing the CIA staff, stressed that the "human factor"—that is, recruiting—was still the CIA's primary activity. There was a chance to reduce that factor and perhaps even work out new rules of conduct in the intelligence field, but the ball was not in our court.

In November 1994, when I was at the head of the Foreign Intelligence Service, I left for the United States to take part in a conference of a Soviet-American task force on problems of future security. Participating in the meeting on the American side were General John Shalikashvili, then deputy chairman of the Joint Chiefs of Staff; some senior officials of the State Department, the Department of Defense, and the National Security Council; and Fritz Ermarth, chairman of the National Intelligence Council, whose participation was of special importance to me. At that stage the CIA director preferred not to meet with me; I took that as a signal.

At the meeting I pointed out that there was a large area of common interest for the intelligence communities of both countries: fighting against international terrorism, drug trafficking, and organized crime. I dwelled on specific methods of cooperation—exchange of information, preparation and conduct of joint operations aimed at preventing or detecting and detaining persons involved in criminal activity, cooperation in preventing the proliferation of nuclear, chemical, and biological weapons of mass destruction, and cooperation in stopping the illegal trade in weapons.

I also spoke about the "rules of conduct," among which I mentioned abstaining from violence (abduction of individuals and forcing them to cooperate) and psychotropic drugs. I declared that the forms and methods of intelligence work should conform to the principles of humane treatment, of respect for human rights and personal dignity. They listened carefully but no one offered a specific proposal.

The opportunity might have been seized because the mood was changing considerably in our service. Yes, some lived in the past and even dreamed of returning to the days when the KGB practically controlled the country. But they were in the minority. The majority, to which I belonged, sincerely welcomed the changes, the spread of democracy and rejection of ideological fetters.

This mood did not imply indiscriminate rejection of everything in the past or the naive notion that confrontation between the states had disappeared with the end of the Cold War. The substance and the form of that confrontation had changed, however, and those changes had to be recognized.

THE NEW APPROACHES

What impact did this situation have on the Intelligence Service? The new leadership of the FIS clearly understood that in the new conditions there was no main adversary (or MA, as we used to say) set once and for all. Adversaries could appear anywhere if other states planned and carried out actions that conflicted with Russia's vital interests—territorial integrity, defense potential, integration of the CIS countries, stability along the borders, guarantee of conditions to permit Russia to join the world economy as an equal participant.

At the same time we accepted another reality. With confrontational opposition at an end, the field of mutual interests was widening and interest in international cooperation against common threats—regional armed conflicts, terrorism, organized crime, narcotics trafficking, proliferation of weapons of mass destruction—was growing.

The need to adapt to new conditions led us to abandon the view of foreign intelligence work as taking a total global approach. During the Cold War its activities were directed mainly toward acquiring information about anti-Soviet actions planned by the United States, our main adversary at the time, and acquiring data on U.S. weapons and examples of the weapons themselves to bolster our preparedness. That was what determined the global nature of intelligence operations, their unscrupulousness, if you will. Now the priorities of intelligence were definitely shifting.

In November 1991 I gave instructions to cancel the program aimed at revealing indications of nuclear missile attack against our country (VRYAN). For a decade large financial and human resources had been spent to prepare purely formal but mandatory bimonthly reports to the Center about the absence of signs of preparation for a surprise nuclear attack, which included such "indicators" as lights in the windows of the Pentagon and other countries' defense ministries late at night.

That program was a typical anachronism. But does this mean that we are altogether abandoning attempts to acquire data about the development of weapons, especially in view of the possibility of gaining knowledge about new systems that might destabilize the situation?

It is widely known that Foreign Intelligence assisted in the development of atomic weapons in the USSR, and in securing machinery that enabled us to reduce the noise of submarines. At the same time I was never among those who credited almost all our successes to intelligence, voluntary or otherwise, belittling the role played by our outstanding scientists in the production of nuclear weapons and in the sharp growth of the country's defense capability.

The FIS has never hesitated in respect to industrial espionage, in which essentially all intelligence services in the world engage. Whether we want it or not, it will go on as long as there are military or commercial secrets to be learned. But what a fuss was kicked up over the "revelations" by the traitor

Oshchenko! I mentioned him earlier; he was involved in science and technology intelligence. Yet when five CIA agents were caught in industrial espionage and expelled from France, the reaction was so muffled that few people have heard about it.

In the 1990s our science and technology intelligence was aimed mostly at analytical work. It proceeded along two lines. First, it kept track of the changing approaches in the so-called critical technologies and of the changing priorities in the leading industrial states; and second, it evaluated the state of various branches of science and technology in Russia and the level of interest of industrialized states in direct cooperation with Russia. Obviously, this information is of importance to the political leadership of the country, because it advances our efforts to reorganize our currently limited resources.

At the same time, such information has a counterintelligence dimension. One of the confidential American documents obtained by the FIS stated: "All Russian technologies of interest to us were created by the military-industrial complex. . . . A number of technological concepts do not have analogues in American industry." Among the subjects singled out for special attention in the document were the process of creating turbulence to dissipate the heat generated by turbines; innovations in metallurgy; the development of monocrystalline structures; the creation of exotic materials; the question of developing antenna designs and laser mirrors to ensure uninterrupted communication with space vehicles when they reenter Earth's dense atmosphere; the purification of medical materials in space; the development of protective layers for insulators; and the mathematical algorithms for processing images.

I wouldn't want to give the impression that the FIS meant to close those areas to international cooperation. Not at all. We realized full well that isolationism could lead to a dead end in the development of science and technology in our country. In Russia's present situation, retaining our scientific personnel and maintaining the level of research we had achieved were among the main motives for developing cooperation with our foreign partners. We knew that our foreign partners were honestly interested in developing scientific ties with Russia and were offering help and support to our science programs in such difficult times. At the same time, some aspects of the Russian scientific research institutions' cooperation with the outside world caused justifiable concern. We focused on two problems in particular.

1. In most cases the amount that foreign clients pay scientific research institutes and engineering design offices in Russia is considerably less than they pay in a developed Western country. In the opinion of intelligence specialists, foreign partners often take advantage of Russia's laxity in protecting intellectual property.

2. Many hidden obstacles impede the exchange of science and technology between Russia and the West. The U.S. Department of Energy, for example, prepared a report in September 1993 stating that the program of scientific and technological cooperation with Russia, created for the "stabilization of Russian science," would be used to find unique technologies that could be introduced into American industry and national laboratories. At the same time, the United States and some other countries tended to bar Russian specialists' access to advanced technologies.

Despite the growing importance of scientific and technological intelligence, however, political intelligence remained the FIS's top priority. We focused on obtaining information on the intentions of other states, especially with respect to Russia. The Russian leadership was interested, and quite justly so, in whether any groups in other countries were involved in attempts to cause Russia to collapse, and if so, which ones. Providing a correct answer to this question was of extreme importance. After a thorough analysis of the problem, the FIS reported that at the time of the report it had no information to the effect that the government of the United States or of any other leading Western country was pursuing that kind of policy. It is considered too dangerous to reach a point beyond which events may become unpredictable, especially in a country bulging with nuclear warheads. But in general the FIS did not deny the existence of an external threat to Russia's territorial integrity. This threat emanates mainly from foreign groups and nationalist or radical religious organizations that directly support separatist sentiments and movements in Russia (the FIS supplied information that was as concrete as possible).

As for the situation in the CIS countries, on the basis of materials we had acquired and analyzed we came to the definite conclusion that the leaders of a number of Western states were trying to prevent Russia from playing a special role in the stabilization of the former Soviet republics and to frustrate their movement toward closer relations with Russia. U.S. politicians tend to consider Latin America and even Europe to fall within their zone of special interest, but they are unwilling to concede that Russia's special interest extends to the former Soviet republics—not to impose its will on them but to ensure that no threat to Russia's interests and security exists along its borders.

At that time we had reliable information that the U.S. special services had begun to strengthen their positions in all the CIS countries by establishing intelligence stations there. Russia was the main focus of their operations. In a large number of documented instances, agents functioning in Russia were to communicate via CIS countries or the Baltic states.

Using the means and methods of intelligence to acquire such information was, in our opinion, a normal intelligence activity that met international standards. But nobody in the United States was shocked when on August 23, 1998, it was announced that on the basis of available information, the CIA had informed President Clinton that Yeltsin was about to fire Prime Minister Sergei Kirienko and replace him with Viktor Chernomyrdin.

For the FIS, under the accepted standards such intelligence activity completely canceled out the zero-sum game that had been played up to then and that was the foundation of our attitude toward the United States and other Western countries; that is, anything good for them was almost automatically bad for Russia, and vice versa. Our opponents played by the same rules.

The shift of emphasis in intelligence objectives called for the FIS to intensify its analytical operations. It also had a positive effect on the quality of the materials we reported to the country's leadership.

The emphasis on the analytical aspect of intelligence activity brought some structural changes. In addition to the old analytical subdivisions of the PGU period, a new department (directorate) was formed to carry out a special mission. It dealt with the growing problem of the proliferation of nuclear and other weapons of mass destruction and the means for their delivery.

That department was actively engaged in getting information as efficiently as possible to develop an objective picture of the proliferation of nuclear weapons. On the basis of our own information, in contrast to unclassified publications, and on the basis of expert analysis, we developed the criteria that were used to determine the progress in possessing nuclear weapons made by states outside of the "nuclear five."

At that time we also decided to publish open reports from time to time in order to familiarize not only the leadership but also the public, both in Russia and abroad, with the conclusions reached by intelligence analysts on the hottest issues. Of several such reports, two, including the first, were devoted to the threat of nuclear proliferation.

An FIS report published in 1992 named three unofficial nuclear states: Israel, India, and Pakistan. Potential nuclear states were classified as "threshold states" and "prethreshold states." The report described the methods used for classification and the indicators that allowed us to put various states in the three groups. We were told that the Indian government expressed displeasure with our inclusion of that country among unofficial nuclear states on the basis of data in our possession. There was nothing we could do about that because the FIS could not and would not use a double standard.

The appendix to the second report, published at the beginning of 1995, included the lists of threshold and prethreshold states.

The work of the FIS on nuclear proliferation problems was met with great interest by our Western colleagues, and it seemed to play an important role in securing the cooperation of the special services of several countries with our foreign intelligence.

The new department, together with other FIS subdivisions, had not only to follow the processes of the proliferation of weapons of mass destruction but also to oppose attempts by some foreign intelligence agencies to take active measures connected with the so-called leakage of nuclear materials from Russia. As a rule, such moves were motivated by a desire to increase the intelligence agencies' funding or to influence the outcomes of internal political struggles in their countries. That said, one of their objectives undoubtedly was to compromise the Russian government, which allegedly was unable to guarantee the security of nuclear materials. A classic operation of this kind was an attempt by a German intelligence agent to organize the acquisition of plutonium in Russia in order to "intercept" it later in Munich. Soon after that operation was exposed, the wave of accusations about the leakage of nuclear materials from Russia calmed down.

More attention than ever before was paid to economic intelligence. A subdivision was formed in the FIS to control the implementation by foreign states of agreements signed with Russia; if such agreements were not being implemented, to determine why; to find out the real (not the bargaining) positions of our foreign partners in the process of preparing the appropriate documents; to take actions to facilitate the payment of debts owed to Russia (which roughly equal the debts Russia owed); to verify the true financial and legal status of each company offering services to a Russian state organization; and so on.

Economic intelligence has worked and is working also to remove artificial barriers erected to prevent competitive Russian products from entering international markets; to counter efforts to push Russia out of its established positions in the area of military-technological cooperation with other countries; and to search for new markets for Russian armaments. At present the latter task is vitally important for Russia, since to a large extent the market for the goods produced by the military-industrial complex determines the economic well-being of over 20 million Russians and in general affects the social situation in the vast regions of the Russian Federation.

Here is an example. In 1995 Pakistani representatives, using all channels, kept insisting on a large purchase of Russian military aircraft. The issue was brought to the attention of the FIS director. By that time we already possessed data suggesting that a multipurpose operation was under way. Pakistan wanted to apply pressure on the United States, which had expressed its displeasure with Pakistan's stand on the nonproliferation issue by refusing to release the $500 million appropriated for Pakistan's purchase of U.S. equipment for its air force. A further goal of Pakistan's operation was to undermine the military and technological cooperation between Russia and India.

In order to provide a complete report to the Russian political leadership, we asked the Pakistanis whether they had enough cash to pay for the airplanes.

"We have received a large credit in Saudi Arabia," they replied.

The FIS economic department thoroughly checked this claim and established that Pakistan had received no loans or credits from Saudi Arabia for that purpose.

A DIFFICULT BREAKTHROUGH

Perhaps the most crucial innovation in Russia's foreign intelligence was the development of contacts with the intelligence services of other countries, including members of NATO. During the Cold War years, cooperation was established between the KGB and its partners in the socialist countries, as well as with a number of developing states that we regarded as part of the "anti-imperialist camp."

The cooperation was very close and intensive, but did not necessarily extend to a totally open exchange of all files and archives, and certainly not of agents. For instance, the Stasi, the East German secret police, conducted some operations behind the KGB's back and on a number of occasions provided the PGU with only partial information. I can't say that we ourselves were completely open to our partners. It's a peculiarity of intelligence work that even the special services of the same country are not entirely candid with each other.

All the same, the cooperation was quite intensive and was undoubtedly beneficial to the parties involved. But now we intended an entirely different kind of contact, now with countries we once regarded as our enemies.

I have to admit that in the beginning a considerable number of FIS officers accepted the policy of establishing such contacts reluctantly. There were also direct opponents of this policy in the special services of other countries. Of course, much depended on the progress achieved in this area with the CIA as well as with German, French, and British intelligence.

In accordance with a previous agreement, the CIA's director, Robert Gates, visited Moscow and St. Petersburg from October 15 to 18, 1992. He was accompanied by a high-ranking delegation that included John McGaffin, head of the CIA's Central Eurasian Operations Department, and John McLaughlin, head of the CIA's Central Eurasian Analysis Department, among others. Because of the importance of the relations that were being established between the FIS and the CIA, I asked Yeltsin to receive Gates, who brought a message from President George H. W. Bush. The Russian president stressed the need for cooperation between the special services in solving issues of importance to both countries. Bush's message contained similar ideas. The exchange of notes was interpreted as approval of contacts between the two intelligence services by the political leadership of both countries.

Gates met with the minister of the interior, the minister of security, and the chief of the General Staff of the Russian armed forces. The head of the Army Intelligence Directorate (GRU) participated in the last meeting. As they usually say on such occasions, the talks were mutually beneficial and were held in a constructive atmosphere. Gates invited me to come to Washington for a return visit.

Half a year later I was ready to go to the United States. We had an intense exchange of opinion about the agenda of the visit, but the day before my departure I was advised that President Clinton was too busy to receive me. I decided not to overdramatize the situation, and said so to the CIA representative in Moscow, D. Rolf, whom I invited to lunch. But at the same time I could not help saying, "I intend to invite the new CIA director, James Woolsey, to Moscow in November, and there is every reason to believe that the Russian president will find time to meet with him, despite his heavy work load solving domestic political and economic problems."

During that period the FIS and the CIA maintained working contacts, including those between the experts and at the level of the deputy director of the FIS, Vyacheslav Trubnikov, and the first deputy director of the CIA, William Studemann. In general I can say that by 1993 notable progress was achieved in our cooperation with the Americans, with each party treating the other with greater trust. Processing of documents and replies to queries were speeded up. Personal contacts between representatives of the special services became stronger.

On the whole, CIA representatives highly valued the materials provided by the FIS, and especially noted the speed of their preparation. We were told that some FIS memos were brought to the attention of President Clinton, and that he took them into consideration in making decisions.

Of course, there were very serious, sometimes almost insurmountable obstacles on the road to the exchange of information between the agencies. Both intelligence services were reluctant to include in this exchange any data that could be detrimental to their source. But on the whole I can say that a mutual hope for cooperation gradually prevailed over the prejudices accumulated over many years.

The Yugoslav issue became a high-priority item during the "intelligence summit" between Director Woolsey and me that took place in the United States between June 12 and 18, 1993. On my visit to Washington I was accompanied by leading experts of the FIS, including the "open" station chief in Washington, Aleksandr Lysenko. We discussed many topics. Apart from the crisis in Yugoslavia, we talked about the situation in the Middle East, Islamic fundamentalism, the problems of fighting against the narcotics business, and the nonproliferation of weapons of mass destruction. Discussions took place at CIA headquarters in Langley, Virginia. This very fact already meant a lot.

Good personal relations were being established between the leaderships of the FIS and the CIA. I very well remember the atmosphere at the country residence of our ambassador in Washington, Vladimir Lukin, where we entertained our American colleagues. I think the embassy's chefs surpassed themselves. We sat outside on benches at wooden picnic tables. Shish kebab was prepared right there. Toasts followed one another; there was no end to the stories and jokes. From the outside it could hardly be imagined that that was a meeting between (to put it mildly) competitors.

The return visit to Russia of the CIA director and his colleagues took place August 7–10, 1993. The guests flew first to St. Petersburg and then to Moscow. Our official talks in St. Petersburg, where I went to meet the Americans, alternated with cultural events. After a visit to Peter's palace and the Hermitage, dinner was served at the Kamenny Ostrov reception mansion. Mikhail Pyotrovsky, director of the Hermitage and my former colleague at the Institute of Eastern Studies, attended the dinner and guided us through some of the Hermitage collection of masterpieces. Later he told me, "Nobody will believe me when I tell them I was sitting at a table between the directors of the FIS and the CIA."

The visit was quite useful, with many important exchanges of opinion. Unfortunately, the stay of the CIA delegation in Russia had to be cut short on August 10, when Woolsey had to leave for Georgia after the murder of the CIA station chief in Tbilisi.

The CIA director delivered a message from the U.S. president to Yeltsin, an indication that he highly valued the contacts between the special services of the two countries, which were becoming increasingly frequent. The very fact of sending this message was important in itself. According to some American writers, the top U.S. leadership knew that the FBI had exposed a Russian agent and was working on him for more than a year before Ames was actually arrested. Thus Bush was already aware of the case that subsequently dealt a serious blow to cooperation between the FIS and the CIA, but did not overestimate its negative impact on relations between our special services. But perhaps he knew nothing about Ames, and the story that Ames was shadowed for many months was nothing but mystification devised to show the "unsurpassed professional skills" of the FBI?

The seriousness of the cooperation is seen in the fact that the Americans were seeking the FIS's assistance in getting reliable information on what was going on in Russia, especially when the situation in our country was deteriorating. It is not out of the question that Washington officials wanted to compare their information with the FIS's interpretation of such a development as the tough confrontation between the president and the Federal Assembly in 1993. On September 24 I received J. Morris at his request. The day before, Woolsey had called him from Washington and instructed him to ask the head of Russian Intelligence to evaluate the events taking place in Russia, for later report to Clinton. As the CIA resident admitted, the very fact of the phone call was quite unusual.

After one of my trips to the Middle East, on November 11, 1993, I sent a message to Woolsey, stressing the serious negative consequences for a Middle East settlement of the lack of progress in the Syrian direction, which it seemed to me the United States was obviously underestimating, especially after some success in negotiations between the Israelis and the Palestinians. On November 19 I received Woolsey's reply:

"I very much appreciate your thoughts on the results of your trip to the Middle East. Your comments are very interesting and deserve further discussion. I would ask you to personally receive in Moscow Deputy Director of the CIA G. McGaffin and the head of the Middle East Department, Frank Anderson, and discuss with them the problems of the Middle East settlement, that being an important first step in the cooperation of our agencies in this new direction. Following this meeting we could organize consultations by the experts."

When McGaffin delivered Woolsey's message, he said my thoughts on Syria had been submitted to President Clinton, who familiarized himself with them with "a great deal of interest."

In general everything was shaping up well—so well that some people suggested that perhaps the traditional methods of intelligence operation should be replaced by cooperation between the intelligence agencies. It was too early for that. Intelligence activity in the present and future world can be halted only in an utterly improbable situation, when all countries sign appropriate agreements and, more important, adhere to them. That scenario is unrealistic. Under the new conditions, however, the means and methods of intelligence gathering could be changed, but strictly on a bilateral basis. This task is quite achievable. And we were moving toward it.

ABOUT THE AMES CASE

The breakthrough in relations between the FIS and the CIA came in connection with the Ames case. Certainly the arrest of Aldrich Ames was an extremely unpleasant event for us, since we lost our most important source at the CIA. It was also unpleasant for the United States, since it turned out that he could have been supplying us with very important information for many years. But still it was possible to keep emotions under control, since nobody was immune to such failures, especially at a time when no one was giving up intelligence gathering.

Ames's personality is very interesting in several respects. I am not among those who believe that Ames worked for the Soviets and then for Russia simply for material rewards. Certainly he was well paid, but there is evidence of an entirely different interest. For instance, in the 1970s Ames approached Thomas Kolesnichenko, a *Pravda* correspondent in the United States. When Ames was arrested and his picture was published in American newspapers, the Kolesnichenko family was shocked. They had known him as Fred Madison, of the New Hampshire Institute for Russian Studies. He had been visiting their home for years. Thomas and his wife, Svetlana, had never suspected the real reason for "Madison's" interest in them. But, Kolesnichenko recalls, little by little Ames not only was showing interest in developments in the Soviet Union but also was sincerely happy about the many changes that were taking place in our country. Wasn't that the reason Ames dropped the Kolesnichenkos so abruptly?[3]

At the same time, Ames did not pass on to us any information other than on agents recruited by the Americans in Soviet and Russian government bodies or special services.

Russian intelligence turned out to be so highly professional that the FBI was unable to uncover any of Ames's secret dead-drops, of which there were many. By the way, an attempt to seize one of them was to have taken place literally a few days before Ames's arrest. But the FBI was not sure about it; otherwise they would certainly have wanted to catch him with material evidence. I could also add that not long before his arrest Ames flew to one of the Latin American countries to meet with our liaison. Later the United States claimed that its agents knew about that and were closely following him, but they still could not document the fact of the meeting between Ames and our representative. And the meeting did take place.

I don't want to speculate on what caused the loss of this extremely valuable source. It is possible that an American special service received some kind of signal from their source in Moscow. Obviously, Ames's carefree spending habits helped U.S. counterintelligence to uncover the mole. In any event, the circle around him began to tighten, and in the end he was arrested.

On February 24 Trubnikov came to FIS headquarters to receive two special CIA envoys, G. McGaffin and Paul Lofgren, sent to Moscow by the CIA director to discuss Ames's case. In the course of the conversation the Americans tried to apply pressure on us, demanding that we recall the FIS station chief in Washington, Aleksandr Lysenko, even though they knew he had nothing to do with Ames. Trubnikov firmly rejected the demand. If the Americans expelled Lysenko, he said, reciprocal measures would be taken with regard to the CIA station chief in Moscow.

Unfortunately, the exchange took place.

After all these events, we received information that the CIA was trying to recruit the FIS station chief in Bern. Rolf Mowatt-Larssen took part in the operation. He was the one who had maintained partnership relations between the CIA and the FIS in Moscow between 1992 and 1994. Characteristically, in response to our protest, the American side acknowledged the recruitment attempt and said it was a "routine affair in special forces work."

In fact, after Ames's sensational case, a number of CIA agents resigned or were fired. The mood at the U.S. intelligence establishment was far from jovial. We in the FIS leadership decided not to rub salt in our American partners' wounds. We did not initiate a single comment in the press regarding the long success of our foreign intelligence. Perhaps, and this may seem strange to someone outside the intelligence community, some kind of corporate loyalty played a role. Besides, these were new times and we did not want to jeopardize our bilateral relations by making thoughtless statements.

We did not give up our interest in cooperating with our American colleagues after the Ames case.

TROUBLES WITH MI6

Our relations with the very experienced and dangerous British MI6 were evolving with difficulty. The British initiated a preliminary confidential contact with the FIS in 1991, in Oslo. The probing sessions to clarify our positions and to define future relations between the two intelligence agencies continued until the summer of 1992.

But then the British began to act in accord with their own scenario. In June 1992 British Ambassador Bryan Foll informed me that the political leadership of his country had decided to establish cooperation between the Russian and British intelligence agencies. Without any prior notification, he had introduced a so-called contact group in Moscow, consisting of the MI6 station chief, D. Scarlett, and a representative of MI5 (British counterintelligence), Andrew Slutter. At the same time, the British government did everything to block similar moves by our side. Naturally, the imbalance did not satisfy us. Furthermore, we gave the British side a list of thirteen individuals —ten British intelligence officers and three MI6 agents—who were actively recruiting Russian citizens. On March 9 we delivered a statement to the MI6 station chief in Moscow regarding an attempt to recruit the FIS station chief in Stockholm.

In these conditions we decided to stop cooperating with MI6 temporarily. Still, I decided to write a letter to Roderic Braithwaite, the British prime minister's councilor and coordinator on intelligence service operations, with whom I maintained good relations during his time as ambassador in Moscow. I received a reply to the effect that R. Braithwaite was coming to Moscow for negotiations with the FIS director. The meeting took place on June 2, 1993. He admitted that our assessment of the imbalance in the relations between the FIS and MI6 was justified and informed us that our proposals would be satisfied—on condition that the FIS representation in London would be considered in conjunction with that of the GRU.

Here I will allow myself a brief digression. During my time as the FIS director not only the English but many others tried to play foreign intelligence against our colleagues in the military. They never succeeded in any way. As for the English, I told Braithwaite bluntly that the GRU was an independent organization and that they could contact it directly to sort out their differences.

We decided to put the Britons' amorphous promises into practice. On July 23 I gave Ambassador Foll the name of our nominee for the position of "open" station chief in Britain. He was Vyacheslav Gurgenov, deputy director of the FIS. But the English continued their game.

On October 1 the *Daily Mirror* ran a story saying that the arrival of the "prominent Russian intelligence agent" Vyacheslav Gurgenov in London for a permanent assignment was undesirable. We realized that his visa application would be turned down. That was precisely what happened.

On March 2 the British ambassador was summoned to the Second European Department of the Russian Foreign Ministry and told that in view of the fact that the official representative of the FIS in London was denied an entry visa, the open representative of MI6 in Moscow, Scarlett, was required to leave Russia. The British retaliated by ordering Nikolai Yavlukhin, a councilor of the Russian embassy, to leave London.

But then things began to move. The head of the Regional Department of MI6, Andrew Robert Fulton, and the director of MI5, Charles Blent, visited Moscow on September 8–9. The British were brought to Barvikha, a countryside resort near Moscow, where I was on my regular vacation. Opening the conversation, Fulton confirmed the intention of the British side to restore "sincere relations of cooperation with the Russian special services, leaving behind the flops that have occurred for known reasons." I replied that we were also interested in that, but on the basis of complete equality, including the number of future representatives of the FIS and MI6 in London and Moscow.

Citing what I innocently called a hypothetical example (I certainly wasn't about to reveal any of our sources), I told the British we would hardly object if they sent Michael Shipster to Moscow. In fact, the British were indeed planning to send Shipster to Russia as an open representative. At the same time, we assumed he would not (as he had done in India) attempt to smuggle the recruited Czech intelligence officer out of the country and take him to the West. My reference to Shipster seemed to puzzle Blent, judging by the glance he shot at Fulton. And when I mentioned Shipster's involvement in Indian operations, Blent appeared to lose control over his emotions for a moment. The British counterintelligence officer hardly expected information leakage of that kind from MI6 (whence but MI6!).

When I was minister of foreign affairs I visited London and met with my old friend Rostislav Yushuk, with whom I used to work in the Middle East. At that time he was an open FIS station chief in Great Britain. He introduced me to Shipster, who was his partner on the MI6 side. I jokingly apologized to Shipster for interfering with his career in Moscow.

Another "surprise" prepared for me in London when I visited the English capital in March 1997 as minister of foreign affairs was a meeting with John le Carré, who to my mind is one of the very best authors of political thrillers. At my request, our ambassador, Anatoly Adamishin, invited him and his wife to lunch. The meeting was quite informal. My wife and I very much enjoyed speaking with this outstanding man. As an old admirer of the works of the former intelligence agent David Cornwell, who became world-famous under the name John le Carré, I was especially pleased to receive a copy of his recently published *Smiley's People*, with the author's inscription: "To Evgeny Maksimovich Primakov with my sincere warm wishes and with the hope that we will live in a much better world than the one which is described here."

THINKING OUT LOUD

Can foreign intelligence be ideological? There is no clear-cut answer to that question, especially if one examines the work of intelligence in retrospect. I knew Donald Maclean and was even on friendly terms with him. He was one of the brilliant "Cambridge Five," who perhaps have no equal in the history of world intelligence. As deputy director of the Institute of World Economy I spent many hours with this talented man, who worked at the institute as

Mark Fraser. When he reappeared in the USSR twenty years later (he and his family had been evacuated under the nose of British counterintelligence, which had picked up the scent of the high-ranking Foreign Office executive who was working for Moscow), he once again became known as Donald Maclean, or to be more exact, Donald Donaldovich Maclean, as he was called at IMEMO.

A Scottish lord, he would never have gotten mixed up with Soviet intelligence for money. In fact, he probably had enough money to maintain the USSR's foreign intelligence. Maclean began to cooperate with Soviet intelligence for purely ideological reasons.

One cannot say that Maclean did not like Britain, and especially Scotland. But he was a patriot of the Soviet Union. I would not want to simplify things, however. Together with us he lived through the drama of the exposure of Stalin and the crimes that did not fit into the framework of ideologically pure socialism, in which he believed so reverently. We spoke a lot on this subject, but there wasn't even a trace of complaint about his fate in anything he said.

A fatal disease with which Maclean struggled courageously finally took the life of this outstanding man. The entire institute and all of Maclean's colleagues in the intelligence community attended the funeral.

Another famous intelligence agent, George Blake, worked and continues to work at IMEMO as a researcher. When he was in Moscow I helped him join our institute. One day Donald Donaldovich told me that the famous Blake wanted to apply for a job at IMEMO. He had recently escaped from a London prison, where he was serving time for cooperating with Soviet Intelligence, and turned up in Moscow. That was the same Blake who had given us the blueprints of the Berlin tunnel leading to the secret communication lines of our military command and information on how the Americans were intercepting all the conversations transmitted by those communication lines. George Blake rendered other services to Soviet Intelligence. Interceding for his friend, Maclean narrowed his eyes and said, "Trust me, even though Blake is a counterintelligence officer, he's smart." It turned out that in Great Britain, intelligence agents, who considered themselves to be highly intellectual, liked to make fun of their colleagues in counterintelligence.

Indeed, George Blake proved to be a clever and charming man. He was welcomed at IMEMO. After my transfer to the Intelligence Service, my friendship with Georgy Ivanovich, as we called him, continued. At FIS parties Colonel George Blake was always among the most welcome guests. As a matter of fact, he was not a guest at all, he was among his own flesh and blood, and I say that with no reservations.

Did the material factor become the sole attraction for recruiting foreigners or keeping them on the job as FIS sources after ideology ceased to play a role in international relations? Life itself gave a negative answer to that question.

A few months after my appointment to the post of director of foreign intelligence I got a report that a source who had been working in one of the European countries for quite a long time told the Center that inasmuch as Russia had given up the communist ideology, he no longer saw any reason to go on working for our intelligence. He was a valuable source. Furthermore, the message seemed to indicate that he was an honest man. In such cases, all contacts of the refusenik are immediately frozen, a comprehensive analysis of the entire period of cooperation is conducted, and the person who has "filed for divorce" is removed from the pool of secret agents.

I decided not to rush. I dictated a letter to him in which I did not simply talk about the foreign policy objectives of the nonideological Russia but also tried to show how important a strong Russia was for world stability in the new conditions.

We did not receive a response right away. But when it came, its author said he was ready to continue cooperating with us; and so far as I know, he carried out important assignments for us for many years. True, soon after his reply he used a special channel to send the Intelligence Service greetings on November 7, the anniversary of the "Great October Socialist Revolution." But then no other similar messages followed. . . .

Generally speaking, the history of intelligence indicates that ideology has never been the sole motivation of sources; it has always contained some element of politics. At various times we were offered assistance by people motivated by their hatred of fascism, for instance, or their desire to preserve peace. And even today many don't want to live in a unipolar world and be subjected to unilateral dictates. Other individuals also support us in our attempts to find political solutions to various crisis situations and sympathize with Russia's opposition to Islamic extremism and religious fanaticism in general.

Now let's address another issue. May a country's foreign intelligence participate in its domestic processes? I categorically insist that it should not. But the only way to guarantee that it does not is to keep foreign intelligence separate from all law enforcement bodies, which by the nature of their functions cannot escape being involved in internal political conflicts. It was because the FIS was an independent agency, separated from the KGB, that the direct confrontation between the Federal Assembly and the president in October 1993 affected Yasenevo only slightly.[4] Naturally, we didn't stuff our ears with cotton and didn't follow the events as outside observers, but we did not get directly involved in the events. I did not convene the directorate to issue political verdicts. I simply called a meeting of the FIS department heads and instructed them to tighten the security of our headquarters and ordered the officers not to carry guns off FIS premises. Any political involvement could cost us dearly, as we could lose a considerable number of our agents.

Yeltsin appreciated this position. In fact, the FIS was the only special service that he did not call during the events.

I would like to reiterate—it had nothing to do with deliberately looking the other way. On the eve of the events Yeltsin signed Decree 1400, dissolving the Federal Assembly. I learned about it a short time before I was supposed to meet some friends. I was driving along Leninsky Prospekt to meet them when Yeltsin called me.

"What do you think about my decree?" Yeltsin asked.

"I don't think it's well thought out."

"I expected a different answer from the director of the Foreign Intelligence Service."

"I told you what I thought. It would have been much worse if the head of the Foreign Intelligence Service lied to his president."

Yeltsin hung up. He never mentioned that phone conversation.

The fact that Foreign Intelligence is completely independent of any law enforcement body is also important because it enables it to supply the country's political leaders with its unedited opinion. When I was an alternate member of the Politburo and later when I joined the Presidential Council and the Security Council, I often had opportunities to read the KGB's classified reports about the international political situation. Many of these reports had nothing to do with the information supplied by the PGU through established channels. The PGU had no direct access to the country's leadership; it was required to submit its reports to the KGB. At times that situation was useful to people who, for political reasons of their own, wanted to distort reality.

Allegations that some of the perestroika leaders were CIA "agents of influence," for instance, caused quite an uproar. As director of the FIS, I responded to the inquiry by the prosecutor general's office by ordering intelligence departments that could have this information to make a thorough check of all their materials relating to these allegations. The answer was unequivocal —although the allegations were said to be based on data attributed to Foreign Intelligence, the FIS never had any information of that kind.

An important achievement of the FIS was the fact that in 1992, for the first time in its history, it acquired legal status. The Duma passed a law that established a legal framework for the FIS's activities. On the one hand, the legal status provided by the law entails certain guarantees and rights. On the other hand, under the law the FIS is supervised by the Federal Assembly. That was another important step toward creating the necessary public conditions for the operation of an organism as complex as the Foreign Intelligence Service.

SECRET TRIPS

During my tenure at the FIS I made secret or half-secret trips abroad. During the Cold War so much distrust accumulated that many Western politicians had trouble believing that any secret trips by the FIS director had no relation to the United States, or that when they were indirectly related to it, as in the case of my trip to Cuba, we were not guided by hostility to the United States. It is very important for the United States to understand that Russia's interests often lie far beyond the framework of Russian-American relations.

In this book I can't discuss all the trips that helped to resolve some of the most vital issues. But still . . .

On July 30, 1993, my airplane flew to Kabul. This was not my first trip to Afghanistan, but it was my first visit as director of the FIS. This time the landing was a far cry from the one before our troops were withdrawn. Back then everything was much more complicated. We had to make steep turns to avoid the green wooded areas, to descend rapidly and fire "heat traps" to protect ourselves from heat-guided missiles. Now we landed without any tricks. But the next day when we were leaving Kabul, we took off from the landing strip quite steeply, because the airport was under fire. The withdrawal of our troops did not herald the coming of peace to war-torn Afghanistan; armed clashes between various groups continued.

The extreme instability of Afghanistan metastasized to neighboring countries. The situation in Tajikistan was especially dangerous; there bloody clashes between regional clans intertwined with the struggle between Dushanbe, its capital, and the Islamist opposition, based almost entirely in neighboring Afghanistan. It was from Afghanistan that the militants made their daring attacks and that they got their weapons and money.

For Russia the situation was especially alarming because our border guards patrolled the Tajik-Afghan border. Their presence there was inevitable, not only because of our interest in stabilizing the situation in this CIS country but also because the Tajik-Afghan border was the border of the Common-wealth and so in a sense of Russia herself.

Our frontier posts, which served as a barrier to the movement of militants and drug dealers—they were often the same people—were under constant attack from the Afghan side. The number of casualties was growing. We had to neutralize weapon emplacements in Afghan territory. Air attacks were also used.

My trip to Kabul was occasioned by all those circumstances. We stayed in the half-ruined Intercontinental Hotel, in the only wing that was functional. A few hours after I arrived I was invited to a meeting with President Burha-nuddin Rabbani. I realized, however, that the main talks would be with the defense minister, Ahmad Shah Massoud. One of the principal field com-manders, he once fought against our troops in Afghanistan. Since he made most of his raids from the unassailable Panjsher gorge, he was called "the lion of Panjsher." Like Rabbani, Ahmad Shah was a Tajik. I think that emo-tionally the situation in Tajikistan affected them more than the others.

But I began my conversation with him with something other than events in Tajikistan. On the way to his residence, my Afghan colleague told me that "one of Ahmad's bodyguards, a Russian by origin," had recently married an Afghan and started a family. Naturally, I was intrigued by this story. At my request, Ahmad Shah summoned the "Russian bodyguard." I had brought an interpreter who was fluent in Dari. A sturdy fellow wearing an Afghan uniform and toting a machine gun walked in. A thick black beard framed a face that no one would recognize as European; he looked Oriental. (Later I was told that he dyed his hair and beard black.) When I questioned him, he answered in good Russian, but with some effort. He spoke to Ahmad Shah and the others in fluent Dari. Ahmad Shah told me that very few people knew that his bodyguard was a Russian. The Russian bodyguard himself told me the following story: He had been on a reconnaissance mission when a fire fight broke out and he was seriously wounded. Unconscious, he was taken prisoner. Ahmad Shah's fighters nursed him back to life ("How can I forget that!" he said). He adopted Islam and became Ahmad Shah's personal bodyguard ("I shall give my life for him!"). His mother and sister visited him and tried to persuade him to come home, at least for a visit. The boss gave his permission, but he refused.

The three-hour talk with Ahmad Shah was altogether businesslike. I described our view of the situation in Tajikistan and Afghanistan. I told him candidly, "Our military operations will inevitably intensify if Russian and Tajik border guards are attacked. But we have learned a bitter lesson and we're not going to bring troops to Afghanistan again. However, we are capable of protecting our interests without a ground operation."

I told Ahmad Shah that we were looking for a political rather than a military settlement in Tajikistan. At the same time, we believed that negotiations between Dushanbe and the opposition must start without delay, with simultaneous multilateral meetings involving Russia, Afghanistan, Tajikistan, Uzbekistan, and Iran. The participation of other Central Asian states was also possible. In order to create the best possible conditions for a peaceful settlement, both sides should stop their military operations on the border. Infiltration of Tajikistan by Islamic militants should be avoided and the return of refugees should be started with guarantees of their security and assistance in settlement.

My partner agreed with most of what I said and was expressly interested in organizing my meeting with the leader of the Tajik Islamic opposition, Said Abdulla Nuri. My confidential contact with him took place on July 31. That was the first time a Russian representative had ever met with the head of the largest antigovernment force, which had made an armed challenge to the president of Tajikistan, Emomali Rakhmonov. The talk was extremely frank. We communicated through an interpreter, but when I met Nuri in Moscow later I realized his Russian was quite good.

In general, my opinion of Nuri was positive. I found out how he became engaged in active antigovernment activities. He was an ordinary mullah, but perhaps differed from his colleagues in speaking openly against corruption and ended up in jail for his pains.

"I hope you understand that it's not in your interest to get Russia involved in the fighting against opposition troops based in Afghanistan," I said. "But we'll be forced to get involved if the attacks against border guards continue. But there is a real alternative: Russia can be helpful in setting up negotiations with President Rakhmonov."

Nuri seemed to appreciate my frankness. "The Tajik government in exile," he said, "didn't aim to overthrow the Dushanbe leaders. What they wanted was a coalition cabinet, with themselves as part of the coalition." According to Nuri, now that our meeting had encouraged him to hope for negotiations with the Dushanbe leadership, he would focus on preventing further complications at the border. "But I don't control all the field commanders," he added.

It seemed to me that Nuri had sent a very important signal. My conversation with him was perhaps the starting point of a difficult, lengthy process with many digressions, but one that might lead to a settlement between the Tajik leadership and the Islamic opposition. Subsequent events proved me right. I continued to meet with the leaders of both sides in Moscow and Dushanbe. I believe that my talks with President Rakhmonov, who was rapidly gaining experience and political weight, and with Hajji Akbar Turjanzoda, who was the second man in the opposition but often set its tone, were of paramount importance. Turjanzoda agreed to a representation of 30 percent for the opposition to the Tajik leadership's 70 percent in government bodies. Rakhmonov supported this ratio. Then Turjanzoda removed the other obstacle to peaceful settlement when he said the opposition would support a clause in the Tajik constitution providing that the state could be neither Islamic nor Communist.

The peace process in Tajikistan made good progress and resulted in an agreement that was signed in Moscow in 1996. I was directly involved in preparing the agreement and spent many difficult hours revising it until it was acceptable to both sides.

And now about my meeting with Fidel Castro.

When I arrived in Havana on October 25, 1994, I thought I would be talking mainly with the head of Cuban intelligence, Eduardo Delgado. We did have a comprehensive and businesslike exchange of opinions, but my meetings and conversations with Fidel Castro lasted much longer—ten hours altogether. Except for a three-hour private meeting, other participants included Raúl Castro, the first vice president of the Council of State and of the Council of Ministers (in essence, the prime minister); Carlos Lage Dávila, a vice president of the Council of State; the minister of economy and planning, José Luis Rodríguez García; and the minister of the interior, Abelardo Colome Ibarra, among others.

People of my generation, at least most of us, saw Cuba in a romantic light. The image of heroic Cuba was inseparably associated in our minds with its leader, Fidel Castro. His passionate four- and five-hour speeches, enthusiastically received by hundreds of thousands of people who flooded Havana's central square and the adjacent streets, kindled the imagination. People liked his simplicity. Everyone in Cuba addressed him as "Comrade Fidel!" Fidel's picture was nowhere to be seen, but Che Guevara's was everywhere. Castro's whole life had a romantic quality: his forced exile, his triumphant return to his homeland as a leader of armed compatriots who overthrew the hated regime of Fulgencio Batista, the defeat of armed intervention at the Bay of Pigs. I remember the delight with which our people watched the visits of Fidel Castro to the Soviet Union.

The glory overshadowed the other side of the coin—the pervasive low living standards of the Cubans and the extremely severe restrictions imposed on the country's economy and its society in general. Certainly one should not forget that Cuba was subject to an economic blockade by the United States. Cuba also suffered from severe curtailment of its economic ties with the Soviet Union and the countries of Eastern Europe after the Warsaw bloc dissolved.

Some of Cuba's economic difficulties could be attributed to Castro's dogmatic conservatism in economic policy and his slowness to adapt to the new international realities. But the situation took a turn for the better when the Cuban leadership introduced economic reforms—not only some liberalization of the country's economic life but encouragement of foreign investment. Large investments flowed into Cuba from Canada, Spain, Mexico, and other countries.

That was my second trip to Cuba. I first visited Cuba in April 1981. Much had changed since then, but the romantic spirit, although less pronounced, was still there. It was that spirit, or perhaps simply the character of the Cuban people, that brought smiles to their faces, in spite of all their hardships. You can't resist the excitement around you. It's hard for anyone free of prejudice or anger not to have good feelings for Cuba and its people.

The first time I met Fidel Castro he immediately suggested that we speak face to face. As soon as the conversation began, I realized that he was in real need of a frank exchange of opinions, appraisals, and ideas. No such meetings with the Russian leadership were possible, whereas Fidel, a candid man not constrained by protocol, was anxious to get the information he was looking for and to share the ideas that overwhelmed him.

"First of all, I'd like to give you my view of Russian-Cuban relations," I said. "We need to understand [I said "we" deliberately] that under the new conditions the ideological factor is gone. And this is not a sort of historical break. But does that mean we have to run in opposite directions? Of course not."

Fidel was listening attentively. He nodded approvingly when I said, "Not only Russia but many other countries, especially Latin American states, need an independent Cuba. At the same time, taking account of the new realities, we are interested in normalizing Cuban-American relations. The time has passed when we viewed Cuba as an anti-American outpost. Normalization and positive development of your relations with the United States will enable the Russian Federation to expand its relations with the Republic of Cuba in all directions."

Fidel replied at once, "I fully share these views. You should know that we don't want to aggravate our relations with the United States and we're ready to compromise. Furthermore, we're not overreacting to America's toughness toward Cuba when we talk about the émigré issue—we realize it's linked to the November elections in Florida. Using an established communication channel, we've told the U.S. leadership we won't open the borders, something they dread because the émigrés might well include people who were by no means desirable."

According to Castro, he realized very well that he should base his policy on the new realities. That was why Cuba refused to support any antigovernment forces in Latin America and shut down all its operations on the African continent. Cuba also needs to normalize its relations with the United States as a prelude to lifting the quarantine, which is opposed by practically all Latin American countries and by Canada as well as by some European states.

"We are also interested in creating a situation that would encourage Cubans living in the United States to begin investing their money here," Castro continued. "According to our information, changes are taking place in the minds of Cuban émigrés. By no means all of them are against normalizing relations between Cuba and the United States, and one of the reasons is their desire to go into business in Cuba. But there are also irreconcilable opponents among the émigrés. It is very unfortunate that that is the group that has access to the U.S. administration."

Castro went even further: he asked me to ask the Russian leadership to inform their American counterparts about Cuba's readiness and desire to improve its relations with the United States. "We'd be very much obliged to you if you'd do that."

After my talks with Carlos Lage, any doubts that the Cubans were committed to introducing the basic elements of a free market economy vanished from my mind. Everything I heard and saw told me that the Chinese and to some extent the Vietnamese models of a transition to a free market appealed to them—models that, in their words, "allow them to preserve their political structures." I was also convinced that nobody questioned the absolute authority of Fidel Castro; without his initiative any changes in the country would be simply impossible.

Both Fidel and Raúl expressed interest in meeting again with me and the FIS colleagues who had accompanied me from Moscow. Castro invited us to a reception where almost the whole Cuban leadership was present. The dinner at our embassy was unforgettable. It was held in our honor by Arnold Kalinin, my good friend from our student days and now Russian ambassador to Cuba. The Cubans learned that I turned sixty-five that day. I was very touched that Fidel Castro came to the embassy. Raúl came with him, despite the fact that for security reasons the Politburo did not permit them to attend such events together. It was a wonderful party. We all sat there for three hours, talking about anything and everything, telling jokes.

At the table Raúl Castro paid special attention to my assistant Robert Markaryan, who he said reminded him of Anastas Mikoyan. I don't know why, they don't look anything alike. Then Fidel Castro told me about his meeting with Mikoyan during the Cuban missile crisis.

"It is widely known," Castro began, "that for a long time we resisted Khrushchev's plan to deploy missiles with nuclear warheads and medium-range bombers in Cuba. Finally we were persuaded to go along 'in the interests of the entire socialist camp.' But then Mikoyan suddenly arrives and tries to persuade us to agree to remove the missiles and the bombers. Difficult talks are going on. I disagree with the suggested option, backed only by a verbal pledge by the U.S. president that we won't be attacked after the missiles are withdrawn.

"At this moment I receive a message that Mikoyan's wife has passed away. I immediately call a recess and say: 'Comrade Mikoyan, I have terrible news for you. Your wife has passed away. I'll give orders to prepare your plane for departure.'"

"I'm not leaving," said Mikoyan. "I can't interrupt the negotiations. Great values, the world's destiny depend on our decisions."

Mikoyan turned around and walked over to the window, but Fidel saw tears streaming down his face. "The recess is over and we accept the Soviet proposal."

Thus ended the tragic page in international affairs that could have brought humankind to the edge of destruction.

We were moved by the story, but we were embarrassed, to say the least, when we heard its postscript.

"After Mikoyan resigned," Fidel continued, "I went to Moscow and asked the comrade from the CPSU Central Committee who accompanied me to arrange a meeting for me with Anastas. A few hours later I received a reply indicating that I should not pursue the matter."

Upon my return to Moscow from my second visit to Cuba, in 1994, I gave Yeltsin a detailed report about my meetings and impressions. He decided to inform Clinton about them. As far as I know, that message stressed our belief in Castro's sincerity when he said he wanted to normalize relations with the United States, and that if he succeeded, normalization in turn not only would help to stabilize the situation in Latin America but also would bring about democratic changes in Cuba itself.

The Cubans again showered me with kindness when I visited Cuba as foreign minister. The schedule of this visit called for me to head for the airport immediately after dinner with Fidel Castro. I was about to bid him farewell when he said, "I'll see you off." I thought he would walk me to the staircase. When we reached the ground floor, I thought he meant to see me to the car. To my surprise, Castro's car pulled up to the door and he said, "Get in with me."

I can only imagine how surprised the journalists who came to the airport must have been when they saw Fidel Castro together with the Russian foreign minister near the airplane.

"Won't you come aboard to have one for the road, as we say in Russia?"

"Well, do you want the journalists to think you're taking me away from Cuba?" said Castro, smiling.

When I resigned from office as head of the government in 1999, I received a touching invitation from Fidel Castro to come to Cuba with my family for a vacation.

CHAPTER SIX

In the Ministry of Foreign Affairs

FROM YASENEVO TO SMOLENSKAYA SQUARE

On the morning of January 5, 1996, the special phone with a dedicated line rang in the office of the director of the Foreign Intelligence Service in Yasenevo.

"The President will talk to you."

In a few seconds I heard his voice.

"Could you come over right away?"

"Sure. I'll bring the briefing documents and I'll come immediately."

"No, don't bring the documents today."

On my way to the Kremlin I couldn't help wondering what was behind this invitation.

Yeltsin welcomed me warmly. After an exchange of the usual pleasantries, he asked, "What would you think about being appointed foreign minister?"

I admit I had thought of this possibility on my way to Yeltsin. Television and newspapers had carried numerous reports that Andrei Kozyrev was about to resign. Names of possible successors were also mentioned. At some point my name was among them, but then it disappeared from the list of nominees. But I had no desire at all to join the Foreign Ministry, and I said so to Boris Nikolaevich. I gave him what I thought were convincing arguments, among them an easily predictable negative reaction by the West, where I was often called "a friend of Saddam Hussein's" and "an old-school apparatchik." Besides, President George H. W. Bush used to head the CIA, and before Klaus Kinkel became Germany's foreign minister he had headed the BND, Germany's intelligence service; a similar appointment in Russia, especially on the eve of a presidential election, could easily be used as a propaganda tool by our enemies.

Yeltsin listened to all my arguments and then said, "Perhaps the minuses you're focusing on may change to pluses. . . . Well, all right, if you refuse flatly, we can wait. But I'm not closing the question yet."

Four days later, on January 9, when I was giving the president a regular briefing, he asked, "Well, have you changed your mind?"

"No," I said as flatly as I could.

"But I have. I ask you to accept my offer."

The offer was too persistent and I could not reject it. True, I was assured I would be able to work for a month or two at my old place. But as soon as I returned to the "woods" (that's what the staff calls the place where the FIS is located), the officer on duty rushed into my office and said, "Is it true? They just announced on TV that you've been appointed foreign minister!"

Later the president's assistant called and apologized for not letting me know. He had been instructed to release the decree immediately, and its text was handed to the news anchor while she was on the air.

The next day at noon a meeting of the Foreign Ministry Board was called in the Kremlin, where Yeltsin introduced me to my future closest colleagues. In the evening I had a previously scheduled meeting with the former head of East German intelligence, Markus Wolf.

I knew a lot about this undoubtedly talented man, who for many years headed one of the most effective intelligence services and was a gifted analyst. "Misha" Wolf spent his childhood in Moscow, where his anti-Nazi parents had had to move before World War II. He went to a Russian school and spoke Russian without an accent.

This time Wolf came to Moscow for a few days with his charming wife immediately after he was "temporarily" released from prison, to which he was sentenced after the unification of Germany. He was arrested against all logic. He had served his country, which was not annexed to the other state but was united with it; he was not personally involved in any actions that could be construed as criminal. In fact, he was involved in something his colleagues were doing in West Germany, and it didn't occur to anyone to indict *them* after unification. Furthermore, in the last years of Erich Honeker's rule, Wolf resigned because of serious political differences with him.[1] Moscow didn't go far enough. When negotiations on the unification of Germany were held, it would have been prudent to put in writing Bonn's obligation not to prosecute persons who had been connected with East German government bureaus.

I went to the meeting with Trubnikov. His future was already decided. During my last conversation with Yeltsin he accepted my suggestion of appointing Trubnikov, my first deputy, as head of the Foreign Intelligence Service.

The evening was quite a success. It was my first meeting with Wolf, and we both had been looking forward to it. We made jokes about everything, including life's vicissitudes. The first toast to the new foreign minister was made in this company. I remember Wolf's words: "Doubtless there will be speculations on account of your FIS connection. But believe me, serious politicians will appreciate the indisputable fact that your work experience as the intelligence chief, which under the circumstances lasted a long time, has secured a fairly good data base for the head of the Foreign Ministry."

Of course, throughout my earlier career I was closely connected with foreign policy, and in many instances was involved in it directly. I had close contacts with the diplomats and knew many of them personally, including such outstanding ones as Anatoly Dobrynin and Oleg Troyanovsky.

I formed relationships with various foreign ministers. I'd like to single out one of them, Andrei Andreevich Gromyko, who occupied the foreign minister's chair for more than a quarter of a century. I met him on many occasions when I worked at the Academy of Sciences. I was deeply touched by his letter when I suddenly lost my son in 1981. It was not a formal letter of sympathy but a very deeply felt, heartwarming message. I remember with gratitude that in his monograph Gromyko mentioned my son's book on the activity of oil companies in the Arabian Peninsula, published after my son's death. How inconsistent all that is with the image of an emotionless iceberg that emerged from some people's portrayals of him!

Of course one's attitude toward a person always depends on how that person has treated one, especially if he occupies a high position in the state hierarchy. But in my assessment of Gromyko I am guided not only by my subjective reasons. For instance, the idea is widespread that he was one of the three people who masterminded the invasion of Afghanistan, the others being Dmitry Ustinov and Yury Andropov. Indeed, he may have put his signature on the appropriate document sent to the Central Committee. But I clearly remember, and so do many other people, a plenary meeting of the Foreign Ministry in 1982, at which I delivered a report as the director of the

Institute of Oriental Studies. The subject of the report was the situation in Afghanistan after the introduction of our troops there.

In it I stressed the utter absence of a "revolutionary situation" in Afghanistan, from which it followed that agrarian reform in that country was sheer adventurism and that bringing about "revolutionary changes" there by military force was impossible. Some participants, obviously mindful of the presence of the foreign minister, reacted to my report with puzzlement and anger. I think they were dumbfounded when Gromyko agreed with many provisions of the report and essentially supported the idea of the futility and groundlessness of the presence of our troops in that country from the viewpoint of the internal situation in Afghanistan. Meanwhile official propaganda, and especially the Central Committee apparatus, claimed that our troops were "preventing imperialism from strangling the Afghan revolution."

Politics is the art of the possible. This well-known truism is usually interpreted as indicating the dependence of politics on the appropriate economic, military, and geopolitical conditions. All that is certainly true. But the art of the possible should probably take into account the limitations created by the predominant ideology, the type of regime, and the state of the society. It seems that Andrei Andreevich was quite aware of these limitations.

I came to the Foreign Ministry at an altogether different time. The country had taken the path of market reform and political pluralism. Changes in Russia resulted in the end of global confrontation. The Warsaw Pact and the Council of Mutual Economic Assistance (CMEA) disintegrated. That was the starting point.

Some people believed this point would mark the beginning of Russia's incorporation in the "civilized world," but as a second-rate power. As the successor of the Soviet Union, bearing all the consequences of its defeat in the Cold War, Russia was admitted to the company of nations for the most part silently but sometimes quite noisily. In that case, its relations with the United States had to follow the pattern of those between the United States and the countries that lost World War II, principally Germany and Japan, which went on to become America's allies. But their postwar policies were controlled by Washington, without any visible concern on their part.

That point of view was relatively widespread among Russia's democratic circles after 1991. Moreover, it was believed that such an understanding of Russia's place in the world would help in the fight against the old regime.

It has always been my philosophy not to lay blame on my predecessors under any circumstances. But in order to clarify the atmosphere among the Foreign Ministry's top executives at the beginning of the 1990s I shall tell the story of a conversation between the Russian foreign minister and former president Richard Nixon as the American political scientist Dimitri Simes, president of the Nixon Center for Peace and Freedom, told it. "Nixon asked Kozyrev to outline the national interests of the new Russia. And Kozyrev said: 'You know, Mr. President, one of the problems of the Soviet Union was that we were obsessed with national interest. Now we are thinking more about human values. But if you have some ideas that you can share with us about how to determine our national interests, I will be very thankful to you.'"

Nixon, who felt a bit embarrassed, asked Simes's opinion about what he heard. Simes answered: "The Russian minister is a man who sympathizes with the United States, but I am not sure he understands the nature and interests of the power he represents, and at a certain point that may lead to mutual problems."

Nixon replied, "When I was Vice-President and then President, I wanted everybody to know I was a son of a bitch who would fight as hard as he could in the name of American interests. Kissinger was such a son of a bitch that I could learn from him. As for this man, he wants to show what a wonderful and pleasant man he is at a time when the Soviet Union has just fallen apart and when new Russia needs to be defended and strengthened."[2]

Naturally, not everyone in the Foreign Ministry, let alone other foreign policy institutions, was of the opinion that the world should be divided into the "civilized" and the "trash," and that the new Russia's most urgent goal should be to attain a strategic union with the "civilized"—our former adversaries in the Cold War—at any cost. At the same time, the implied format had Russia as the follower and the West as the leader. The danger of that approach was becoming increasingly evident because it matched the aspirations of many American politicians.

Those who favored rapprochement with the civilized West at any cost proceeded from the assumption that in the circumstances the only alternative was to slide toward confrontation. That was not so. When I took office at the Foreign Ministry I was confident that Russia could and should actively seek an equal partnership with everyone, look for and find areas of common interest, and work them with the others. And when interests don't coincide (and experience teaches they won't always), we should try to find solutions that will neither sacrifice Russia's vital national interests nor lead to confrontation. Clearly that is the dialectics of Russia's post–Cold War foreign policy. If areas of common interest are ignored, the result may at best be another Cold War. The alternative is partnership.

There were and still are those who think that today's Russia cannot even afford to carry on an active foreign policy. We should first, they say, concentrate on internal affairs, improve the economy, reform the military, and only then present ourselves in the international arena as a major player. I realized that this view could not withstand criticism, mainly because without an active foreign policy it would be difficult or impossible for Russia to carry out radical reforms domestically, preserve its territorial integrity and security, and become integrated with the world economy as a full and equal participant.

Three days after my appointment as foreign minister, on January 12, 1996, a press conference was held. The Foreign Ministry's press center, on Zubovskaya Square, was packed. Journalists' anxiety was stirred up by reactions in the United States and some other countries to my transfer to the Foreign Ministry. Comments kept coming in after the press conference. William Safire's column in the *New York Times* was typical. He said that my sudden appearance as Russian foreign minister sent "shivers" up the collective spine of the West. The choice of a "friendly snake" who had headed the espionage agency, he wrote, signaled the end of "Mr. Nice Guy in Russian diplomacy."[3]

But not everyone agreed. There were some positive comments as well, some in U.S. papers—the *Washington Post,* for one—and some in London papers. Our ambassador to Washington, my old friend Yuly Mikhailovich Vorontsov, wrote that he was sincerely happy about my appointment. We were both cadets at the Baku Naval School when we were fifteen- and sixteen-year-old boys. Later on, in the 1970s, we laughed at the tricks of fate—in the Naval School, headed by Rear Admiral Mikhail Vorontsov, his son Yuly was privileged to wear longer hair, while the rest of us were shaved clean. Today, in our more mature age, we've traded places—now it's our ambassador who has lost his hair. Incidentally, the senior Vorontsov was the naval attaché in Berlin who informed Stalin of the exact day when Hitler would invade the Soviet Union, but Stalin did not believe him.

In general I was happy about the article in *Obshaya Gazeta* by the former foreign minister A. A. Bessmertnykh, who said that my appointment was the best choice. But he ended the article with the following words: "Yevgeny Maksimovich can become a solid professional in diplomacy, if his political lot gives him enough time."

That allusion to the forthcoming presidential elections, half a year away, appeared in other publications as well. I am absolutely sincere when I say that the duration of my term in office as foreign minister was not uppermost in my thoughts. Throughout my life and in a wide variety of positions, some for years, others for months, I have never felt like a temporary replacement. When I was transferred to the Foreign Ministry, I was prepared to work hard.

From the very beginning I made my plans in close cooperation with my foreign colleagues. Perhaps my sociable disposition played a role there. I established frank relations with the foreign ministers of France—first Hervé de Charette and then Hubert Védrine—Germany's Klaus Kinkel, Italy's Lamberto Dini, Canada's Lloyd Axworthy, Sweden's Lena Elm-Vallen, Finland's Tarja Halonen, Switzerland's Flavio Cotti, Mexico's José Ángel Gurria, India's Inder Kumar Gujral, Japan's Ikeda Yukihiko, and others. With some of the ministers, such as those of Egypt and China, I had a long history of relations.

Upon examining the situation in the Foreign Ministry, I realized that the overwhelming majority of top executives, especially the deputy ministers, were excellent professionals who merited the high positions they occupied in the ministry's hierarchy. But some regrouping was needed. Igor Ivanov was appointed first deputy foreign minister. He performed ministerial duties while I was away from Moscow and in general worked in tandem with the minister. It was a good choice. When I was abroad I kept in close touch with him and was fully confident that he would perform his daily administrative duties with care and initiative. In view of the importance of the CIS, I appointed Boris Pastukhov as another first deputy. Pastukhov is a man with extensive experience and a strong sense of responsibility.

THE EXPANSION OF NATO: A HOT ISSUE

At the time of my transfer to the Smolenskaya Square office, our relations with NATO became one of the major foreign policy issues.

As far back as two years before my appointment to the Foreign Ministry, the Foreign Intelligence Service prepared a report on the expansion of NATO. Quite possibly some of the people who attended my press conference then were misled by my avoidance of answering the question whether Yeltsin had seen that report in advance. He did see it. Therefore the answer had to come from the president's press secretary, Vyacheslav Kostikov, who declared that Yeltsin shared the Intelligence Service's negative reaction to the expansion of NATO.

On one of my first days at Smolenskaya Square, my deputy Sergei Krylov told me that the Foreign Ministry's archives had records of conversations suggesting that the expansion of NATO was conceived not during the Cold War but after it was over. I asked him to give me those archive materials. They dated back to the time of German unification and the disintegration of the Warsaw Pact. The leaders of all the Western countries that belonged to NATO assured the Soviet leaders they did not intend to expand NATO. The reasons were obvious—to encourage Moscow to withdraw its troops from East Germany and to take the edge off the anticipated sharp reaction to the collapse of the Warsaw Pact.

Here are documented statements made by Western leaders in 1990 and 1991:

James Baker: "We believe that consultations and discussions within the framework of the 'two plus four' mechanism should guarantee that the unification of Germany will not lead to expansion of the NATO military organization to the east." (Record of a conversation between M. S. Gorbachev and Secretary of State J. Baker, February 9, 1990.)

Note that the secretary of state himself suggested that the nonexpansion of NATO could be legalized through the agreement on the unification of Germany. I well remember Gorbachev's words during a Politburo meeting in the spring of 1990. Gorbachev said we could try to tie our agreement to withdraw our troops from the DDR with the withdrawal of the unified Germany from NATO. It was clear from the very beginning that the West would not agree to this linkage. This was Gorbachev's bargaining position. In the end we finally received guarantees that no nuclear weapons would be deployed or foreign troops permanently stationed in the territory of the former DDR. These provisions became part of the Treaty on the Unification of Germany. But Baker meant something more than that; he was talking about a guarantee that NATO's military organization would not expand to the east!

Helmut Kohl: "We think that NATO should not expand the sphere of its operations. We must find a sensible solution. I appreciate the security interests of the Soviet Union and realize that you, Mr. General Secretary, and the Soviet leadership will have to clearly explain these events to the population of the USSR." (Record of a conversation between M. S. Gorbachev and Chancellor Helmut Kohl, February 10, 1990.)

According to a statement by the *British prime minister,* he "does not anticipate conditions under which the East European countries could join NATO at present or in the future." (Report of D. T. Yazov to M. S. Gorbachev on his conversation with Prime Minister John Major, March 6, 1991.)

Douglas Hurd: He confirmed that NATO had no plans for the countries of Eastern and Central Europe to join the North Atlantic Treaty Organization in any shape or form. (Information by the Minister of Foreign Affairs of the USSR A. A. Bessmertnykh on the results of a visit to the USSR of the foreign secretary of Great Britain, D. Hurd, March 26, 1991.)

François Mitterrand: "There is another consideration. Each of the states I mentioned [the former Warsaw Pact members] will strive to guarantee its security by concluding a separate treaty. With whom? Obviously with NATO. But this prospect will reinforce the feeling of isolation and even encirclement on the part of the Soviet Union. I am convinced this path is not the right one for Europe." (Record of a conversation between M. S. Gorbachev and President of France F. Mitterrand, May 6, 1991.)

It is a great shame that we failed to insist that these assurances by the Western leaders be legally formalized in a treaty. There is every reason to believe that move could have succeeded at that time.

What was it that caused the countries playing leading roles in NATO, especially the United States, to change their positions so radically? Why did they make a 180-degree turn from their previous assurances, seemingly supported by serious arguments against acceptance in NATO of the countries of the disintegrated Warsaw Pact? The answers are not simple.

Indeed, the leaders of the Central and East European countries declared their firm desire to join NATO. Indications are that a considerable part of their populations—indeed, the majority—supported that position. Public opinion polls and a referendum in Hungary confirm that impression. What was behind the desire to join NATO? Was it fear that the situation in Russia could pose a threat to their security? I don't think that was a major reason or even a valid one. Besides, many leaders of those countries stated emphatically that their choice was not motivated by fear of Russian aggression. Today, as a result of the democratic development of Russia and fundamental changes in the international arena, any talk about Russia as a potential military threat to Central and East European or any other countries seems like nonsense. That is true regardless of any actual, I repeat actual, combination of forces exercising power in Russia.

It is worth mentioning in this connection that during the most critical period of the socialist camp's disintegration, Moscow did not exert any pressure on its allies to remain in the Warsaw Pact. I took part in the Politburo meeting at which Gorbachev said that in a fit of hysteria Nicolae Ceausescu demanded that Soviet troops be sent to Romania. (The Warsaw Pact was still in existence.) But this was not 1968, when Soviet tanks invaded Prague; this was 1990. The matter did not go beyond informing the top Soviet leadership of Ceausescu's request. None of those present at the meeting even raised a question about a possible military invasion of Romania. In the present circumstances, the prospect seems totally unthinkable.

The Central and East European countries' desire to join NATO probably has a different explanation. They want to be identified as part of Europe, not of the East but of the West, and to join the European structures, mainly the European Union. There is reason to believe that joining NATO seemed to be the shortest and least burdensome way of entering the European structures.

We share the blame for that. After the Warsaw Pact and the Council of Mutual Economic Assistance were liquidated, we didn't pay enough attention to our former allies; we put our relations with them on the back burner. It was not willful neglect, it was simply that our attention was focused exclusively on our own problems. But the fact remains: by abolishing the CMEA, we threw the baby out with the bath water.

True, the council was imperfect in many respects and was criticized by its Eastern European members. Nevertheless, it maintained the long-established cooperation between Soviet and East European industries and provided stable markets for East European products. When all that ceased to exist, those countries found themselves in a vacuum.

It's not beyond the realm of possibility that some countries' interest in joining NATO was motivated by concern over pressure from Germany, which was flexing its muscles. That motivation does not seem to be realistic, however, especially in the context of the emerging European security system. The leaders of some Central European states wanted their countries to join NATO for their own political reasons and in an attempt to strengthen their regimes for years to come.

But no country would even think of joining NATO if it did not realize that its aspirations were in line with U.S. policy. NATO survived the Cold War, but was that enough to ensure the United States' continued presence in Europe in full force? It was not an idle question. The situation was changing rapidly. Europe was and is taking steps toward integration. The outline of one of the strongest centers of a multipolar world is beginning to take shape. In the North Atlantic Treaty Organization the European element was gaining prominence and historical perspective. It was that situation that must have made Washington think of strengthening its position in NATO and consequently in Europe. Expanding NATO by accepting new members that were subservient to the United States undoubtedly improved America's chances in Europe.

With the United States embarked on the expansion of NATO, our side was also required to take appropriate measures. Therefore a meeting between me and the secretary of state was imperative. I was ready to initiate such a meeting myself, but Secretary of State Warren Christopher made the first move. He called me from Jerusalem, where he was stopping during a Middle Eastern tour, and proposed that we meet in Geneva.

SLEEPING WITH A HEDGEHOG—IT'S NOT FOR US

I won't deny I was glad to get that call. But the choice of the meeting place was made too firmly. I checked and learned that Christopher had no other business planned in Geneva in the near future. I've never cared too much for protocol, but in this case I was a bit concerned. My staff added to my anxiety when they told me that the last time Christopher had met with a Russian foreign minister, he had also initiated the meeting, and it had taken place in Geneva.

The subsequent back-and-forth on the preparation and conduct of the talks persuaded me that my concern was not completely groundless. Perhaps the events I am about to tell about were not orchestrated by the secretary himself. Probably they were an exercise by his staff. But he had his own style, one that Madeleine Albright was to discard.

So I immediately confirmed my interest in discussing a number of bilateral and multilateral issues with the secretary of state and offered a choice of three countries—Belarus, Bulgaria, and Finland. At the same time I emphasized that our meeting did not cancel Christopher's scheduled official visit to Moscow. As I expected, the State Department chose Finland. The hospitable Finnish foreign minister, Taria Halonen, issued invitations without delay.

But the protocol duel—who needed it?—was not over yet. Washington suggested that the meeting should take place at the residence of the U.S. ambassador in Helsinki. We replied that the last meeting in Geneva took place on American territory, in the U.S. consulate, and now it was our turn.

Therefore, another choice—either the Russian ambassador's residence or the hotel on the outskirts of Helsinki where I intended to stay.

Several days of silence. Twenty-four hours before my scheduled arrival in Helsinki, on February 9, we received a message agreeing to meet in the hotel.

A couple of hours before the secretary was to appear at the Hotel Kalastajatorppa, which in Finnish means Fisherman's Shack, a State Department representative arrived. He gave me the following scenario: I meet Warren Christopher in front of the hotel. Dozens of American reporters who have accompanied the secretary, mostly TV crews, will already be there. I will be wearing a coat, as will Christopher. We will both enter the hotel. Our talks will take place during dinner in one of the hotel rooms.

Why should I be told to wear a coat? Was the American chief of protocol so concerned about my health? When the outside temperature is −12°C (10°F), most people do wear a coat. Once again my assistants helped me understand what was going on. Christopher always viewed an event as a performance. In any case, according to his advisers' scenario, in the images captured by the media when we met in front of the hotel it would not be clear who was the visitor and who the host. Unfortunately, much attention was paid to such details.

I met Christopher with a warm smile at the entrance to the hotel wearing a suit, as befits a proper host.

The face-to-face negotiations took place during dinner. Four people sat at the table, two on each side: the principals and their assistants, who took notes of the discussion. Christopher spoke English and I spoke Russian. The discussion was scheduled to last an hour and a half, but in fact it lasted over three hours.

The conversation began with the secretary's suggestion that we call each other by our first names. "Friends usually call me Chris," he said. Everything suggested Christopher wanted to establish normal relations and at the same time was trying to feel me out. These two different tasks determined the content of our conversation. I had the impression that he had decided not to bring up any hot issues this time. As for me, I was not going to refrain from direct questions about things that aroused our concern.

I listened very attentively as he told me how much snow there was in North Dakota, where he had been born; I learned that his wife was Finnish and that his ancestors came from Scandinavia, and that he was a naval officer during World War II, although he did not see action. Speaking about the war, Christopher pointed out that the United States and Russia had been and are the most powerful states.

Using these words as a springboard, I launched into concrete issues and suggested that we should agree on five points to govern the relations between these two great powers: first, regular consultations; second, exchange of information on matters of concern to the other side; third, no surprises; fourth, implementation of the agreements reached; fifth, finding solutions to issues in which our interests do not coincide. At the same time, I stressed that Russia must have advanced, developed, and diversified relations with the United States, but speaking frankly, I said, it looked as though the American side was not paying enough attention to maintaining the parity of the two members of this relationship.

"I think that's just not true," Christopher said. "Looking at Clinton and Yeltsin standing shoulder to shoulder at their press conference, nobody can say our president treats yours as anything but his equal."

I had to point out to Chris that any head of state who visits the United States stands next to the American president on the podium.

I went on to express our concerns about American policies in several areas. In this connection I remarked that the presidents of the two countries had agreed, after some difficulty, to differentiate between strategic and tactical anti-ballistic-missile systems. Otherwise it would be impossible to preserve the anti-ballistic-missile treaty of 1972, and therefore to continue the reduction of strategic weapons. However, the United States had made no move to pursue the negotiations, and the suggested agreement hung in the air.

Christopher interrupted me. "Let's instruct our deputies Georgy Mamedov and Lynn Davis to resolve this issue today."

"No," I replied, "this is a subject for negotiations, and not an easy one."

I mentioned Bosnia separately. I said much had been done at Dayton, and the State Department deserved credit for that. However, one of the important items of the agreement was still up in the air. We agreed that sanctions against Yugoslavia would be lifted thirty days after the Serbs withdraw their troops to their former positions. Forty days had now passed, but the sanctions were still in place. I warned that this was a matter of principle, and that it was very important to resolve this issue; otherwise we would have to lift the sanctions unilaterally.

Although at the beginning Christopher tried to approach the issue like a lawyer and to confuse the definition of the "zones of separation" in Bosnia and Herzegovina, I did realize that he took my words about the need to lift the sanctions against Belgrade seriously. He even noted that he wanted to strengthen cooperation with us not only in Bosnia and Herzegovina but also in the Middle East peace process, and that he was going to send his main negotiator, Dennis Ross, to Moscow for consultations. (Ross never came to Moscow.)

The future of NATO was one of the most important issues we discussed.

"You know that Russia isn't going to bang its fists on the table, as both you and we unfortunately did during the Cold War," I said. "But that doesn't make our serious concerns about the expansion of NATO any easier. We're told that NATO is not going to conduct any military operations against Russia. But you also know that Russian missiles are not targeted at the United States. But does that mean that Washington would be ready to support Russia if it increased its nuclear potential, even if it's not aimed at the United States? In any case, the very fact of NATO approaching Russia's borders creates an entirely new military and geopolitical situation that is extremely unfavorable to us."

In response Christopher cited a set of assurances and arguments that were already very well known to us, putting the main emphasis on the assumption that the expansion of NATO was not intended to create new division lines.

But he sounded tough now.

"Beginning in 1993, President Clinton clearly stated that NATO would expand," said the secretary. According to Christopher, NATO members proceeded from the facts that, first, Russia wanted the expansion to be gradual, and second, a way to incorporate Russia in NATO in some form should be found. That was how Washington interpreted the signals from Moscow. "If that has changed," Christopher said, "then you'll have to sleep with a hedgehog."

I don't know what he thought about my answer, but I replied that I prefer to go to bed with something other than hedgehogs.

My discussion with Christopher left no doubt that our opinion would be ignored during the expansion of NATO. It was not the process of expansion that would have to take Russia's position into account but Russia that would have to adapt to the process.

Strobe Talbott was the first to tell me there were no "different classes" for passengers in NATO, when he and the future U.S. ambassador to Russia

James F. Collins visited the Foreign Ministry in January 1996. Therefore, he said, no limiting regulations could be introduced for new members of the organization.

To Talbott's credit, he said nothing and just smiled when I replied, "Strobe, what are you talking about? If NATO is compared to an airplane, then it has passengers of different classes on board, and Americans are in the pilot's seat. Is that evidence of equality for everybody? As for the rights and responsibilities of NATO members, who allegedly are absolutely equal," I continued, "I'll give you the example of Norway, which has neither nuclear weapons nor foreign bases on its territory. It can be argued that that is a self-imposed limitation. But how about Germany, then? Under the German Unification Treaty, the United States, the USSR, England, and France agreed that no nuclear weapons or foreign troops could be deployed on Germany's eastern territories—the former DDR."

During my contacts with Western representatives such arguments remained unanswered. So what? We had to ask ourselves a sacramental question: What shall we do next?

Hypothetically we could consider three options.

1. To oppose the expansion of NATO and give up any relations with it. This option was a road to nowhere, or more precisely a road back to a gradual resumption of the Cold War.
2. To accept the expansion of NATO and make no attempt to influence it. We were pushed toward this option by NATO members, especially the United States, and by some Russian politicians. This option looked like unconditional surrender, with potentially grave consequences.
3. To maintain our opposition to the expansion of NATO and at the same time to conduct negotiations to minimize the consequences most threatening to our security and counter to our interests. In other words, to focus on influencing the expansion process.

We at the Foreign Ministry agreed to pursue the third option, considering it the optimal course in this situation.

Now about the possibility of Russia's joining NATO. Speculation on that subject was extensive in some Russian media.

It is obvious to me that no Western politician has seriously considered or is considering the possibility of accepting Russia as a member of NATO. As one of my Western European colleagues told me frankly, NATO's leadership proceeds from the assumption that Russia's membership would lead to the collapse of the alliance. NATO was established to ensure the collective security of its members from any threat in the European theater, and it is absolutely inappropriate to give Russia guarantees against any threat coming from Asia. If Russia were to join NATO, such guarantees would be necessary. In any case, does anyone want to think of this huge country of Russia shouldering its way through all the other European countries? And then what—would two centers form in NATO, the United States and Russia?

ON THE EVE OF NEGOTIATIONS

It appeared that after our first meeting with Christopher, our opponents launched a reconnaissance in force to determine how strongly Russia opposed the expansion of NATO. It became crystal-clear during Warren Christopher's official visit to Moscow on March 21–22, 1996. It was hardly a coincidence that almost on the eve of his visit to Moscow, the secretary of state made a "conceptual" statement in Prague, in which he emphasized that a real threat to the countries of Central and Eastern Europe existed; that U.S. leadership in Europe was a necessary condition for stability in that region; that Ukraine could become one of the second-stage candidates for NATO membership in the context of its integration with the European structures; and that no pauses in negotiations with NATO candidates were possible because it was a permanent process.

During my first discussion with Christopher I told him that Yeltsin's reaction to Christopher's speech in Prague had been very critical. I also referred to the president's tough discussion with Javier Solana, the secretary general of NATO, whom he received in the Kremlin a day before the secretary of state arrived, and said Solana's reaction to Christopher's Prague statement was probably the same. I added that the United States seemed to be gambling on Yeltsin's losing the election. If that was really the case, they were making a mistake.

Christopher, who admitted he knew from Solana that Russia was taking an extremely tough position, tried to vindicate himself by the usual devices, saying that in Prague he had also talked about the vital importance of establishing normal, forward-looking relations between Russia and NATO. He asked me to make appropriate preparations for his meeting with Yeltsin the next day. He appeared to be very nervous about that meeting.

Yeltsin must have decided that the signals given to NATO's secretary general and through me to the secretary of state were sufficient to remove any doubts regarding the "weakness" of our position. Yeltsin's discussion with Christopher was cordial. They touched upon the matters of bringing the nuclear security summit in Moscow to an appropriate level and transforming the Big Seven to the Big Eight in Lyon.

It is characteristic that when we and our advisers met with Christopher at the Foreign Ministry right after his Kremlin meeting, neither the secretary nor his colleagues said a word about NATO. We didn't bring the matter up either.

But things were different in Jakarta, where a regular meeting of the Association of Southeast Asian Nations (ASEAN) was held on July 23, 1996, and where I met the U.S. secretary of state once again. Christopher began the conversation by saying, "We don't discuss the issue of expanding NATO with third countries, nor do we talk about different classes of membership in NATO."

"You shouldn't present us with an ultimatum," I said. "If you tell us you don't wish to discuss this issue, we shall have to pay more attention to our own security—by revising some of the previously signed disarmament treaties, for instance."

"I haven't presented any ultimatum, I've simply clarified the situation," responded the secretary of state.

We were not overly hopeful about the situation. We realized that the United States in essence was coordinating all parallel contacts of Western countries with us, but at the same time all of them believed that the extreme position promoted by the secretary of state was perfect. Here are some examples of dialogues in which some changes in Western European ideas were gradually becoming evident.

During my first meeting with the British foreign secretary, Malcolm Rifkind, on February 27, 1996, in Strasbourg, I decided to warn him against two misconceptions regarding Russia's position, since they were then becoming widespread in the West. I said that there would be no change in our position in regard to the expansion of NATO after the presidential elections in Russia. "You're making another mistake if you believe that our position will change as a result of our cooperation with NATO in Bosnia. There should be no illusions about that, either."

Malcolm Rifkind, a brilliant lawyer, produced a host of arguments: expansion was in the very nature of NATO, candidates for membership don't even think about threatening anybody's security, and so on and so forth. But the main thing for me at that time was these words: "Of course, if nuclear weapons were deployed near Russia's borders, we would understand your anxiety."

On July 30, 1996, in Paris, where we met again, Rifkind said, "The dialogue between you and NATO has begun." The issue of the nonproliferation of nuclear weapons could be discussed in the 16 + 1 format. But the issues of broader relations between Russia and NATO should still be raised on a bilateral basis, and not only with the United States but also with Britain and France. The United States was certainly the most important partner, but it could not speak for all of NATO.

This conversation took place two months after our meeting with the NATO members' foreign ministers in the 16 + 1 format in Berlin. That was what Rifkind was referring to. In Berlin I also talked with the German foreign minister, Klaus Kinkel.

"What I am about to say I haven't coordinated with anyone," said Kinkel. "Why don't we think about forming a Russia-NATO Council, where Russia will have equal representation? It can become part of a proposal on signing a Russia-NATO charter."

That was another new and extremely important initiative.

But the most important one was Jacques Chirac's idea of a "chain" of actions; that is, reforming NATO, then holding negotiations between Russia and the reformed North Atlantic alliance to establish special relations between Russia and NATO, and only then to begin talks on the forms and content of NATO's expansion. During a meeting of the Big Eight in Lyon, Chirac stressed that Chancellor Helmut Kohl of Germany shared the chain idea.

I told Foreign Minister Hervé de Charette, whom I met separately in Lyon, that we were prepared to go along with that idea. Unfortunately, President Chirac's idea was subsequently eroded. Because as we saw it, its main feature was not only the three actions he outlined but also the order in which they were carried out.

SOLANA ONSTAGE, THE UNITED STATES BEHIND THE SCENES

At that juncture the Americans began to show their irritation over the fact that Russia was conducting many parallel talks. Judging by the reactions of my European colleagues, they were aware of that irritation. Perhaps that was where the American proposal to begin the negotiation process without delay and on the NATO track—that is, with Solana—originated.

We were preparing for those negotiations very seriously. Throughout the summer of 1996, working closely with representatives of the Ministry of Defense and the Foreign Intelligence Service, we prepared various optional positions and agreed on our negotiating tactics. However, we all agreed that the situation was not yet ripe for negotiations. We had more probing to do.

Extremely important meetings were to take place in New York, where I was to attend the U.N. General Assembly. I was informed that I would be received by President Bill Clinton. On September 20, on my way to New York, I stopped in Vienna and had a talk with Javier Solana.

Later I established good relations with Solana, but at that time everything suggested we were incompatible. When I asked concrete questions, Solana replied he could not speak for the sixteen NATO members without first consulting them. Yet he wanted me to give him specific answers to his questions. It was quite obvious he was trying to discover just how flexible our position was. I told him, "Please don't take it personally, but I feel as though we're both in a prison cell and one of us is a stool pigeon."

As he was aware of Russia's interest in Chirac's chain idea, Solana brought up the question of parallel negotiations. I tried to explain to him that we understood the transformation of NATO, the development of relations between Russia and NATO, and the expansion of the alliance not as three independent processes but as interdependent parts of one process. Then to illustrate his point Solana put three pens down on the table and said, "As a physicist I insist that these three parallel lines will meet somewhere in infinity." I answered that as I am not a physicist, I don't live in infinity. I live on the Earth, and I'd like these issues to meet in the course of a discussion on them. It was clear that at that time Solana had no mandate to conduct negotiations —an indication that the chosen strategy was to "hurry without haste."

My meeting with Christopher on September 23 in New York provided an additional indication. Once again he started talking with anguish (by then I realized it was his negotiating style). "Today we are having perhaps the most important conversation in the history of our relations," said the secretary of state. "Our time is limited. Many events will take place this fall, such as the summit in Lisbon,[4] and then in December the meeting of the leaders of the NATO countries. The schedule is tight, so we intend to help speed up the dialogue between NATO and Russia in order to widen the forms of our cooperation. It would be great if we could do it at the same time the new members are accepted."

Then Christopher asked point-blank whether we were going to continue the dialogue with France, England, and Germany. "It's important to agree," he said, "that the Russian-American channel is the principal one, but the Americans can and will inform their allies as well as Solana about the process."

I said calmly that Russia needed a detailed document that would clarify its relations with NATO, "not just declarations that we won't attack each other. As for informing other partners in the dialogue, we'll keep doing that, but the main thing is to rule out any distortions." I added, "The main thing for us is to prepare a document that will define a mutually acceptable development of our relations with NATO, will help to transform the alliance from an instrument of the Cold War to a new organization, and will also minimize the negative effect of a possible expansion for us. If we fail to produce such a document, we won't sign any other."

In response Christopher decided to give me a cold shower by confirming that he did not view the charter in question (he persisted in using that word) as a binding or even concrete and detailed document.

The next day I met with Klaus Kinkel. He asked about my impressions of the meeting with the Americans. I answered, "I get the feeling that we're moving backward." Having sensed my mood, Kinkel put his hand on my shoulder in a friendly gesture. "As German foreign minister," he said, "I reject any dictate with regard to Russia." Kinkel agreed that it was necessary to discuss with Russia the details and the terms of NATO's expansion, including, of course, the military infrastructure on the territory of new members.

I would not say that this rather obtuse tactic of applying pressure was approved by all the top American officials. In any case, my meeting with President Clinton on September 24 convinced me that it was not. We were informed that he delayed his departure after addressing the General Assembly in New York to talk with a few select representatives of other countries, including me.

The meeting took place in the building of the U.S. mission to the U.N. The president met us at the entrance of a specially prepared room. Then followed the alternating waves of photo and TV journalists customary on such occasions. Some of them called out questions over the security officers' shoulders. President Clinton answered patiently and with a smile. He could handle the press perfectly. Finally we left the floodlights behind. The meeting was scheduled to last twenty minutes, but we spoke for an hour. Warren Christopher; the president's national security adviser, Anthony Lake; Madeleine Albright, the U.S. representative to the U.N. at the time; and Strobe Talbott, deputy secretary of state, were present at the meeting. Our side was represented by the Russian ambassador to the United States, Yuly Vorontsov; Russia's representative to the U.N., Sergei Lavrov; my deputy, Georgy Mamedov; and the head of the Ministerial Secretariat, Robert Markaryan.

Clinton spoke warmly about Yeltsin, who at that time was preparing for heart surgery. Then, having said that the secretary of state had reported our conversation on NATO to him, the president must have decided to smooth over the impression that the conversation with Christopher might have left.

"From my first days in office," said Clinton, "I've adhered to the idea of creating a democratic Russia so it could become a reliable and strong partner of the United States in the twenty-first century. It's important for a number of reasons." Clinton singled out the special importance of our joint and co-ordinated action, something I admit I had not expected. "In the next twenty-five years," he said, "the conflict between India and Pakistan may threaten to develop into a nuclear attack. The same is true of the Middle East," he added. "Peaceful settlement there is impossible without the joint participation of Russia and the United States."

In less than two years after those words were spoken, India and Pakistan held their nuclear tests, and I recalled the words of the U.S. president again and again and quoted them to my colleagues. Indeed, the prospect of nuclear proliferation created an entirely new situation, one that I considered no less dangerous than the one we faced during the Cold War. And it was not limited to the India-Pakistan conflict. Other conflicts could go nuclear, including those in the Middle East. In all probability, Israel already possesses nuclear weapons, while the Arabs, at least some of the Arab countries, will strive to acquire them, especially in view of the development of the so-called first Islamic nuclear bomb. Hence the extreme importance of coordinating the efforts of the two most powerful nuclear states to prevent the development of a new deadly threat to humanity by using diplomacy; by applying export sanctions; by encouraging correct behavior, including assistance in the peaceful use of atomic energy; by promoting disarmament; and by democratizing international relations.

Clinton smoothly switched from the threats of the twenty-first century to current European affairs, and stressed his desire to help build a united Europe to replace separate states hostile to one another. Such a Europe is needed for peace and security beyond its borders. "This is achievable," the president continued, "if we manage to create special and clearly defined relations between Russia and NATO, to which I am personally strongly committed."

The meeting was obviously taking longer than scheduled. Christopher began looking pointedly at his watch. I decided to help my colleague out and asked the president whether, at the end of a conversation that had lasted longer than expected, which I had enjoyed very much, he would like to hear one of my favorite jokes.

"Certainly," said Clinton.

"A chicken was asked what the biggest achievement in her life was. 'I laid an egg that weighed five kilos,' she replied. 'And what is your greatest wish?' 'To lay a seven-kilo egg.'

"A rooster was asked the same questions. To the first he replied, 'My hen laid a five-kilo egg.' To the question about his greatest wish, the rooster answered, 'To beat the hell out of the ostrich!'"

I don't exactly remember why this joke came to my mind as an informal closing statement. Perhaps because the secretary of state was so obviously trying to end the conversation. Everybody laughed. The president smiled and turned to Albright: "Is that about me?"

True to his friendly nature, Clinton escorted us to the elevator and said good-bye warmly.

In my coded cable to Moscow about my conversation with Clinton I stressed there was every reason to believe that while the president was wholeheartedly in favor of expanding NATO, he did not share the views of those in the American establishment who wanted to isolate Russia and rule out any possibility of our influencing the terms of that expansion. The message said an important condition had been created for preparing a document that in the end we could approve.

The cable also proposed that Russia's foreign policy be more active on a broader scale, in an effort to create a new architecture of European security. Such a universal system could reduce the effect of the new division lines that threatened to appear in Europe as a result of NATO's expansion.

In recent years NATO had become cluttered with various new branches and connections. As a result of the Partnership for Peace program (PfP), various states that had absorbed its lessons were drawn to NATO, both those that did not plan to join it and those that sought admission.

The Council for Euro-Atlantic Cooperation was also formed. On the surface everything looked fine. NATO was creating a political forum where both members and nonmembers could jointly discuss issues important for their security and stability. But all those NATO-sponsored organizations were created at a time when both the Organization for Security and Cooperation in Europe (OSCE) and the Council of Europe were already in existence and operating quite successfully.

Russia has taken part in these NATO structures and will continue to do so in the hope that they will have a positive effect on the reorganization of NATO itself. But Russia's participation has nothing to do with agreement to a NATO-centered model of European security.

Taking all these ideas into consideration, I approached Yeltsin with a proposal for the Russian foreign minister to address the Permanent Council of the OSCE in Vienna. Such speeches were common practice, but no Russian or Soviet minister had ever addressed that forum before.

The huge hall, with a gigantic round table seating the delegates of fifty-four countries, was very impressive. There were many familiar faces among those present, including representatives of the CIS countries, who became members of this unique organization whether they belonged to Europe or Asia. I won't deny that warm greetings across the table gave way to a certain coolness as soon as the speeches began. It was not even what the CIS representatives said in their speeches, but the fact that some of them chose to speak in broken English or French into the microphones standing before the delegations, though they knew Russian perfectly well, having worked at the Soviet Foreign Ministry for several years. And simultaneous translators worked in all six official OSCE languages, including Russian.

In my statement I said that the events taking place in Europe in the post-confrontation period proved the necessity of a new mechanism to guarantee its security. The epicenter of threats had shifted from the global to the regional level. Then I dwelt upon some features inherent in the model of European security and stressed that all the international organizations working in this sphere, such as the U.N., the OSCE, the Council of Europe, NATO, the E.C., and the CIS, should get involved in it. For that purpose it was necessary to discuss questions of concrete cooperation among them.

At the same time, we supported the idea that the OSCE should play the central role in the new model of European security. It was the only truly universal organization of European states, and it also served the function of providing a means for solid cooperation between the countries of Europe and North America. Of equal importance was the fact that the OSCE was an organization based on the principle of consensus, which guaranteed the rights of all its member states, both large and small. Contrary to the superficial assertions by some politicians and journalists, I did not offer to create a hierarchical system of security headed by the OSCE, which was to issue orders to other organizations, including NATO. Yes to the OSCE's system-forming and coordinating functions but no to its assuming command.

I delivered that speech at a time when preparations for the OSCE summit in Lisbon were well under way.

The OSCE Lisbon summit allowed us to begin working on the Charter of European Security, whose importance can be compared with that of the final Helsinki Accords. At the same time, it became clear in Lisbon that the path to creating an architecture of European security was thorny and the adoption of the charter was by no means an easy matter. All those standing behind the idea of expanding NATO were well aware that the fewer the supporters of the European Security Charter, the closer they would be to achieving their goal.

But other sentiments were abroad, and still are. Much later, on July 26, 1998, at the time of the E.U.-Russia meeting in the troika + 1 format[5] in London, I made a speech at Chatham House (the Royal Institute of International Relations). It was not my first speech at this world-renowned research center. I had established and maintained close relations with the institute and its director, Admiral James Eberle, since my days as head of IMEMO. We remained close friends after his retirement.

I was very happy to meet him once again, especially because the new director of Chatham House met Sir James's request—he chaired the meeting during my speech. In his concluding remarks he said, "Why don't we focus on the idea of future integration of NATO and OSCE, especially because the latter is doing so much in preventive diplomacy, human rights protection, and conflict resolution."

Perhaps that is indeed an idea for the future.

MAGICAL MESHCHERINO, AND SO ON

An official offer to conduct negotiations on a document that would define our relations with NATO was presented by its members on December 11 at a meeting of foreign ministers under the formula of 16 + 1. We invited the

NATO delegation, headed by Solana, to Moscow. I don't remember whose idea it was to hold the meeting at Meshcherino, the Foreign Ministry's country residence, but that proved to be the right move. Negotiations were conducted away from the journalists, so nobody played to the public. But the reporters did not appreciate that, and some of them criticized us for "hiding from the mass media" (I have to say that they often confused the need for privacy in confidential talks with lack of the long-awaited glasnost).

Meshcherino is a magical place. The mansion where our meeting took place is a magnificent old country estate built by Count Meshchersky in 1830. It is surrounded by an enormous forest on the bank of the Pakhra River. In January the river is covered with ice. Everything around was under sparkling white snow. In their thickness stood conifers, proudly upright both winter and summer, and wistful larches with their naked branches. Everything was wrapped in ringing silence. In the house firewood was softly crackling in the fireplace. The talks opened in the living room and continued during the Russian dinner with pickles, mushrooms, meat pies, salads, herring, boiled potatoes, soup served in clay pots, and countless other dishes, and of course cold vodka in misted bottles.

The dialogue that began at the work desk went on during the meal and then outside for almost two hours when Solana and I took a long walk in the chilly air along forest paths cleared of snow.

Before our talks began I was thinking about how tricky life could be. From 1924 to 1946 this building where we had worked and had dinner had been the home of the so-called All-Union Elder, Mikhail Kalinin, successively chairman of the Soviet Executive Committee and chairman of the Presidium of the Supreme Soviet of the USSR. His neighbor was the general secretary of the Comintern, Georgy Dimitrov. Mao Zedong and Kim Il Sung visited here. And now we are hosting here a delegation of the North Atlantic Treaty Organization, formed originally to fight communism and socialism.

From the very beginning both sides demonstrated their desire to make the meeting as businesslike as possible. Solana started out by saying, for the first time, that he had a mandate to conduct negotiations on behalf of sixteen members of NATO.

I had a feeling that the fireplace and even the chilly winter forest had thawed Solana a bit. And yet he remained rather tense, probably because he felt that he could not be flexible enough, dependent as he was on the opinion of the NATO leaders and the instructions he had received. But still, during our two-hour walk I felt for the first time that Solana wanted our negotiations to move forward.

Solana expressed many ideas that could be of interest to us. However, the NATO secretary general persistently avoided any substantive discussion of military issues. Apparently that was not sanctioned by the alliance at that time. Solana must have appreciated our state of mind and uttered a key phrase that explained the limits of his authority: "You'll meet with American representatives. Make sure you clarify their position on that score."

Solana left Meshcherino bearing our main message, that an agreement on military issues must be an inseparable part of the general document. Obviously, he came to yet another conclusion after our talks, including the one during our stroll in the woods: no matter how eager Russia was to turn the Big Seven into the Big Eight and to join the World Trade Organization (WTO) and the Paris and London clubs (Solana spoke with passion about how much closer this prospect would be if we signed the charter), we would not accept any payment for the softening of our position toward NATO, and these questions should in no way be connected with the document that we were preparing or be any part of it.

The second round of negotiations with the NATO delegation took place in Brussels, where we gave NATO our drafts of all sections of the document. We included all NATO suggestions that we found acceptable. We were confident we could begin working on the texts at the next stage of negotiations.

The third meeting of the Russian and NATO delegations was scheduled for March 9 in Moscow. Just before the meeting we were visited by Gebhardt von Moltke, assistant secretary general for political affairs. His conversations with Nikolai Afanasievsky indicated that the pendulum was swinging back. Moltke adamantly refused to discuss our proposals on military issues.

In the meantime, my meeting with President Clinton and Secretary of State Madeleine Albright in Washington was already scheduled. But the NATO members were probably waiting for the outcome of the Russian-American summit in Helsinki, which was scheduled for March 21–22, 1997.

Yeltsin and Clinton discussed my trip to Washington over the phone. It was decided that before the Helsinki summit Ms. Albright and I had to make progress in preparing the summit documents, including joint statements by the presidents on issues of European security; on further reduction of nuclear arsenals; on strengthening the ABM treaty; on Russian-American economic initiatives. Each of those documents was of utmost importance.

As for the first document, on European security issues, we were to find framework approaches to those problems of Russia-NATO relations that could not be put on paper.

In essence, all these documents were interconnected. An agreement on serious progress in weapons reduction would undoubtedly lead to resolution of a multitude of issues involved in NATO-Russian relations. As a matter of fact, Ms. Albright openly said as much a bit later. Thus disarmament issues that were undoubtedly very important by themselves acquired new meaning in the context of the preparation of the joint Russia-NATO document.

The schedule in Washington was extremely tight. I met with Albright and Talbott, then Talbott invited me, Ambassador Vorontsov, my deputy Georgy Mamedov, and Albright to his home, where we talked business all evening. The charming Mrs. Talbott deliberately stayed out of the conversation when she appeared in the living room bearing extremely hot Mexican dishes. But it turned out that she was not at all indifferent to the subject under discussion. The next day Talbott said that his wife listened with great interest to "history in the making."

Despite the fact that Clinton had had surgery on his leg the day before and was limited in his movement, he invited me to a meeting that lasted over an hour. The very fact that I was invited to the living quarters of the White House by a president who had to keep taking painkillers, as well as the nature of the conversation, proved that Clinton was genuinely interested in the success of the forthcoming talks with Yeltsin.

Our visit to the Pentagon's situational room was an extraordinary event. The Russian foreign minister was allowed to enter this holy of holies of the U.S. military establishment to meet with the secretary of defense and the chiefs of staff of all branches of the military. The chiefs of staff made their reports, illustrating various points with diagrams that were projected on a wide screen.

The military are always more straightforward than the politicians, a proposition supported by the reports. I came to two conclusions. The Pentagon was interested in making progress in nuclear arms reduction; in other words, in preparing for the future SALT III. But the defense effort was directed at creating an antiballistic-missile (ABM) defense system capable, as one of the speakers put it, of providing reliable protection to American soldiers in case of a regional military action, such as Desert Storm.

On the first question our interests obviously coincided, although the problem of balancing the reductions in the context of the national security of both sides and global stability still remained. As for the ABM, our challenge was to find a solution that, while allowing for the creation of a nonstrategic ABM system, would not at the same time lead to the development of Star Wars weaponry.

The Americans, especially at the early stages of negotiations in Washington, resorted to pressure tactics. Attempts were made to remove from the draft of the joint statement on European security provisions prohibiting the deployment of conventional weapons close to Russian territory and replace them with a NATO statement that was so vague that it was unacceptable to us. (This statement was made in Brussels on the eve of our negotiations in Washington.)

After arduous discussions, we finally agreed on the following points:

- The document on NATO-Russian relations, to be signed by the top leadership of Russia and all the NATO member countries, was binding.
- The joint statement would include the U.S. president's assurance that there would be no increase in the number of NATO troops permanently deployed near Russia's borders.
- The Statement on European Security would provide for nonproliferation of nuclear weapons and acknowledge the need for inclusion of these assurances in the Russia-NATO document.
- The joint statement would describe the OSCE as a universal organization that could play a special role in the system of European security and state the need to develop a charter of European security based on the decisions of the OSCE Lisbon summit.
- The joint statement on strategic nuclear weapons would include an extension of the terms of arms reduction reached in SALT II (the Americans offered 2006 as the date and we offered 2008; we agreed to leave it for the presidents to decide). At our insistence the extension of the deadline was not linked mechanically to the signing of SALT III. A ceiling of 2,000–2,500 warheads was set for SALT III.

A document on ABM systems was the only one we failed to produce, although our discussions in Washington mapped out an area of agreement, which at least the presidents could mention at a press conference in Helsinki. Both parties agreed to adhere to the ABM treaty at present and in the future.

We felt that the Americans attached special significance to the preparation of the ABM document, which of course we also needed.

Economic issues were touched upon for the most part during our discussion with the U.S. president. Clinton confirmed his intention to support Russia's plans to join the WTO and the Paris Club and to give more prominence to the Big Eight. But he just outlined those items; he must have intended to elaborate on these issues during his meeting with Yeltsin in Helsinki.

All things considered, one could say the doors to Helsinki were practically open.

THE TWO POST-OP PRESIDENTS MEET IN HELSINKI

"Boris, have mercy on the cripple." That was President Clinton's response to Yeltsin's complaints about the United States' persistence in supporting the expansion of NATO.

Clinton had to make an enormous effort to fly across the ocean for the summit in Helsinki. With the aid of crutches Clinton walked to a special wheelchair, extended his leg, and . . . smiled, even though it was perfectly obvious that he was in great pain, despite the painkillers he took regularly.

Not long before the meeting Yeltsin had had heart surgery, but he looked great. It was his first trip abroad after surgery, too.

And anything could happen. I recall Yeltsin's election campaign. I was among those who met the president at Vnukovo II airport after his trip across the country before the first round of voting. That day he made a blitz tour of several cities, and upon his return to Moscow he decided on a frank exchange of opinions right there at the airport. Both those who accompanied him and those who were meeting him were invited to a dinner table prepared in a closed area. The mood at the table was elated, to say the least. Indeed, such presidential trips were productive. As a result, public opinion polls throughout the country showed Yeltsin's rating rising day after day. I don't know what made me cut into the conversation and put a fly in the ointment. Perhaps it was a vivid picture of carelessness resulting from unreasonable enthusiasm.

"Boris Nikolaevich," I said, "I don't think you'll win in the first round. But you may carry the runoff election."

"I'm not quite physically fit enough to keep up this work load till a runoff election," the president replied. "And I'm not ready psychologically, either."

As we were leaving the airport, where we spent little time, Yeltsin's wife, Naina Iosifovna, who had been silent at the table, thanked me for my remark. It was clear that the people closest to Boris Nikolaevich were worried about his health, and they had reason to worry.

Word spread later that in the middle of March Yeltsin was going to issue a decree dissolving the Duma, banning the Communist Party, and postponing the presidential elections, but then he gave up that idea. Anatoly Kulikov, former minister of internal affairs, has given a detailed account and named everyone who was invited to Yeltsin's office in connection with the affair. The minister of foreign affairs was not among them, and I was not involved in the intricate designs of the presidential elections, although I suspected that something was afoot.

Yeltsin became ill between the first and second rounds. Nevertheless, he won the elections, but surgery was becoming inevitable. The heart surgery was performed by a team of Russian doctors headed by Sergei R. Akchurin.

So now the two post-op presidents were meeting in Helsinki. The exchange of greetings was traditionally friendly, although Yeltsin began by stating that the results of the meeting would determine whether we would begin slipping back toward the Cold War. Clinton's opening remarks also suggested that he considered this meeting with the Russian president to be of exceptional importance, since it could contribute substantially to the resolution of a multitude of issues, both bilateral and global.

The highest point of the talks was the discussion of the document on the differentiation of strategic and tactical ABM systems. In fact, by adopting the joint statement on this complicated issue Clinton ensured progress in other important disarmament directions and the success of the Helsinki meeting in general.

By the time of the Helsinki meeting, negotiations on antimissile defense had been going on for four years. Their goal was to preserve the ABM treaty signed in 1972, which for objective reasons was circumvented when the proliferation of missiles and missile technologies, particularly in unstable regions, called forth preparation of a nonstrategic ABM system. In the process some elements are bound to appear that can be used for a strategic ABM system. If so, that development not only implies evasion of the ABM treaty but eliminates the very possibility of a substantial and consistent reduction of strategic nuclear weapons. It is quite obvious that if one side is strengthening its defense against strategic missiles, the other side will strive to possess missiles of sufficient quantity and quality to enable it to reach the target despite a modernized ABM system.

In Geneva, American and Russian experts resolved the issue of the differentiation of strategic and nonstrategic low-velocity ABM systems. Differentiation of high-velocity systems, however, came to a standstill. It turned out that the two remaining problems could be resolved only at the summit. First, the Americans proposed to soften the requirement of some limitations of nonstrategic ABMs. As a result, a number of important restrictive parameters would fall into the category of merely desirable "trust-building measures." Second, our partners wanted this "restrictive agreement" to be the last one. But with the inevitable development of new technologies in the future, the creation of a strategic ABM system would no longer be restricted and the ABM treaty would not be protected.

After strenuous discussions, the presidents took a brief break and instructed Ms. Albright and me to find a way out of the impasse. As he left the room, Yeltsin turned to me and said, "Find a solution."

It was quite obvious the American side needed fresh troops, because the regular negotiators had exhausted all their potential for flexibility and assumed that since the president had given us a direct order, we should finally slip away. Madeleine Albright helped recruit John Shalikashvili, chairman of the Joint Chiefs of Staff, who usually kept a low profile and was highly respected by the American military. With an effort we finally found formulas that covered both U.S. concerns and our own.

Criteria were determined that would block the development of a strategic ABM system—restrictions on the targets used during tests, on the speed of the interception missiles, on the use of space-based interception missiles. At the same time we reached agreement on a mechanism for determining the compliance of any newly created system with the ABM treaty, with future technological developments taken into account. We also agreed to exchange information on tests of the ABM systems and to invite observers to witness them.

Negotiations were not at all smooth. We appeared to have reached an agreement, approved by both the secretary of state and the chairman of the Joint Chiefs of Staff. As they say, we shook hands on it. Then one of the American negotiators returns and demands that another amendment be added. We don't agree. There comes a dramatic moment when everything hangs by a thread. Albright declares that if we don't accept the American wording, with which we disagree, there will be no Helsinki documents at all, no Joint Statement on European Security. I answer, "Don't drive us into a corner."

Finally passions cooled down and we managed to find wording that, although not entirely satisfactory to the Americans (as they told us), they could still accept.

After a break, President Clinton was the first to appear, rolling into the room in his wheelchair. He was sincerely happy that a solution had been found and that the summit would be successful in all respects. Yeltsin, in turn, thanked all the participants in these talks, which were "so tough at the finish," for all the work they had done.[6]

So all the drafts that were prepared for the Helsinki summit turned into documents. All the white spots were painted over. The joint statement on the parameters of the future reductions in nuclear weapons established the following timetable: deactivation of strategic carriers of nuclear warheads by detachment of the warheads or by other mutually agreed-upon measures before December 31, 2003, and their liquidation, in accordance with START II, before December 31, 2007. The presidents agreed that after START II came into effect, Russia and the United States would immediately begin negotiating on START III, which would provide for bringing down the aggregate levels of strategic nuclear warheads on each side to 2,000–2,500 before December 31, 2007.

That September, in New York, Ms. Albright and I signed legal agreements on strategic nuclear weapons and ABMs based on the Helsinki documents. They opened the way for ratification of START II and for the beginning of negotiations on even deeper cuts in Russian and U.S. strategic offensive weapons within the framework of START III.

Javier Solana had called me on March 26. He certainly had heard about the outcome of the Helsinki summit from the Americans, but he must have wanted to hear it from me as well, probably in order to compare our impressions.

I said we took a positive view of the agreements reached in Helsinki. I also thought it necessary to tell Solana we were still waiting for comments on our written proposals regarding the transformation of NATO, the mechanism for Russia-NATO consultations and decision making, and the spheres of cooperation between us. As the positions of the two sides on these issues were fairly close, it would be good if we could proceed to draft the texts of appropriate sections of a Russia-NATO document. But it was most important that we concentrate on its military and political section, which we practically had not even addressed.

Solana agreed with this approach in general.

A few days before this telephone conversation with the secretary general, the first contact between our and NATO's military took place. The deputy chief of NATO's Military Committee, Klaus Naumann, visited Moscow and made a good impression by his rationality and openness. Some of his ideas were close to ours. That was reassuring , but in the absence of written offers from Solana on military matters, it was still too early to talk about progress in negotiations in the military sphere. After we and the Americans agreed in Helsinki that nuclear weapons would stay within the borders of the sixteen NATO member states and that no threatening number of NATO troops would be stationed close to our borders on a permanent basis, definitive statements of these provisions and an agreement on the terms of their implementation were needed.

Yeltsin discussed this issue with a number of European leaders by phone. I received invitations to visit Germany and France. Those visits might be especially helpful if Kinkel and Charette could talk to Solana before he came to Moscow. Indeed, both of them expressed their willingness to help advance the negotiations. They thought the secretary general would not come to Moscow empty-handed.

On April 9 I was received by the president of France, Jacques Chirac. He seemed to want to do his best to remove obstacles to the signing of the document in Paris, nowhere else, and precisely on May 27; that was a couple of weeks before the NATO session in Madrid, where the forthcoming expansion of the alliance would be announced. We were also interested in signing the document laying down certain conditions for the expansion of the alliance and neutralizing its most unfavorable consequences for us without waiting for an announcement of NATO's new members. However, I told President Chirac that the date of the signing was of no particular significance to us.

Of special importance was the bilateral Russian-American meeting set for May 1–2.

We received the American delegation at the Foreign Ministry building on Spiridonovka Street. The delegation included Secretary of State Albright, Deputy Secretary of State Talbott, Under Secretary of State Lynn E. Davis, and Assistant Secretary John Kornblum; the president's special adviser on the CIS, James Collins; the president's special adviser and director of the European Department of the National Security Council, Alexander Vershbow; the head of the Military and Political Section of the State Department, Craig Gordon Dunkerly; the State Department press secretary, Nicholas Burns; two deputy assistant secretaries of defense, Jan Lodal and Frank Cook; and the assistant to the chairman of the Joint Chiefs of Staff, Richard Meyers, among others.

Our side was represented by the minister of foreign affairs and Deputy Ministers Nikolai Afanasievsky and Georgy Mamedov; our ambassador to the United States, Yuly Vorontsov, who was summoned to Moscow for the meeting; the directors of the five Foreign Ministry departments, Sergei Kislyak, Robert Markaryan, Nikolai Spassky, Oleg Belous, and Gennady Tarasov; and the head of the Department of International Military Cooperation of the Ministry of Defense, Leonid Ivashov, among others.

I have listed the visiting American delegation and our participants in order to demonstrate that both sides believed this meeting to be of vital importance.

The importance of this meeting was enhanced by President Yeltsin's telephone call to us. His conversation with Albright and then with me encouraged us to achieve an agreement.

MADELEINE ALBRIGHT, ANOTHER IRON LADY

By the time of the meeting, very cordial relations—unlike those with Christopher—had begun to form with the clever and charming Madeleine Albright.

Many people believe that Albright's views were shaped by Zbigniew Brzezinski, who not only was her professor at Columbia University but also invited her to work at the National Security Council when he was President Jimmy Carter's national security adviser.

In my opinion, it would be superficial to think that Albright was a devoted follower of Brzezinski's views and ideas. What relates her to Brzezinski is the idea of promoting active American leadership in international affairs and her sharp criticism of isolationist attitudes. At the same time she attaches great importance to taking advantage of the United States' "special status" in international organizations, of its dominance in relations with its allies, and of the unwillingness of many countries to oppose the powerful United States. I think Albright believes that such an arsenal is quite enough to enable the United States to take a firm stance in the international arena. In any event, for all her toughness in defending America's interests (as she perceives them, of course), Albright is not one to begin rattling her sword without good reason or to be reluctant to sheathe it.

Quite by chance I learned that Seweryn Bialer had supervised Ms. Albright's dissertation. I mentioned that when I sat next to Madeleine at the farewell dinner after the ASEAN forum on security in Manila in July 1998. "I consider myself to be Bialer's student to a certain extent," said Albright. At that moment she did not know how well I had known this exceptionally interesting man in the 1970s, when I worked as Academician Inozemtsev's deputy at IMEMO.

Bialer had been awarded a Soviet military medal for his work with the Polish resistance in World War II. He was not only a member of the Polish United Workers' Party but served as a technical secretary of its Politburo. When the Berlin Wall went up, he escaped to the West. In the United States he became one of the most preeminent Sovietologists. He headed Columbia University's Institute of International Affairs, where he was considered a counterbalance to Brzezinski, who also worked there. I appreciated the nature of this man during our numerous meetings in Moscow, Suzdal, New York, Washington, and other Soviet and American cities where symposiums were held. Between discussions we had ample free time to exchange views on a wide range of issues. I can only add that he knew the lyrics of all the Soviet songs about the Red Army better than we did, and like us, he had no doubt at all that the Red Army's contribution was decisive in liberating the world from the "brown plague."

Albright, both as permanent U.S. representative at the U.N. and as secretary of state, was tough and forceful in conducting U.S. foreign policy. Sometimes her emotions and biases affected her attitude toward international events. She acknowledged that one of her goals was to make the countries of Central and Eastern Europe part of the Euro-Atlantic structures as soon as possible. Could her motivations have been colored by her sentiments as an immigrant from Prague? But at the same time, I am absolutely confident that Albright is by no means anti-Russian.

I saw Ms. Albright on many occasions and exchanged many phone calls with her during her tenure as secretary of state. My numerous conversations with her allowed me to learn a lot about her. I felt immediately that one should speak frankly to her, without double talk, marking time, or trying to avoid sharp corners. We maintained this style in our business relationship. I am confident that Madeleine Albright realized, as I did, that if one of us said yes, we were not merely voicing an opinion, either personal or theoretical, but intended to act to implement the agreement reached. At the same time we both understood that a definite no meant that the negotiating partner was honestly drawing a line he or she would not cross without some movement by the other side.

That became clear during our very first face-to-face conversation, in Moscow on February 20, 1998. After stating firmly that NATO's timetable for permanent expansion would be observed, she said that in preparing the Russia-NATO document we would have to take several steps toward each other. She summarized my observations in four distinct groups: nonexpansion of the military presence, consultations and their mechanism, nonproliferation of nuclear weapons, and the transformation of NATO. "That can provide the basis for our future work. We have ideas in each of the four directions," she said.

She seemed to attach special meaning to what she said next: "As we all know, in the past there were opportunities to improve our relations with Russia, but they were wasted. Let's not waste them now."

Ms. Albright touched upon this subject when she met with Yeltsin on February 21. "When I worked at the university," said Albright, "I lectured on the lost opportunities in Soviet-American relations and explained how their worsening could be avoided. I assume we agree there is every opportunity not to repeat the mistakes of the past and to build a relation of partnership between our countries."

And another detail: On the eve of Albright's arrival in Moscow my granddaughter was born. When Madeleine learned about that, she gave me a photograph of her and President Clinton with a note: "Mashenka, when you were born your grandfather and we were trying to do something to make the world a better place for you to live in."

Among Madeleine Albright's other characteristics are lack of pomp and a pleasing ingenuousness. How different she is from her predecessor! On the closing night of the ASEAN forum on security in Jakarta in 1996, all the delegations put on skits (this is an annual tradition). Christopher burst onto the stage in an athletic outfit, waving an American flag, as a demonstration of American victory in the Olympic Games, which were in progress at the time. The next year in Kuala Lumpur, Madeleine, accompanied by the rest of her delegation, sang a funny song about U.S. foreign policy to the tune of "Don't Cry for Me, Argentina," from the play and film *Evita*. The audience burst into applause.

But that was later. Now on May 1, our meeting with Ms. Albright was to resolve the questions remaining from the negotiating marathon aimed at reducing the negative consequences of NATO expansion for us.

The stumbling block was the problem of the Conventional Forces in Europe Treaty, signed in 1990. We agreed with the need to bring that treaty up to date but not to cancel it. The Conventional Forces in Europe Treaty set limits for NATO and the Warsaw Pact. We feared that a switch from group to national limits would enable the expanding NATO to increase the number of conventional weapons above the ceiling set by the treaty.

The Americans proposed that their "basis for discussions" by experts serve as the "basis for negotiations." They certainly had a positive element —they lowered national ceilings considerably in comparison with the current levels. But again there were no provisions for group limits. There were territorial limitations, but only "flank limitations." When it was to their advantage, our partners wanted to hold onto the bloc psychology that otherwise they deplored. They rebuffed all our arguments that a departure from bloc estimates presumes the elimination of flank limitations.

Despite these difficulties, we decided to follow the text of the American proposals. But soon it became clear that any concrete comments on the wording would be rejected. Ms. Davis was especially tough in this regard.

On the evening of May 1, I invited the Russian and American negotiators to dinner at my home. My colleagues suggested that we dine either at our headquarters building or at a restaurant, but I wanted to socialize with our American partners in an informal atmosphere, especially since Ms. Albright and her deputies would be leaving early the next morning. My wife and a friend prepared everything with the help of some cooks and joined the waiters in serving the food.

Before the guests arrived, our street was cleared of parked vehicles for security purposes. The elevator was checked and quickly fixed. (A few days later our building's superintendent asked my wife whether the elevator could be replaced at the city's expense, as part of the bill for the reception of such distinguished guests. We had to disappoint him.) Albright and the others came in with numerous bodyguards. I asked Colonel Gennady Khabarov, who served as my head of security for twelve years, to take care of his colleagues, and they seemed to have a good time in my study.

The dinner was a smashing success. Strobe Talbott admired the *pelmeni* (Siberian meat dumplings), which go so well with vodka. We joked a lot.

Madeleine Albright understands Russian, and she was trying to catch the words of a TV newscast. It was discussing the Russian-American talks. The reporter stood at the gate of the Foreign Ministry building on Spiridonovka and berated the ministry for not letting him in during our talks. "So much for your glasnost!" he said. But still he had learned what was going on from "reliable sources." The Iron Lady has come and imposed her conditions on the Russian side, saying there was "no more room for concessions." So what could the Russian foreign minister do? He could not resist the tough and forceful Madeleine Albright, who not only knows her position well but is also very good at defending it.

I asked Madeleine, "Tell me the truth. Do they sing your praises so much in the United States?"

"Never," she replied, smiling.

We took a little break between courses. Albright, Talbott, Vorontsov, and I stepped to the side. We had a completely frank conversation.

I said, "You see, I can't simply go to the Duma—and we'll have to do that—and tell them we accepted a proposal that calls for us to ignore the Conventional Forces in Europe Treaty and agree that NATO's arms level can rise as the alliance expands. That's what will happen when you undermine every chance for cooperation and generally normal relations between Russia and NATO. That's what will happen when a new division line inevitably runs across Europe, and not only Europe."

"What needs to be done to avoid this?" asked the secretary of state.

"We need a formula that will limit the growth of NATO's military potential after the inevitable switch to national ceilings. I can't think of anything else."

Albright asked Davis to join us. "Let's think again about such a formula." And then, addressing Vorontsov and me, she said, "I'm going to delay my departure from Moscow. Could we meet again tomorrow morning?"

On May 2 the talks were held at the Foreign Ministry building on Smolenskaya Square. The secretary of state agreed to include in the document a statement about the need to consider "all levels" set by the original Conventional Forces in Europe Treaty. Combined with the principle of consensus for the setting of new national levels, it allowed for setting a limit on all NATO conventional forces in the event of its expansion.

We also reached a compromise on the important issue of limiting the future military infrastructure in Central and Eastern Europe. In the end, the

Basic Principles included a provision stating that this infrastructure must be "adequate" to the commitment made by Bill Clinton back in Helsinki not to station "considerable" additional military forces on the territory of the new members on a permanent basis.

FINDING A WAY OUT OF THE LABYRINTH

On the whole, the May stage of negotiations with the secretary of state laid the foundation for the subsequent agreement on the key number of articles on arms reduction in the Russia-NATO document.

Time was growing short before the document was to be signed in Paris. We also felt the pressure of time during our next meeting with Solana in Luxembourg on May 6, but for an entirely different reason. As it turned out, the Luxembourg airport closed at midnight and the secretary general had at all costs to get to his plane and take off before then.

The talks in Luxembourg left me with a vaguely disconcerting impression. On the one hand, we seemed to have made some progress, because we included in the text some important elements of the agreements reached with the Americans. On the other hand, there were still quite a few points on which we could not reach an understanding. Solana was obviously nervous and constantly whispered into the ear of his deputy, Gebhardt von Moltke. During one of those protracted whispering consultations I had to say, "Friends, have we come to Luxembourg to sit around or to conduct negotiations?"

We arranged to resume negotiations in Moscow.

As soon as I met with Solana on May 13, I realized that NATO had made a political decision to arrive in Paris with a complete document. This was evident in both Solana's mood and his first words: that he had come to Moscow not just to search for an appropriate solution but to find one. However, many problems needed to be cleared up.

We worked till late at night. The military on both sides also worked hard on the wording. The wording was simultaneously passed on to Brussels for approval by the North Atlantic Council, which remains in permanent session at the ambassadorial level. The ambassadors, for their part, were in constant communication with their respective capitals. The members of the NATO delegation in Moscow called Brussels on their cell phones from the rear of the Foreign Ministry building on Spiridonovka. In the opposite corner our military were on their own cell phones, discussing sensitive military issues with the Central Command. Some secrecy!

So the marathon negotiations that enabled us to minimize the negative consequences of NATO's expansion for Russia's security and made it possible for the Western states to avoid a dangerous worsening of relations with Moscow came to an end. As soon as the happy negotiators appeared on the front steps of the building, the lawn was flooded with journalists carrying TV and still cameras and tape recorders. After an improvised press conference, all the participants in the negotiations posed for a group picture on the steps. The document on the basic principles of mutual relations, cooperation, and security between Russia and the North Atlantic Treaty Organization was signed on May 27 in the Main Hall of the Élysée Palace, the residence of the French presidents, which was built over a century ago and where the most important receptions and other ceremonies take place. In front of the rows of ministers, other foreign officials, members of the diplomatic corps, and journalists, sixteen seats were arranged in a semicircle with an opening in the middle. The heads of state of the sixteen NATO members occupied the semicircle; in the opening between the two parts of the semicircle sat Yeltsin, Chirac, and Solana.

The ceremony was opened by the president of France as head of the host country. Then he gave the floor to Yeltsin for a ten-minute address (twice as long as the time allotted to the others). The elevated mood of all those present at the ceremony and at Chirac's official reception was evidence of the tremendous importance of the event that had taken place (I prefer not to call it a "historic event"; we use that cliché too often and too casually).

Bilateral meetings between Yeltsin and the heads of other countries also took place in Paris. Apart from congratulations, many tried to persuade the Russian president to come to Madrid, where the announcement on the beginning of talks on NATO's enlargement was to be made at the NATO summit. "If you are there," Chirac kept telling him, "the expansion problem will move to the rear and the opening of the Permanent Joint NATO-Russia Council will take the foreground. The Russian president will be the main figure, just as in Paris." When Clinton insistently called upon Yeltsin to go to Madrid, I could no longer keep from breaking in (the foreign minister and the secretary of state took part in that meeting). "It seems to me there's no need for the president to do that. The undoubtedly attractive idea of opening the meeting of the Joint Council doesn't outweigh the negative impact, especially for Russian public opinion, of being present in Madrid at the time NATO announces its enlargement."

"You see, Bill, it's not that simple," said Boris Nikolaevich.

During the reception Helmut Kohl, who sat next to Yeltsin at the table, leaned toward him and told him quietly, "Boris, I understand your decision not to go to Madrid. You are absolutely right."

The beginning of the summer of 1997 marked a switch to practical cooperation within the framework of the Joint Permanent Council (JPC). It was finally decided that the council would be chaired jointly by a representative of Russia, the secretary general of NATO, and a representative of one of the NATO members, which would rotate. For the first time I took the chairman's gavel and approved the agenda of the JPC meeting at the foreign minister level on September 26, 1997, in New York. The representative of Russia would give the floor to the foreign ministers and the U.S. secretary of state and then would comment on the speeches, summarizing their main ideas and inviting everyone present to concentrate on them. It turned out that this format was not customary at NATO and there were some murmurings, but they had to reckon with the complete equality of all signatories of the Basic Principles.

It was clear that the success of NATO's cooperation with Russia would be essential not only for bringing true stability to various regions but also for the direction and rate of evolutionary change within NATO and the Russian Federation. This reality colored the attitudes of different groups of people toward the JPC. There was a tendency to turn the JPC into a discussion club, which was unacceptable to us. It wasn't acceptable to some NATO members, either.

A year later Solana and I met in Luxembourg. The occasion was a reception in honor of the foreign ministers who took part in the North Atlantic Council. We stepped aside. I told Javier, "It seems to me that if it weren't for the expansion of NATO, so that you and Russia are always fearing unpleasant surprises from each other, the Joint Council could become the center of European security."

"I've been thinking about that too," replied Solana.

I remember a joint performance by the Russian and American delegations in Manila in July 1998, after the conclusion of the ASEAN regional security forum, which takes place annually between the ASEAN countries and the so-called equal partners in dialogue, among them the United States, Russia, China, India, Japan, Canada, Australia, New Zealand, South Korea, and the European Union. I mentioned earlier that traditionally each delegation, headed by the foreign minister, puts on a skit at the farewell dinner. This time we and the U.S. delegation had agreed in principle almost a year earlier to perform together. We corresponded with each other and revised the script, but we could rehearse only once in Manila, not long before we went onstage.

"NATO accepted Hungary!" sang Madeleine Albright to a tune from Leonard Bernstein's *West Side Story.*

"That was the biggest mistake," I sang in reply. The audience of delegates thundered their approval.

When I reread this section describing in detail the tough and lengthy negotiations that finally led to the signing of the Basic Principles, I thought, Should I put it in the book at all? because so many unprecedented events have taken place since then. The bombing of Yugoslavia dealt a serious blow to NATO-Russia relations. Perhaps in that context our enormous efforts to achieve constructive mutual understanding with the North Atlantic alliance should be termed a mistake. I say it definitely was not, mainly because the role played by Russia interrupted the NATO military operation. And I say that Russia's voice in the area of peacekeeping would not be so strong and effective if not for the stages in the history of its diplomacy that were devoted to exhausting but in the final analysis completely justified negotiations on the preparation and signing of the Basic Principles.

The ability of Russia and NATO to reach a compromise, which was proved by the signing of these principles, undoubtedly increased the ranks of those who considered NATO's operation against Yugoslavia an obvious mistake. And the prospect of a sharp deterioration in relations with Russia, particularly the disruption of the work of the Joint Permanent Council, must have deterred the escalation of military action and a ground assault against Yugoslavia.

Furthermore, the Russia-NATO Council resumed its work.

I believe that without the Basic Principles and the creation of the JPC it would have been impossible to move forward. That we did move forward was evidenced by the signing in May 2002 of a new agreement with NATO on the Russia-NATO Council, with many of its provisions based on a consensus of all its members. It should be recognized that many of the functions of this council had been stipulated by the agreements on the JPC operation.

CHAPTER SEVEN

Force or Other Methods

MY TENURE at the Foreign Ministry was not confined to negotiations aimed at regularizing relations between Russia and NATO. We focused on measures to neutralize a shift by some states to a course that conflicted with internationally accepted legal norms. How were we to react? Did we have to rely on military force, or should we simply ignore it as a part of international life? Neither of the above.

The new conditions that have evolved since the end of the age of global confrontation make it possible to coordinate political measures. Such measures have to be resolute, sometimes tough—whatever it takes to encourage every state to adhere to the commonly accepted norms of civilized behavior. Of course, if worse comes to worst, force cannot be ruled out, but only on two conditions. Force or a demonstration of force should be secondary to finding a political solution. And force should be used only after an appropriate decision by the U.N. Security Council.

Is it difficult to pursue such a combined and coordinated course? Of course it is. But it has to be pursued, especially when real opportunities to do so are available. Incidentally, viewed in the proper light, Russia can certainly play a very positive role here. And finally, that course is especially necessary when refusal by one state or a group of states to comply with a joint resolution on the most difficult regional situations does not encourage the positive forces to stand together in the fight against international terrorism.

IRAQ: HISTORY REPEATS ITSELF?

The situation in Iraq at the end of the 1990s is instructive in this regard. After Iraq had evacuated its troops from Kuwait in 1991, a special commission (UNSCOM) was formed to inspect military and industrial installations in Iraq and order the destruction of any weapons of mass destruction found. The mood among the members of the Security Council varied. Although everyone wanted to see the special commission succeed, some thought it was not carrying out its work effectively, not only because of Iraqi interference but also because the commission's leadership was often programmed to fail.

The head of the special commission, Rolf Ekeus, who had fairly good relations with Iraq, was replaced in 1997 by Richard Butler, Australia's former representative to the U.N., who back then had a good reputation and whose appointment was supported by everyone, including Iraq. But the initial high marks for his performance soon began to fall.

In 1998 I met Butler in Moscow, where he came for an exchange of views before a discussion of UNSCOM's regular report to the Security Council. We began the discussion at Smolenskaya Square by talking about the nuclear file. Many observers believed the time was ripe to turn inspections into permanent monitoring (that was what we meant, rather than "closing" one or another file, as the media often reported). Butler preferred to remain silent. When we turned to the missile file, I asked, "Do you have any evidence that Iraq has missile launchers or their engines?"

"No," Butler replied.

"In that case, why do you insist on maintaining the inspection phase and oppose switching to permanent monitoring? Instead you're piling up questions addressed to Iraq. That can be carried to absurd lengths. With no launch pads and no engines, the Special Commission can demand, say, that missile covers and then perhaps the hooks that keep them in place and so on and so forth must be found and destroyed."

Butler's answer puzzled me. "Everything depends on whether you can reach an agreement with the United States," he said.

"But wait, that agreement would be possible only after you provided us with objective information, not the other way around."

These words hung in the air.

On October 23 the U.N. Security Council passed Resolution 1174, based on the Special Commission's report condemning the Iraqi government's repeated refusal to allow access to the sites identified by UNSCOM. The vote was 10 for and 5 abstaining (Russia, France, China, Egypt, and Kenya). It should be noted that although not everyone agreed with the content of the resolution, none of the permanent members of the Security Council had vetoed it and not a single nonpermanent member had voted against it. It was a clear indication that a foundation existed for measures that would force Iraq to honor the U.N. mandates.

After that, events developed quite rapidly. On October 29 the Iraqi government declared that it would not admit American citizens as participants in UNSCOM activities in Iraq and demanded that American U-2's be banned from oversight flights and replaced with the aircraft of other nations.

In response, the Security Council *unanimously* supported its chairman's statement that Iraq must fully cooperate with the Special Commission without preconditions or limits and warned of "serious consequences if Iraq fails to immediately and completely fulfill its obligations."

The United States cocked the gun. On November 8, President Clinton said that he did not rule out "any measures" against Iraq in response to its violation of the Security Council resolution.

When Iraq refused to allow U.S. inspectors to visit the sites, inspections by the Special Commission were actually frozen. As a result, the Security Council passed another resolution condemning Iraq and banning foreign travel by Iraqi officials and military officers who were responsible for Iraq's failure to comply with its obligations under the Security Council resolutions. In other words, the escalation of political measures had begun.

Iraq responded by expelling U.S. citizens who worked with the Special Commission.

Now the world community once again found itself at a crossroads: use military force against Iraq or increase the pressure in an effort to make it abandon its destructive and defiant posture?

Supported by Great Britain, the United States began intensive preparations for a military strike against Iraq. Russia, China, France, and some other countries believed there was still room for political pressure to be effective, especially after Madeleine Albright's trip to Qatar, Bahrain, Kuwait, and Saudi Arabia showed that nobody had given unconditional assent to the military action that was under way.

On Sunday, November 9, Yeltsin departed for Beijing. I accompanied the president on this trip. As soon as the plane gained altitude and the seatbelt sign went off, Yeltsin's aide-de-camp leaned over me and said, "Boris Nikolaevich asks you to come over."

At Yeltsin's request I expressed my view of the situation in the Middle East: that extraordinary measures had to be taken to reduce tension and at the same time force Iraq to implement the directives of the world community, prescribed by the U.N. Security Council resolutions. That is where we conceived the idea for Yeltsin to send a tough message to Saddam Hussein.

The message said: "I would ask you not only to publicly confirm that Iraq is not refusing to cooperate with the Special Commission, but also to invite Special Commission inspectors back to Iraq to continue their regular work." Of course the return of its original staff was implied. The message stressed that if Hussein agreed, Russia would take steps to improve the work of the Special Commission, and with Iraq's constructive attitude would try eventually to close the nuclear file.

Yeltsin informed Clinton about his letter to the Iraqi leader and once again called upon him to refrain from the use of force. Clinton replied by phone that the use of force was not a priority and that he wished success to Russia's diplomatic mission.

On November 17 I spoke on the phone with Iraq's foreign minister, Mohammed Said al-Sahaf. He said that after a discussion with the Revolutionary Command Council, Saddam Hussein approved an answer to Yeltsin's message, and it would be delivered to Moscow in a few days.

"Why in a few days? Don't you understand how hot the situation is? Ask Tariq Aziz to bring the reply right away."

"Tariq Aziz is in Morocco. He'll have to fly to Amman first and from there to Moscow, because Baghdad's airport is closed."

A strange reply. Couldn't Baghdad deliver the information to Tariq Aziz in a coded message via Rabat? Or via the Iraqi embassy in Moscow?

I said firmly: "Tariq Aziz must be here tomorrow."

On November 18 Aziz arrived in Moscow. Our talks went on for two days. They were not easy ones, although one would think we needed no preliminaries. I told him immediately: "Tariq, you and I know the situation pretty well, so let's get down to it."

After complaining at length about the work of the Special Commission, Tariq Aziz nevertheless hinted and then, after consulting with Baghdad, declared directly that Iraq agreed to the return of the Special Commission in its full strength, including the Americans, and that they could resume their work immediately.

It was only to be expected that Russia had to make some commitments as well. But I must stress that Russia made those commitments for itself alone, not on behalf of the Security Council's permanent members, for which it clearly had no authority. Our commitments boiled down to a promise to raise some issues with the Security Council: a more balanced membership of the Special Commission, special forms for inspection of the so-called sensitive sites in Iraq, and rotation of the planes that patrolled Iraq. We also said that after the extraordinary session of the Special Commission, Russia would raise with the Security Council the questions of moving from inspections to monitoring of the nuclear and missile situations and speeding up the Special Commission's work in the chemical and biological areas. This activity by the Special Commission was to be supported by scientific seminars in which Iraqi representatives would take part.

This list suggests that Russia simply tried to bring the sides closer together without budging an inch from the basic stance on Iraq approved by the world community.

On November 19 Yeltsin took a helicopter to his residence in Gorky, where he had a meeting with Aziz. We briefed him on the work that had been done and familiarized him with the joint Russian-Iraqi statement that we had prepared. He reacted very positively to Aziz's announcement that at 10 A.M. the next day, November 20, Baghdad would announce the Revolutionary Command Council's agreement to the return of the Special Commission in its full strength.

I immediately phoned Albright, British Foreign Secretary Robin Cook, and French Foreign Minister Hubert Védrine and informed them of the radical change in Iraq's position. They all insisted on a meeting of the foreign ministers of the permanent members of the Security Council. On top of everything else, they seemed to suspect we were up to something.

Things were taking a difficult turn for me. Late on the night of November 19 I was to leave for Latin America. In Brazil, my first stop, I was scheduled to meet with the president immediately upon my arrival. Albright, who was in Deli, called me several times that day. She said she was ready to cut her stay in India short in order to organize a meeting with the British foreign secretary, the foreign ministers of Russia and France, and China's ambassador to Switzerland in Geneva on the night of November 20. Finally we agreed to meet at 2 A.M. at the Geneva airport. But since the Geneva U.N. head-quarters is only a short distance from the airport, we decided to meet in the Hall of Nations in the U.N. complex.

I have not often seen so many reporters from so many countries gather at such a late hour. Of course they were not present at the talks, but they waited patiently for the press conference.

Madeleine Albright took me aside and asked, "Yevgeny, is there anything else behind your agreement with Baghdad?"

"Madeleine, you can trust me, there is nothing. I've never lied to you and I'm not doing so now. I'm not even trying to embellish the situation."

We introduced the draft of a statement of the "five" to our colleagues. We came to an agreement on every proposal. Robin Cook, who chaired the meeting, played a large role in reaching the compromise. After the meeting was over I told him that in view of his undeniable talent, we'd be glad to have him chair every tough discussion. He jokingly parried, "A hard job should be rewarded."

"I don't know about Great Britain, but back in Russia those who do hard and dangerous work are given milk."

I don't think Robin found this explanation very inviting.

The Russian participants kept checking their watches. We were ungodly late with our departure, and we had already changed the time of my meeting with the Brazilian leaders once. But the Chinese ambassador had to receive Beijing's approval of the wording of the joint statement before he could sign it. Albright, for her part, was constantly communicating with Sandy Berger, the president's national security adviser. At long last the text was signed. It emphasized the importance of the joint efforts of the five permanent members of the U.N. Security Council in achieving Iraq's complete and unconditional fulfillment of all corresponding U.N. resolutions.

All those who signed the document hailed Russia's diplomatic initiative, undertaken with all other permanent members of the Security Council. It is important to point out that the statement supported the idea of discussing and preparing recommendations on ways to increase the efficiency of the Special Commission.

Thus ended one of the most dangerous moments in the crisis surrounding Iraq. It happened because the permanent members of the Security Council were united.

An extraordinary session of the Special Commission on November 21 adopted our recommendations for improving the efficiency of its operations —the possibility of a shift from inspections to monitoring, the problem of clarifying the remaining questions on expanding the number of countries participating in the Special Commission, the possibility of using additional planes, and so on. The next day the inspection groups resumed their work in Iraq. U-2 flights were resumed.

Iraq decided to allow "guests" from among the representatives of the Security Council members to visit presidential palaces and "sensitive sites" to convince them of the absence of prohibited materials and documents there. It was specified, however, that the guests could not include any members of the Special Commission inspection groups. A strong political démarche in response could be used without disrupting the solidarity of the permanent members of the Security Council. However, events took a different turn.

In the middle of December a delegation of the Special Commission headed by Butler went to Baghdad. Butler said in a prepared statement that the problem of inspecting the presidential sites was not resolved.

Tariq Aziz gave the number (eight) and locations of the presidential sites and provided descriptions of them, but he rejected the proposed options for their inspection until after the technical evaluation conference was over— that is, until April at the earliest.

According to the New York Times, Clinton approved a military operation against Iraq on November 24. Operation Desert Thunder envisioned four days of round-the-clock air strikes against Iraqi military sites by bombers and missiles.

It seems to me that at that time Butler was once again adding fuel to the fire. In an interview with the New York Times he said that Iraq possessed bacteriological agents capable of destroying Tel Aviv and means to deliver them. Butler's statement spread all over the world, while Baghdad's categorical denial was all but ignored.

In this environment a special representative of the president of Russia, Deputy Foreign Minister Viktor Posuvalyuk, was dispatched to Baghdad to encourage the Iraqi leadership to find compromise solutions on the inspections of the presidential sites. Despite Posuvalyuk's highly professional skills, this assignment looked difficult to carry out, because the presidential palaces had not been included among the sites to be inspected during earlier talks. For the Iraqis, that was a tremendously sensitive issue, a risk of losing face at the highest level, and on many occasions they had categorically refused to allow inspectors into the palaces. But this time Washington seemed to be intent on delivering a military strike.

On January 28 I went to Paris for talks with Hubert Védrine. Then I was received by President Chirac, who said France was ready to join Russia in an effort once again to achieve a political solution without the use of force.

I told the president that Posuvalyuk was supposed to meet with Hussein to deliver Yeltsin's message.

"You think Posuvalyuk will be able to meet with Hussein?" asked Chirac.

"Yes, I think so. Especially because the message was devised in a way to enable Posuvalyuk to meet with him personally. Direct contact with Hussein is very important."

On February 2 Posuvalyuk was received by Hussein. In the course of his daily contacts with the Iraqis an agreement was reached regarding the need to enlist the services of the secretary general of the U.N., Kofi Annan, an experienced politician who was well known throughout the world and whose objectivity was beyond question. During the month of February we maintained almost daily contact with him. He was increasingly inclined to step up his activities to resolve the conflict surrounding Iraq.

Meanwhile the Americans and the British were seeking to gain the Security Council's approval of a tough anti-Iraqi resolution that included the term "material breach," which not only established Iraq's "substantial breach" of the Security Council resolution but also gave a green light for strikes against Iraq. At the Security Council, in notes, and in numerous telephone talks with Albright and Cook we kept repeating that such a resolution was unacceptable. We in Moscow doubted that the persistent effort to get it passed was impelled solely by the need to increase pressure on Baghdad, especially when attempts to disrupt Annan's mission, which was ready to go to Baghdad, were being made just as persistently. When the attempt to foil that visit failed, they tried to turn Kofi Annan into a messenger of sorts, whose mission was not to negotiate with Saddam Hussein but to deliver categorical demands that he obey all U.N. resolutions.

Kofi Annan's trip to Baghdad as a negotiator may have been furthered by a joint statement by Yeltsin and Prime Minister Romano Prodi of Italy, which supported his diplomatic efforts to find a political solution. This statement was published during Yeltsin's official visit to Italy on February 10. Susan Anielli, Italy's former minister of foreign affairs, came up to me after reading the statement and said, "If I were foreign minister, I would never let this one pass."

"Why not, Susan?" I asked.

"Because it cancels out a military strike against Iraq. Saddam should be punished for everything he has done."

Fortunately, Lamberto Dini was foreign minister; Romano Prodi was prime minister then. Despite objections by some Italian Foreign Ministry officials, the prime minister gave orders to consider the text of the statement agreed upon with such difficulty to be final.

But the Americans continued to resist.

In a telephone conversation on February 12 Albright told me, "I think it's too early for Annan to go to Baghdad. Until Iraq is prepared to cooperate, such a trip will be counterproductive."

"I have every confidence that if the secretary general goes to Baghdad with his plan, the Iraqis will agree to it. Posuvalyuk met with Aziz again today in Baghdad and told him on behalf of our country's leadership that Kofi Annan's trip must be successful. We don't see any other peaceful way out of the situation," I answered.

I'll skip all the twists and turns that followed, but I'll mention the basic elements of the work done. First, Posuvalyuk reached a general agreement with Tariq Aziz on a format for the inspection of the eight presidential sites. Then at a meeting between Annan and Hussein in Baghdad on February 22, the secretary general repeatedly consulted with Posuvalyuk, who in turn was in contact with Aziz and other representatives of the Iraqi leadership. Annan and Aziz signed a memorandum of understanding on February 23. Iraq affirmed its commitment to cooperate with the Special Commission and allow a full-scale inspection throughout the country. Access to the eight presidential sites was provided for a "special group," selected by the U.N. secretary general, the chairman of the Special Commission, and the director of the International Atomic Energy Agency. The need to make the Special Commission more efficient was also mentioned, and the commission's obligation to respect Iraq's legal rights to its sovereignty, territorial integrity, and national security was confirmed.

Boris Yeltsin received a letter of thanks from both Hussein and Annan. The secretary general called me at home from Baghdad that night and said two words in Russian: "Spasibo, Rossiya [Thanks, Russia]!"

The fact that this tale does not end there by no means implies that the search for a balanced political and diplomatic solution was a failure. Baghdad clearly understood that when Iraq went too far, it rallied all permanent members of the Security Council against it. But if, despite this understanding, the Iraqis still sometimes unnecessarily provoked tensions, they did so when they felt that the situation had reached a dead end. Often they worked themselves up to hysteria, but sometimes their conclusions were not far from the truth.

The next Iraq crisis, no less dangerous than the previous two, has confirmed all that.

On October 30 the Security Council supported the U.N. secretary general's proposal of a comprehensive review of Iraq's observance of the Security Council's resolutions. By that time I was the head of the government, with an office in Moscow's White House, while Igor Ivanov was appointed foreign minister. We both thought that such a review would be useful provided that Baghdad abrogated its decision of August 5 to restrict the activities of the U.N. Special Commission. As a result, the landmarks for lifting the sanctions could be mapped out. Instead of revoking those restrictions, however, on October 31 the Iraqi leadership once again suddenly introduced a complete ban on the Special Commission's operations. The Iraqis referred to the fact that under pressure by the United States and Britain the Security Council allegedly had rejected the possibility of lifting the sanctions.

On November 5 a Security Council resolution was once again passed unanimously. It condemned the Iraqi decision and qualified it as a flagrant violation of the Security Council's resolutions. The United States declared that all options, including the use of force, were open. A strike against Iraq was scheduled for November 14.

On November 13 a note from Yeltsin was delivered to Hussein along with one from me. Both contained resolute calls for Iraq to immediately reestablish complete cooperation with the U.N. Special Commission and the International Atomic Energy Agency. Baghdad showed some signs of prudence on November 14. After a meeting of the Iraqi leadership, Aziz sent a message to Annan declaring Iraq's decision to allow the normal activities of the U.N. Special Commission and the International Atomic Energy Agency. The message noted that in reaching that decision the Iraqi leadership had taken into account "the letters of Yeltsin and Primakov."

Iraq's decision was welcomed by many members of the Security Council, who noted that Iraq once again failed to find a crack in the relations among the permanent members of the Security Council. Besides, every forced retreat by Iraq weakened Saddam Hussein's position both internally, despite the regime's propaganda efforts, and especially externally. However, Washington declared that Baghdad's regime was acceptable.

The situation was getting visibly strained. Viktor Posuvalyuk called me at 3:00 A.M. After that phone call, negotiations with Baghdad and New York went on all night. I instructed Posuvalyuk to approach the Iraqi leadership and tell them there was a limit to our peace initiatives. That was a sleepless night.

On November 15 Baghdad gave an official explanation that "Iraqi proposals" regarding the parameters of the comprehensive review were not connected with the Iraqi government's "definite and unconditional decision" to resume its cooperation with the Security Council and the International Atomic Energy Agency. To our general satisfaction, President Clinton declared that Iraq unconditionally yielded to the demands of the international community.

But a month later the United States and Great Britain carried out a series of strikes against Iraq, this time without any apparent or sufficient reason. Another sleepless night on December 16, with calls on the special line from President Yeltsin, telephone conversations with Igor Ivanov in Madrid and the chief of the General Staff of the Russian Armed Forces, Anatoly Kvashnin. Washington did not inform us of H hour, but the General Staff followed all movements of the U.S. Navy and Air Force. Yeltsin called Chirac that night, hoping that together they could persuade the Americans not to take this step. The French president agreed that a strike against Iraq without obvious provocation, especially during a session of the U.N. Security Council called to discuss the relations between Iraq and the Special Commission, was totally counterproductive. Yet Chirac said there was nothing he could do to stop the Americans: the strike had been scheduled for four o'clock Moscow time; cruise missiles and self-targeting bombs had begun exploding in Baghdad almost three hours earlier.

In his evaluation of the situation at the U.N., our representative, Sergei Lavrov, pointed out that the Americans had been unable to provide the Security Council with any argument in support of their decision. They referred to an obscure report by Richard Butler, who, as it turned out later, had been given instructions that originated in Washington to withdraw all members of the Special Commission from Iraq without delay. As I mentioned earlier,

I had met with Butler when I was foreign minister. Two weeks before the strikes against Iraq, Butler visited Russia again and, our foreign minister told me, assured us that right after the forthcoming discussion at the Security Council he would be able to close three of the four disarmament files on Iraq: nuclear, missile, and chemical.

Could we trust Butler, who spun like a weathervane, depending on which of the Security Council's permanent members he was talking to?

I would like to quote from the transcript of my telephone conversation with Vice President Al Gore. He called me late in the evening of December 17, 1998.[1]

GORE: Yevgeny, the main thing we want to avoid is for the situation surrounding Iraq not to undermine our relations with Russia. I know that Foreign Minister Ivanov had a very difficult conversation with Secretary of State Albright. As our ambassador in Moscow, [James] Collins, informed me, Deputy Foreign Minister Mamedov warned him today that many issues that are important for our relations are currently being threatened. I want you to understand that the United States has done something we've been warning about for a long time. In November when Saddam Hussein refused to cooperate with the U.N. Special Commission, we allowed ourselves to be persuaded to give him a last chance. Now that we've made the decision to strike, we've had to use the advantage of a surprise attack, so we couldn't warn anybody in advance, except for a small circle of countries directly involved in the preparation and execution of the strikes.

PRIMAKOV: You referred to the Iraqi situation in November. Perhaps you had reasons to react sharply at that time. Similar reasons existed in August, too. But at that time we acted together, and that allowed us to successfully find an optimal solution, a political settlement. To take Butler's report at face value would be naive, at the very least. He said something entirely different in Moscow a few days ago and drew opposite conclusions about the situation in Iraq. He is not an objective man and he's acting as instructed.

GORE: I would like to comment on Butler. We were not familiar with the final draft of his report. Nobody in Washington knew, until we received the text. Butler told the Security Council that Iraq failed to fulfill its obligations and that the Special Commission was unable to perform its duties. How else could we react to such statements? I'm aware of your serious efforts to make Iraq fulfill its obligations. But Saddam refused to do so. As a result, if we didn't act immediately, all the control procedures would have collapsed before our eyes.

PRIMAKOV: Your words may sound convincing, but not to us. We have information that you've been preparing for these strikes in advance. It wouldn't have happened if Butler's conclusions had been a surprise to you. I can assure you that your actions have dealt a serious blow to those in Russia who want to have good relations with the United States. We all should think about how to get out of this situation. The first thing to be done is to stop striking Iraq. Second, the problem needs to be transferred to the sphere of political discussions in the U.N. Security Council. It has to be understood that Butler is now persona non grata to everyone. We need to seek a solution.

GORE: You said we've been preparing for the operation in advance. Yes, we've been ready since November. We waited for Butler's report. Our president didn't make any decision to act until Butler stated in his report that Hussein was not fulfilling his obligations and that the Special Commission was unable to carry out its mandate. I want to stress once again that our relations with Russia remain a top priority for us.

PRIMAKOV: I agree that our relations are of fundamental importance for our peoples and for the world at large. But the ball is on your side of the court now. You can't do anything you want against any country. It's this approach that leads to global destabilization. You insist that you want to liquidate weapons of mass destruction in Iraq. Do you really think your strikes improve working conditions for the Special Commission? We've worked hard to get an opportunity to monitor Iraq. Are you sure that monitoring will be preserved? We have a common goal, to secure the liquidation of weapons of mass destruction in Iraq. Please understand that your attacks do nothing to help us reach that goal.

GORE: You and we approach the situation differently. I would disagree with your statement that the United States believes it has the right to use force at will. This is where our main difference lies. We are deeply convinced we are acting in accordance with the mandate of the U.N. Security Council. We've said that on many occasions.

PRIMAKOV: Not only Russia, but China, France, Brazil, Costa Rica, and other countries disagree with this position of yours.

GORE: I want you to understand that we absolutely sincerely believe that we have every reason to act as we do.

At the end of the conversation we agreed that we should stay in touch with each other.

Two days after this exchange, an American arms-control expert, Scott Ritter, talked on the BBC. Before August 1998 he was one of the Special Commission's leaders. He accused Butler personally of intentionally provoking military strikes against Iraq. Giving a general overview of the work done by the Special Commission, Ritter declared that "the inspection sites in Iraq were selected not for the purpose of finding weapons there but rather for provocational reasons." In Ritter's words, Iraq was expected to react as it did, thus providing a reason for a military strike. It was Butler who "allowed the United States to manipulate UNSCOM in order to justify air strikes."

As we predicted, strikes against Iraq did nothing to weaken Saddam Hussein's regime. On the contrary, he gradually began to emerge from his isolation in the Arab world. A number of countries increased their demands for the lifting of sanctions against Iraq. In some cases they were lifted de facto.

Then, in March 2003, came the U.S. military operation in Iraq, undertaken without the sanction of the U.N. Security Council. The Iraqi armed forces showed little effective resistance. But the situation grew worse. Strikes against occupation forces led to American casualties many times heavier than those suffered during the war itself. Other problems stemmed from the necessity of rebuilding a postwar Iraqi state.

Until the very beginning of the operation against Iraq, Russia tried to avert war. President Putin summoned me late one night three weeks before the American invasion. When morning came, I was on my way to Baghdad with his verbal message for Saddam Hussein. The message suggested that Hussein resign and urge the Iraqi parliament to hold democratic elections. "If you have the interests of your country and your people at heart, you should do this in order to try to stop Washington"—that was what Putin asked me to tell Hussein. Saddam mumbled some phrases incoherently, tapped me on the shoulder, and left the room.

Seven months into the American occupation of Iraq, Saddam Hussein was arrested. This was done with great fanfare, but questions remain unanswered. American tanks rolled onto intact bridges and eventually into Baghdad, meeting hardly any resistance. When the Americans started the operation, they knew the combat capabilities of the Iraqi National Guard. Yet it offered no resistance. And the Iraqi air force and armored units were not engaged at all.

I have no doubt that the Americans captured Saddam Hussein and not one of his numerous doubles. But did they lay hands on him at the time of the announcement or somewhat earlier? Madeleine Albright is surely not one to make extravagant statements, yet she said that with the U.S. elections in sight, President Bush now has to produce the arrested Osama bin Laden. Cornered by questions, Albright said she was just joking. To my mind, this could be called a joke only if we compare the hypothetical situation regarding the prime suspect in the September 11, 2001, terrorist attacks to the real arrest of Saddam Hussein.

I can speculate about what happened. The United States could have contacted a member of Saddam Hussein's inner circle to tell Saddam that his life would be spared if the military operation met with no resistance. The fact that he was given POW status seems to uphold this.

If this version is true, the American secret services should be highly praised for excellent work that saved many lives. But what is to be done with Iraq itself, which was occupied without a clear-cut plan for the aftermath of a successful military operation? And what's in store for the unilateralist pacifiers?

KOSOVO IN THE SIGHTS

I told President Slobodan Milosevic in 1996, "Take a look at Kosovo. An explosive situation is building there that will be hard to deal with." I know I was not the only one to arrive at that conclusion. Many people warned the president of Serbia about Kosovo's potential threat.

He either failed to notice that threat or just brushed the warnings aside. Perhaps the American diplomats' flirtation with Milosevic went to his head. They realized that without Milosevic, no one would be able to produce the Dayton Accords, which ended the war in Bosnia and Herzegovina. Milosevic could very well think of himself as an omnipotent politician because practically nobody could oppose him in Serbia, or in Yugoslavia in general. So Kosovo didn't worry him too much. But the situation there was heating up.

As far back as the early 1990s, postwar Yugoslavia was cut in half when Croatia, Slovenia, Macedonia, and Bosnia and Herzegovina declared their independence. The world community—including Russia, unfortunately— welcomed those developments immediately, without any feeling of tension or concern for the future. Meanwhile the knife that cut them apart separated peoples. Ethnic conflicts could cause bloodshed.

On the basis of the Dayton Accords, international forces, including a Russian team, pacified the warring parties in Bosnia and established a cease-fire. While this book was being written, the process of forming national structures in Bosnia was far from over, but the situation there was gradually stabilizing. In Kosovo the situation developed differently. The conflict first smoldered and then burst into flame.

During the long presidency of Josip Broz Tito, Kosovo, with its largely Albanian population, was a part of Yugoslavia, but it enjoyed broad autonomy. After the disintegration of the Yugoslav federation, Serbia's new constitution significantly curtailed Kosovo's rights. As a result, dual power was formed in Kosovo, which Serbs consider to be a historical center of their statehood and spirituality (ancient Serbian monasteries are located there). Pristina, Kosovo's administrative center, refused to recognize the authority of the Belgrade government and created its own power structures. But Albanian extremism was still at its embryonic stage. In fact, Serbian police basically controlled the situation, while Milosevic ignored warnings that the Kosovar Albanians were about to erupt.

However, Albania lay just across a border that was far from secure. In 1957, as a Moscow radio correspondent, I accompanied Nikita Khrushchev to Tirana, Albania's capital. I was the editor in charge of programs for the Arab countries. I don't know why I was sent on that trip. Perhaps somebody at the top confused Albanians with Arabs. During that visit we were shown a monument to Stalin and were told that the Albanians revered him because he had saved Albania's independence from Tito's encroachments. Indeed, Tito had been about to annex Albania to Kosovo, but an ultimatum from Stalin foiled that attempt. Now some Albanians nurtured a plan to create a Greater Albania, this time by annexing Kosovo to Albania. Belgrade's unwillingness to take the Kosovo problem seriously, in the hope that it would work out by itself, strengthened the position of the Albanian separatists in Kosovo, who turned to terrorist tactics against the Serbian authorities and the police.[2]

At the same time, Albania itself was falling apart. As a result, an unrestrained flow of volunteers and weapons began to move across the border to help their "brothers" in Kosovo.

The Serb police who were "cleaning up" the territory did not handle the situation as intelligently as they might have.

When socialist Yugoslavia was about to collapse and military operations on its territory were at their peak, a so-called contact group was formed by Russia, the United States, and a number of major European countries. A meeting of the Contact Group at the foreign minister level, in which I participated, was held during the fifty-second session of the U.N. General Assembly on September 24, 1997. There for the first time Klaus Kinkel suggested the adoption of a separate statement on Kosovo. We worked on the text and it finally became fairly objective. The statement was passed unanimously. It expressed concern at the way events were developing, called for reconciliation, and appealed to Belgrade to carry out its responsibility for maintaining security in the territory.

By the end of February 1998 the situation in Kosovo had sharply deteriorated. An attack by the Kosovo Liberation Army (KLA) on a Serbian police patrol led to a series of armed clashes with special units of the Yugoslav police. Casualties mounted, among them a growing number of civilians. From that time on, armed clashes in Kosovo were continuous.

This was the situation when the Contact Group met again in London on March 9. The United States, Great Britain, and a number of other countries spoke in favor of imposing economic and other sanctions against Yugoslavia. We expressed our views frankly during the meeting as well as in the lobby. Russia claimed a special position on a number of issues that it considered unacceptable and supported only provisions that included temporary restrictions on the supply of weapons and military hardware to the former Yugoslavia, with the understanding that they would apply to Kosovo as well.

It was vitally important to persuade the Westerners not to exacerbate the situation in Kosovo by thoughtless actions and we did our best, but obviously it was not enough.

During my tour of the four republics of the former Yugoslavia, I met with Milosevic in Belgrade on March 17. Our one-on-one discussion was very heated. Russian colleagues in the next room said later that when our voices rose, one of the Yugoslavs went to the door and tried to shut it more firmly.

I was trying to persuade Milosevic to come up with an initiative regarding Kosovo's autonomy; pull his troops back to where they were originally stationed; assume personal responsibility for the beginning of talks with Ibrahim Rugova, the leader of the relatively moderate wing of the Kosovar Albanians, and make this intention public; and agree to the arrival of a group of OSCE observers in Kosovo.

At dinner in our honor that evening, hosted by Milan Milutinovic, the recently elected president of Serbia,[3] he said that Milosevic accepted our proposals. In the morning, however, the statement about their intention to begin negotiations with the Albanians was issued in the name of Milutinovic. Milosevic seemed not to be involved. Despite the fact that some of our proposals were not reflected in Milutinovic's statement, we were pleased with the result, since it was a step forward made by Belgrade.

Although on the whole the tension in Kosovo had subsided somewhat, our Western partners in the Contact Group insisted on increasing pressure on Belgrade. The United States and some other members showed a clearly biased approach to the parties involved in the Kosovo conflict. The Albanian terrorists were presented almost as fighters for justice.

By that time we had received information on some American politicians' flirtation with the leadership of Montenegro, which was facilitated by Belgrade's policy on that small republic. (Characteristically, when the president of Montenegro came to Belgrade to meet with me, the official media failed to notice his arrival, although this was his first visit to the capital in a long time.)

In any event, we could not help feeling that some of our Western colleagues' view of the Kosovo problem was colored by the thought that Yugoslavia might finally be about to collapse, depriving Serbia of much of its strength.

A meeting of the Contact Group at the ministerial level was held in Bonn on March 25. That was a stormy meeting. Madeleine Albright firmly insisted on increasing the demands and measures against Belgrade. It was difficult to convince her of the fallacy of this position. At one point I even said, "Sign whatever you want, but Russia will publicly declare that we're against it and that we're leaving the Contact Group." The host of the meeting, Klaus Kinkel, called a break and asked me to follow him into his office. We spoke in English without translators.

"Let's agree on wording that is acceptable to you," said Kinkel. We worked on it together. Kinkel summoned his political director, Wolfgang Ischinger, a very smart and well-disposed man, and instructed him to check out the wording with the other participants.

While we were sitting in Klaus Kinkel's study, passions were raging outside the windows, where members of the Albanian diaspora were shouting anti-Serbian slogans and some were urging a march on Belgrade.

"You see what pressure we have to live under," said Klaus.

"Let me give you some advice," I said. "Announce that you've issued instructions to the police to write down the names of all the demonstrators. Just say it through a loudspeaker, and you will see them fade away and disappear. What these people most fear is going back home to Yugoslavia or Albania. Do you seriously believe that even if Kosovo hypothetically becomes independent, Albanian refugees will want to return there from Germany?"

I felt that Kinkel had a realistic view of the situation, but parliamentary elections were coming up and the Albanian refugee card was being played, along with the idea of "restoring order in Kosovo" so they could all go home.

In the end we managed to adopt a document in Bonn that stated that the solution of the Kosovo problem had to be based on preservation of the territorial integrity of the Republic of Yugoslavia and observance of OSCE standards, the Helsinki Accords, and the U.N. Charter. The sanctions imposed on March 9 remained in place, but that was it.

The package of so-called stabilization measures was approved at the Rome session of the Contact Group on April 29. Simultaneously, parallel missions were initiated, one by Richard Holbrooke and Robert Gelbard for the Americans and another by Nikolai Afanasievsky for Russia. The parallel but fairly closely coordinated trips to Belgrade and Pristina produced some results. On May 15 in Belgrade, Milosevic and Rugova agreed to start negotiations on a political settlement of the Kosovo problem between representatives of the Serbian and Yugoslavian leadership on one side and the Kosovar Albanian community on the other.

The first work session of the delegations took place in Pristina on May 22. The tension was noticeably lessening. But exactly a week later the situation in Kosovo exploded once again. It was undoubtedly provoked by the Albanian militants of the KLA, who attempted to gain control over the regions of Kosovo that bordered on Albania. In response the Serbs launched a broad police operation in western Kosovo. Both Albanians and Serbs suffered casualties, some of them civilian. The number of displaced persons and refugees in Albania had increased considerably. The leaders of the Kosovar Albanians refused to continue the talks.

The danger that NATO would use force against Yugoslavia was becoming more and more real, although a number of European states, some NATO members among them, were hesitant about such action, especially without the approval of the Security Council. Once I told Ms. Albright, "Russia has been present in the Balkans for two hundred years, maybe more. It's beyond me why the Americans want to force their recommendations on the Balkans without consulting us, or to resolve local conflicts in their own way."

When tensions reached their peak, Milosevic was urgently invited to Moscow. The presidents met in the Kremlin on June 16, 1998. The outcome was that we agreed to issue a joint statement. Its text was prepared right there in the Kremlin by Milosevic and his colleagues and the Russian foreign and defense ministers with their colleagues.

We managed to make the Yugoslavs declare their readiness to resume negotiations on a whole range of issues, including the form of the region's autonomy, without delay. They agreed not to conduct any repressive measures against the civilian population; to allow freedom of movement throughout Kosovo as a trust-building measure; to guarantee full access to the region by humanitarian organizations, including the International Red Cross and the Office of the High Commissioner for Refugees; not to hinder any attempts by diplomatic representatives accredited by the Federal Republic of Yugoslavia and international organizations to familiarize themselves with the situation. There was also a provision on unlimited repatriation of refugees and displaced persons under programs agreed upon with the Red Cross and the Office of the High Commissioner for Refugees. This was the most important breakthrough.

The withdrawal of Yugoslav special forces from Kosovo developed into a sore point. When we persisted in urging Milosevic to agree to their withdrawal, he said, "Please understand that until the KLA stop their active military operations, even the mere announcement of the possibility of withdrawal will now result in a wave of Serbian refugees from Kosovo."

In the end we agreed on the following wording: "As terrorist activity diminishes, the security forces will reduce their presence outside the area of their permanent location."

Yugoslavia also declared its readiness to negotiate the admission of the OSCE mission into Kosovo, which was to occur simultaneously with Yugoslavia's reinstatement as a member of that organization.

Unbiased observers came to the conclusion that Russia's diplomacy eliminated the need for the use of force against Belgrade. After the joint statement was signed in Moscow, the situation in Kosovo began to improve. Trips by the diplomats and representatives of humanitarian organizations accredited by Belgrade to various regions of Kosovo contributed to that improvement. The Russian ambassador said that after such trips, many of his

Western colleagues no longer shared the pessimism and obvious bias that continued to prevail in their capitals.

The situation seemed to be moving toward a political settlement. It was announced that a new negotiating team of Kosovar Albanians had been formed with the assistance of an "informal mediator," Christopher R. Hill, U.S. ambassador to Macedonia. Hill maintained close contact with Afanasievsky. But at that moment NATO's sword again rose over Belgrade. The epicenter of the struggle was the U.N. Security Council, where the United States and Britain kept insisting on passing a resolution on Kosovo. They referred to Chapter VII of the U.N. Charter, which provides for the escalation of sanctions and the possible use of force in the event of a threat to world peace. Chapter VII had been used only once, to authorize war in Korea under the U.N. flag. Back then our representative was absent and the resolution was passed. But now we tried to apply the lessons of the past and openly declared that we would veto such a resolution.

In September I was vacationing in Sochi, on the Black Sea. Strictly speaking, this was hardly a vacation. In any event, the Abkhazian leader Vladislav Ardzimba and others visited me for negotiations and for other reasons, and I was constantly on the phone with Moscow and other places. Kinkel asked me to meet privately with his representative Wolfgang Ischinger, who would "bring and comment on an extremely important personal message on Kosovo."

We agreed that I would meet Ischinger at the airport in order not to attract the media. He came with an interpreter on a regularly scheduled airliner from Moscow on August 21 and gave me a long message from the German foreign minister. Criticizing our position in blocking a reference to Chapter VII in the Security Council resolution, Kinkel wrote threateningly about an escalation of risks for relations between the West and Russia, including Russia-NATO relations; for Russia's position in the Security Council and Russia's ability to play its role in settling international crises; for Russia's role in the Contact Group; and for our ability to cooperate jointly and constructively in other areas, including economic and financial issues.

Trying to justify Germany's "exceptional interest" in passing the reference to Chapter VII, Kinkel referred to the growing number of refugees coming to Germany ("We proceed from the fact that 400,000 Kosovar Albanians live in Germany and 2,000 more people keep applying for asylum every month").

"I am writing all this to you," Klaus Kinkel said at the end of his extraordinary message, "as a man who, as you know, holds relations with Russia close to his heart. And it is because I am so concerned that as your friend I think I must tell you everything so frankly."

I read the letter in Ischinger's presence and told him, "Please tell Kinkel that we differ in our understanding of current events in Kosovo. Tensions are not growing there, the situation has somewhat stabilized. We should keep looking for a political solution, all of us—we, the Americans, and the European Union. I agree that urgent humanitarian measures are needed. Russia's position is not going to change. Figuratively speaking, it consists of four no's: no to NATO's military operation against Belgrade; no to Kosovo's leaving Yugoslavia; no to an escalation of sanctions against Yugoslavia; no to maintaining Kosovo's current status, which deprives it of autonomy. We must seek an immediate cease-fire by both sides and begin negotiations."

After I was appointed to head the Russian government, our successful efforts to achieve a political settlement in Kosovo were continued by the new minister of foreign affairs, Igor Ivanov. But the main events were still to come.

CHAPTER EIGHT

Middle East Settlement

LOST OPPORTUNITIES

MYTHS AND REALITY

It is both easy and difficult for me to write about the Middle East conflict. I was involved in it for years, observed the situation from close up and from a distance, wrote about it in articles, reports, and books. One would think I must know quite a lot about it. But sometimes it's very hard to know what's behind events in the Middle East, even when you are familiar with its history, the character of the people, and the true reasons for many clashes. Nevertheless, I have something to say about lost opportunities, overlooked situations, and thoughtless decisions. Misconceptions rooted in the consciousness of politicians and widely accepted throughout the world have had a lot to do with the failures.

The first myth is that the Middle East has never been able to sustain a state of either war or peace that might eventually lead to the establishment of territorial stability.

The string of wars has continued without a break.

I edited Moscow radio programs for Arab countries when the joint forces of Britain, France, and Israel attacked Egypt in 1956, after Nasser nationalized the Suez Canal. Back then we found ourselves on the brink of a world conflagration. Such effective démarches as Washington's outright displeasure with Britain, France, and Israel and a simultaneous warning by the USSR stopped the war but did not prevent developments that, after regrouping (the United States sided with Israel), led to a string of new armed conflicts.

I worked in Cairo as a *Pravda* correspondent during the Six-Day War of 1967, launched by Israel after an unsuccessful and unjustified show of strength by Cairo. Nasser may have misinterpreted a thoughtless remark by Marshal Andrei Grechko, then commander in chief of the Warsaw Pact forces. Probably intending to show how well Soviet military advisers were doing in Egypt, Grechko said during a visit to Cairo that the Egyptian army could "successfully settle a variety of tasks in this theater."

The war broke out on July 6. At nine in the morning, in a voice breaking with agitation, I was reporting by phone to my editor that a plane had been shot down right before my eyes. The missile drew a line in the bright-blue sky, there was a flash, and the plane disintegrated before the eyes of the cheering citizens of Cairo. The radio endlessly reported fantastic figures of Israeli losses, but it turned out that the plane was Egyptian and so was the missile. My Cairo friends gathered in my apartment. By that time I had learned from some of our experts who had come in from the Cairo west military base that the Egyptian air force never took off from the airfield and was destroyed on the ground. Many Egyptians cried when they heard that news.

The complete and humiliating defeat of the Egyptian army and Israel's capture not only of the Sinai Peninsula but also of the West Bank of the Jordan River and East Jerusalem seemed to move the prospect of a new war into the distant future. Many Americans, even those who dealt with problems of the Middle East (with the possible exception of Henry Kissinger), probably assumed that the territorial division that resulted from the Six-Day War was in effect final.

We thought differently. In May 1973 Vitaly V. Zhurkin and I addressed the Council on Foreign Relations in New York. The audience consisted of highly professional scientists, analysts of the State Department, CIA, and other organizations, both state and private, who worked on the Middle East problem. Our prognosis that an Arab-Israeli war was inevitable in the very near future was met with hostility, as was the prediction that Arabs would initiate the war and for the first time use oil as a weapon by blocking its delivery to the West. One of the participants ridiculed that idea: "The Israelis are in full control of the situation. The Arabs would never dare and never be able to start a military action, and even worse, challenge the whole Western world." When half a year later events began to unfold according to our scenario, Zhurkin and I went again to the United States, and if it weren't for our friend Marshall Schulman, who worked at the State Department, our visas wouldn't have been extended. Of course neither I nor Zhurkin had been informed of the Arabs' intentions. Even our military advisers in Egypt and Syria didn't expect the Arabs to start a war. It incurred the serious displeasure of the Soviet leadership.

During the October War in 1973 I went to Beirut and then by car to Damascus, where I saw three Israeli planes shot down by anti-aircraft fire. But the Arabs were not successful in that war, either.

Many Western politicians believed that military defeats would force the Arabs to accept terms dictated by Israel. Thus was born another myth that did not stand up under scrutiny. A series of wars betokened no change in the mentality of either party. I became convinced of that after numerous conversations and discussions with many leaders of the countries of that region, with whom I had long since developed relations of confidence and sometimes even friendship.

Hafez al-Assad was one of them. On February 23, 1966, the left wing of the Ba'ath party came to power in Damascus. That was probably the first bloody coup in Syria, and I was immediately instructed by the editors of *Pravda* to get there from Cairo. The Damascus airport was shut down. I came on a Czech plane that was making a technical stop. They wanted to deport me immediately, but a phone call to one of the men who had just come to power helped. As a result, the next day I became the first foreigner to meet with the new prime minister. On March 8, during a parade organized by the Ba'ath Party, I was introduced to Air Force Commander Hafez al-Assad. After he became president of Syria we met on many occasions and talked for hours on the hot issues of the moment.

Since the late 1960s and early 1970s I have had many discussions and arguments with a number of Palestinians, among them Yasir Arafat, Abu Aiad, Abu Mazen, and Yasir Abed Rabbo, and enjoyed their friendship.

I have known the Iraqi leadership since the end of the 1960s, but I have already mentioned that. I was introduced to the Lebanese leaders, both Muslims and Christians, whom the civil war placed on different sides of the barricade—Camille Shamun and Pierre Gemayyel and their sons, Kamal Jumblat and his son Walid, Rashid Karame, and others.

In December 1975 I talked for three hours with Anwar Sadat in his residence together with the late Arabist Igor Belyaev. After Belyaev and I received an international Nasser Award for our book about the Egyptian leader,[1] we were invited for a frank discussion and were practically the last Soviets Sadat met with. By that time Sadat had already made up his mind to turn his back on Moscow, but our discussion was friendly.

I had three lengthy night meetings with King Fahd of Saudi Arabia, who usually received his guests at night. He gave me his beads, saying, "I am the keeper of two major Muslim holy objects. Make sure you don't give these beads away to anybody." In 1991 King Fahd told me he enjoyed watching the TV news program from Moscow called *Vremya* (Time), which he said covered events in the Middle East without bias. He asked, "Would it be possible to translate this program into Arabic every day?"

I brought a unique documentary film to the King Faisal Museum, which showed the Saudi foreign minister and future king during his visit to Moscow in 1930. I received thanks from his sons, who occupied top positions in Saudi Arabia at the end of the last century.

On many occasions I met King Hussein of Jordan, for whom I had very warm feelings. Our mutual sympathy and I presume to say friendship began in 1970. I arrived late for an audience with him because I miscalculated the time it took to get there. The king met me wearing a bright shirt with rolled-up sleeves and laughed when I tried to explain why I was late. "Jordan is the only Arab country where you can't drive on a red light," he said. Here is another story suggesting the closeness of our relations. Once I went to see the prime minister of Jordan at his home, and when Hussein learned I was there, he came over alone on a motorcycle (he could also fly various planes extremely well). His Caucasian bodyguards, angry and scared to death for their beloved sovereign, rushed after him.

I have been corresponding and meeting with the king's brother Hassan for years.

I also had good relations with another descendant of the prophet Muhammad, Morocco's King Hassan II, who played an outstanding role on the Palestinian front, trying to bring the parties closer together. Unfortunately, both King Hussein and King Hassan II are no longer with us.

I also established frank and trustful relations with President Hosni Mubarak of Egypt.

I met privately with Golda Meir, Moshe Dayan, Shimon Peres, Yitzhak Rabin, and Menachem Begin,[2] and had official meetings with Yitzhak Shamir, Biniamin Netanyahu, Chaim Weizmann, Levi Eshkol, Anatoly (Natan) Sharansky, and Ariel Sharon. It is impossible to name them all.

Having plunged into the whirlpool of Middle Eastern events, I absorbed the information I was receiving from the most well informed people—straight from the horse's mouth, as they say. And because so much blood has been shed, so many destinies have been broken, so much fury has accumulated, and so many eyes have been blinded by hatred, I am convinced that a Middle East settlement is impossible without active intervention from the outside.

In developing our Middle Eastern policy and bilateral relations before the 1990s, we had to take the Cold War into consideration and sometimes even to use it as our departure point. I imagine our opponents did the same. The Cold War undoubtedly colored the way the United States with its allies and the USSR approached the Middle East peace process.

In this connection another myth, this time created by the Soviet side, interfered with a Middle East settlement—the Arab-Israeli conflict occasionally took on ideological tones. No, it was not only a matter of geopolitical competition. The theory of "socialist orientation" was advanced, which declared a presocialist stage of development in Egypt, Syria, and other countries of the so-called Third World.

Some Arab leaders grasped the ideological hand extended to them. Many of them took advantage of the Soviet mind-set and began playing the role (it was literally a role) of a kind of ideological partner, mouthing such sweet words as "the whole socialist [or progressive] world led by the Soviet Union," "the USSR is the leader of the world national liberation movement," and so on and so forth.

Interestingly enough, Stalin, who in 1948 instructed Gromyko to recognize the state of Israel without delay, was also guided by ideological considerations. He believed that since Israel had welcomed large numbers of immigrants from the socialist countries and established such "communist" settlements as kibbutzim, it would become a socialist cell in the Middle East. But eventually the inconsistency of such brave assumptions could no longer be denied. The irrationality of an ideological approach to the conflict became all too clear in the early 1990s.

All that was true, and yet I can say as a professional that even during the Soviet period we were interested in establishing peace between the Arabs and the Israelis. We were not simply interested but took steps in that direction without forgetting (nobody ever forgot) about our many-sided interests in the Middle East.

But how could a settlement be reached? Certainly Moscow understood very well that compromise was necessary. But what was the limit for a compromise that could lead to a settlement and, more important, keep it afloat? In the most general terms, such a compromise was found: the territories occupied by Israel during the Six-Day War in exchange for peace between the Arab countries and Israel, including not only recognition of Israel but the establishment of full diplomatic and other relations with it.

I must say that the affirmation of this approach at the Madrid Peace Conference in 1991 signified general recognition of a truth that had seemed indisputable to us from the very beginning, that Israel's return of the Arab territories on the one hand and the strengthening of Israeli security on the other were the only way to a Middle East settlement.

The process of political settlement has stretched over decades. Certainly the mentalities of the parties involved are playing their roles. At the same time, I believe there is another myth that makes the road to peace even longer: the idea that the United States can achieve peace in the Middle East single-handedly, without coordinating its actions with Russia and the European Union.

LOST OPPORTUNITIES

It seems to me that a realistic chance for a comprehensive settlement of the Middle East conflict appeared for the first time in 1973. But for a variety of reasons it was decided to prepare a separate agreement between Israel and the strongest Arab country, Egypt. In other words, the U.S. approach prevailed. The idea was to pull one Arab country at a time to peace with Israel and later add the Palestinians to the process.

During my conversation with Sadat at the end of 1975 he told me about the 1972 war and drew the following picture of its last days: "The battle front was like a puff-pastry pie. My Third Army was surrounded by Israelis in Sinai. For their part, the Egyptian troops surrounded General Sharon's tanks that broke through to the western bank of the Suez Canal. They connected with the main Israeli forces by a six-kilometer corridor and a few pontoons across the canal. Our generals put pressure on me to cut the corridor and strike at Ariel Sharon's foothold. We had everything we needed for that, including a two-to-one advantage in artillery and tanks. But Henry Kissinger informed me, 'Mr. President, if the Soviet-made weapons defeat the American, our game with you will be over.' "

"What game?" Belyaev and I asked in unison. Sadat evaded the question and changed the subject.

The next day we were in Amman, where the situation was clarified by King Hussein and Prime Minister Said Rifai, who accompanied him. During the informal breakfast I brought up my conversation with Sadat.

"I have no doubt that a game was indeed being played," said the king of Jordan.

Prime Minister Rifai chimed in: "I remember my visit to Cairo sixteen months before the war broke out. I went to see Sadat to restore diplomatic relations, which the Egyptians had severed the year before. Sadat told me candidly that he had a secret arrangement with Kissinger. Then Sadat confided the idea of thawing their conflict with Israel. 'It can be done by means of a limited action aimed at capturing a small foothold on the east side of the canal. After that I can sit at the negotiating table.'"

Finally Assad, the president of Syria, put the dot over the i. During my meeting with him on June 2, 1983, we touched on many aspects of the Middle East conflict. We also brought up the possibility of settling the conflict immediately after the 1973 war. Here is what Assad said: "We had a preliminary agreement with Sadat to act honestly and jointly. Naturally, he failed to inform us that he conceived this war only as a means to break the deadlock and begin separate negotiations. In Syria we believed that the war's end result must be a comprehensive political settlement, based on the decisions of the U.N. Security Council. However, our plans rested on the assumption that by the time the U.N. intervened in the conflict, we would have recaptured the territories Israel occupied on both fronts in 1967. But that's not the way things turned out," Assad concluded.

One of the most outstanding and skillful politicians of the second half of the twentieth century, Henry Kissinger denies in his memoirs that he knew in advance that Sadat's ideas "were aimed not at securing territorial gains but at creating a crisis that could change the frozen positions of the involved parties and thus open up the road to negotiations."[3] But even if the U.S. secretary of state had not been playing a game with Sadat from the very beginning, the plan seems to have appealed to him: thaw the conflict by a very limited action on Sadat's part; America takes control of the situation; create conditions that will increase Sadat's prestige so that he can negotiate a separate agreement.

When Kissinger was in Moscow before the signing of Security Council

Resolution 338, on the cease-fire in the Middle East, which was prepared jointly by the USSR and the United States, he said he agreed with the Soviet leadership that a link must be established between the end of the war and the beginning of a *comprehensive* settlement. In reality he distanced himself from the linkage idea, as became apparent during the Geneva peace conference, which according to Kissinger was to become a means to bring together all the interested parties for a symbolic act that would enable each of them to go its own way, at least for the time being.

In 1978, when Kissinger was no longer secretary of state, Israel and Egypt signed a bilateral treaty. But it did not put an end to a series of wars and military clashes. In 1982 Israel carried out an incursion into Lebanon that in scope and number of casualties on both sides was comparable to all the preceding wars in the Middle East. Exchanges of gunfire, air raids, armed clashes, and terrorism are still everyday occurrences in the West Bank, the Gaza Strip, and East Jerusalem. In the years since the Camp David agreements of 1979 there have been no effective changes in the Middle East peace process. That speaks for itself.

At the same time a gradual shift in the correlation of forces was taking place; or to be more precise, while maintaining its military superiority, Israel was paying an ever-greater price for its military victory, or at least for control over the situation that resulted from the military clashes.

A Middle East peace conference convened in Madrid in 1991 pressured the conflicting parties to become more active in seeking peace. Several rounds of secret meetings between representatives of Israel and the Palestine Liberation Organization took place in Oslo in the mid-1990s.[4]

Some progress was taking shape in the direction of Syria, but contacts were insignificant and did not go beyond probing. Despite the importance of moving forward along the Palestinian track, peace in the Middle East is impossible without a settlement with Syria. Furthermore, failure to resolve problems with Syria actually threatened retreat on the Palestinian front. During one of my conversations with Assad, I told him about my vision of Syria's position in the existing circumstances. On the one hand, Syria doesn't want to be the first to reach an accord with Israel; on the other, it doesn't want to be the last, as in that case it would have to deal with Israel all by itself. Such a dialectic leaves very limited room for maneuver. Assad agreed with me and said, "Perhaps we won't be able to bring about a comprehensive settlement, but in any event, we're in a position to avoid having to face Israel alone."

I met with Edward Djerejian, whom I consider one of the best American Middle East specialists, in Moscow in 1993. We used to see each other periodically in Syria when he served as U.S. ambassador there and in Washington when he was appointed assistant secretary of state for Near Eastern and South Asian Affairs. I remember calling the U.S. ambassador when I was in Damascus. The hotel staff somehow managed to learn about that and insisted that Djerejian and I meet in a room reserved for that purpose. I preferred to sit with him in the lobby. We refused coffee, and then tea and fruit. Then a waiter came up to our table and put a small vase of flowers in front of us. But we never even intended to make any deals behind the backs of our cordial hosts. The conversation was purely social. We exchanged reminiscences, asked each other about people we both knew.

In 1993, by contrast, when I played host to Djerejian in the FIS guesthouse in downtown Moscow,[5] the entire conversation was devoted to the prospects of a Middle East settlement. We focused on Syria. I told Edward, "It's important to understand that Damascus won't agree to peace with Israel unless the Golan Heights are returned, however slowly, step by step with some concessions on Syria's part. But the understanding that Israel will withdraw from all of the Golan Heights must be mapped out very early in the process. This approach could cover the questions of demilitarization, the locations of observation posts, joint patrols, and other measures that obviously have to be agreed upon with Damascus."

I was very surprised to see that Djerejian was unprepared even to consider Syria's possible agreement to Israel's gradual withdrawal. He was making notes in his notebook throughout our conversation. Recalling this extremely useful discussion—useful for me, at least—I once again think how far we could have advanced toward a Middle East settlement if the United States and Russia had coordinated their diplomatic and political efforts. Unfortunately, the central figure in the development and implementation of U.S. Middle East policy was Dennis Ross, who seems to have been thinking in different terms.

By the time I left Yasenevo for Smolenskaya Square, the situation in the Middle East was still complex and even explosive, although there was some room for optimism. The positions of Israel and the PLO came closer together. The steps of the Israeli troop withdrawal from a considerable part of the West Bank were outlined; basic features of Palestinian self-government were discussed, as were such issues as the creation of a corridor between Gaza and the West Bank and the building of an airport in Gaza. According to Syrian leaders, they received firm assurances from the United States, which in turn referred to the Israeli leadership, that Israel was prepared to withdraw its troops from the Golan Heights eventually.

But by that time it had become clear that the United States was once again insisting on their solo performance in the peace process. This time Washington, in essence, not only turned its back on the Russian co-chairman of the Madrid peace conference but also did not wish to cooperate with the Europeans in carrying out its peacemaking mission in the Middle East. As I mentioned earlier, the subject of the Middle East used to come up in my discussions with Christopher and Albright, but that was as far as it went.

As Russia's minister of foreign affairs, I toured the Middle East three times, and each time I became convinced all over again that great opportunities had been lost because of the United States' unwillingness to relinquish its role of sole mediator between the parties involved in the Middle East conflict.

In April 1996 the heads of the Big Eight came to Moscow just as the crisis in Lebanon exploded. The exchange of fire between Hezbollah militants' Katyusha rockets against northern Galilee and the Israeli air force and artillery against the villages of southern Lebanon foreshadowed the escalation of military operations. There was even a forecast of a large-scale Israeli ground operation.

Chirac was insisting on sending me to the site of the conflict. U.S. Secretary of State Christopher and Italian Foreign Minister Anielli were already there. My French colleague Hervé de Charette went there as well. Clinton also supported the idea of my trip, adding that he would give Christopher instructions to work closely with me and the others. Yeltsin sanctioned the trip, and literally the next day, April 20, I was in Damascus.

I immediately phoned Christopher. I assumed that, under Clinton's instructions, he would quickly turn to a joint effort. When I proposed that we four ministers get together and coordinate our actions, however, he reacted with reserve. I never met with him on that trip. I don't think Charette had any more luck than I did. After he talked with the secretary of state, he told me indignantly that Christopher looked reserved and did not lay his cards on the table, didn't even care to inform him of the nature of his talks with the Syrian leaders. In a word, he was pulling the blanket over his head. Susan also looked discouraged.

That being the case, we decided to keep in close touch with each other and try to act in concert to facilitate a settlement. Both Charette and I had quite a few opportunities, and we took advantage of them. The foreign minister of Iran, Ali-Akbar Velayati, who undoubtedly had influence on Hezbollah, came to Damascus. Charette met with him once and I had several meetings with him; Christopher couldn't squeeze one in. My talks with Velayati hadn't an iota of diplomacy. This was by no means the first time we had met, and we called a spade a spade.

Finally, I was the only one who met with Hussein al-Halil, a member of the Hezbollah leadership who came to Damascus from Beirut for this meeting. I was pleasantly surprised by his lack of bias, his willingness to listen, and his realistic approach to the situation. The conversation was very practical and useful. Afterward Halil immediately returned to Beirut.

On the surface, then, it looked as if the United States, acting alone, had brought the parties to compromise: both sides agreed to a cease-fire and an international commission of observers was set up. Incidentally, the Americans did not include Russia in this commission, although I must admit we didn't seek to be included, because we thought the commission was stillborn, an assessment that was subsequently confirmed. In reality there were more authors of the settlement than one, but not all of them were in the spotlight. By the way, the Syrians preferred to remain anonymous. It was to their advantage that the United States could try to influence Hezbollah and Iran only through Damascus.

I left Damascus for Jerusalem. During my meeting with Shimon Peres on April 22, 1996, the prime minister, who had met with Christopher not long before, told me, "We need only one mediator, and it should be the United States." But even that unequivocal statement did not make us lose heart.

I made another trip to the Middle East in October, visiting Syria, Lebanon, Egypt, Israel, and Jordan. In preparation for that trip we had a series of meetings and decided that the main problem was to keep the peace process from stalling. This tendency became more prominent when the Likud government came to power in Israel. In those circumstances, an intermediate agreement on two issues could acquire special meaning. The first was an obligation to continue in force the agreements reached by their predecessors. Since the settlement process is so protracted, that issue acquires strategic importance not only for the Arabs but also for the Israelis. Israel cannot afford to ignore the need for continuity in its policy when changes in the leadership of the

PLO and some Arab countries are imminent. The second issue is simultaneous progress on all facets of the settlement.

We had prepared a document and proposed to sign it serially, without gathering everyone together. In Cairo President Mubarak and Foreign Minister Amr Musa assented to the proposed agreement. In Damascus the Syrians were receptive, but they wanted to add provisions that Israel was unlikely to endorse. After talking with Assad and later with the Israeli leadership, I became convinced that the proposal could not be reduced to writing just now. (We called it a "cross," where continuity was a vertical line and simultaneous progress was a horizontal one.) But I think the discussions with the leaders of the parties involved in the conflict were beneficial.

On October 31 in Tel Aviv I met the new prime minister of Israel, Biniamin Netanyahu, whom I had heard a lot about. Clearly he was departing from agreements that had been reached with the Arabs by his predecessors Yitzhak Rabin, murdered by a Jewish terrorist, and Shimon Peres. The Arab leaders I had a chance to meet with at the time stressed that it would be unrealistic to move toward peace with Netanyahu in power, since it was impossible to reach an agreement with him and even less so to implement an accord even if one was reached. The Americans were also annoyed.

Frankly, that's not quite the way I saw it. Not that I did not actively oppose Netanyahu's abandonment of efforts to reach a political settlement. I told him so directly, mincing no words. I made my attitude doubly clear by going to Gaza after my meeting with Netanyahu and meeting with the Palestinian leadership, headed by Arafat. At the press conference I stated (as I had done publicly in Israel) that Russia categorically insisted on the implementation of the Madrid formula of territories in exchange for peace and was against any attempts by the Israeli leadership to depart from any agreements reached earlier. At the same time, it seemed to me that one could do business with Netanyahu in seeking to settle the conflict.

First, he was altogether different from Peres. Netanyahu told me, "My position is that Russia must take a more active role in the Middle East political settlement. These are not just words, this is my position."

To my mind the fact that Netanyahu did not fear any blows from the right, since he himself stood at the extreme end of Israel's right-wing political forces, bore some promise for the future. History shows that a lack of such fears often facilitates the solution of the most difficult issues. Characteristically, peace between Egypt and Israel was signed when such right-wing politicians as Sadat and Begin were at the helm in their countries. I wouldn't want anyone to think I advocate the idea that right-wing politicians, especially those on the extreme right, should rule countries involved in a conflict. But that's life.[6]

Bibi, as he is known in Israel, linked all issues of conflict resolution with the problem of Israel's security, as he saw it. When I first met him he was far from understanding that Israel's security was ensured not by the presence of its troops on the Golan Heights but by peace with Syria, which was impossible unless those troops were withdrawn. Nor could Netanyahu rise above himself when I said to him, "Listen, why don't you declare that you will agree to withdraw from the Golan Heights with many ifs? Formulate those ifs in a way that links them to Israel's security. But their fulfillment must first be linked to your readiness to withdraw completely from the occupied territories."

I must say that even back in 1996 Netanyahu realized the need to resume the negotiation process not only with the Palestinians but also with the Syrians. He agreed with me that while Israeli troops were being withdrawn from Lebanon, a direct or indirect agreement with Syria should be reached, and that the withdrawal should in no way threaten Syria's interests.

At our second meeting, a year later in Jerusalem, Netanyahu began talking about the possibility of mediation between him and Assad. This time we were dealing with a concrete situation.

At that time anxiety was written on the faces of many Israelis. The mass media spread rumors about the movement of elite Syrian troops, ready to attack the Golan Heights at any moment. A few months later the Israeli press revealed that Israeli military intelligence, in an attempt to inflate its accomplishments, misinformed the country's leadership regarding Syria's alleged preparations to capture some of the Golan territory. But that was later. When I met with him on October 26, 1997, Netanyahu, without naming his source, insisted he had reliable information about the Syrians' true intentions. He may have even assumed that we knew about Syria's plans. When we confronted the journalists after our meeting, he openly enjoyed my answer to one of the questions: I said Russia was against any violation of the ceasefire in the Golan Heights, no matter who was responsible. At the same time, I told Netanyahu that I did not believe Syria would initiate a military operation. But fueled by mutual suspicion, the tension was really growing. Before I arrived in Israel I was told in Damascus that the Israeli army, reinforced earlier, held military exercises on the Heights.

"Could you tell the Syrian leadership we shall not be the first to start military action?" asked Netanyahu.

"I will do it personally, and I will arrange a meeting with Hafez Assad," I replied.

So I made a shuttle trip to Syria and met with the president, who asked me to convey similar assurances to the Israelis.

And when we met in Moscow early in 1999, when I was serving as prime minister, Netanyahu spoke of the need for "general mediation" by Russia. I would not say he was against the U.S. mission, but he did want to dilute it. Doubtless he also understood that Russia was acquiring greater potential for an active role in the peace process. Long gone were the days when we stood on one foot, essentially without having any position in Israel. I met with Natan Sharansky (by tradition we called him Anatoly Borisovich), the same Sharansky who had spent nine years in Soviet prisons and camps for his "Zionist ideas." After he emigrated to Israel, he created a "Russian party" of immigrants like himself and became a minister in Netanyahu's government. Sharansky told me with a touch of pride that he represented a diaspora of almost one million; that the Russian-language press was the most interesting and popular in Israel; that Russian immigrants were gaining political weight; and that they felt nostalgic about Russia and were sure it could play an important role in the Middle East peace process.

When Ehud Barak's government came to power in Israel, in May 1999, the United States actively pursued a Middle East settlement. President Clinton, stepping in as heavy artillery, made special trips to the region and received the leaders of Israel and the Palestine Liberation Organization in Washington on many occasions. The Palestinian parliament removed from its charter the statement that the PLO's goal was the elimination of the state of Israel. With the help of Secretary of State Albright we succeeded in moving closer to an agreement on the content of the various stages of the Israeli withdrawal from the West Bank. We welcomed these diplomatic and political successes of the United States. I kept saying so to Madeleine and publicly at press conferences.

But was that the end of the peace process?

Unfortunately, events at the end of 2000 revealed that the answer was no. After Ariel Sharon, Likud's new leader, made a well-publicized tour of the Temple Mount, site of Al-Aqsa Mosque, a holy place to the Muslims, the situation in the West Bank and East Jerusalem exploded. The negotiation process was torpedoed. The number of casualties, most of them Palestinians, grew daily. The Israeli soldiers who fought against them suffered casualties as well. Then followed terrorist attacks against Israeli settlers on the West Bank and Israeli gunfire against Palestinian villages.

What next?

In mid-2001, after several visits to Middle Eastern countries, I realized that we faced the prospect of continued violence, even an escalation of violence, and that conclusion horrified me. In that case, the street would take over and politicians would often be forced to follow its will. It would be especially tough for Egypt and Jordan, which have already established diplomatic relations with Israel.

How to break this circle of violence? Both sides have adopted the Mitchell Plan, according to which both the Palestinians and the Israelis were to declare a cease-fire. They have done so many times, but Israel insists on a pause between the cease-fire announcement and the beginning of talks. During that pause the Israelis will allegedly make sure that the cease-fire is stable. Only after that will they be ready to sit down and talk.

The suggested prenegotiation regime (and this was secured in the Israeli position) can only torpedo the idea of a peaceful settlement. Sharon must know that Arafat would like to stop the violence from the Palestinian side, but is unable to build a dam strong enough to hold back the streams of terrorists determined to break through it. That is beyond his power. Such a dam could be built only by a compromise Israeli-Palestinian agreement to create a Palestinian state in the West Bank and Gaza Strip. Only then can there be any realistic chance for Israel's security, not just Arafat's desire to assist in it.

This approach has nothing in common with even indirect support of violence against civilians. As a matter of fact, not only Russia but the Soviet Union as well condemned such actions. I recall a time when I worked at the Academy of Sciences and the Central Committee of the Communist Party assigned me and Yury Gryadunov, the future ambassador to Jordan, to go to Beirut. We met with the leadership of the People's Front for the Liberation of Palestine (PFLP) and demanded that they stop hijacking airplanes. That was at the very end of 1970. The hijacking did stop, and later the PFLP admitted that they had bowed to Soviet pressure. We have always believed that no attack against a civilian population can be justified by any idea of national liberation, as some people were trying to establish.

At the same time it should not be overlooked that the Israelis also act against civilian populations. Palestinian villages are being targeted by tanks and missiles.

In order to break the circle of violence, the parties have to sit at the negotiating table. With shifting chances for success, they could be brought there by an expanded mediation group including the United States, Russia, the European Union, and the United Nations.

By the time I moved to the high-rise building on Smolenskaya Square, the task of resolving conflict situations not only in the Middle East but elsewhere, this time on the territory of the former USSR, such as the conflicts between Georgia and Abkhazia, Georgia and Southern Ossetia, and the situation around Nagorno-Karabakh and Moldova, had became one of the highest priorities for the Foreign Ministry. For all their differences, these conflicts had a common underlying cause: the aspiration of a national minority to separate from the region to which it was unwillingly bound.

What should be done in such cases? Taking into consideration that two thousand nationalities and peoples live in more than 150 states, one can conclude that the general policy should be to ensure the rights of national minorities in multinational states. This became Russia's guideline. We did not confine ourselves to making general statements on the need to resolve these conflicts, but advanced concrete proposals to safeguard the territorial integrity of Georgia, Azerbaijan, and Moldova while providing wide-ranging rights to such national formations as Abkhazia, Southern Ossetia, Nagorno-Karabakh, and Pridnestrovie within the framework of those states.

Unfortunately, we have failed to resolve those conflict situations. But if full-scale wars have been stopped, if the conflicting sides have begun to negotiate with each other and are still doing so now, if the sprouts of mutual understanding are beginning to appear, then I can confidently say that these advances are due to Russia's policy and its direct political and economic involvement. Much of my hair turned gray as a result of meetings, negotiations, and trips to conflict zones, especially in my capacity as foreign minister. I was in Baku in 1990, when anti-Armenian pogroms were taking place, the People's Front threw off all restraint, and Russian troops were brought in. I made shuttle flights between Baku and Yerevan, flew by helicopter to Nagorno-Karabakh to exchange POWs on the Red Cross lists—over two hundred of them, some of whom had been sentenced to death. Taking every precaution, I used my plane to bring the Abkhazian leader Vladislav Ardzimba, who had been outlawed, to Tbilisi for talks with Shevardnadze. It is simply impossible to mention everything—the list is far too long.

CHAPTER NINE

Chairman of the Government

DECISION IN THE CORRIDOR

The eight months I served as head of the Russian government were the most difficult period of my life. For two days Yeltsin urged me to head the government and I flatly refused. The last conversation on the subject took place in his office on September 12, 1998, in the presence of Viktor Stepanovich Chernomyrdin and Yury Sergeevich Maslyukov.[1] A few days earlier Chernomyrdin, who had been asked to resign as prime minister in March, had been named prime minister once again when Sergei Kirienko was ousted after less than six months in office.

By September 12 Yeltsin had proposed Chernomyrdin for the post twice, and twice the State Duma had rejected him. There was no doubt that a third vote would go the same way. Yet Viktor Stepanovich decided not to withdraw his name, principally because Yeltsin had told him that he'd made a mistake when he asked him to resign in March.

Yeltsin was not about to retreat, either. Retreating was not in his nature. If the Duma rejects a candidate three times, it is automatically dissolved, so there wasn't much room for maneuver. Suddenly Chernomyrdin said, "I'm willing not to go to the Duma a third time if Primakov is offered as candidate." I once again refused.

Chernomyrdin's offer came as a surprise to me. Viktor Stepanovich and I had worked together a long time. I was part of the cabinet he headed and

I was one of those whose opinion he listened to. He knew I was very much against the attempts to cause dissension between the president and the chairman of the government. Those attempts were made constantly by the people who surrounded Yeltsin.

The pressure against Chernomyrdin mounted when he started to gain prominence abroad, especially in the Russian-American commission that he and Vice President Gore headed. Yeltsin's annoyance was also aggravated artificially by the independent role the prime minister played in negotiations to save the hundreds of hostages held by Chechen terrorists after they captured the Budennovsk hospital in 1995. The whole country watched Chernomyrdin, not Yeltsin, on TV as he talked by phone with the Chechens. This was unacceptable to the Family.

As a human being I wanted to support Chernomyrdin after his March resignation. An opportunity presented itself within a few days. A big party was thrown to celebrate Chernomyrdin's sixtieth birthday in an effort to flatter the ousted prime minister. The reception was held in a state-owned mansion and the Russian elite were invited. There was a wonderful concert, and tables groaned under culinary delights. The president himself presented a bouquet of sixty red roses to Chernomyrdin. It was obvious that Chernomyrdin felt awkward. Not far from him sat the new prime minister, Kirienko, who soon left the party with Yeltsin. I don't think Viktor Stepanovich, having just turned sixty, appreciated the speeches about the need to "make way for the young." Then I went up to his table and offered a toast. (This toast was not aimed at Kirienko, whom I respect as a very capable and, no less important, honest man.)

"An old man and a young man argued about who was smarter. The old man proposed that they see who could climb up a tree and take an egg out of a bird's nest without moving the little bird that was hatching the eggs. The young man tried, and the bird flew away. The old man said, 'Watch how it's done.' He took off his coat and sable fur hat, climbed up the tree, and took an egg from under the bird, which did not move. When he climbed down, he found that neither his coat nor his hat was there. So let's drink to the young generation!"

Everyone, including the young, laughed loudly.

But on September 12, 1999, I wasn't laughing. When I came out of the president's office I ran into a few people who were waiting for me: the head of the Presidential Administration, Valentin Yumashev; the head of Presidential Protocol, Vladimir Shevchenko; and Boris Nikolaevich's daughter, Tatiana Dyachenko. I spread my hands, saying I couldn't accept Yeltsin's offer. Volodya Shevchenko, with whom I have been friends for years, almost exploded. I have never seen him so agitated.

"How can you think only of yourself? Don't you understand what we're facing? August seventeenth destroyed the economy.[2] There is no government. The Duma will be dissolved. The president may be physically unable to perform his duties at any moment. Don't you have any sense of responsibility?"

"But why me?" I answered.

"Because today, of all the candidates, the Duma will be satisfied only with you, and because you will succeed."

When I impetuously agreed, they rushed to hug me. Someone ran to tell the president.

There is no doubt that the president and I got along well. Up to the time I received the offer to become prime minister, over many years of working together, I never detected suspicion, annoyance, or even a commanding tone from Yeltsin. Yeltsin was not famous for level-headed relationships with the people under him. I was never included in the narrow and ever-changing circle of people who surrounded him. I had no wish to be included in that circle. He kept a certain distance as well and never invited me to his home or to impromptu feasts with his friends. However, I had reason to believe that Yeltsin valued me for my work and as a colleague and wanted me in the most critical posts. Not too many people received, as I did, the new Russia's highest honors, the medals "For Service to the Fatherland" in the third and second degrees. At the time it didn't occur to me that I might be viewed simply as a transitional figure, someone whose job was simply to keep the lid on. In my opinion, Yeltsin did not plan such a fate for me. Even after everything I have lived through, I have trouble believing he had such underhanded motives for pushing me forward for the post of prime minister.

I won't describe in detail what my family and friends thought about my decision to agree. My wife said, "What's done is done, stop crying over it." My friends were divided; some thought I had made the right decision and some thought I had not. But this negative attitude was immediately replaced by unconditional support from my wife, children, grown-up grandchildren, and all my friends, without exception.

On the same day, September 12, the president sent my name to the State Duma.

While the Duma was considering my appointment, I made no gener-
ous promises. I said I was not a magician, and that the government I would
head would be unable to bring prosperity and affluence to a country in deep
crisis. At the end I made a remark that was more prescient than I realized:
"As far as I personally am concerned, I don't know what's best for me: whether
you vote for or against me."

I received 317 yea votes, more than the constitutionally required majority.
This was a record of some kind. The nay votes were cast only by Vladimir
Zhirinovsky's Liberal Democratic Party of Russia (LDPR). A few days later
Zhirinovsky came to see me in the White House, the seat of the Russian
government, to tell me, "Pay no attention, this is politics. I personally have
a wonderful opinion of you and I'll support you."

Such strong support from the State Duma helped ease the process of
forming a government. Things were easier also because both the president
and his advisers decided not to force any candidates on me as deputies, ministers, or other high government officials, the usual practice before and after
I was prime minister. The Kremlin's unusual restraint was attributable to
some confusion, fear that I might dig in my heels, and unwillingness to take
responsibility for the tragically grave economic situation. The government's
inability to pay its accumulated multibillion-dollar debts was made even more
painful by the refusal of the International Monetary Fund (IMF) and the
International Bank for Reconstruction and Development (IBRD) to keep
their commitments to extend new amounts of credit. It was decided to let
the new head of government and the ministers he picked untangle that mess.

It was clear to me that the government would be unable to function
without close ties to the Duma. But how could those ties be developed? In
some countries this question is solved simply by creating a governmental
majority. In others, such as the United States, the elected president supervises
the formation of the government. In a number of countries, a parliamentary
plurality creates a coalition government. In Russia there were no constitutional or political provisions for any of these solutions. That is why I gave
the highest priority to the candidates' professionalism when I formed the
government. But membership in the parties and movements represented
in the State Duma could not be ignored either. At the same time, it was vital
to prevent the government from becoming hostage to those parties.

Maslyukov's candidacy was predetermined. I offered him the position
of first deputy prime minister for economic affairs. The reason was not only

that he was a member of the Communist Party of the Russian Federation (CPRF), which had the largest representation in the Duma. In him I saw a good specialist who possessed detailed knowledge of industry, especially the military-industrial complex. He was open to new ideas, but at the same time he was balanced and practical. I knew that in his work he was guided by common sense and an interest in getting things done.

At first I thought the other deputy should handle social issues. Who could be the leader in this crucial line of work?

As if he had heard my question, my secretary came into the office and said Grigory Yavlinsky wanted to talk to me for a few minutes. We had a very detailed talk. It appeared that the movement he headed, Yabloko, was ready to help the government. The conversation was frank, since we had known each other a long time and we treated each other well, or so I think, despite occasional clashes when Yavlinsky made remarks I considered ill advised.

I offered him the post of first deputy prime minister, along with Maslyukov, to be in charge of social issues. Yavlinsky refused.

The government was formed in September.

I had no hesitation regarding the candidacy of Viktor Gerashchenko, or "Hercules," as he was nicknamed, for chairman of the board of the Central Bank. This key position was of special interest to those in the president's circle; they played their own game, which had nothing to do with the interests of society.

In view of the severity of the economic situation in the country, which was to a large extent due to the activities of the former leadership of the Central Bank, it was especially important to put forward a candidate who was not only an excellent banker but also a reliable man who was not prone to taking unnecessary risks. Gerashchenko satisfied those demands better than anyone else.

The government included people who belonged to various political organizations, such as the CPRF (two), the Agrarian Party (two), the LDPR (one), Yabloko (one), and Regions of Russia (one). Some of the new ministers were sympathetic to different parties and movements though not official members. Was this a coalition government? I don't think it was, mainly because everyone included in it obeyed the rules of the game as we set them up among us. From the very beginning we agreed that it was unacceptable for any political organization to force any obligation on a cabinet minister. I won't deny that the leaders of many factions in the State Duma presented candidates, but we never gave political considerations higher priority than professional criteria.

The administration made some indirect attempts to influence my choice of candidates. For instance, Yeltsin's daughter, Tatiana Dyachenko, very much wanted to see someone other than my candidate as minister of health. Her candidate was not a doctor and was dependent on certain financial circles, according to some sources. Dyachenko even asked my wife to use her influence on me. My wife answered that she never discussed my work and had no influence over me.

Yury Zubakov became chief of staff. He had worked with me previously for ten years as a consultant in the Presidential Council and had also been deputy director of the Foreign Intelligence Service and deputy minister of foreign affairs. I immediately ordered him to put all documents in order, make sure that all meetings and government decisions were organized and prepared accurately, and prevent any leaks of information. Information leaks were almost daily occurrences at that time.

Strange people were loitering about the government building. Nobody knew who had issued them passes, when they had issued the passes, or why. These people could easily walk into an office and out again with any documents they found there. We lost a lot of information about government plans. Similar damage was done when drafts of documents in preparation were copied by persons unidentified and then published in newspapers and magazines as decrees already adopted. In reality, preliminary drafts often bore very little resemblance to the eventual decrees.

When we strengthened the rules governing visits to the White House, a number of newspapers and magazines complained that we were resisting glasnost. Far from resisting it, I decided that every Saturday I would meet with government-accredited journalists and tell them in detail about the work that was under way. We had a few such meetings, but they could not go on because some participants demonstrated a complete lack of journalistic ethics and published information that was given to them off the record.

Rumors spread about my presumed unaccommodating and even confrontational attitude toward the press. It was said that I couldn't bear criticism. There were even stories that I showed Yeltsin a collection of articles critical of me that were underlined with different-colored markers. That, by the way, was what he wrote in his memoirs. It was all nothing but idle gossip.

Certainly I find it unpleasant when an article provides deceptive information or misquotes me. That's all. As for my cooperation with journalists, I never avoided them even before I came to the government. Furthermore, I attended ITAR-TASS dinner meetings with heads of the mass media and answered their questions frankly. These meetings continued even after a staff member who accompanied me discovered that my answers were being recorded on tape in the next room, though we had previously agreed they were not meant for the press.

I was a professional journalist for fifteen years. I respect and value the selfless, difficult work of journalists, without which a normal society cannot exist. And I firmly believe that journalists who permit themselves to be bought will soon become exceptions to the rule in Russia.

WHAT WE INHERITED

The tasks that were facing the government were truly immense.

By mid-1998 processes were fully developed in Russia that pushed the country toward the abyss. Production was declining; unemployment was rising; month after month state-employed workers, members of the military, and pensioners were not being paid. Strikes not only were breaking out all over the country but were becoming increasingly dangerous. In May strikers started to block railways and roads, threatening to shut down the factories that were still operating. When I came to the White House, miners had organized a tent encampment in front of the entrance. Periodically they pounded their hard hats against the pavement, demanding their pay. The floor of the Central Bank's currency exchange-rate band, within which the ruble traded against the dollar, began to shatter.

There is reason to believe that this was the logical result of the course of economic development initiated in 1992. Those who took responsibility for Russia's economic policy at that time called themselves liberals, stressing their connection to the Chicago school, whose representatives were widely known in the West. An important factor was that these people enjoyed full support in the West; nobody there seemed to realize the grave consequences of the policies forced on Russia by these "liberals."

Generally speaking, modern liberalism as a school of thought advocates free competition with minimal interference by the government in market activities. This approach narrows the function of the state to quite distinct and limited tasks, such as reducing the burden of taxation and ensuring fair competition, which should result in the optimal use of revenue by enterprises and consumers.

International experience shows that the matrix of the liberal approach to the economy can never be universally applied to the pulsing reality of any country without consideration of its particularities, its history, and the state structures that are already built into the economy. All this was ignored in the case of Russia. As home-grown liberals destroyed the existing production mechanisms, they conducted a shock liberalization of prices accompanied by privatization for the sake of privatization, and its main concern was the broad scope of the operation rather than its connection to the efficiency of production. The economy was opened up all at once. The internal market was exposed to the toughest international competition, and no thought was given to the ability of Russian enterprises to survive.

The approaches taken to create the market infrastructure were unorthodox, to say the least. An obvious example is the manipulation of state bonds, known as GKOs. The following strategy was developed: The Finance Ministry put its financial resources into selected banks at low interest rates. The banks bought GKOs with the state's money. The profits came from an unimaginable 150–200 percent annual interest rate. Huge sums were transferred to the West, in many cases deposited in the accounts of corrupt officials who had promoted this strategy.

The development of a securities market is undoubtedly important and necessary for the development of a market economy. But this is the case only if this market becomes an instrument to attract domestic and foreign investment in the development of industry. In Russia capital went into the highly profitable GKO market and practically turned its back on financing Russian industry, agriculture, transport, and construction. It was used mainly for short-term speculation. Production and the availability of finished products declined sharply in Russia. People with low incomes were the hardest hit.

Sure enough, reforms facilitated the appearance of a middle class and an entrepreneurial social stratum. Because these reforms were carried out in a rather peculiar way, however, they enriched a small group of people with unprecedented speed. Among them are the people who have come to be called "oligarchs." Within a few years they managed to create fortunes in billions of dollars.

Promoting the interests of this small group of oligarchs, the pseudoliberals redistributed Russia's natural resources in their favor. The oligarchs received support during privatization and auction winners were determined in advance. Using the holes in the budget as an excuse, state officials transferred state-owned enterprises to the oligarchs at prices that were clearly too low.

The oligarchs in turn did everything they could to preserve the political power of those who helped them skim the cream without having to make their money on the growth of production and development of the service sector. Their tentacles reached the circles that were close to Yeltsin. The oligarchs were instrumental in his 1996 reelection and as a result had a say in economic and personnel policies, either directly or through their representatives, and so made the policies more beneficial to them.

In his book *The State and Evolution,* Yegor Gaidar explained the necessity of an "exchange of power for property." But as the exchange was conducted in the 1990s, the result was not a giving up of power in exchange for property but a merging of state power with ownership, this time on a new, postcommunist basis. This process was seen most clearly in the circles close to the president. It is possible that he was not aware of all the details.

It became obvious that the people who formulated and implemented the economic course in the 1990s chose goals and methods that had nothing to do with the liberal approach and sometimes were directly opposed to it. The state intervened in ways that balked the creation of conditions of equal competition between producing entities. The government selectively supported certain enterprises by setting exclusive export quotas, especially for oil, relieving them of customs duties, giving them tax exemptions and credits for specific purposes, and so on. All this did nothing to provide incentives for people on the cutting edge of scientific and technological progress or to encourage investment in the production of badly needed products—steps that had to be taken at the beginning if the economy was to flourish.

Privileges were offered to commercial banks in accordance with their closeness to the people in power. Some of these banks received the right to service state programs, including such immensely profitable ones as arms trading.

The financing of Russia's regions was carried out on the basis of subjective decisions by the federal government. I was flabbergasted to discover that the resort city of Sochi was among the group of "depressed" regions. That's where the country's leaders go for their vacations. Meanwhile Bryansk oblast, whose population suffered most acutely from the Chernobyl tragedy, was not on the list.

The situation was worsened by indifference to unwarranted budget expenditures. It should be enough to cite the number of people employed by the various ministries and departments of the central government (not counting security agencies). They number more than 300,000, and in addition to their salaries they are provided with cars and apartments paid for by the state.

Emphasis on macroeconomic policy was most likely an end in itself for Russia's "liberals." In any event, macroeconomic regulation did nothing to develop the industrial sector (production continued to decline) and did not result in positive social changes (standards of living declined; pension and health reforms never got off the ground). It is believed that in a market economy, a 30 to 40 percent reduction in inflation should be accompanied by a rise in production and an increase in investment. In Russia inflation was reduced far below that threshold, but production continued to decline.

Naturally, all this exacerbated social tension. The liberals tried to vent some pressure by borrowing money from abroad. The money borrowed became a necessary support for the ugly economy and in effect made the whole country dependent.

Generally speaking, the pseudoliberals' reforms cost Russia a great deal. The economic model that was created was characterized by a lack of balance between domestic production and consumption, supported mainly by exports of raw materials and imports of food and other products.

The amount of investment was too low to assist in development. The amount of Russian capital sent abroad far exceeded the money that flowed in from lenders. Domestic producers depended on domestic suppliers and vice versa; the amount of money that changed hands was low and falling.

It cannot be overemphasized that the economic course chosen by the pseudoliberals provided a lot of room for corruption, economic crimes, and arbitrary rule by state officials. Billions of dollars were illegally appropriated, stolen in the course of machinations, and siphoned abroad. All this incredibly hampered the transition to market relations in Russia and made the transition even more painful for the majority of people. The development of a market economy, unavoidably accompanied at first by inflation, decline in production, and reduction in living standards, was achieved by other countries in a relatively short time. Russia became a champion not only in the depth of the problems encountered during the transition process but also in the duration and intensity of the hardships suffered by the people and society in general.

To a large degree the fundamental unwillingness of the Russian pseudoliberals to fight economic crime fostered this situation. By mid-1998 it became clear that their economic program had brought the country to a dead end. On August 17 a moratorium was declared on payments to owners of GKOs and government bonds (OFZs). This move catastrophically aggravated Russia's numerous economic, social, and political problems.

I think the people who made those decisions on August 17 did not foresee what the consequences would be, and they thought that asking the advice of people of other economic schools of thought was unnecessary and even humiliating. Unfortunately, this was a common failing among the reformers, who found themselves in leading economic positions after the events of the 1990s but had no significant experience in the field. They often disregarded the opinions of others in Russia and let their power go to their heads as they plunged into thoughtless and finally irresponsible experimentation on a huge scale.

The decisions made on August 17 were a tragic mistake. But were they a mistake for everyone who had a hand in them? To this day I can't find an answer to this logical question: Why, on the eve of those decisions, in the summer of 1998, was $4 billion put into euro bonds at very high rates? Why was the leadership of the Central Bank ready to spend so many dollars, which were so expensive at that time, on the eve of the inevitable devaluation?

Was the president informed of the upcoming government and Central Bank decisions? Later I was told that a few people told him in general terms about what was about to be done. But they assured the president that the Treasury would receive an additional 80 billion rubles, that the exchange rate would fall and inflation might increase a little, but only briefly, and that in a short time all negative consequences would vanish, everything would return to normal, and the budget would receive the funds it so crucially needed.

I don't know whether Yeltsin was told about this, but the IMF was informed about the preparation for this joint action by the government and the Central Bank. By the way, when I later met the deputy director of the IMF, who came to Moscow and talked down to us, I had to interrupt him to say that the decisions of August 17 had been discussed with the IMF representative (I got this information from Finance Minister Mikhail Zadornov), so there was no cause to represent the IMF as a supreme arbiter that had nothing to do with what happened.

When the stunning outcomes of those decisions became clear, Yeltsin in conversations with me was not shy about saying what he thought of the people who made them, although no names were disclosed.

When I became head of the government, I thought—and in essence this is how it really was—that Yeltsin had not been privy to the events that brought the Russian economy to its knees. Answering a journalist's question on whether the president was aware of the move that was being prepared, I said no. Yeltsin's advisers were extremely sensitive about this statement, probably suspecting that I wanted to show Yeltsin as being removed from the events that were taking place in Russia, and not sufficiently involved in the key issues of economic policy. Well, I did my best to help him.

It is possible that the Family had a different reason for their negative reaction: they may have feared that acknowledgment that Yeltsin had nothing to do with the matter would remove the shield they used to cover themselves.

Meanwhile the real price that Russia and the Russians paid for the unprofessional, to say the least, decisions of August 17 was huge. The gross domestic product (GDP) sharply declined, production went into free fall, the banking system stopped functioning, and payments virtually ground to a halt. Even the railroads stopped delivery of cargo. The national economy was on the brink of total collapse.

In the first week of September, inflation exceeded 15 percent, and despite urgent measures taken by the government, it was up to 38 percent by the end of the month. In essence the country faced hyperinflation. The uncontrollable devaluation of the ruble exploded consumer prices. As a result, people's real income in September 1998 was 25 percent less than it had been in September 1997. The value of citizens' savings in rubles shrank alarmingly. People whose savings were in banks that went bankrupt lost everything.

Because the country was dependent for food and medicine on imports and money was not available to pay for them, the supply of basic goods was threatened.

Perhaps the most serious consequence of August 17 was a crisis of trust. Loss of trust was a disease that struck all links of the economic system: relations between producers and consumers, debtors and creditors, managers and owners, population and security forces, as well as various branches and levels of the executive power. The unilateral moratorium on payments for state-issued securities announced on August 17 completely undermined confidence, both at home and abroad, in the possibility of stable cooperation with Russia's financial institutions and commercial banks.

The very possibility of Russia's transition to a market system was in doubt.

Official circles in the West clearly supported the policy that was implemented in Russia in the 1990s. The prevailing view seemed to be that any departure from the centrally administered system of the Soviet period toward a market economy was an absolute blessing, regardless of the forms and methods used to bring it about. I can't exclude the possibility that some forces refused to criticize the pseudoliberals because they hoped that Russia would remain for many years a supplier of raw materials to the states that were already well advanced in the postproduction phase of their development.

The lack of criticism of Russia's economic policy by the leaders of Western states was motivated by politics. It is difficult to imagine that Western leaders absent-mindedly neglected to mention this subject when they talked with their Russian colleagues and those who stood at the helm of Russia's economic policy. Perhaps they simply didn't want to irritate their "friend and brother Boris." I doubt that this was the main reason. I think it goes much deeper. The West seemed to fear that any criticism would strengthen the proponents of a stronger state role in the economy, even those who were firmly on the side of market reforms and privatization but wanted them to be implemented in a way that took the needs of production into consideration. The West feared them because the increased influence of such forces over foreign policy would inevitably lead to a more assertive defense of Russia's national interests. In my opinion, the Western politicians in power at the time made a serious mistake when they shied from developing contacts with those politicians in Russia.

Was I aware of the true state of the Russian economy in the 1990s before I was appointed prime minister? Certainly I saw and felt a lot, and disagreed with many things, and criticized them among my friends. I could not remain an indifferent observer. I never joined the "liberals" and I had no respect for many of them. I did not include them among my friends. But I did not make public statements against the economic course they were taking. I could not do that when I headed the Foreign Intelligence Service and then the Foreign Ministry. On many occasions, however, I told the president the impartial opinions of our foreign sources, especially regarding actions of the "liberals" that bordered on the criminal. He listened to those reports but had nothing to say about them.

Of course the full picture became clear to me when I became head of the government during that difficult time.

STRATEGY AND TACTICS

What is to be done? This eternal Russian question once again demanded an answer, this time from me. Keeping in mind that the main goal was to calm down the society and stabilize the situation, I decided first of all to determine what should not be done in these circumstances.

The Russian economy fallen flat on its back, the knockout blow against the country's living standards, the burning anger over the 1990s economic policy that enveloped society, the president's confusion, the desire of those who had made their way to the top of political power to slip into the shadows —all these factors untied the government's hands. Later on, when I was lumped with the extreme left, I thought they didn't understand a thing. Back then I could have started nationalizing everything, instituted comprehensive punishment for economic crimes, put sharp limits on the convertibility of the ruble, refused to pay foreign debts. And all dissenting voices, if any dared to speak, would have been drowned by shouts of public support. But such measures could not be reconciled with the worldview I hold. I also understood that they would have torn the society apart, destabilizing the situation even further. In this situation, here is what I decided to do:

1. I determined not to start with a public examination of the undoubtedly faulty policies pursued throughout the 1990s that had brought the country to the brink of the abyss. Of course it would have been easy to find public support by coming down hard on the authors of "shock therapy." But in Russia's situation, people would immediately start slinging mud at each other, erecting barricades (perhaps not literally), igniting a war in the mass media. This sort of thing would only increase the bitterness of the majority of the population that was suffering from that policy. That is why I rejected advice to "clearly demonstrate the fundamental nature of those who brought the country to such a state." Therefore, in none of my public statements, and I made plenty, did I name anyone who was to blame for what had happened. An evaluation of Russia's economic policies in the 1990s was of course not removed from the agenda. But it had to come later, when passions had cooled.

2. We could make no decisions that could be interpreted as a return to the "good old days," despite the fact that the events of August 17 swelled the ranks of people who said and, more important, believed that "it was better in the past." Exploiting such a mood would simply have been dangerous from a strategic point of view. My colleagues in the government

and I were firmly convinced that retreat from the path of reform would inevitably lead to the restoration of the command-administrative system that had opened the door to totalitarianism and caused the Soviet economy to fall farther and farther behind. But here I am speaking specifically about the decision in favor of reform, not about the way it was implemented in the 1990s.

3. Despite the negative and sometimes criminal way privatization was carried out, which robbed the society, the state,[3] and the common people and disrupted production, we could not call for its sweeping abolition, which would result in a massive new redistribution of property. This could plunge the country into bloodshed, deal a blow to the nascent middle class, and knock honest entrepreneurs off their feet. In Russia millions of people had already become owners of apartments, dachas, kiosks, small enterprises in the service sector, and stocks in larger enterprises. We could not ignore that.

4. The macroeconomic policy followed by earlier governments should not be ignored, but we needed to make corrections in it. The main thing was to subordinate it to the task of stabilization and macroeconomic development. While rejecting administrative limits on the convertibility of the ruble, we had to strengthen the ruble by letting it float and hold inflation in check by not allowing sharp and unpredictable shifts.

5. We should not start by promulgating some final program of economic development. The government and I personally were criticized, especially in the mass media, for coming to the White House with no such extensive program. In general, I don't care for any of the various plans that have become so popular in Russia recently—and only in Russia, not in other countries. A system of approaches that identify the principles of policies to be implemented is absolutely necessary, and so are concrete programs. But not a selection of statements that are artificially united into a pseudoscientific document, which in my opinion offers little practical help but gives great scope for criticism, especially by people who have no responsibility for the state of economic affairs. We chose another path, which was gradually but steadily to familiarize the public with our ideas in the area of economic policy and simultaneously to tell people about the concrete measures envisioned by those policies.

The decision not to issue a premature economic plan by no means signified that we chose to conceal our thoughts about the key issues. The government confirmed that the high road for Russia was the creation of a civil society and political pluralism, continuation of market reforms, and de-velopment of production as an integral part of our economy. This was very important, especially in that period. At the same time, we realized that in order to truly move along that path and not to slip back, which didn't seem so impossible then, reforms had to have a social orientation to ensure that they served the interests of Russia's citizens by improving conditions and raising living standards.

How could we do that? First, by strengthening the state's role in the economy—not to curtail market processes but to facilitate the transition to a civilized market.

This approach envisioned the establishment of a reasonable order that would stimulate the growth of the industrial sector and ensure a level play-ing field, regardless of the form of an enterprise's ownership; firm control over practices of accounting for revenues and expenditures and the use of state property; elaboration and implementation of measures against illegal activities in connection with privatization, false bankruptcies of enterprises, and illegal transfers of funds abroad; and creation of conditions that would encourage Russian banks to support the development of Russian industry and agriculture and attract foreign investment in the Russian economy, chiefly in its industrial sector.

State intervention was propelled by the fact that Russia needed to find a way out of a very serious crisis. The market could not do the job alone. The United States' experience offers a vivid example. In his efforts to overcome the impact of the Great Depression, Franklin D. Roosevelt leaned heavily on state levers. In defending his New Deal policy he stressed that he did not mean the comprehensive regulation and planning of economic life but rather the need for authoritative intervention by the state in economic life in the interests of various regions and population groups and also between the vari-ous sectors of the country's economy. Our government could have put its own signature under those words.

State intervention in economic life was the foundation on which Ludwig Erhard, finance minister and then chancellor of West Germany, built his policy. Certainly, after World War II West Germany was aided by the Marshall Plan, but if not for Erhard's purposeful policy, it would hardly have been pos-sible to turn a country that lay in ruins into one of the world's economic lead-ers in such a short time. Otto-Wolff von Amerongen, one of the most promi-nent German industrialists, my old friend from IMEMO days, told me that

Erhard twisted the arms of entrepreneurs such as himself to get them to comply with state controls.

The government's ideology did include measures to support Russian producers. Implementation should start with a well-thought-out and fairly flexible customs policy and end with equally well-calculated tax reform. The state should also support Russia's exporters.

But to support domestic producers is not to oppose or simply ignore the participation of foreign capital in the development of the industrial sector of the economy. We in the government understood that global business in our era develops on the transnational level. We also did everything we could to attract foreign investment, especially in the form of joint ventures and joint projects as well as direct investment. At our insistence, the State Duma passed a law on product sharing that foreign investors had long hoped for and amended twelve other laws to conform with it.

Of course we could not disregard the problem of competition of products made by enterprises under various forms of ownership. State regulation in this case is far from irrelevant. It is well known that the process of modernizing production assumes that obsolete technologies cannot be scrapped without scientific research and development. In the 1990s the state almost completely stopped financing scientific research. Despite its shortcomings, the Soviet Union had an unquestionable advantage over many developed countries in advanced theoretical research. Instead of focusing the state's efforts on speeding up research that would have offered practical benefits for the scientific and technological advancement of our economy, the pseudoliberals placed their bets on something else. They decided to push not only the economy but science into the market, believing that only scientific activities that bring immediate profit will survive.

These principal positions became the basis of the government's activities from the start. But the first task was to deal with the critical situation in Russia and try to feed the country.

Serious problems with food and medicines were imminent. One result of the pseudoliberals' policies was the country's dependence on imports of essential products. By the middle of 1998, over half of all food products consumed in Russia were imported. Russian agriculture was collapsing. Production of medicines in Russia went into sharp decline. When the crisis of August 17 shrank the volume of goods imported into the country, we had to take decisive steps.

The government lowered customs duties on seven critical imports. We demanded that governors restore free circulation of products between regions. We agreed with Ukraine and Belarus that their debts for deliveries of Russian natural gas would be partially covered by foodstuffs. We negotiated with the United States for assistance with agricultural products, even if we had to buy American grain to get it. And we had to go along with this condition.

We took serious steps to support domestic producers. Despite resistance by the Ministry of Transport, we lowered the 50 percent tariff on rail deliveries for a number of essential agricultural products. We lowered the value-added tax (VAT) on foodstuffs. We decided that the regions could repay previously issued federal loans by providing foodstuffs, at (and I would like to stress this) market prices.

We also managed to deliver fuel and food to Russia's northern areas before ice halted navigation on Siberia's rivers and the adjacent seas. We inherited a tough situation, since nothing had been done on time and people could have frozen to death.

But perhaps the most painful thing for the whole country when we came to the White House was the halting of payments of the money owed to state-employed workers, pensioners, and the military. Many single pensioners were doomed to starvation. On TV one could see desperate army wives who had nothing to feed their children. Imagine trying to establish stability in such an environment.

My deputies and I told each other that if we failed to solve the problem of timely salary and pension payments to all categories of the population immediately and if we didn't start to catch up on payments long overdue, we had no business being in the government. Some voices advised us to start up the printing presses and solve all these problems by printing money. Perhaps we would have gained an immediate public relations advantage, perhaps even a political advantage. But within a few months, inflation would have consumed all the money we printed. We had to find another way. In the initial stages we had to redistribute budget expenditures and look for budgetary reserves. Strategically we could solve the problem only by establishing financial order in the country and launching the industrial sector of the economy.

Starting in October we issued monthly pension and salary payments to state workers and the military. At the same time we made payments on the arrears owed.

In September, 7 billion rubles were allocated to finance the army, which constituted half of all federal budget expenditures. In October over 5 billion was spent to cover part of the debts of the defense industry, which contributed to a general revitalizing of the economy. These payments were accompanied by real cuts in the armed forces. Numerous statements regarding the reduction of the armed forces did not reflect the real state of affairs, since the government had no funds to pay the people who were let go. According to federal law, an officer who is removed from service must be paid a sum equal to twenty-one months' pay. We found the funds to pay 30,000 officers who were transferred to the reserves.

But unfortunately these were not the only difficulties. We needed to secure the timely payment of salaries from *local* budgets to doctors, teachers, cultural workers, and people employed in the nonbudget sector.

Addressing a session of the government, I said that we could no longer provide enormous assistance to the regions by either selling state property or accumulating debts, as had been done in 1997. We proposed to take extraordinary measures and oblige the regions (with the exceptions of Moscow, St. Petersburg, and Samara, which were solving their problems independently) to allocate no less than 40 percent of their budgets to salaries. Governors were warned that if this instruction was not followed and if transfers of money from the Center for teachers, doctors, and the rest were used for other purposes, the regions would be put under the direct control of the Treasury. However, we promised that additional funds would be allocated from the federal budget to depressed regions unable to implement this instruction. The Ministry of Finance immediately provided a list of these "disaster" areas.

Paralysis of the economy was the root cause of nonpayment in the nonbudget sector, which accounted for 80 percent of total nonpayments. But not only that. During one of my trips around the country I visited a plant where the manager introduced a third shift. In fact, he was not just the plant's manager but owner of 5 percent of its shares. If a third shift was needed, obviously the product was selling. When I asked about wage payments, the manager said they were delayed by two to three months.

A few days later I addressed a meeting of union leaders: "You often take the federal government by the throat. But at the same time you're not nearly so active in enterprises that have signed a collective bargaining agreement but are not paying their workers." Nonpayment is even more important in the many institutions and enterprises that keep two sets of books, one official and one unofficial, The unofficial books show wage payments without employer deductions for the pension and other social funds and without employee deductions for income tax.

The pseudoliberals simply ignored this antisocial practice, which is absolutely uncharacteristic of civilized market relations. Upon instructions from the leadership of the Cabinet of Ministers, the tax police checked 70,000 enterprises and began to investigate banks and commercial structures. Someone did not like this at all.

THE FIRST TASK: DEVELOPING THE INDUSTRIAL SECTOR

A fundamental shift in economic policy was impossible without creating conditions for development of the industrial sector of the economy. Therefore, the first thing we had to do was to restructure the banking system, not only to restore it but also to change the emphasis of its activity. Theoretically, at that time the state could have decided to save certain banks and specific bankers. That was what the oligarchs wanted. Some bankers even offered to nationalize their banks, a move that of course would have shifted the burden of accumulated debts to the government. Instead we offered to conduct intensive negotiations with creditors, both domestic and foreign, about restructuring the banks' debt. We realized we wouldn't be able to manage without increasing the percentage of foreign capital in Russian banks or without widening the scope of foreign banks' activity in the Russian Federation.

The government and the Central Bank put their hope in supporting financial institutions that were still viable while ridding the market of crippled, half-dead, and disreputable banks.

A solution to the nonpayment problem was among the most important questions on the agenda. By the time our government came to power, the federal budget debt to enterprises and institutions amounted to 50 billion rubles. In turn, the debt of the enterprises and institutions before the budget was 150 billion rubles. Interenterprise debt was also accumulating. The situation was aggravated by the general sharp demonetarization of the economy during the time the pseudoliberals were in control. At the time reforms were initiated in 1991, money in circulation constituted 66.4 percent of GDP, generally in line with international practice. On July 1, 1998 (before August 17), money in circulation constituted only 13.7 percent of 1997 GDP.

Federal authorities demanded that payments of money owed by one enterprise to another be made exclusively in cash, as is normal in a market economy. The problem was that so little money was in circulation that most enterprises could not comply. In a vicious circle, mounting debts prevented the growth of production, and stagnation and decline of production precluded the growth of money in circulation.

Going against the opinion of the IMF and previous practice, the government began mutual debt payments between the budget and enterprises, which quickly freed up 50 billion rubles. The fact that mutual payments were made through the Treasury rather than the commercial banks prevented the flight of financial resources. The transactions were conducted on the basis of clearing. This was a major difference from mutual debt payments between various enterprises, many of which were conducted on the basis of barter.

By clearing the mountain of debt arrears by means of mutual payments, we created an important impulse for the functioning and development of industry. Interestingly enough, the head of RAO EES (Russian Joint-Stock Company "Unified Energy System of Russia"), Anatoly Chubais, who during his days in the government was one of the most vocal opponents of noncash payments, switched sides. When the government spoke of the results that could be expected from mutual payments, he insistently urged that this practice be followed until both the government and the enterprises had accumulated sufficient financial resources.

Now a few words about tax reform. In the government we did not have to convince each other that tax reform was needed. Our predecessors had made little progress in this area. They emphasized collection of taxes owed, which, while important, was not enough. Boris Fyodorov, who was responsible for tax collection at that time, often appeared on TV wearing a camouflage uniform and accompanied by tax police. But the taxes collected increased very little.

In any case, squeezing taxes out of citizens and enterprises may not help replenish the budget. When I came to the government I encountered a paradoxical situation. It turned out that for many months, in some cases years, modern equipment purchased abroad and paid for by the enterprises (with a total value of about 2 billion dollars) was kept locked in customs warehouses because the enterprises couldn't pay the VAT and, in some cases, customs duties. Of course all taxes and customs duties must be paid. But how can one expect payment from enterprises that have ceased production for want of the equipment they have bought and paid for? I instructed the Customs

Committee to release such equipment and sign an agreement with each owner setting a timetable for repayment of the debt and accepting either the equipment or a bank guarantee as collateral. Many enterprises sighed with relief. Experience showed that this was the right decision. Repayment of debt soon began.

Administrative measures that are not supported by economic stimuli certainly can't improve the situation. That is why we adopted measures aimed at lowering the number and amount of taxes. The burden of taxation shifted from production to consumption. The government prepared nineteen laws on taxation and six were adopted while my team was in the government.

We also began a serious fight against tax evasion or partial tax payments. This effort was not accompanied by posturing on TV but it turned out to be effective. Georgy Boos, who served as minister of taxation and tax collection, drew my attention to the fact that schemes for using insurance for entrepreneurial risks to imitate the purchase and movement of goods were in wide use. Without investing a ruble, an enterprise could receive reimbursement from the budget for money it had "spent."

This is how wide-scale fraud was carried out in connection with the purchase of sand. AvtoVAZ and other enterprises claimed to be purchasing sand, but it turned out that the sand was not transported (this operation would have required 20,000 boxcars, which would have strained the whole rail system to the limit for months) or even dug from the sand pits. Sharp questions were asked. We offered to let AvtoVAZ issue stock in order to transfer 50 percent of the company's shares to the state for unpaid debts. At the same time the government started negotiating with foreign companies to resell these shares on condition that they make a large investment in production.

An agreement between AvtoVAZ and the revenue service was prepared, but after our team left the government it was not implemented.

Although we had little time, the new and much tougher policy produced results. Some people attributed the substantial increase in collected taxes to inflation. Inflation certainly had an effect, but the increase could be observed not only in absolute figures but also in their share of GDP. This growth had nothing to do with the growth of inflation, which in any case began to decline.

The introduction of state controls over production and distribution of alcoholic beverages was of considerable importance for replenishing budgets at all levels. With the loss of the state monopoly, taxes were collected only on legally produced wine and vodka products. But the black market became so huge that it gained control over many local governments. The cost of producing bootlegged vodka was incredibly low and bore no relation to the sale price, which was still lower than the price of legally produced vodka. People died from drinking that vodka, some of which was produced with methyl alcohol.

We decided to cut this knot by sharply reducing imports of the ethyl (grain) alcohol the underground producers needed; decreeing that plants that produced ethyl alcohol in Russia must be either state-owned or joint-stock companies with a certain number of shares belonging to the government; and establishing quotas for production of ethyl alcohol at these plants. Order was established at vodka plants and the police began a serious campaign against illegal production. As a result, taxes collected from the alcohol industry rose 1.5 times in just two months.

We decided not to nationalize this industry, but introduced state control and state regulation. We decided not to introduce hikes in excise taxes, which without a doubt would have caused vodka prices to rise and encouraged underground production. Unfortunately these introduced practices were discontinued.

By these actions we challenged very powerful forces connected to extremely profitable underground industries. But they did not dare to resist the government openly at that time.

The focus of the government's attention shifted to questions connected with the sale of state property. While not giving up on privatization, we concentrated on bringing order to the process.

Previous formulas for selling government shares were not properly calculated. We had questions about the percentage of shares to be transferred to private property and the price of those shares. For instance, we disallowed another sale of 25 percent of state shares in Sviazinvest. Three months earlier, the same number of shares had sold for $1.2 billion. Someone tried to convince me that now the price of those shares should not exceed $600 million and that I should agree to that price. Later, when *Moskovskye Novosti* published a chapter from a book by George Soros, a lot became clear. According to Soros, Berezovsky "sincerely believed that while he and other oligarchs paid for Yeltsin's re-election, the government now refused to fulfill its part of the deal by conducting a fair auction of Sviazinvest."[4]

The rational use of funds in enterprises that belonged to the state or were joint-stock companies in which the state participated remained beyond the reach of the Ministry of State Property. In Russia there are still about 14,000 state enterprises, 23,000 organizations, and four joint-stock companies of which the state owns a share; in 50 percent of cases it owns a controlling share. Yet the budget was receiving less than a billion rubles a year in dividends from all these state enterprises!

A question was raised about our stance toward national monopolies, including Gazprom, the Ministry of Railway Transport (MPS), and RAO EES. What approach should we choose at this stage? Should we privatize and break them up, as the IMF suggested, or keep them intact with significant participation by the state? Those who favored the breakup of natural monopolies, mainly the leadership of RAO EES and MPS, usually argued that the privatization of separate parts of the monopolies would attract investment for modernization of worn-out equipment. At the same time, they denied that such privatization would stop the rapid increase in rates. In that case, why couldn't the state use the income from rate increases exclusively for the modernization of equipment? Opponents of the privatization of natural monopolies claimed that international experience had demonstrated that breaking up such monopolies hindered technological advancement. The government firmly supported that position. Finally, it should be noted that Russia's natural monopolies help to unify the disparate parts of our huge country.

But a desire to preserve natural monopolies as single organisms does not mean allowing them absolute power. Our government was strongly opposed to the unjustifiable increases in the prices for the products and services of natural monopolies. With such unsupported increases it would be impossible to reduce production costs, increase the competitiveness of local products, or facilitate economic growth. We realized that.

At the end of 1998 the economy began to inch upward. It appeared to be stabilizing in October. The decline in production was consistently slowing. In April 1999 production was ahead of the level of April 1998. There are grounds for believing that by the time the government left, the positive dynamic was leading to a stable increase in production.

Many found it beneficial to represent this development as exclusively a consequence of the devaluation of the ruble, which indeed pushed the growth of the export sector of industry. The need for import substitution also played a role when the volume of finished imported goods declined after the crisis of August 1998. But the measures we took to exploit this favorable state of affairs were decisive for progress in the economy. By the way, analysis showed that import substitution accounted for approximately one-fourth of total production growth during the eight months our government was in power.

Attempts to explain this turn for the better by pointing to the rise in world oil prices are groundless as well. The economy stabilized and was moving ahead before oil prices shot upward. The increase in oil prices began in March 1999 and its main effects were felt after I left office.

The positive dynamic in the economy allowed the government to propose a tough but realistic budget for 1999, and it was approved by the State Duma. It was the first time this had happened in the 1990s. For the first time, budget revenues exceeded budget expenditures. For the first time, 2 percent of revenue was earmarked to cover the debts amassed by our predecessors.

Of course the government did more than work on the economy. We wanted to do more to bolster science, education, and culture than ensure timely payment of the salaries, current and in arrears, of the people employed in those fields and finance them strictly in accord with the federal budget. A lot had to be corrected.

I was told that, literally on the eve of the default, our predecessors adopted a law, No. 600, that mandated a program of minimizing state expenditures. There is no doubt that the idea behind the program was on the right track. The unjustified and sometimes excessive expenditures of the bureaucratic apparatus, mainly the high-level bureaucrats, had to be reined in. Of particular interest was construction of state-owned dachas, especially at a time when the country lacked housing and educational facilities for its citizens. But we needed to dig deeper by reforming the ineffective system of social benefits, reducing the cumbersome governing apparatus, eliminating duplication in the work of federal executive organs, and establishing strict order in the use of federal funds by the armed forces.

Meanwhile, along with justified and necessary measures, the zealots of economizing hit upon the idea of abolishing all bonuses and additional payments to college professors and high school teachers, who received meager material rewards for work that is very hard but very important for society. The small stipends for college students were to be cut 30 percent as well. By a decree of December 11, 1998, our government overturned all such measures.

We also did away with the preceding government's proposal to cut expenditures on basic research and assistance in science and technology. While our government was in office, the funds allocated for the Academy of Sciences of the Russian Federation were paid in full. They were certainly not enough, but the release of funds that earlier had been withheld still led to a long-awaited breakthrough.

I still find it hard to believe that a man as well educated and intelligent as Kirienko made a conscious decision to include all this in the list of items to be cut in the name of economizing. Besides, the money saved in science and education was meager, while the damage dealt to the country was immense. Perhaps he did not read this thick document attentively. Or perhaps its authors were guided by the slogans of the liberals, who were wedded to the idea of keeping the state's investment in education, culture, and art to a minimum.

But economizing was not limited to state expenditures. At the beginning of 1999 I was visited in the White House by Oleg Yefremov, Mark Zakharov, and Galina Volchek, the outstanding directors and leaders of three famous theaters, MKhAT, Lenkom, and Sovremennik. It pained me to realize that Russia's best theaters had to fight for their lives, look for sponsors, beg for assistance, rent out parts of their buildings to buy props and finance new productions without sending ticket prices through the roof. So what did the government do? The Finance Ministry demanded that all their funds be taken from accounts in commercial banks and put into non-interest-bearing accounts in the Treasury.

"If they don't believe we're not using that money for personal expenses, let them control every ruble," said Oleg Yefremov. "But this is money we got ourselves, and we're afraid the bureaucrats will decide which particular production expenses it can be used for."

I called the minister of finance and instructed him, over his protests, to withdraw those orders. I added that we should be looking for thieves not among the intelligentsia, especially its best representatives, but among the entrepreneurs, from whom our ministries often coyly look away.

Since I've touched upon this topic, I want to make it clear that I was never against honest entrepreneurs and business people, and gave them all sorts of support. Their emergence and strengthening are good for Russia. But along with honest business people there are enterprising thieves and economic criminals, whom I always thought had to be fought, and fought as hard as possible.

So this is how our government was creating conditions for the political and social stabilization of Russia, while the rest of the world was wondering whether the country would collapse.

When I became prime minister and for some time afterward, the most important task was to find a path between dictatorship and chaos. I think we found it by strengthening the role of the state and increasing its effectiveness.

For a market economy and society in general the danger lies not in a strong state that relies on the law and democratic processes, but in a weak government that, even with the best intentions, tries to interfere in private life and in the workings of the society and becomes a tool of influential groups. As FDR used to say: "A strong, active state will never degenerate into a dictatorship. Dictatorship always replaces a weak and helpless government."

THE BLEEDING WOUND OF CHECHNYA

The crisis in Chechnya coincided with my work in the Foreign Intelligence Service, the Foreign Ministry, and the government. Although the FIS and the Foreign Ministry were not directly involved with the Chechen crisis, at that time I also worked at the Security Council, which was in the thick of it. Unfortunately, these bloody encounters are not at all a thing of the past. This is how everything started.

In 1991, General of the Soviet Army Dzhokar Dudaev, an ethnic Chechen, was sent to Grozny by people in Yeltsin's circle to replace an "unacceptable" old Soviet leadership. The people in charge at that time were not concerned about keeping Chechnya calm and orderly, which the government of the old Chechen-Ingush Republic had managed to do with great effort.[5] The priority for the people close to Yeltsin was to show the power of the new government. Thus began the "Chechen experiment," which turned out to be so costly for Russia.

Meanwhile, in the republic and outside its borders, processes were going forward that tied the Chechen knot even tighter. The Ministry of Defense withdrew all federal forces from Chechnya, leaving a plentiful supply of arms for Dudaev, and not only guns. Abandoned equipment included 108 armored units; 51 military and training planes; anti-aircraft units, including anti-aircraft missile and artillery systems and about 750 guided missiles; 153 units of artillery and mortars, including mortar rocket systems; and much more besides. Dudaev grew stronger and started pushing for independence.

Practically from the first days of its existence, Dudaev's regime took on criminal overtones. Violence and arbitrary rule prevailed. Criminals were released from prisons. The economy was destroyed. The oil sector was plundered. Agriculture collapsed. Unemployment reached unheard-of levels—

more than two-thirds of able-bodied men and women had no jobs. About a quarter of the population left the republic. Many became refugees.

At this time Mafia and criminal connections were established between certain groups of Russian businessmen and the Chechen leadership, which they used to build fortunes. They had plenty of opportunities. Since Chechnya was part of the Russian Federation, they could bring in raw materials from Russia and then export finished goods without payment or collection of duties. The arms and drug trades flourished. A large proportion of the illegal and criminal operations were connected with the extraction and refining of oil and with banking. Connections between certain oligarchs and Dudaev's representatives grew tighter. So this is how the transition from the old regime to the "democratic future" was carried out in Chechnya.

Inside forces in Chechnya resisted Dudaev's regime and organized a movement against him. They were particularly strong in the summer of 1994, when they organized an anti-Dudaev movement and formed the Provisional Council and government. Clashes between the Chechens broke out. The federal central government did not remain indifferent, but its efforts were slapdash and inexpert. So-called volunteer tanks entered Grozny without infantry support. The operation ended with the tanks burning on the streets of the Chechen capital.

The question of bringing in federal forces was raised. Rumors are still afloat about how this question was decided in December 1994. True, Pavel Grachev, then the defense minister, made some careless remarks about cleaning up the situation in a few days with one paratrooper regiment. But as one who took part in the meeting where the final decision was made, I can attest that neither Grachev nor Viktor Yerin, the interior minister, expressed any enthusiasm about launching a military operation.

Who was unreservedly for military action? I don't want to reveal their names, especially since some of them are no longer with us and others are no longer in politics. The minister of justice doubted the wisdom of using the military. So did I, as he confirmed in an interview with *Komsomolskaya Pravda*.

The discussion was not to the point. Two main topics were discussed: how much time was needed for preparations—seven days, ten days, or two weeks—and who should be in charge of the action, Grachev or Yerin. At Grachev's insistence, he was appointed coordinating commander of the operation.

I asked Yeltsin to step outside with me for a moment so we could talk privately, and we went to the adjoining reception room. I said, "We should not bring in the troops. We don't know how we can withdraw them later. In any event, before we begin military operations, I think we ought to send Dudaev's former commander, Marshal of Aviation Yevgeny Shaposhnikov, to talk to him. That would be useful."

"Don't worry," said Yeltsin. "We'll probably do that. I hope we won't have to use force."

After that a vote was called for, and everyone without exception raised his hand for the military operation.

But I have to say that the president's role in all this was far from simple. I believe he was sincere when some time later he said he was prey to doubts. On the one hand, as a guarantor of the Constitution he could not passively observe the emergence of a criminal Chechen state within a state, which did not recognize federal laws and essentially withdrew from Russia. On the other hand, he was dismayed by a sense of guilt for the deaths of human beings.

Only a few people know that Yeltsin launched one of the Security Council meetings in 1995 by announcing that he was submitting his resignation because he felt guilty about the events in Chechnya. All members of the Security Council spoke, categorically demanding that he do no such thing. I don't think this was a game Yeltsin was playing. Everything connected with Chechnya was painful to him.

What happened next? I am opening the records I made during those years. They reflect the moods of various people at meetings called by the leadership, prominent among them a realistic view of the situation combined with a desire to project optimism. But the main thing one can see from those records is lack of a coherent policy laid down to be rigorously implemented, an inability to gather all necessary information and act together to work out and adopt comprehensive, adaptable plans that took the country's future into consideration. The decisions made then have had far-reaching effects on Russia and all Russians.

A meeting was held on December 16, 1994, with Premier Chernomyrdin.

NIKOLAI YEGOROV *(appointed the president's representative in Chechnya):*
The military operation should be completed without negotiations with Dudaev. It's impossible to come to terms with him at all. The antigovernment tone in the major mass media reflects their fear that they themselves created a positive image of Dudaev in the past.
PAVEL GRACHEV: If we express things in numbers, 70 percent of

the population favor Dudaev. As for Grozny, only 500 representatives of the Chechen opposition will be with us. Furthermore, we failed to approach Grozny from the south. If we go from any other direction, we have to strike against populated areas. Without bombardment and artillery fire against Grozny, I won't attack it. There will be big losses.

VIKTOR YERIN: We shouldn't just be thinking about the situation in Ingushetia and Dagestan but exerting influence over it. The operation in Chechnya should be completed, but we need to assume that we'll have to work there for many years.

SERGEI STEPASHIN *(chairman of the Federal Counterintelligence Service [FSK]):* We can't withdraw from Chechnya, we can't leave Grozny. At the same time, if we liquidate certain separate sites within the city, we may be able to do without an assault.

IVAN RYBKIN *(chairman of the State Duma):* If we decide, we must do so without delay.

Nobody summarized the discussion or suggested any option that could have been offered to the president.

On December 26 the Security Council met again. In my notes I underlined the words of Grachev, who said Dudaev could still put up determined resistance. He received weapons and ammunition from Abkhazia and Azerbaijan by hidden channels. There was no breakthrough to our advantage in Grozny.

I said that if we didn't expect to capture Grozny in the next few days (the military should determine the probability), we definitely needed to announce that blockading the city was our main goal and stop at that. Afterward it would be reasonable to stop bombing Grozny, announcing that we're opening corridors for civilians who want to leave the city. At the same time, with the help of the Ministry of Internal Affairs and FSK, we would need to sort out the people coming out of the city and then prepare and carry out special operations to capture the leaders of Dudaev's group. This would by no means prevent negotiations with those Chechens who might take it upon themselves to start disarming.

During a meeting with Yeltsin on January 6, 1995, Grachev painted a gloomy picture: violent resistance from Dudaev; according to our information, plans for guerrilla war were being prepared; Dudaev had 11,000 militants in Grozny alone; his supporters infiltrated government organs on territory controlled by federal forces; and infiltration from abroad continued. "It seems we need two to three years to bring the situation under control."

Quite a difference from the promise to crush the enemy in a week.

According to Yerin, 15,000 Interior Ministry troops in addition to 37,000 troops from the Defense Ministry were not enough to ensure success in Chechnya. "Let's be realistic," he said.

Yegorov spoke about the negotiation process. Was there any? "Hadzhiev established contacts with some field commanders.[6] So you can say the negotiation process has started. We should bring in the head of the Chechen General Staff, Maskhadov, who still keeps his distance."

Stepashin added that a good background for negotiations was that eight out of eleven regions supported us.

That was it. The matter remained undecided.

On January 10, 1995, I went to make my weekly report to the president. Chechnya was the first issue we discussed. Although the Foreign Intelligence Service was not one of the power structures directly involved in the Chechen problem and its work did not cover Russian territory, we had sources abroad who were well informed about the situation in Chechnya. Several FIS employees who were ethnic Chechens knew the situation very well, and a strong team of specialists analyzed the information we received.

Yeltsin agreed that the military operation alone would not solve the problem and that the military and political costs, both internal and external, were much greater than expected. It was very important to combine the military operation with the negotiation process in order to preserve stability in Russia and keep our country from being isolated.

I offered to make a few trips. I had a preliminary agreement that the king of Morocco, Hassan II, who as chairman of the Organization of the Islamic Conference (OIC) would grant me an audience, as would the president of Algeria, Libya's Muammar Qaddafi, and President Mubarak of Egypt.

I also told the president that I thought it would be a good idea for him to go public with an analysis of our shortcomings, blunders, and mistakes during recent events in Chechnya. At his request, I enumerated them:

1. For three years no decisive measures were undertaken. One difficulty was that the "Chechen question" became part of the general political crisis in Moscow. But the Russian government's obvious lack of realistic information also played a role.

2. Part of our heavy military equipment was taken over by Dudaev's regime after our troops withdrew from Chechnya.
3. There were shortcomings in the work of the General Staff and intelligence services in preparing the military operation in Chechnya; in coordinating the various components of the military forces and, on a wider scale, military construction; and in producing the weapons needed to carry out the present tasks.

Yeltsin sat lost in thought. I could feel that he had thought about all this often.

My trips to the Middle East and North Africa confirmed my feeling that the heads of many Arab states not only did not support terrorism but very clearly understood the need to fight against separatism. The king of Morocco almost brought an urgent meeting of the OIC devoted to Chechnya to a standstill, and Qaddafi even phoned Dudaev in an effort to calm him down.

But calming down Chechen militants proved to be impossible either before or after Dudaev's death.

This time the Security Council gathered on June 29, 1995, after the terrorist operation in Budennovsk, which began with the capture of a hospital by Shamil Basaev's militants and ended with the deaths of dozens of hostages and Russian soldiers. It was agreed that all remaining hostages still held by the bandits would be freed in exchange for a promise of free passage for the terrorists.

The governor of the Stavropol region, Yevgeny Kuznetsov, spoke first. "For the people of Budennovsk the main question is why the bandits are not being eliminated." The border with Chechnya, he said, was guarded by only 236 local police, and the border between Chechnya and Dagestan was completely porous. Thus the entire area between Chechnya, Dagestan, and the Stavropol region was wide open to the terrorists. According to Kuznetsov, the operation in Budennovsk demonstrated a complete lack of cooperation among all power structures. No information was coming from military intelligence, and the governor doubted that the situation would improve soon.

Yerin spoke after that. He honestly admitted serious shortcomings in the Interior Ministry's work and offered to submit his resignation. Stepashin described the situation and said he had already decided to resign. Grachev said his worst failing was that from the very beginning he was unable to coordinate the activities of the power structures. His other failing was that he did not finish destroying the remaining groups of bandits that retreated into the mountains. His main fault was that he did not find and destroy Basaev's detachment. As for Budennovsk, Grachev frankly admitted that he was hiding behind his colleagues' backs. "And I want to apologize for my sharp words to Yerin and Stepashin," Grachev said bluntly. He added that he, too, was ready to resign.

Yegorov and Oleg Lobov, secretary of the Security Council, also stated their readiness to leave their posts.

"The price of your mistakes is very high," said the president.

Some resignations followed, but the Budennovsk scenario was repeated when the terrorists captured the maternity hospital in Kizlyar. Negotiations then began spontaneously, without the preparation and planning necessary for success. In August 1996, the rather ambiguous Khasavyurt Agreements were signed.[7] Federal troops left Chechnya and everything stayed as it was, with criminal authorities still in place.

When I write of the events of 1994–96, I can't help comparing them with the operations in Chechnya that started in 1999, which in general were much more successful. I keep wondering whether a serious analysis of the first war in Chechnya was conducted and whether military and political conclusions were drawn. I don't know if an in-depth examination of these events guided the way the situation unfolded in Chechnya and neighboring countries and among the peoples of the Russian Federation, or whether various options were considered. When I was foreign minister and then chairman of the government, I was not involved in such comprehensive and focused discussions.

At a Security Council meeting on August 30, Yeltsin announced that a "shift toward a peaceful resolution" was taking place and pointed out that he was ready to talk to everyone who exercised authority in Chechnya, including Ruslan Khazbulatov.[8] At the same time he appropriately criticized the Ministry of Defense for withdrawing its forces too soon. He was also displeased with the border guards for not arranging with Georgia to close its border with Chechnya and for failing to establish control over that border.

"After Budennovsk we should have taken Basaev at the border," said Yeltsin. "This is where our area of responsibility ended. Special forces, first and foremost the Defense Ministry, should strengthen all administrative borders with Chechnya."

The new minister of internal affairs, Anatoly Kulikov, addressed the meeting to propose strengthening our positions on the Terek River and returning two districts that had been given to Chechnya under Soviet rule back to the Stavropol region.

But these were just contributions to a deep and detailed scrutiny of the situation in an effort to determine the actions to take.

At that time oil was becoming a determining factor in the changing situation in Chechnya. The press speculated freely about the construction of the Baku-Ceyhan pipeline. This project has purely geopolitical rather than economic importance. From an economic point of view it was incomparably more profitable to transport not only the "early" oil (the amount agreed upon) but also the "main" oil from the Caspian via the Baku-Grozny-Novorossysk pipeline. By the way, the dynamics of the predictions seemed to indicate a sharp decline in optimism regarding oil reserves in the Caspian. At the same time, the construction of a Caspian pipeline from the Tengiz oil field in Kazakhstan to Novorossysk was under way. It was carried out by a consortium consisting of Russia, Kazakhstan, and eight transnational corporations, including such giants as Chevron and Mobil. Thus the issue of moving Kazakh oil through Russia was decided.

The pipeline issue was the cause of a bitter struggle among Tbilisi, Baku, and Ankara. The sharp lowering of expectations for the Caspian Eldorado oil field undermined the Baku-Ceyhan project, which was extremely detrimental for Georgia, Azerbaijan, and Turkey. In these circumstances, the Chechen leaders joined the game in pursuit of political as well as economic goals. The project "Caucasus Our Common Home" was born, established by Chechnya, Azerbaijan, and Georgia. After the Chechens captured and murdered some foreign nationals, however, Tbilisi and Baku turned their backs on the Common Home project, and Chechnya once again found itself alone, with no hope of breaking out of its isolation by participating in anti-Russian pipeline projects.

By the time I had formed a government, terrorism was sweeping over Chechnya. At the beginning of October 1998 four representatives of a British firm—three British citizens and one New Zealander—were captured and later brutally murdered in Chechnya. This outrage was a blow to the pride of Aslan Maskhadov, the elected president of Chechnya, especially because London was the only Western capital where he had been officially received as one of the founders of the Common Home project. He ordered a search for the four kidnapped foreigners, and after the four severed heads were found, he ordered a search for their murderers.

From that moment, conflicts among the Chechen field commanders intensified. Maskhadov ordered all irregular military units to disband, and ordered his forces to immediately liquidate the bases of the rebels Shamil Basaev, Ibn-ul-Khattab, and Abumuslim Israpilov in Serzhenyurt, Vedeno, and Urus-Martan. Simultaneously, the head of Shariat Security demanded the liberation of all hostages and said certain populated areas would be surrounded and "criminal groupings destroyed."

When the deadlines announced by Maskhadov passed, the large-scale operations he had threatened did not begin. Meanwhile, his opponents did not remain inactive. The head of the Department of the Fight against Kidnappings, Ministry of Shariat Security, was killed, and the mufti of Chechnya, Ahmed-Khadzi Kadyrov, was assaulted. At that time Kadyrov was known for his opposition to the extremist Wahhabists and his support of Maskhadov.

Taking all this into consideration, I asked Yeltsin if I should invite Maskhadov to meet with me. Yeltsin agreed. I consulted with Aleksandr Dzasokhov, president of North Ossetia–Alania, and Ruslan Aushev, president of Ingushetia. Maskhadov and Aushev came to Vladikavkaz, where we decided to hold the meeting.

The meeting took place on October 29, which was both my and Ruslan Aushev's birthday. Dzasokhov, our host, was an old friend, so we had a good setting for negotiations. But I spoke with Maskhadov one on one.

From this conversation I gathered the following:

1. Maskhadov and Basaev were separated not only by their struggle for leadership in Chechnya but also by strategic interests. When I questioned him directly about this, he said: "I think an independent Chechnya must exist within its current borders. Basaev disagrees. He wants to spread the Chechen experiment, particularly to Dagestan, and get access to the Caspian and Black seas."
2. Some circles in Russia maintained close contacts with Maskhadov's opponents. To be precise, according to Maskhadov, Boris Berezovsky "supports them financially by paying ransom for hostages and also offers them radio equipment." After talking about Basaev in this connection, Maskhadov pointed out that Berezovsky's main partner was Movladi Udugov, who at that time was Chechnya's foreign minister.[9]
3. Basaev's program makes him an unappeasable enemy of Russia, whereas Maskhadov expressed readiness to discuss many problems connected

with "Chechnya's independence within a common economic space, common currency, etc." with Russia.

We agreed (Minister of Internal Affairs Stepashin and Minister of Nationalities Issues Ramazan Abdulatipov were with me) about cooperation between security organs in the fight against kidnappings and crime, reconstruction of a number of plants in Chechnya, payment of compensation by the central government to citizens who were deported in 1944 and who live in the territory of Chechnya, and payments to Chechen pensioners from the Federal Pension Fund.

The main result of the meeting was Maskhadov's promise that these and earlier commitments between us would be fulfilled within a month, and he would "engage in an open struggle and defeat the terrorists."

I gave the president a detailed account of the discussion with Maskhadov. I gave corresponding instructions to the Ministries of Finance, the Economy, and Energy. Yeltsin supported the prepared draft of instructions to the Ministry of Internal Affairs.[10]

Upon his return to Grozny, Maskhadov either wouldn't or couldn't act against the field commanders, who were independent of his regime and gaining strength. Whereas during the first days after the Vladikavkaz meeting he tried to demonstrate his determination to act—for instance, on October 30 he removed Movladi Udugov from the post of foreign minister without explanation—later Maskhadov's decisiveness evaporated. Perhaps he feared that tension in Chechnya might grow into a civil war, which could be even more dangerous than sharp deterioration of relations with Russia. That deterioration was inevitable when Maskhadov's inaction, either deliberate or forced, freed the hands of the extremist elements who wanted to export the Chechen "experiment" to Dagestan and carry out large-scale terrorist attacks deep within Russia. I don't think Maskhadov chose to support these actions, but I think he knew about them and did not take decisive steps to prevent them.

It seems to me that Maskhadov failed to calculate the real consequences of terrorist attacks in Russia and aggression against Dagestan. He could hardly have predicted the scale of Russia's reaction. With almost the complete support of Russian public opinion, Russia sent troops to Chechnya. The anti-terrorist operation in effect turned into a war against Chechen terrorists and separatists. The goal of the operation was to destroy the terrorists' capability as well as (and I think there is nothing to conceal here) to return Chechnya to Russia and frustrate the plan to remove the North Caucasus from Russia's territory and cause the Federation to disintegrate.

The need for tough action was beyond argument. It would be evidence of the unwillingness or inability of the federal government to defend the interests of Russia and the Russians just to kick the Chechen militants out of Dagestan without chasing them, or to limit the response to criminal investigations, or to make fruitless demands of the Chechen government to extradite the people who blew up apartment buildings, killing and wounding a thousand civilians. When Putin, who was prime minister then, took responsibility for decisive action against the militants in Chechnya, his approval ratings soared. It's not surprising that he won the presidential elections in the first round.

Many people suspected that the explosions in the apartment buildings were connected with the presidential campaign. Some even pointed their fingers at the FSB. I am absolutely convinced that there is nothing to such talk. For four years and four months I headed the special forces and I am certain that any such thing would simply not have been possible during my time. I am not even talking about the completely changed moral climate; there is no mechanism for carrying out such an operation. No one would risk sanctioning it even if he wanted to. An operation of that scope can't help being discovered; the preparations alone for this hypothetical operation would involve dozens of people.

At the same time, the way the FSB discovered the Chechen trail needs to be widely publicized. A lack of information always encourages rumors and lies. So in September 1999 federal forces entered Chechnya's territory. Were there different ways to continue this operation? Yes, there were. Yury Luzhkov, the mayor of Moscow, and I exchanged views on many problems. We thought the best option was to stop at the Terek River, close to Chechnya's borders with Dagestan and the Stavropol region as well as the border between Ingushetia and Georgia. This would establish a security zone. We did not need to enter the south of Chechnya. We did need to carry out precision air and missile strikes against military targets and the infrastructure used by the militants.

As for the liberated north of Chechnya, we needed to do our best to demonstrate the advantages of a peaceful life by building hospitals and schools, paying pensions and salaries, and providing order and security. In the meantime, the southern part of Chechnya faced a cold and hungry winter.

If the plan succeeded, there was a real opportunity to split up the Chechen field commanders and, more important, distance the population from the militants. This seemed to us to be our major task in Chechnya, for it would open the way to a political resolution.

Together with Yury Luzhkov I discussed all this with Putin before the State Duma elections. He did not disagree. But one should not forget that the logic generated by the military operations continued in force.

The option that we proposed did not find support. Some people feared that the earlier situation would be repeated (remember that Grachev said that one of his mistakes was not finishing off the bandits and instead letting them escape into the mountains) and some military commanders gave too much weight to the fact that federal forces moved to the Terek with minimal losses, which encouraged them to continue on to the south. The fact that Chechen militants began to infiltrate the liberated territories also played a role. Intelligence reported that they were literally turning inhabited areas into fortified bases. Georgia refused to let Russian border guards enter its territory so they could close the Russian side of the Chechen-Georgian border.[11]

The crossing of the Terek and the struggle to liberate Grozny and other populated areas under the militants' control resulted in numerous casualties among civilians and the federal forces, despite measures taken to avoid them. Although in the end this large-scale operation routed some of the militants' detachments, they were still quite capable of carrying on guerrilla warfare.

After I left office I visited Germany and France, where I was received by Chancellor Gerhard Schröder and President Chirac. They were both surprised that Russia had not accepted the West's kind offer to start negotiations to resolve the "Chechen tragedy." Certainly, in the end we will have to conduct serious negotiations in order to determine the status of Chechnya within the Russian Federation. So far I agreed with them. But they in turn agreed when I pointed out that the Chechen side in the negotiations must meet two requirements: it must publicly dissociate itself from terrorism and be able to control the situation in Chechnya.

The Moscow Chechens—in other words, the Chechens in the diaspora —satisfy only the first of those requirements. At the time of my talks with Schröder and Chirac, none of the field commanders, including Maskhadov, was able to reject terrorism unequivocally and support this stance with action.

Hope for negotiations may rise if the Chechen field commanders are drawn to them by the hopelessness of their situation. It seems to me that the statements of some of our military—that under no circumstances will they agree to conduct negotiations with field commanders—is just rhetoric. Life is much more complicated.

What about the West? There were strong forces that took an anti-Russian position on the Chechnya issue. I would divide them into two groups. The first group consists of those who either don't know the true state of affairs or are not aware of the barbarity of the Chechen militants' methods. I am willing to believe that many people in the West were sincerely shocked by the scale of the destruction and civilian casualties that resulted from the military operations in Chechnya. The second group consists of those who do not understand the strategic situation and the inevitable change that would result from either the success or failure of the federal forces in Chechnya. I'd better go into a bit more detail here.

Current developments suggest that the Chechen separatists' rebellion is not an isolated event. This is evident in the presence of foreign mercenaries among the militants, who were themselves trained abroad, are supplied with money and weapons from abroad, and have connections to Osama bin Laden and Al-Qaeda.

Chechnya cannot be seen in isolation when there are parallel attempts to establish Greater Albania as an extremist Islamic state in the center of Europe. Here one may speak of a strategic extremist Islamic triangle: Afghanistan, the North Caucasus, and Kosovo. I wonder about those who zealously criticize Russia for actions aimed at, among other things, preventing a corner of this triangle from being established in the North Caucasus.

The war in Chechnya by no means fits the definition of an anti-Chechen or religious war. The more people understand this, the less needless criticism of Russia there will be. When I say all this I am obviously not trying to justify the civilian casualties and destruction that are associated with the Chechen war.

The latest developments lead to two conclusions. First, the creation of local authorities is well advanced. Kadyrov has been elected president of the Chechen republic. He was with the guerillas in the first Chechen war but later, upon discovering the actual intentions of its leaders, switched sides. Supported by the federal authorities, Kadyrov focuses on spurring the Chechen militia, which is augmenting its fight against the bandits.

Second, the impossibility of negotiating with former Chechen leaders —neither Basaev nor Maskhadov—was proven yet again. It is widely known that terrorists took more than eight hundred people hostage in a Moscow theater in 2002. This tragedy resulted in loss of lives. To keep the whole theater, together with the hostages, from being blown up, a rescue operation was mounted. Gas had to be used, and 128 people died. Was the rescue operation necessary? The answer is yes, unequivocally. Several hours before the rescue operation at the request of the hostages, I met with Baraev, the leader of the terrorist group. He said that starting at noon the next day he would begin killing hostages one by one until the federal troops were withdrawn from Chechnya. He mentioned the name of his "emir"—it was Basaev. Later it was speculated that Maskhadov could have been unaware of the terrorist act beforehand. I cannot believe that such a sophisticated operation with more than fifty terrorists involved (all were killed during the assault) could have been masterminded and worked out without Maskhadov's knowledge. If in fact Maskhadov did not know of the terrorist attack, that is further proof of his inability to control the situation.

So, with whom do we negotiate?

NEGOTIATIONS WITH THE IMF: MARKING TIME

The Chechen problem began to have an increasingly negative impact on our relations with a number of Western states after the government I headed resigned. However, the bombing of Yugoslavia by NATO forces took place while my government was still in power. This did not create the most favorable international climate for the work of the Cabinet. There was also little reason for optimism about our negotiations with the IMF.

By the time our government was formed, Russia already had a long history of relations with the International Monetary Fund. We received loans. They came with recommendations with which Russia's economic decision makers agreed, as a rule, even when they were obviously unfeasible. They were grateful that no one set firm rules for the use of the credits. I would call this a mutually beneficial cooperation, where both partners shut their eyes and were happy with each other.

The situation began to change after August 1998. In front of me is an interview that Michel Camdessus, director of the IMF, gave to *Le Monde* on October 27, 1998. He stated that in managing the crisis, one should not be limited solely by a macroeconomic approach. His next eye-opener was that he was voicing some of his retrospective evaluations of Russia for the first time. He said we had liberalized capital in a way that was disorganized and sometimes contrary to common sense. The IMF never welcomed excessive liberalization of capital for speculation at a time when administrative barriers for foreign investment were in place. Finally, in Camdessus's opinion, international financial institutions such as the IMF and the World Bank have a mission to make decisions that go beyond the purely financial and directly affect the life of a society.

These words were probably motivated by a desire to answer growing criticism of the IMF for its unwillingness to condescend to consider the diversity and difficulties of the countries to which it offered credits, and its propensity to view all of them, starting with Indonesia and ending with Russia, as fitting a single model where universal, mainly macroeconomic rules of behavior apply but do not always guarantee social or political stability.

But words are words. A dialogue with the director of the IMF might improve my understanding of the IMF's position. I met with Camdessus at the beginning of December 1998. The exchange of views did not disappoint me. In particular, Camdessus said that in general he approved of our strategy in regard to the accumulated debt. "For our part, we will do more than before to support your negotiations with the Paris Club, since we realize that the Soviet-era debt must be restructured and at the same time all obligations on the Russian debt must be met. Despite statements in the Russian press, your government did a lot in a very short time."

Our conversation during dinner at our White House was completely informal and even frank. Afterward we went to a shooting gallery. I knew that Chernomyrdin had invited Camdessus to go hunting in one of the forests near Moscow while he was prime minister. Some people said that not all the wild pigs that fell had been hit by the IMF director's bullets—hunters who crouched in the bushes were much better shots. I have to say, however, that at the shooting range Camdessus was a good shot. All in all, we were elated; we thought the $8 billion transfer that was promised to us earlier would be arriving any day now.

We would soon be disappointed. True, there was no shortage of meetings. Visits to Moscow by various IMF officials alternated with visits by our representatives to the United States. At Camdessus's request, Mikhail Zadornov was appointed to coordinate Russia's interactions with the IMF. Yeltsin talked to Schröder about speeding up the signing of an agreement with the IMF to enable Russia to receive the next transfers. President Chirac phoned me and promised to convince Camdessus.

Did Russia need the IMF loans? Obviously we managed to survive without them, but the lack of them made life more difficult, especially in view of our need to pay our debts. In eight months we paid more than $6 billion, money we very much needed ourselves. The IMF credits were only a part of the story. Without signing an agreement with the IMF, we couldn't restructure our debts with the London and Paris clubs, receive the loans from the International Bank for Reconstruction and Development agreed on earlier, or even receive credits and loans on a bilateral basis.

I remember when Prime Minister Keizo Obuti of Japan called me before his visit to Moscow. I had had cordial relations with him since the times when we were both foreign ministers. Half-jokingly he told me, "For the bravery you demonstrated by agreeing to head the government at such a critical time, I promise that Japan will issue Russia a credit for a total of $800 million." Naturally, I thanked my colleague profusely. A few days later, however, when the Japanese finance minister got in touch with Zadornov to confirm Japan's commitment, he said it would be implemented after Russia and the IMF had signed an agreement.

That agreement kept being delayed. We in the government tried our hardest to patch the holes in the social sphere, stimulate the economy and both industry and agriculture, rebuild the collapsed banking system, maintain the fighting ability of the armed forces, and guarantee the repayment of debts. And we were lectured over and over again and presented with requests and demands that were sometimes impossible to fulfill. I don't say that everything that came from the IMF was incorrect or unusable. But its main objective seemed to be to amass enough arguments to delay the signing of the agreement and demonstrate our incompetence.

Here are some excerpts from documents that I think reveal a great deal. From Camdessus's letter dated March 3, 1999:

Dear Mr. Prime Minister:

To follow up on your suggestions regarding the possible continuation of our joint work that I received through Ambassador Ushakov, I sent an IMF expert to Moscow to discuss the financial program for 1999 with representatives of the government.
The above-mentioned expert already made a report for me from

which I learned with satisfaction that discussions in Moscow were open and honest and that they contributed to our understanding of the prerequisites for the 1999 budget. However, unfortunately the discussions did not lead to an agreement on the major fiscal measures. As for revenues, I was disappointed to learn about the government's decision to abolish the export duty on gas, lower the taxation of the gas industry, and reject the export duties on the export of oil due to the fall in oil prices.[12]

I am also alarmed by the fact that so far no steps have been taken to close the major banks that are potential sources of additional losses in the public sector, and that the law on the restructuring of banks is still waiting to be adopted. Finally, as you know, I am concerned about the reports about possible misuse of reserves of the Central Bank, and we would need guarantees that the funds that have already been allocated by the IMF will be used appropriately. . . .

I answered Camdessus calmly and with restraint, attempting to show specifically and in detail that some of the questions he posed were already being resolved upon our own initiative; his other questions did not escape our attention either. To make a long story short, a lot was being done to clear a path toward an agreement. In conclusion, I once again confirmed that we thought it would be extremely important for an IMF mission to come to Moscow within the next few days. For our part, we were ready to issue instructions to our ministries and departments to encourage them to work productively and constructively.

On March 9 Camdessus sent me another letter, informing me that he was sending a "vanguard group to try to narrow the differences in evaluations and to develop and agree on additional measures in the area of taxation." The arrival of the IMF's vanguard group was a positive development, and we in the government agreed to do everything possible for successful contacts between them and our ministries and departments.

Yury Maslyukov headed the work with IMF missions on our side. At first the top management of the IMF were cool toward this decision. Gradually these suspicions evaporated, however, as our partners saw that he wanted to achieve an agreement with the IMF. Personally, I had no doubt that he would act precisely as he did. I was firmly of the opinion that the first deputy prime minister should lead our day-to-day work with the IMF, regardless of what some people in our country and abroad thought about it. This is precisely what happened.

I met with the IMF mission on March 19. After mutual greetings I offered to discuss concrete issues. At first we discussed the 32 billion rubles to add to Russia's budget that Gerard Belanger and Maslyukov agreed on during the preliminary exchange of views.

But where could we find those additional revenues? I said I was ready to discuss and try to follow the IMF's recommendations, if it was possible to do so. For instance, we liked the idea of introducing an additional tax on the most expensive foreign cars. That measure was acceptable because it would not hit the broad masses of the population. Obviously, we had to consider the question of raising gasoline prices, but only for high-octane gasoline, because we couldn't deal a blow to agricultural production, the army, and the part of the population that was not affluent.

I emphasized that difficulties with the revenue part of our budget were to a large degree due to nonpayment by the CIS countries for oil, gas, and electricity. Their debt was $7 billion, of which Ukraine owed $2 billion. When I was foreign minister we also delivered gas to Sarajevo on credit, at the request of several countries, including the United States.

"We have some reserves," I continued, "but we would prefer not to reduce them. Although these reserves are small and insufficient, we would like to invest them in the industrial sector of the economy. Because if we do that, we'll be taking care of tomorrow."

Belanger said he would help us, and asked if we were ready to consider a situation in which Gazprom contributed less to the budget than it was required to contribute by law. I tried to explain that Gazprom is a joint-stock company that makes contributions to the state budget in the form of taxes and export duties. If we demanded more money, which would be against the law, Gazprom might say that it would no longer deliver gas to Belarus, Ukraine, and Georgia until they covered their debts. It could also set domestic prices equal to export prices and stop deliveries of gas to power stations that couldn't pay for it, and that would be most of them. All this had to be taken into consideration.

Belanger's advice took on moralizing overtones. He said we needed to force everyone to pay their debts in monetary form and to create conditions in which all companies as well as Ukraine would pay for gas and public utilities in monetary form. I had to explain that the share of monetary payments was growing, but it was impossible to solve the problem at one go. For instance, the share of "live money" payments by Gazprom increased, but we could not immediately demand that it rise to 100 percent. This problem could not be solved by Gazprom alone, since its resolution depended on the general state of the economy. The economy had started to revive. I had to stress that Russia was not isolated from the world economy; quite the contrary, it was being incorporated into it. The government pushed several important laws through the Duma, including the law on product sharing, the law on investment, and the law on concessions. Didn't the IMF see the real difficulties we were facing and the efforts we were making to overcome them? That was the question I asked Belanger, and I added that this was the moment when we needed to sign an agreement with the IMF, and that the agreement ought to be based on mutual understanding.

Belanger played his own game. He said he wasn't asking us to raise pensions, simply to adjust them for inflation. He said he wanted us to find a way to do that. As if we hadn't tried!

I decided to cross all my *t*'s and dot all my *i*'s: "There are three scenarios. The first is the one we would like to implement, which is to reach an agreement with the IMF. The second option is to conclude that the IMF is unwilling to provide loans for us. This scenario would be bad for the country in general and for the government in particular. I doubt that it's in the interests of the IMF, either. However, there also is a third scenario, which is absolutely unacceptable to us, which is a wait-and-see attitude on the part of the IMF and endless negotiations. So far our government's relationship with the IMF consists of pleasant talks and nothing else. So far there is no progress toward practical results."

That was the end of that conversation.

At the end of March the managing director of the IMF visited Moscow again. By phone I had urged him to visit, since I had been unable to go to the United States, where we were supposed to meet. I talked to Camdessus first with the full delegation in attendance and then face to face. The conversation took place in the White House on March 29. Camdessus had already met with the heads of the Federation Council and the State Duma, party leaders, and Patriarch Alexei II,[13] not to speak of Viktor Gerashchenko, head of the Central Bank; government ministers; and Rem Vyakhirev, chairman of Gazprom, among others. Camdessus also spoke by phone with the president.

"I wanted to thank you for organizing the trip so well," said Camdessus at the beginning of our meeting. "I was able to meet with a record number of officials."

And then everything went down the tubes again.

"Mikhail Zadornov told me about the additional 17 billion rubles you need for a reasonable increase in expenses and a 2 percent increase in revenue. But to these 17 billion we need to add the full amount necessary to bring salaries and pensions to a level commensurate with inflation," Camdessus said, smiling maliciously.

With the help of Maslyukov, Zadornov, and Georgy Boos, minister of tax collection, I tried to demonstrate that we couldn't overcome all the catastrophic consequences of August 17 in a single year (1999), and that those expenses amounted to 30 percent of revenues. By the second half of 1998 we had resumed regular payments of salaries and pensions and made a decisive start on reducing arrears in salaries and even eliminated some of them. In 1999 we began salary adjustments, which were not small. We allocated funds for them in the budget. But in 1999 we couldn't compensate people for everything they had lost as a result of August 17, 1998. It should also be borne in mind that it would only be worse if we went to indexation without supporting it by budget revenues and continued to accumulate debts on salaries, pensions, and payments to the army.

Camdessus and his team listened to our explanations, and then they came up with a new figure for the needed increase in revenue: "at least" 45 billion!

"We keep returning to our initial positions. From one IMF mission to another we first narrow our differences and then suddenly go back," I said. "Yesterday we reached the figure of 17 billion, but today it turns out that you want to triple it."

"I know you have a very difficult problem with indexing salaries and pensions," said Camdessus. "But let's look at what you'd get if you completely indexed your revenue. In other words, what if the buyers of gasoline at the pump and buyers of alcohol paid the same amount in real terms as they did in July 1998?"

Camdessus said he "wanted to show us the easiest ways to replenish the revenue side of the budget." But in effect he did not respond to my explanation that if the price of a bottle of vodka was $4 in 1998, that would be 20–30 rubles, but in 1999 the same bottle of vodka would cost 100 rubles, which amounted to one-tenth of the average salary. At the time of our conversation the exchange rate was 23–24 rubles per U.S. dollar. "If we followed your recommendation, this government would cease to exist within a few days," I said.

"I don't understand why those who like alcohol should pay less than in 1998," insisted Camdessus.

"No, they don't pay less. Their incomes are smaller. If we set a price of 100 rubles per bottle of vodka, it would be illegally produced and illegally sold. It would be made out of garbage and people would get poisoned. This is real life."

"By restoring the excise tax to the level of 1998, you will receive an additional 3.5 billion rubles," Camdessus continued to push his line. "In August of last year people did not get poisoned."

I could no longer restrain myself: "Indeed they did. Do you know that during 1997 and 1998 alone we lost more people to rotgut than we did during the whole of the Afghan war?"

"It is simply shocking," said Camdessus, changing the subject, "that in Russia the tax on high-octane gasoline is 1 cent per liter, while in Europe in general it's 25 cents per liter and in the United States, which is also a producer, it's 10 cents per liter. If you managed to raise the excise tax to the U.S. level this year, you'd add 20 billion rubles to the budget."

"Show me how you'll do this. You're talking all gasoline. But let's talk about only high-octane gasoline and show me how we'll receive 20 billion. We can't raise the excise tax on all gasoline. That would hit agricultural workers and the army. In addition, we have millions of people who own ten- to fifteen-year-old cars. They keep patching them up and filling them with low-octane gas."

"I'm sorry," Camdessus said. "Let me clarify the numbers. We received incorrect information."

"You understand that in general we simply can't compare prices here and in the United States. You should compare these prices' share of average income in the United States, Russia, and France. And if you show me that this share is smaller in Russia than in France and the United States, then I'll throw up my hands."

"You're saying that you can't get as much money as I said by raising the tax on gasoline," said Camdessus. "All right. But there are several sources from which you could get the money. Gazprom, for example. Also, we agreed that you would think about an export duty of 5 ECUs[14] per ton of oil, regardless of the price of oil."

"We've already set a 5 ECU duty, but only for prices over $12 a barrel. We can't take more. But we think prices will go up. That's why the government decree says bluntly that duties will be adjusted to price dynamics," I answered.

It turned out that the director had not seen this decree. He was not aware of many other things the government had been doing. In the course of our conversation I got the feeling that certain politicians—or to be more precise, political intriguers, mainly from Russia—deliberately supplied him with information that did nothing to encourage Camdessus to reach an agreement with our government.

I don't want to accuse Camdessus, although some complaints would be justified. Still, in general he was in a constructive frame of mind. I am sure that behind his not altogether skillful attempts to increase budget revenues, which were not always made with knowledge of our situation, stood a desire not to let the Russian budget collapse. He remembered that in the past, unrealistic budgets were presented to the State Duma with full awareness that corrections were inevitable and that the necessary funds would come mainly from the International Monetary Fund. He did not believe that we wouldn't follow the same course. When I said we were expecting revenues to increase because the economy was improving, he took my words with a grain of salt. To give him an example, I purposely said nothing about production of raw materials and talked instead about machinery construction, which received three and a half times more orders in January 1999 than in January 1998. His face expressed skepticism. I thought it over and decided the time had come for an energetic conclusion. I said:

"Mr. Camdessus, I agreed that we will definitely have a 2 percent increase in revenue. You have my word on that. That means we will need to increase revenues by 11 or perhaps 18 billion rubles. I don't want to set a specific figure at this time. However, I can state my views on the surplus. That's it. Do you understand? Let's agree on this, because we keep talking in circles.

"Furthermore, the government will do its utmost to preserve the purchasing power of the population in 1999 at a level that will be no less than 85 percent of what it was between January 1 and August 17, 1998. By 2000 all losses that people suffered as a result of the August 1998 crisis should be compensated. The government will do everything in its power to ensure constant—and I would like to stress that word—increases in real incomes. If you want, we can write in the communiqué that the IMF recommends that all additional sources of revenue be used to achieve this goal. Are you satisfied?"

"OK," the director agreed. But he also reserved the right to "state an understanding" on problems other than the budget. Some of them, he said, would be identified during the next IMF mission. When I asked what mission he was talking about, Camdessus said that meetings should be continued in both Moscow and Washington until we could produce a joint statement in the IMF format. "We're getting close," said Camdessus. That statement was to serve as a basis for allocating a loan to the Russian Federation.

"I don't want to complicate the situation," added Camdessus, "but in the future we shouldn't transfer our funds earmarked for Russia through a third bank in London, Zurich, or New York. I don't want to do that because I believe it puts you in a kind of a triangular relationship with them."

The only thing I could say was that if the reason for the delay of credits to Russia lay in the "triangular relationship," then the solution was easy. No control would be needed over the funds we received if the IMF simply transferred them from one of its accounts to another and counted it as Russia's payment on its debt.

Despite the difficult negotiations, Camdessus and I parted on a pleasant note. By that time it was clear that the possibility of realistic progress toward an agreement with the IMF, while depending on the personality of its head, was determined largely by the position of the United States.

Our meetings with the president of the World Bank, James Wolfensson, took place practically at the same time as the negotiations with Camdessus. Negotiations with his team were constructive and successful. We agreed on large loans from the IBRD to develop the mining industry and the social sector. But according to the bank's charter, receipt of these funds depended on an agreement with the IMF.

My colleagues and I had only the best impressions from the meetings with Wolfensson, an outstanding, benevolent man who endeavored to grasp the heart of every problem, to learn the details of our Russian reality, and to help us to the best of his ability. I very much appreciated the letter Wolfensson sent shortly after my removal from the post of prime minister. It gave high marks to the activities of our cabinet and expressed bewilderment at its dismissal.

I was also touched when in June 2000 Wolfensson came to Moscow for a day and a half to meet with President Putin and Chairman of the Government

Mikhail Kasyanov. He did not leave without looking me up. We spent an hour and a half in pleasant talk.

WASHINGTON'S CONFUSED POSITION?

On the eve of my trip to Davos, Switzerland, where an annual forum brings together representatives of business and political elites and heads of governments and even states, I received a message from Al Gore, vice president of the United States. The date was November 14, 1998. He wrote that he was sending me a "frank and even strongly worded" document that included recommendations for Russia. Later we figured out that the author of the "Memorandum on the Question of the Russian Economic Crisis" that was attached to Gore's letter was Larry Sommers, one of the prominent American experts, then deputy secretary of the treasury.

I could hardly believe my eyes when I read this document because so many of its assessments of the reasons for the economic crisis in Russia were in tune with our own. Let me quote some of it verbatim:

> *Lessons from reform efforts undertaken up to now.* The crisis demonstrated tendencies that became clear some time ago. Russia lacks the basics of a market economy: trust in the national currency as a source of value (or even the means of payment in large transactions); a banking system that issues credits to private firms that are not connected with it; a legal system that protects the rights of owners and investors; a just system of regulating and collecting taxes which would provide a predictable, competitive and transparent business climate, supply the government with financial resources and would not serve as a mechanism for state corruption.
>
> There are at least two schools of thought in Russia that explain why these foundations are not developed in Russia. The first one asserts that much time is needed to develop these foundations anywhere, even in the West. Moreover, Russian reformers had unrealistic expectations about the timetable for developing market instruments, laws and accumulation of the market experience which never existed in Russia. According to the other school, the USA and Western, Central and Eastern Europe cannot serve as models for Russia. The Asian paths of development are more

important, since they to a larger extent depend on cooperation and interconnection of the state and private sectors.

Both are probably right. But for Russia the role of the state is paramount.

Russia is facing a long struggle not only to create effective state institutions, but also to overcome deep-rooted resistance to the very idea of strengthening the civil state. As happened in the history of our country, part of the final solution to the problem of legality of power could very well be the transfer of governing authority from the central government to the regions and local governments.

The model of a market democracy remains the right choice for Russia. However, it must receive support from the state, which creates a competitive, orderly, predictable and transparent environment.

There are no cultural or specifically Russian peculiarities that explain the fact that the country was unable to move toward investment and growth during the past six years. No, deplorable economic results are explained by the natural reaction of a part of the Russian population and business to obvious failures in the areas of policy regulation and the legal system.

The following was the key phrase: "Prime Minister Primakov and his government are facing the extremely difficult but unavoidable task of determining a new economic course."

All this sounded like an obvious criticism of the authors and executors of Russia's economic policy earlier in the 1990s. But why hadn't the American leaders been so direct with either Gaidar or Chubais or Fyodorov or Chernomyrdin or, finally, Yeltsin? Why hadn't they favored the regulating and controlling role of the state *back then*, before we came to power? Certainly this was to be carried out in a civilized manner and accompanied by the country's full transition to market relations, but still with a sharp strengthening of the role of the state.

During the preelection period of 1999–2000, the Republicans criticized Clinton and Gore for "giving Russia too much." In fact those criticisms were groundless. In the economic sphere they gave practically nothing, not only financially but in real advice. In the area of science and technology they received a great deal dirt cheap, among other things via the brain drain from Russia. The president of the Russian Academy of Sciences, Yury Osipov, said in an interview, with bitterness and pain, "We must realize that many representatives of the most promising trends in science for the twenty-first century received wonderful education and training in the scientific schools of the Academy of Sciences, and the best universities of Russia today replenish the scientific communities and companies of the United States, Germany, France, Canada, and other countries."[15]

The policy of "taming" Russia that the U.S. leaders counted on in the 1990s cost them very little. I support Bill Clinton and Al Gore on this issue.

But let's turn again to the memorandum the vice president sent me. Apart from the assessment of the current state of affairs and the reasons for the crisis in Russia, it suggests a whole series of measures. Many of them were already being employed. For instance, strict limits on the amount of money put into circulation; rejection of issuing money to finance the indiscriminate rescuing of banks; refusal to take steps that would limit the convertibility of the ruble; transition to a floating foreign currency exchange rate, "with the possibility of fixing it in the future, when adequate macroeconomic conditions are created"; liquidation of debts in unpaid salaries and pensions; audit checks of banks "to determine a few of them that should be preserved in accordance with recommendations of the Central Bank"; a change in ownership and management of insolvent banks; establishing more competitive and transparent "procedures for privatization"; an increase in collection of taxes in monetary form; and so on.

Other suggestions concurred with our intentions, such as tax reform with reduction of the level of taxes and their collection on a wider, predictable, and more honest basis in order to "bring the subjects from the shadow economy into the official sector"; changing the "system of Russian tax federalism into a better combination of revenues and responsibility"; separation of banks from large financial-production enterprises; "de facto implementation of the law on product sharing in order to remove the barriers for the flow of billions of dollars in the form of direct foreign investment into the Russian energy sector"; allowing "wider participation of foreign banks in building a healthy, governable banking system that issues credits to the industrial sector of the economy"; and guaranteed protection of intellectual property. Other suggestions included making "concrete irresponsible actions of majority stockholders illegal" and fighting crime and corruption in the police.

It was as if the Americans heard our discussions at government meetings and presented our own plans as their advice!

But there were other recommendations that we were unable to implement at that stage; for instance, advancing the retirement age, abandoning subsidies and direct credits, and a special taxation program for foreign investment in the energy sector.

After receiving Gore's message and the accompanying memorandum with its many statements I agreed with, I left in good spirits for Davos, where I was to meet the vice president of the United States. After delivering an address to the forum in which I outlined the main directions of government activity, I headed off to the house where Gore was staying. He received me very cordially. The conversation revolved mainly around the events in Kosovo. Suddenly Larry Sommers entered the hall of the wooden two-story chalet. I told him that the memorandum we received was a very interesting document. To my great surprise, he smiled and said, "But you are so far from implementing the recommended key measures." So this is how the wind was blowing. Remember that this meeting took place after our first contacts with the IMF.

Obviously trying to relieve the tension, Gore emphasized the importance of this talk. But my heart was still heavy. Was it really possible to program the direction of a conversation regardless of what the person you were talking to was saying or was going to say? As it turned out, it was possible.

I was convinced of this all over again during my meeting with Strobe Talbott on February 23, 1999, in the White House in Moscow. Before the meeting I was handed a memorandum by Talbott headed "Economic Issues." It opened with the claim that the United States had initiated a "comprehensive package of assistance" to Russia from the Big Eight. Then there were direct threats. During the past year, the memo said, discussions on economic issues had begun to remind the Americans of a dialogue of the deaf. If we mistakenly concluded that they didn't wish us well, that they wanted us to fail, then it seemed unlikely that we would be able to agree on other issues.

The Russian government, the memorandum went on to say, had failed to demonstrate true readiness to engage in the purely technical discussions necessary if we were to achieve agreement on the new program of credits. As a result of my meetings with Madeleine Albright, Vice President Gore, and others in Davos, the United States was under the impression that we viewed it as a political question, as if Bill Clinton could just declare that Russia needed to receive IMF support and the other members of the Big Eight would fall in line.

Then came a whole series of arguments against an immediate agreement with the IMF. According to the memorandum, within a few months the money would be either eaten by inflation or lost as a result of capital flight. At the same time, the burden of Russia's debts would become even heavier and the economy would be in an even worse situation. Regardless of support from the IMF, if Russia didn't have a rational economic program, it would have to either turn on the printing press to pay the bills or pile up debts.

An analysis conducted by the IMF made it absolutely clear, the memo concluded, that our current budget did not allow payments of salaries and pensions. The IMF did not want to reduce these budget expenditures, but in order to protect salaries and pensions Russia needed a new plan for expenditures and a higher level of revenues flowing into the budget. Also, the IMF program was necessary to open the way for the restructuring of debts.

Just as during negotiations on arms control, the memo went on, talks with the IMF required a great deal of difficult technical work. Both sides needed to build up trust and work through a large number of difficult questions. At the time, however, despite the great interest of the parties, there was still no foundation for building mutual trust and resolving the basic technical issues. Work toward laying that foundation was to serve as a starting point in Russia's cooperation with the IMF.

"You need to," "it is imperative," "has to be done," "you must"—commands burst forth in full strength in the section headed "What to Do?":

> You and the IMF need to reach an agreement on how to form
> a rational foundation for the budget. It is imperative for the IMF
> to understand how you are going to ensure the receipt of a large
> amount of funds to finance all priority areas of your policy and
> to counterbalance the unfounded provisions regarding the ruble
> exchange rate, inflation and spending. This has to be done on
> the basis of the purely technical and concrete data.
>
> I want you to understand how many political and economic
> efforts we made. We are talking about many billions of dollars,
> and not only in the funds provided by the IMF, but also about
> what kind of assistance is intended for the payment of the debt.

This means that you must demonstrate a similar degree of decisiveness, decisiveness in taking active steps.

I won't deny that I was outraged by this essay on economic issues. What did they take us for? Did Talbott really think the time had come to speak to us in such tones? I had no doubt that he had some help in writing the memorandum. But that didn't matter. Talbott was known to be close to President Clinton. That was why I decided to cross all my *t*'s and dot all my *i*'s during our meeting. I would like to emphasize that Strobe and I are friends. I paid special attention to this meeting, since Talbott's memorandum made it crystal-clear that the IMF's decisions were dictated by Washington.

On February 23, 1999, at the White House in Moscow, I began my conversation with Talbott by saying, "I read your memorandum carefully and I have to say that I'm surprised, at the very least. You write that we've been having a *dialogue* of the deaf. I disagree. This is a *monologue* of the deaf and the blind. Can you think that we are doing nothing? Can't you see what is happening in the country? I don't know, probably the ambassador sends you some information. You also have analysts who follow developments in Russia.

"The government has been in power for half a year. To suggest that political stabilization was the only thing that happened during that time is absolutely incorrect. From the economic point of view we achieved quite a lot. We don't shout about it because we don't see these results as a breakthrough. But the thing is that predictions made in the United States are not coming true. According to your predictions, everything was going to collapse in Russia. Huge inflation was predicted. But in reality, in February it was reduced to 4 percent compared to 8 percent in January and 11 percent in December. It was predicted that the ruble's exchange rate would approach 100 to 120 rubles per dollar. But in reality the ruble exchange rate is now 22.5 to 22.8 per dollar. I'm not saying that the rate won't change, but we are containing it.

"You criticize us for not dealing with the economy. Why, then, during the five months that the present government has been in office, was the extraordinary financing through issuance of currency only $1 billion? This is very little. At the same time we completely settled up with state employees, we paid salary arrears to the army, we're paying pensions, although we still haven't paid pension arrears. If this is not emission financing, where do we find all these funds? Neither you nor the IMF nor anyone gave us a cent. Where did it all come from then? This means that tax revenues increased. It means that revenues from duties increased also, even though imports are lower as a result of the crisis. It also means that we are fighting against corruption and crime. So it's going slowly and gradually, but the economy is reviving!

"You can't be a prisoner of views that have nothing in common with reality. And you can't talk to us in the tone in which that memorandum was written. We are going to meet the IMF requirements. As you correctly pointed out, we had a budget surplus of 2 percent. But they tell us we need more. There are always demands. But at what expense? Those who understand economics answer, How can we do this? By not paying state employees and the army? Or when a pilot is required to have 160 flying hours and receives only enough fuel for 10? That won't happen. This government would rather resign than do that. I won't undermine the social situation in the country; that would provoke chaos. Neither you nor we are interested in that.

"Don't think that we are satisfied with the economic situation in the country. But this difficult situation has a lot to do with your wait-and-see approach to Russia and because the IMF maintains the same attitude, at your insistence. Without an agreement with the IMF we can't restructure our debts to the London and Paris clubs, can't receive loans already allocated from the World Bank, and can't get loans and credits on the bilateral state level.

"Do you want to isolate us? Say so directly and then we'll think about what we should do and what steps to take. Where does this attitude toward us come from? You think we're doing something against the United States? If that's what you think, tell us openly. But we're not even thinking about that.

"You're afraid we may adopt a fake budget? But we can't include in the budget the 'realistic rates' you suggest. Imagine what would happen if the budget assumed the exchange rate to be 40 rubles per dollar. The next week the exchange rate on the street would be 40 rubles per dollar. When Kirienko outlined the upper level that the ruble was to reach by the end of the year, it reached that level the following week. We chose a different approach by insisting that the budget be corrected every quarter. In general I can sense some kind of condescension on your part, as if people from the university came to teach the failing high school students.

"Now I would like to talk about something else. We receive signals from you indicating that you want either to revise the ABM treaty or to create a national ABM system unilaterally. Is this an ultimatum? Now about the Kosovo issue. Madeleine Albright now sees that the Serbs are not solely to blame. What will be achieved by military strikes against the Serbs? You are once again pushing us into a corner. And this strike that's being prepared is groundless from any point of view. I don't know, maybe I'm old-fashioned, but I just don't understand a lot of things.

"Pardon me for being emotional," I concluded, "but all this truly hurts us."

"The only statement that I completely disagree with, Yevgeny Maksimovich, is your apology. Certainly when I came here I knew there were problems in our relationship, but in the last thirty-five minutes my assessment shifted significantly toward pessimism, though still not hopelessness. I think we can use this meeting to really achieve progress in understanding each other and I'm stressing understanding. Stagnation in our relations is unacceptable, especially because it can be avoided. There are both objective and subjective grounds for improving our relations. I think my goal should be to be able to tell the president, the vice president, and the secretary of state that although our meeting was very frank, and perhaps even angry, it was still a good talk that perhaps laid a foundation for future progress.

"Let me start with the economy. I think it's necessary to point out that the intentions of President Clinton and Vice President Gore are 100 percent contrary to what you suspect. If Russia felt isolated, it would indeed have negative consequences for the president and vice president[16] and for the whole world for decades. But if Russia integrates into the rest of the world, then we'll be able to work together to resolve global issues. And there's no limit to what can be achieved through such work.

"Your guests do not represent the IMF," said Talbott. "Currently you are in direct contact with Mr. Camdessus and his colleagues and we hope that in the end these contacts will be successful. We represent President Clinton and Vice President Gore. It's clear to me that this document, to which you reacted in the way you did, was a bad idea. When I return to Washington I'll conduct a thorough investigation, although I'm afraid that the first draft of this document can be found in my computer. It would be even more unpleasant to learn that the president of the United States was involved in the final product. There were two reasons why he wanted to participate in this meeting, even though he is not here. First, he wanted to point out that the political decision he made six years ago to assist Russia—that by all means includes the government you chair. The goal of all the American diplomats who are here today is to build a bridge between a positive political solution and the economic issues that are still to be resolved. And the second reason is to remove any problem that you haven't mentioned in your remarks, namely Iran, in order to disarm the bomb that may explode."

Then Carlos Pasqual, of the National Security Council, joined the discussion at Talbott's request. He essentially repeated what Strobe Talbott had already said. Once again he reprimanded us, although not in the language that was used in the memorandum. I once again explained our point of view.

What aftertaste remained in the wake of this meeting? The Americans, including Pasqual, stressed that they were talking on behalf of the highest government officials of the United States. The arguments they used echoed the reasoning of the IMF, and from their direct statements it was clear not only that Washington and the IMF were tightly connected, but also that the guidelines set by the United States determined whether financial assistance was or was not made available. As a matter of fact, it would be more precise to say that the United States facilitated the IMF's wait-and-see attitude, which in the opinion of many people in Washington was to serve several purposes. One of its goals was to force a weakened Russia, under threat of bankruptcy if IMF debts were not paid, at least not to resist America's foreign policy (events in Kosovo were about to take place, the anti-Saddam operation was not yet finished in Iraq, a movement to create a national anti-ballistic-missile system amounted to unilateral withdrawal from the ABM treaty of 1972). The other goal was internal, connected to an attempt to strengthen the Democrats in their election struggle with the Republicans by showing that the current leadership of the United States was not toothless when it came to Russia.

It seems that by that time two schools of thought had formed in the American establishment. The first, which I believe included Clinton, Albright, and Talbott, continued to think it important to maintain good relations with Russia, because they were necessary for global stability. But the age of "Brother Boris" was coming to an end. Russia should be kept at a distance for now. Who knew how events would develop in that country, where (and this really put Americans on guard) corruption was becoming widespread and the oligarchs were grasping at political power? In America the attitude toward these oligarchs was strongly negative because of their "shadiness." The second school of thought advised ignoring Russia altogether. Their attitude was: Let Russia stew in its own juice.

I think it was no accident that Talbott so pointedly raised the question of Iran, which seemed to have no direct bearing on what we were discussing.

He focused even more sharply on Iran when I talked to him in private after the general meeting.

How did Iran became a subject in Russian-American relations? Iran is a sovereign state in which complex processes are unfolding. There is an internal clash between the strengthening secular movement and the religious extremists, who still wield considerable power. The election of President Mohammad Khatami in 1998 showed that the vast majority of the electorate rejected a strict Islamic organization of state and society. That is one development. Another is that Qum, the religious center of Iran, seems to be rejecting the idea of exporting the Islamic revolution of Ayatollah Ruhollah Khomeini, which was a prominent feature of the Islamists who came to power after they deposed the shah in 1979.

Russia followed all these changes attentively, and not just out of idle curiosity. Iran is a neighboring country with which we have had decades of mutually beneficial relations. These relations have not been interrupted and not only have a strong economic element but since the mid-1990s have also included political cooperation, especially on matters in which our interests converge. Of primary importance, as I have mentioned, was stabilization in Tajikistan and rejection of an extremist position regarding Afghanistan.

I talked about the situation in Iran with Madeleine Albright on many occasions, trying to persuade her that tough policies that tended to turn that country into an outcast of the world community served only to worsen the situation in Iran and were thus completely counterproductive.

Russia's cooperation with Iran in building an atomic power station in Bushehr has long been a bone of contention in Russian-American relations. Washington remained deaf to our explanations that what we were doing in Bushehr had nothing to do with nuclear arms, that we were delivering light-water reactors that in their characteristics and potential were exactly the same as those that the United States promised to deliver to China. A Russian organization had intended—and it remained only an intention—to develop a scientific (nonmilitary) booster and a uranium mine in Iran, but these projects were vetoed by the president of the Russian Federation.

The wave of interest in the United States in Russian-Iranian relations was manifested rather vividly in 1997–98, especially on the issue of the missile industry in Iran. The United States made it a ubiquitous point of discussion during meetings with Russian representatives at all levels. I think Israeli and American intelligence added fuel to the fire, although they could not present any facts suggesting that Russian state institutions violated any international rules or broke any of their international commitments in their cooperation with Iran. The list that was circulated and given to us in its entirety by the Americans, Israelis, and representatives of other countries under their influence consisted mostly of either unverified information about private Russian firms (for instance, the address given for one of them turned out to be a hostel) or farfetched accusations (for instance, that Iranian students were studying in the physics department of one of Moscow's institutes of higher learning).

But still there is no smoke without fire. The thing is that some scientists and specialists not only in the Russian Federation but also from other CIS countries could travel to Iran, sometimes through Europe, and provide various consulting services. When I served as head of the government, the FSB reported that not a single individual who had left Russia in recent years had directly participated on a level of any importance in the production of weapons of mass destruction or means for their delivery. But certainly one could not guarantee that a scientist who studied turbulence, say, would be unable to travel abroad. Prohibition of such travel could not be imposed. If that happened, Western democrats would be the first to criticize us. Furthermore, uncontrolled trips abroad could be carried out via the transparent borders with the CIS countries, such as Ukraine and Kazakhstan.

Some attempts were made in Russia to transfer to Iran some secret military data that it wanted, but these attempts, far from being encouraged, were suppressed by the Russian Federal Security Service, without any hints from the outside. These FSB actions were made public. Thus there were no grounds to accuse Russia of something it never did and was not going to do.

In response to American allegations, which as a rule were general rather than specific, we asked them, also as a rule, to provide clarifying concrete facts. I addressed not only Americans but also Israelis when I visited Israel as Russian foreign minister and at the insistence of my hosts met with the heads of military intelligence. I was told that they could not provide us with concrete data because they did not want to compromise their sources.

But let's return to my discussion with Talbott. I told him that the subject of Iran could not serve as an irritant in Russian-American relations. We would strictly follow all international regulations, but the United States could not force its own rules on Russia.

To my deep regret, the emphasis on the Iranian problem continued. At the end of 2000 the United States began to insist that we cease all military and scientific cooperation with Iran, all of which was within the framework of deliveries of conventional weapons. Russia certainly could not submit to such a dictate.

A month after my conversation with Talbott, a delegation headed by Maslyukov flew to the United States for final negotiations with the IMF. In a statement dated April 30, 1999, addressed to me, the director of the IMF, Michel Camdessus, wrote:

> I am happy that we managed to reach an agreement with
> Mr. Maslyukov and his team on your economic program. I have
> no doubt that the implementation of this program, together
> with the measures that you are planning to implement in regard
> to the credit offered by the World Bank to conduct structural
> changes, will strengthen Russia's macroeconomic stability and
> improve the future of reforms aimed at a transition to a market
> economy, based on monetary growth. This will lead to positive
> economic growth.
>
> I would be happy to recommend that the Executive Commit-
> tee approve the agreement to offer Russia credit in the amount
> of 3.3 billion SDR,[17] as soon as you implement the first-stage
> measures that would facilitate this program.
>
> I can reassure you that the IMF will continue to support your
> efforts to implement the economic program in these difficult
> times. I clearly see the difficulties that you have to overcome,
> and I also know that there is no easy path for restoring economic
> stability and creating conditions for economic growth.

It seemed that the marathon was coming to an end. However, the policy of dragging out the matter of IMF credits was resumed in the governments of Stepashin, Putin, and Kasyanov.

U-TURN OVER THE ATLANTIC

In the meantime, despite the measures we undertook to attract foreign investors and rebuild their trust, and despite the fact that the largest international companies did not leave the Russian market after the August 17 events, Russia's bilateral economic ties with foreign countries were not at their best. Conditions for access of Russian goods to the markets of our trade partners worsened, to the detriment of Russia's industry, which was just beginning to get on its feet, and of our ability to pay our foreign debts.

The government sought to establish equal conditions of access to foreign markets. Once again much depended on the U.S. position. Around March 20 the Russian-American Commission held one of the periodic meetings chaired jointly by Vice President Al Gore and the Russian prime minister of the moment, Chernomyrdin, Kirienko, or me.

We prepared very thoroughly for this trip. Several members of the cabinet flew to the United States in advance to conduct negotiations with the Americans. I was prepared to take part in discussions not only during the plenary sessions of the commission but also in specific committees. At the meeting of the committee on developing business partnerships, I decided to emphasize the export of Russian steel to the United States. The U.S. steel lobby exerted extreme pressure on the administration in an effort to close off access for Russian steel to the U.S. market. An antidumping investigation was started with this goal in mind. The well-being of several of our large metallurgical plants depended on exports of steel, and production in those plants in turn influenced the revival of a significant part of the industry. Before I left for the States, the directors of many such plants visited me to ask me to protect their interests.

Our government inherited the unresolved problem of financing by the U.S. ExImBank of a joint project to create an IL-96 MT airplane. As for us, we fulfilled all our commitments, starting with registering the plane outside Russia and ending with issuing credit from Vnesheconombank.

I was going to pose the question of the American certification of the AN-124–100 plane, which was already certified as a civilian cargo plane by the International Aviation Committee (IAC). American certification of the plane was required for its use in the United States, and its introduction in the U.S. air transportation market was of interest to us. But certification was dragging on and on.

And certainly I was going to mention our old request for permanent most-favored-nation status in trade with the United States. I also wanted to pay special attention to encouraging economic cooperation between the two countries on the regional level, such as between the Russian Far East and the West Coast of the United States.

I wanted to raise the issues of American support for small business in Russia in the form of cheap credit and widening of cooperation in agricultural business, including the entrance of the largest American manufacturers of farm machinery, such as Case and John Deere. Apart from importing agricultural machinery, we wanted joint ventures to be established with them in Russia.

A meeting with representatives of large American businesses was scheduled, during which I was going to invite them to enter into active cooperation with us.

In general, the economic program of my visit to the United States was well put together. I think it demonstrated that our government considered the interests of Russia's businesses one of its most important tasks, regardless of their form of ownership. Most of the projects I mentioned were of interest to joint-stock companies and private entrepreneurs.

And certainly the trip to the United States provided an opportunity to conduct meetings with the president, vice president, and secretary of state on a whole range of Russian-American relations. As the conversation with Talbott had shown, such discussions were very necessary.

On March 18, literally on the eve of the trip, Al Gore called me late in the evening. After an exchange of greetings and remarks about the approaching meeting in Washington, Gore changed the subject to events in Kosovo. First he talked about fears that "Belgrade may start a wide-scale assault at any moment." Russia had received no such information. Gore pointed out that the "Kosovo problem can be solved peacefully," and then added, "Trust me, air strikes are not our choice."

If I understood him correctly, he was asking us to issue a political statement that would make it clear that Belgrade was responsible for the breakup of negotiations.[18]

I said frankly that if we made such a statement, it might be interpreted as our invitation to strike against Yugoslavia. We could not and would not do that.

It became apparent that the Kosovo theme was to be heard more and more distinctly in connection with the approaching meeting in Washington. But we in Moscow still hoped to prevent a situation in which, on the initiative of the United States, NATO would carry out a strike against Yugoslavia.

On March 22 Leon Fert, national security adviser to Vice President Gore, made the following statement to Deputy Chairman of the Government Konstantin Kosachev, pointing out that he was reading a text prepared in advance:

1. Washington believes that the approaching visit of Primakov is very important for both sides.

2. This visit will take place in the background of the very rapid developments in Kosovo.

3. The American side gives one more chance to S. Milosevic by sending R. Holbrooke to Belgrade.

4. If this meeting does not bring the desired results, S. Milosevic will carry the full weight of responsibility for the consequences, including a military operation.

5. The main thing is that Primakov understands the seriousness of the situation so that the possible actions of the American side are not a surprise for him. The American side wants to be absolutely clear on this question.

On his own behalf Leon Fert said this information "by no means was advice to Ye. M. Primakov to cancel his trip."

Kosachev came into my office while Foreign Minister Ivanov and FSB Director Trubnikov were there. I dictated the following reply, which found their full support and was given to Fert to be delivered to Gore: "Primakov also believes his visit to the United States to be very important. He is thoroughly prepared for these talks. But after receiving your message, he asks you to deliver the following: Russia's position is very well known in Washington. We are against the use of force in Yugoslavia. This is especially the case since we think that despite all the difficulties of this situation, political measures are far from being exhausted. If the United States still decides to conduct a military strike, Primakov will have no choice but to cancel his visit."

We came to the conclusion that the positions were clearly defined. I am writing in such detail about this matter, as well as about later events connected with the decision to turn the plane around over the Atlantic, largely because of speculations that later appeared in our mass media. They talked profusely about the "impulsiveness" of the decision to turn the plane around three hours before our scheduled landing at the military base near Washington where government planes were usually received.

Others, including some politicians, criticized me for not landing in the United States and immediately going to address the Security Council to expose the military strike against Yugoslavia that was being prepared. The authors of these criticisms apparently forgot that I was flying to Washington, while the Security Council and the rest of the U.N. were located in New York; and that calling and inviting oneself to make a speech before it can't be done on the spur of the moment. I'm not even sure it could be done at all in that situation.

After exchanging views through Fert, we continued purely technical contacts connected with the details of the visit. Events in or around Kosovo were not discussed in any form either through the embassies of the two countries or by phone or fax.

On the morning of March 23 our plane flew from the government airport, Vnukovo II, headed for the United States, with a stop in Shannon. I flew with Governors Eduard Rossel, Konstantin Titov, Vladimir Yakovlev, several ministers, Viktor Gerashchenko, and several prominent businessmen—Vagit Alekperov, Rem Vyakirev, Mikhail Khodorovsky—along with assistants and others. Work on the documents and drafts of my speeches continued in the air.

After the plane landed at Shannon, I was told that our ambassador in Washington, Yury Ushakov, was calling. Referring to a conversation he had just had with Talbott, Ushakov said, "There is a 98 percent chance that negotiations between Holbrooke and Milosevic will collapse and the United States will use military force against Yugoslavia."

I immediately asked the staff to connect me with Al Gore. The conversation took place at 3:00 P.M. Moscow time (7:00 A.M. Washington time). Gore confirmed that "the possibility of military strikes is constantly increasing, since negotiations with Holbrooke in Belgrade are going nowhere."

"When will the United States know for sure about the results of Holbrooke's negotiations?" I asked.

"Within a few hours," Gore replied.

"In view of the importance of our relations with the United States, I've decided to continue our flight to Washington. But if during our flight America decides to strike Yugoslavia, I ask you to let me know immediately. In that case I won't land in the United States."

"We will immediately inform you about the results of Holbrooke's negotiations and whether he'll stay in Belgrade or not," said Gore.

"I'm not interested in Holbrooke's location, I want to know what the U.S. decides about the strikes. That's what I'd like you to tell me about."

"OK. In any event, I want to confirm that we're not interested in impairing relations between the United States and Russia," said Gore.

"We're not interested in that either," I stressed, "but we'll have to issue an explanation of why the chairman of the government, on his way to the United States, didn't land there but turned around and flew back. I would appreciate a phone call to my airplane."

"Thank you for this conversation. I hope you had some Irish whiskey in Shannon."

"I prefer Russian vodka to Irish whiskey," I said.

"Start the engines!" rang the command. The plane took off for Washington. Everyone felt uneasy while we waited for a phone call from Gore. The conversation took place at 9:00 P.M. Moscow time (1:00 P.M. Washington time). I spoke from the plane as we flew over the Atlantic.

GORE: Yevgeny, I'm calling you in connection with our agreement. Richard Holbrooke just flew from Belgrade. Diplomatic efforts produced no results. We're preparing for a strike nonstop. Milosevic continues his advance against the Kosovar Albanians. This can in no way be justified, especially since the violence has been going on for several days. Every day Serbs are killing innocent people, destroying villages, forcing people out of their homes.

We worked tirelessly on preparing for this visit. Of course, we'll be glad to welcome you if you choose to come. But if you decide to postpone your visit, I suggest making the following points in the press release: American-Russian relations are of vital importance, and the visit is delayed but not canceled. In other words, we'll schedule a new date as soon as possible and we regret that a peaceful resolution of the Kosovo issue has not been found so far.

If these suggestions are acceptable to you, then we could agree on a text with your embassy in Washington. When do you expect to deliver this statement? Where are you planning to land, in Gander or on U.S. territory?

PRIMAKOV: First of all, I want to thank you for your candor. We value our relations with the United States. The evidence is the decision I made to keep on flying to Washington after our first phone conversation when I was in Shannon. However, we are categorically against military strikes against Yugoslavia. I think you're making a huge mistake. This concerns not only our relations. This won't yield any positive results at all. We'll still have to search for a political solution to the problems.

Since you're directly telling me that strikes against Yugoslavia are inevitable, I certainly cannot come to Washington. We'll have to talk later. I'm convinced that not all political tools for resolving the conflict have been exhausted. I hope you'll consider again all the consequences of the actions you plan. I believe that after the strikes it would be much more difficult to go back to seeking a political resolution.

I regret that with your actions you're threatening everything we achieved on relations between Russia and NATO. It was very difficult to achieve this. Now ratification of the SALT Two treaty is threatened. I hope that in taking this step you at least analyzed the situation two or three moves ahead.

GORE: Please understand that we are talking about stopping the murder of innocent people. I am extremely sorry that the use of force against Milosevic may affect our relations. Let's talk later, perhaps when everyone's emotions cool down. So what about my suggestion to report that your visit is postponed to a later date?

PRIMAKOV: I'll ask the president for permission to release a statement that says roughly, "After Al Gore told me that military strikes against Yugoslavia are inevitable, I cannot begin my visit and cannot land on the territory of the United States." Let's leave it at that. Good-bye.

GORE: I'm sorry everything turned out this way. I hope to talk to you soon.

After this conversation I asked the whole team that was flying with me—governors, ministers, assistants, businessmen—if, given the circumstances, they approved the decision to turn around over the Atlantic and fly home. Everyone, without exception, said yes. I called the captain of the plane and asked him to change course. We would not have enough fuel to fly directly to Moscow, so we planned a stop in Shannon. The plane turned around. I asked to be connected by phone with Yeltsin. I told him about everything. The president said straightforwardly, "I approve of this decision." After asking whether we had enough fuel for the return flight, he added, "See you soon."

Upon my return to Moscow I immediately met with Yeltsin. He agreed that I should fly to Belgrade with a few representatives of power ministries to try to convince Milosevic to take a more constructive approach in negotiations during the session of the contact group in Paris.

I immediately called Milosevic and told him about the idea of this visit to Belgrade, with the understanding that after our meeting he would state

his willingness to sign a political agreement in Rambouillet. "That would seriously complicate the implementation of the anti-Yugoslav plans," I stressed.
"I must know your opinion in advance, because if this trip produces no results, it will have serious negative consequences. NATO will then declare:
'The Russians failed. Political methods are exhausted.'"

"I am very thankful for the offer of help and for support," replied Milosevic. "But yesterday the Parliament of Serbia totally rejected the agreement."

In that event and with Milosevic in this frame of mind, it would have
been inappropriate to make the trip.

During the night of March 25 Yugoslavia was bombed and hit by NATO
missiles. On the morning of the 25th I contacted Prime Minister Tony Blair
of Great Britain, who immediately said that NATO had no other option after
the failure of negotiations with Milosevic.

"I disagree with you on that score. But I think that even today it's not
too late to correct the mistake that was made. It would be impossible to force
Milosevic to sit at the negotiating table while NATO air strikes continued.
That's not realistic. We need to find a solution to this situation. If the conflict
escalates, it will become harder to resolve the Kosovo problem," I answered.

The substance and the tone of the conversation indicated that Blair, too,
was interested in finding a way out of the situation. He said, "I hope we'll
be able to formulate some kind of initiative in the coming days. Could you
approach Milosevic and exert pressure on him?"

"If you immediately stopped the strikes against Yugoslavia, we could
create a contact group and discuss what to do next. If you drag out the decision
on halting the strikes, it will be more and more difficult to begin looking together for a way out."

"It would be difficult for us to halt the military action in the absence of
any steps forward by Milosevic." This is how the British prime minister summarized the West's position.

In this situation the key problem was to end the strikes. On the evening
of March 27 I was glad to hear by phone from President Chirac, who said
that an hour earlier he "had a lengthy discussion of the situation in Kosovo,
in particular the continuation of strikes against Yugoslavia, with President
Clinton. I think there is only one decision today and it must come from
Moscow. The Americans will continue the strikes, justifying them by the
massacre in Kosovo. If we want to change the situation, we need at least a
small gesture from Milosevic. Otherwise, considering America's position,

the strikes won't end. Only Russia can influence Milosevic to make some kind of gesture, thus changing the situation. Perhaps you should personally go to Belgrade to get something out of Milosevic."

I asked what I should try to convince Milosevic of and whether his agreement to gather a contact group would serve as a "small gesture." Chirac said it would.

I reported to Yeltsin immediately about the phone call from the president of France. We agreed that I would fly to Belgrade on March 30, accompanied by Foreign Minister Ivanov, Defense Minister Igor Sergeev, FIS Director Trubnikov, and Valentin Korabelnikov, head of the Central Intelligence Department of the General Staff. After negotiations with the Yugoslav leadership we planned to fly to Bonn to meet with Gerhard Schröder, chairman of the European Union.

On March 29 I got a call from Massimo D'Alema, chairman of Italy's Council of Ministers. It seemed that on the eve of my trip to Belgrade, the Western countries were coordinating their actions. Most likely knowing about my phone conversation with Chirac, the Americans wanted to find additional channels to let us know that they were taking a tougher position than Chirac. They would not be satisfied simply with Milosevic's agreement to discuss the situation with a contact group. Behind the desire to increase pressure on Milosevic was a determination not to let Russia's political and diplomatic efforts lead the world out of the very dangerous situation created by NATO's bombing of sovereign Yugoslavia without U.N. sanction. Perhaps the U.S. administration feared that if Russia's peacemaking efforts were successful, the U.S. role would be diminished, especially after Holbrooke's failure. Russia's success would be in even sharper contrast to the widening resistance, mainly in Europe, to the strikes against Yugoslavia, which led to the destruction of civilian targets and numerous civilian casualties.[19]

At the same time, Washington and European capitals had to realize that a blunt dismissal of the Russian mission would strengthen anti-Western sentiments and an isolationist tilt in Russia itself, and in the end would facilitate closer relations, possibly military, between Moscow and Belgrade. Quite a few people feared the conflict would escalate to a land operation against Yugoslavia, which would undoubtedly lead to serious losses for NATO as well as Yugoslav forces. They thought that Russia's contacts with Milosevic could prevent such a development.

Taking into consideration these sometimes contradictory sentiments and thoughts, the United States was not content with the role of first fiddle but wanted to conduct the whole NATO orchestra. It worked out a strategy of not standing in the way of Russia's peacemaking efforts, even encouraging them, while at the same time escalating demands on Milosevic as a condition for halting the strikes. And even if Milosevic shifted his position substantially in response to Russia's mission, the United States would consider them insufficient. The correctness of this analysis of the U.S. position became obvious to me as events unfolded.

On March 30 we flew to Belgrade. From the airport we headed to Milosevic's residence, located within the city limits. It was an ordinary house that did not seem to be under guard.

"Shall we have lunch first and then talk?" asked Milosevic.

I preferred to plunge into the discussion immediately. It went on for more than six hours and was not at all easy. I won't give the details of all the twists and turns. The important thing is that in the end we managed to get a "signal":

- Readiness for a political settlement, which could be achieved by negotiations with representatives of national communities in Kosovo.
- Readiness for a constructive approach toward negotiations that should result in providing equal rights for the entire population of Kosovo, regardless of nationality and religious belief.
- Readiness to start Yugoslavian troop withdrawal from Kosovo right after NATO's bombing is called off.
- Readiness to guarantee the return of refugees from Kosovo.

All these points were reflected in Milosevic's statement that the environment of continued strikes was naturally diluted by political and propaganda messages.

On March 31, as we boarded our plane to fly from Belgrade to Bonn, we understood that if the Americans and other NATO members were serious about ending the strikes against Yugoslavia, they would use this signal to at least declare a pause in the bombing and take initial steps toward a political settlement. But immediately after our plane rose from the runway, the Belgrade airport was bombed.

"But they don't even know what we are flying to Bonn with," said my colleagues, in justifiable outrage. "They're already giving an answer to the signal from Belgrade when they don't know what it is."

The fact that the answer to any signal from Yugoslavia (other than capitulation) was predetermined was made clear during our meeting with Schröder, which took place immediately after our arrival. Essentially even without trying to grasp the heart of the Yugoslav position or determine the possible ways it might develop, the federal chancellor rebuffed our points by saying that signals from Belgrade were not enough. After a few attempts I felt the futility of trying to move him from this fixed position. I learned that before talking with us, Schröder had had a telephone conversation with Clinton. I would like to stress that this conversation, which determined the chancellor's position, also took place before the West learned about the shift in Milosevic's position, since he had not yet issued a public statement.

Schröder tried to soften the uncompromising toughness of his position with words about his interest in the continuation of Russia's contacts with Milosevic; the EC should develop relations with Russia, he said, since "it is so important for the whole world. Unlike others, we think Russia must play a special role in the security of the Balkans."

Two years later, when I accompanied President Putin to Bonn as the leader of a Duma faction, I was present at his meeting with Chancellor Helmut Kohl, who called the NATO strikes on Yugoslavia a "colossal historical mistake."

"If I had been Germany's federal chancellor at that time, I would never have let that happen," added Kohl.

After the negotiations with Schröder ended, we headed to the airport and left for Moscow.

Immediately after our return from Bonn on March 31 I exchanged views with Jacques Chirac.

"Dear friend," said the president of France, "here is my opinion. Even if the result was not all we expected, your mission was still very useful. We need to admit that the United States wanted to solve the problem in Kosovo by itself. We think Russia's participation in the settlement is very important. It is necessary for the unity of Europe. As for the Europeans' approach, we would like to see Kosovo as an autonomous district within Yugoslavia. This is a sensible proposal that would mean a return to the situation that existed before 1989. I am also worried that the leaders of the Kosovar Albanians are once again beginning to demand independence. The number of people who support this idea is growing among the region's Albanian population. This is a bad sign. Are you considering a new mission to Belgrade?" asked Chirac.

"If we decide to go to Belgrade again, we would like to know in advance about the true stance of NATO. But we won't go to Yugoslavia to demand that they wave a white flag," I answered.

As usual, the talk with Chirac ended warmly.

The main subject of a talk with Kofi Annan on April 2 was the possibility of visiting Yugoslavia as a mediator in a search for a political settlement. However, back then Annan replied evasively.

The Yugoslav ambassador to Moscow, with whom I met on April 3, was Slobodan Milosevic's brother. I was sure he would report all the nuances of our conversation to Belgrade. I stressed the importance of a meeting between Slobodan Milosevic and the leader of the Kosovar Albanians, Ibrahim Rugova. The continuation of such contacts strengthened Belgrade's position, especially if Milosevic issued a public statement that the question of granting autonomy to Kosovo was discussed.

Knowing that the Yugoslav foreign minister had sent a letter to Kofi Annan sharply criticizing the U.N., I told the ambassador that I would advise the minister to be more restrained. I knew from my meetings with him that he was too blunt. In the current situation, Yugoslavia needed to look for allies at least among the neutral countries.

After reading the statement Milosevic had addressed to me, I asked the ambassador to deliver my thanks for the kind words about Russia's role and in particular about our mission to Belgrade. At the same time, replying to specific points in the message, I said, "Assure the Yugoslavs that we won't step back from our position, especially during our approaching meeting under the Big Eight framework. But also please ask Slobodan not to go too far," I continued. "It would be counterproductive to reject the option of talks altogether and in advance. De Gaulle in his time had talks with the Algerians, and the Israelis and Palestinians have sat at the negotiating table."

I would like to describe in some detail a conversation with Al Gore that took place on April 6, at his initiative. Usually we addressed each other by first name, but this time he addressed me as "Mr. Prime Minister," probably to give an official tone to our conversation and emphasize its importance.

The vice president named "two circumstances that are a cause of great concern to the United States." Gore said, "I would like to hear assurances, in connection with the sending of a Russian intelligence vessel to the Adriatic, that you won't share intelligence information with the Serbs. The second concern has to do with the fact that despite the U.N. embargo on deliveries of military equipment to Yugoslavia, the Russian Defense Ministry and other government institutions are preparing to provide military gear to Yugoslavia. Such deliveries, as well as the transfer of intelligence information, would deal a tremendous blow to Russia's relations with the West."

"Mr. Vice President," I said, "we are also interested in preserving our relations and not worsening them. But this can't be a one-way street. You're saying that we should not increase our support of Yugoslavia, but at the same time you don't say that the United States and NATO should not build up their military operations. You are a politician, Mr. Vice President, and you realize that these two aspects are interconnected.

"The Big Eight foreign ministers will be meeting soon. I think they will discuss what practical steps can be taken to move from a military solution to the conflict in Kosovo to a diplomatic one. Albright talks to Ivanov almost daily. The tension can be relieved if there is no escalation of military action from either side. In that situation, Russia will do everything possible to preserve its relations with the West."

"Thank you for your comments," said Gore. "But first let me reply to your statements. We are doing nothing against Russia. Our actions are aimed at stopping Milosevic's violence toward Kosovar Albanians, to give the Kosovars an opportunity to return to Kosovo and live there safely, with autonomy. Currently the situation in Kosovo is terrible. Ethnic cleansing is going on, people are being kicked out of their homes and forced to leave all their property and make their way to Kosovo's borders through the mountains. Over a million people have already been forcibly removed from their homes. Men are being separated from women and children and are often simply shot. Yevgeny, all this is just terrible!"

"Al [if he was going to use my name, I would use his], you say you're not doing anything against Russia. Recently a missile exploded 500 meters from the Russian embassy. What would have happened if it had hit the embassy? Another missile exploded 300 meters from the Russian school in Belgrade. What would have happened if it had hit the school?

"Now about the numbers. I don't defend ethnic cleansing. I think these acts are terrible and inhumane. But the mass ousting of the Albanians began after NATO began bombing. You said that more than a million people escaped from Kosovo, but Kosovo's entire population is about a million. As for a land operation, I pray that it doesn't start, because both sides will get thousands of coffins. We must now look for solutions. Let's both think how to find them."

"I want to assure you that in sending our helicopters to Albania we're not preparing for land operations," Gore replied. "We didn't change our stance on this matter. The entrance of ground forces is possible only to enforce a political agreement. Now about ethnic cleansing. We have unambiguous testimony that cleansing began long before the bombing. All refugees, and there are hundreds of thousands of them, say ethnic cleansing is not connected to the bombing. They all say the same thing. It's especially striking when little children say it."

"We just sent Russian humanitarian help to both sides, not only to Serbia and Montenegro, but also to Macedonia, where the camps of Albanian refugees are located."

"We appreciate that. Now about the missiles that, as you said, almost hit the Russian embassy and school in Belgrade and your request for me to imagine what would have happened if they had hit them. We take all necessary safety measures, so there is no need to even imagine anything like that. We don't do anything that could be aimed against Russia. But on the other hand, we see signs that someone in Russia would like to damage us. If you give me your personal assurance that Russia is not planning to transfer intelligence information to the Serbs and send military assistance there, I'll be much obliged."

"You are sending weapons to the KLA [Kosovo Liberation Army]. Your communication officers are in KLA detachments. These are facts. No one is asking you to give your personal assurance that the United States will stop supporting the Albanian separatists. Let's do everything we can to shift the conflict toward a political settlement. Then there'll be no need for us to ask each other such sharp questions. I can assure you that neither the president nor I nor anyone else wants to pull Russia into a military conflict. We will do everything to avoid that.

"We would also prefer a political settlement to a military one. Albright and Ivanov reached agreement on many key issues. The only difference concerns bringing in an international security force and also what Belgrade's first step should be. I'm counting on tomorrow's meeting of the contact group to widen the scope of agreements and narrow the existing differences. After that, at the end of the week we'll hold a meeting of political directors, where we should be able to cement the success we've achieved."

"Yevgeny Maksimovich [toward the end Gore finally found a way to address me that was neither too official nor too personal], we don't have any communications officers in KLA detachments and we haven't changed our position regarding bringing land troops to Kosovo. They can be deployed there only within the framework of agreement on a peaceful settlement."

"Assurance that you're not planning a land operation is cause for optimism. I, too, am hoping that this week's negotiations will be successful."

That was how the conversation with Gore ended. Later developments proved my arguments correct. The leaders of NATO confirmed that they had achieved their goals through the air strikes. But those strikes destroyed the civilian infrastructure of Yugoslavia and killed and crippled ordinary people. Did they really achieve their goals? There is no stabilization in Kosovo. The Kosovo Liberation Army is the most destabilizing force, as the West now has to admit. It makes short work of the Serbian population in its efforts to separate Kosovo from Yugoslavia and create a Greater Albania. Serbs who lived in this historically Serb territory, whose intimate relationship with Yugoslavia is not challenged by even those countries that participated in military operations against Belgrade, have been turned into refugees. Under present conditions there is not now and there never will be a mass return to Kosovo of Albanian refugees from Western Europe—the particular hope of Bonn, which took part in the attack on Yugoslavia.

The fact that the presidential elections of 2000 were won by Vojislav Kostunica is also not a result of NATO's strikes against Yugoslavia. Certainly the election results reflected the widespread dissatisfaction of the Yugoslav population. But what were they unhappy about? Not with Milosevic's efforts to preserve the territorial integrity of Yugoslavia or his resistance to attempts to dictate to his country conditions that were unacceptable to it. The results of the presidential elections prove something else: that the Yugoslavs disapproved of the methods the former president used to govern Yugoslavia and the lack of democratic choice in the regime he created.

But will the election of a new president lead to a solution of the Kosovo problem?

Multinational armed forces are stationed in Kosovo. They control the situation with great difficulty. But they won't stay there forever. And then what? Once again Belgrade will have to sit at the negotiating table with the Kosovar communities. But the new president in Belgrade, who needs to assert himself as the leader of the Serbs, has even less room for maneuver than Milosevic had. The only alternative to the political process is war. If the redrawing of maps is put on the agenda, this war will tear all the Balkans apart. So one should not talk about bombing as a means of reaching internal political goals in Yugoslavia.

This is how my Yugoslavian saga ended. I would like to point out that I by no means acted alone. We coordinated the approaches that we developed with representatives of what we call the "power structures." Every day at 9:30 A.M., including Sunday, the foreign minister, the defense minister, the FIS director, the chairman of the General Staff, and the head of the GRU gathered in my office at the White House. We discussed the situation, the initiatives, and the possible actions we might take. Each day we sent specific suggestions to the president.

As I learned later, someone in Yeltsin's circle strongly disapproved of my daily contacts with the power ministries, which to a large extent facilitated the appointment of Chernomyrdin as the president's special representative on the Yugoslav crisis.[20] As for Viktor Stepanovich, he got actively involved in the peacemaking mission and undoubtedly played a very important role in ending the strikes against Yugoslavia. The appointment of Chernomyrdin as special representative shifted the weight of the work to his shoulders. This was about three or four months before I was forced out.

In discussing the eight months of my work as chairman of the government, I have emphasized my conversations and actions for obvious reasons. I hope I won't be suspected of trying to downplay the statements and actions of the president or Chernomyrdin or anyone else.

At the same time, I hope that as chairman of the government I managed to leave some positive legacy for those who successfully continued to act to end the air strikes and then worked to stabilize the situation in Kosovo. Unfortunately, calm had not yet descended on Kosovo at the time this book was written.

CHAPTER TEN

The Family, the President, and I

TRAPS ALONG THE WAY

At what moment did the president's inner circle begin to stalk me? I can't say the Kremlin began scowling at me as soon as I took office as head of the government. But even then I was put on guard by a media report that the new economic team was unable to repair the critical situation facing the country after August 17, 1998. But so far nobody had touched me. Judging by everything that followed, this was what was supposed to happen: Some time later, say in two or three months, the leftist members of the team would be replaced and I, a person "useful for society" (I received wide popular support and they could do nothing about it), would be turned into a "pocket premier"; responsibility for the economy would be taken over by people who would be imposed on my government and whose views I did not share.

About a month after Yeltsin appointed me to head the Cabinet, without warning he called me in for a "strategy session," as he put it.

"I would like to discuss your future as my successor. What we should do in this regard."

Later, recalling some of my conversations with Yeltsin, I wondered whether that strategy session was held to probe my readiness to be a team player, even to the extent of agreeing to remove the leftist ministers from the government and replace them with the customary "liberals."

In any event, during that conversation I took Yeltsin's words seriously.

"I have no presidential ambitions, and in general I don't think I could do a good job as head of the government if I had a presidential campaign in the back of my mind," I replied, "because the success of my current work hangs to a large extent on the opposition of the leaders of some groups in the Federation and to some extent on the pressure to be applied to them. I don't think they all approve of the idea of strengthening the central power, of tough control over the use of funds allocated from the federal budget, of the requirement to abrogate all local decrees and decisions that violate the Constitution of the Russian Federation and its laws, and of stepping up the struggle against antisocial activities, especially in the economic sphere. But if I intended to take part in the presidential elections, I would have to collaborate on these issues or at least refuse to pursue them seriously. I can't do that. It's contrary to what the government is supposed to do."

At that time Yeltsin did not pursue the subject. Later he returned to it from a completely different angle. But more about that later.

That was perhaps the first trap set for me. I evaded it by not only refusing to play by rules other than my own but by announcing publicly that I would retire if my deputies Yury Maslyukov and Gennady Kulik were fired.

I don't know whether that was the main reason that neither Maslyukov nor Kulik was touched until I was forced out myself in May 1999. Possibly at first Yeltsin's inner circle didn't want to complicate relations with the leftist faction of the Duma, which constituted a majority at that time. Later the Kremlin strategists decided that to force my resignation by expelling leftists who had proved to be good professionals was not the best option. That would be more painful and would cause more popular protest than the quiet replacement of a prime minister who had done pretty well at resolving tactical issues but was now making way for someone better qualified to achieve strategic economic goals. That was how the president publicly explained his decision in May 1999.

Thus my leftist deputies remained in the government for the entire eight months I was in office. But their lives were far from comfortable, and not just because their jobs were tough. They were under constant fire by people who wanted to compromise them, starting with rumors that government positions were given for bribes and ending with unfounded accusations of corruption in their work before they joined my government. I didn't dismiss this talk out of hand; I made inquiries in the Ministry of Internal Affairs

(MVD), the FSB, and the prosecutor general's office. I received official replies that those bodies had no evidence to support the accusations.

As for me personally, I have not been a target of such slander either then or since, perhaps because I have never been connected to any financial or commercial organization, have no hidden income, and have meticulously paid all taxes due. All that was common knowledge.

So a different direction of attack was chosen. Because I had never held any managerial positions in business, my "economic incompetence" became a favorite subject of some media. During one such "debate" on Moscow radio, my grandson, a Moscow University graduate whose name is also Yevgeny Primakov, couldn't stand it any longer. Using the anchor's invitation to call the studio with questions, he said that I had graduated from the Economics Department of Moscow State University and held a Ph.D. candidate degree and the degree of Doctor of Economic Sciences. For several years I had headed the Institute of World Economy and International Relations, where Western economics was thoroughly studied with the aim of finding practical applications in the Soviet Union. I had been elected to full membership in the Soviet Academy of Sciences, in its Economics Department.

He stood up openly in my defense, having first introduced himself. I was deeply touched not only by my grandson's behavior but also by the fact that I learned about it not from him but from a newspaper story.

Meanwhile, all my opponents, who were gradually becoming my enemies, went even further. Acknowledging the obvious and undeniable fact that the government had stabilized a political situation that had threatened at some point to turn into street confrontations, they began accusing me and the Cabinet in general of inertia in the economic realm.

A couple of months after my appointment, Yeltsin complained, "You're surrounded by leftists. As members of the government they follow the instructions of the Central Committee of the CPRF."

"You know me pretty well," I replied. "With all my shortcomings, I've never bent either to Gorbachev or to you. As for the leftist members of the government, they're there in their own capacity. You need examples? Here you are. Maslyukov is against the president's impeachment, while the CPRF is for it. The leftist Cabinet members openly propose that the Duma ratify the START II treaty without delay." But Boris Nikolaevich seemed to be most impressed by these words: "In front of me and Chernomyrdin, Maslyukov declined your offer to become the head of the government. If, as you say, Maslyukov was taking orders from the Central Committee, wouldn't he have agreed to head the Cabinet and become number two in the state hierarchy?"

"Am I being so misinformed?" The president raised heavy eyes that reflected both bewilderment and anger.

They not only suspected but were afraid that I would join forces with the CPRF when neither side showed any inclination for me to do so. I had contacts with Gennady Zyuganov and other leaders of the CPRF, with whom we discussed Cabinet activity. For their part, the Communists never informed me about their actions, intentions, plans, or perspectives. Perhaps that was for the best, and I certainly don't criticize them for that. When I or my colleagues asked them to either pass or ease the passage of our bills through the Duma, we knew in advance that our request would be met only if it didn't conflict with their specific party interests. For instance, that was what happened when we asked them to give up their idea of impeaching the president, since that campaign impeded the government's attempts to stabilize the political situation. That was very important and hardened the Kremlin line, and that was extremely unwelcome.

I gave no signs of readiness to yield to some of the Communist leaders' wishes, such as the dismissal of Anatoly Chubais, chairman of the board of RAO EES, and Sergei Generalov, minister of energy. I had different thoughts on that matter. That is why, when I asked Chubais to refrain from holding political meetings of his right-wing supporters in the company offices, I was not acting on someone's instructions but trying to distance the government and its agencies from political struggles. At the same time I did not want to cause trouble for Chubais, a strong manager whose skill the country needed. That opinion is by no means identical to sharing Chubais's ideas and political approaches, or to approving the way privatization was carried out under his leadership.

I was glad that Chubais agreed with me and faithfully kept his word.

As for Generalov, I worked with him in the government and became convinced that he was a capable man with a sense for a complicated situation, aware of the problems facing the ministry, and ready to solve them at a professional level.

The cabinet I headed was centrist or, to be more precise, left-centrist, and that orientation formed the basis for a certain rapprochement with the leftist forces. But it could take place only if the Communist Party stressed the need for the unity of all supporters of state power, the patriots, and at the same time admitted and reflected in its documents that there was no return to the command and administrative model of the social and economic system that existed when the CPSU was in power.

FALSE FEARS

Soon after my appointment I sensed that the president's inner circle wanted to distance me from the Kremlin, so that I had no part in the president's decisions. At the same time, my independence made them nervous. That view was contrary to mine. I am used to being a team player but I have never accepted the role of puppet.

From my first days in office I publicly stated that any and every measure by the Cabinet would be either discussed with Yeltsin or implemented with his approval. In fact, I did the same when I headed the FIS and the Foreign Ministry. But consulting him was not always easy, because for reasons of health the president was sometimes not readily accessible.

At first Yeltsin supported that practice. Then he would call me at night (the calls often came late at night or early in the morning) and say, "Take more responsibility yourself."

I did, while at the same time stressing the role of the president. But soon Yeltsin began to have doubts. Somebody was advising him that I was playing my own game.

I was just as unsuccessful in my attempts to participate in discussions designed to find an optimal solution for the president, who became less and less capable of leading the country by himself as his health deteriorated. In October 1998 I invited Tatiana Dyachenko to the White House. Yeltsin's daughter was more the Family's manager than its ideological or strategic leader, since she had greater access to him than any of his other close advisers and knew when he could sign this or that paper or write down a necessary resolution. We met in my office. I had no prejudice against her whatsoever. I began by saying, "We have a common goal, to do our best to see that Boris Nikolaevich finishes his constitutional term as president. As things stand now, his premature resignation wouldn't be in the interest of stabilizing the situation in Russia. Let's think together how this can be done in the best possible way. We must also think about our tactics. We have to show the country and the world that the president works uninterruptedly and effectively. If you share my concerns and don't question my sincerity, then why have you withdrawn into a closed circle? Besides, I'm not a novice at situational analysis, making forecasts and developing options."

"Come on, Yevgeny Maksimovich. We respect you so much."

That was what the answer to my bewilderment and my proposal that we work together amounted to. That was how the door I was trying to open was firmly shut. There was only one reason—the president's inner circle realized I was not going to play in an orchestra conducted by the oligarchs.

But that was only half the problem. At the same time they were trying to drive a wedge between Yeltsin and me. It seemed that the Family was doing all that not only because we were not blood brothers, so to speak, but also because they were afraid of my meetings with the president, at which he could get true information, which differed in many ways from what he was getting from his inner circle.

At the end of November, when Boris Nikolaevich was in the hospital with pneumonia, I made several attempts to visit him and report about the situation. Each time my visit was postponed. When I finally succeeded, Yeltsin asked irritably, "Why have you avoided meeting with me lately?" The Family's whispering must have had its effect.

"For God's sake, Boris Nikolaevich, I've been asking for a meeting with you for some time now. They kept putting me off, saying it was doctor's orders. They've even said I shouldn't phone you."

"Get Anatoly Kuznetsov in here right away," Yeltsin barked.[1] Kuznetsov had absolutely nothing to do with preparing Yeltsin's schedule, but when he hurried in, Yeltsin said with steel in his voice, "Put Primakov through every time he calls and bring him right in whenever he asks for a meeting."

He ignored my explanation that Kuznetsov was not to blame and that everything was in Tatiana Dyachenko's hands.

"Well, how did it go?" she asked me in the corridor when I left the ward.

"Boris Nikolaevich is displeased that I don't meet with him more often," I replied.

"But he often feels worse after meeting with you. Please try not to upset him," she said.

During the first months of my premiership the president was in the hospital several times with various health problems and he instructed me to take care of many prominent guests and hold talks with them and arrange receptions. All that did not go unnoticed by the public. Much was said when the president of the People's Republic of China, Jiang Zemin, visited Yeltsin in the hospital and stayed for a little over half an hour but spent the rest of his time in Moscow at meetings where I represented the Russian side.

On October 16 the president canceled a trip to Malaysia, where a summit of the states of the Asia-Pacific region was to take place. Russia was to be represented at the summit, the first since Russia was finally admitted to the Asia-Pacific Economic Community (APEC). I went to Malaysia instead of the president. Ten days later the president's trip to Austria was canceled. The head of the government had to go there in his place for a one-day meeting with the EC heads. A bit later a trip to India scheduled for December 6 and 7 was also canceled, and again I went instead. The main brunt of the visits of Schröder, Netanyahu, and others was transferred to my shoulders as well.

The idea of turning some of the president's functions over to the head of the government began to spread. The media carried a news item saying that during his meeting with the editors of major print and TV media the head of the Presidential Administration, Valentin Yumashev, referred to Yeltsin's health and mentioned the possibility of transferring part of the president's authority to the head of the government.[2] I think it was not by accident that Yeltsin unexpectedly returned to the Kremlin on October 20, earlier than the previously announced date of his return from the hospital.

It was also not by accident that the following conversation took place in December.

"Are you ready to confirm that you're not planning to run in the presidential elections?" Yeltsin asked, looking down.

"I've said so many times."

"Well, then say it again in front of the TV cameras."

"Sure, I'll say it again."

A TV crew came in. Boris Nikolaevich and I stood side by side. When I repeated that I was not going to run for president, Yeltsin nodded approvingly, and then said he fully approved of what the government was doing.

It was also not by accident that the president's last words here were not aired. Later Nikolai Bordyuzha, who by that time headed the Presidential Administration, told me he had been told that the president didn't look quite "photogenic" when he was voicing his approval of the government. Bordyuzha requested the tape. Then it disappeared from his desk.

That happened at a time when my relations with the president were deteriorating visibly. In November, when I was making one of my regular reports to Yeltsin, I told him it would help stabilize the country's situation if the Duma passed a law that guaranteed the security of a retired Russian president and spelled out living arrangements for him.

"You can see it would be inappropriate for me to introduce such a bill," said Yeltsin.

"I agree. I can do it myself."

After that conversation, events suggested the need to take a broader look at the problem of political stability than simply providing guarantees to the president after the end of his constitutional term in office.

It was widely speculated that Yeltsin intended to ban the Russian Communist Party, proclaim a state of emergency, and cancel the forthcoming presidential elections. In his memoirs Yeltsin states directly that he was intending to do just that.

On January 22, 1999, I sent letters to the chairmen of both chambers of the Russian Parliament, which said, among other things:

> Today the issue of ensuring the country's political stability during the preelection period has acquired the utmost importance. Without that it is impossible to overcome the consequences of the social and economic crisis, restore and develop the country's economy, and restore people's trust.
>
> In this difficult period for the country I consider it very important to take all measures necessary to strengthen the institutions of the state and to secure the coordinated efforts of the federal institutions of state power. For this purpose I propose to secure agreement on rules of conduct for the president, the Federal Council, and the government of the Russian Federation and to adopt a joint package.

It was envisioned that the joint statement would contain a set of voluntarily assumed responsibilities to be in effect until the new presidential elections, such as the following: The president will not dissolve the Duma and will not exercise his right to replace the government; the government will not initiate a vote of confidence that could lead to the dissolution of the Duma; the Duma will abandon the idea of impeachment (the campaign was gaining strength at the time); constitutional amendments can be introduced only on the basis of consensus. I attached to these letters a draft law on guarantees of immunity to individuals holding the office of president of the Russian Federation.

The Speaker of the State Duma, Gennady Seleznev, immediately distributed the letter to all the deputies. Naturally, it quickly reached Yeltsin's inner circle, and the Family reacted predictably.

But first a word about why I decided to step forward with what I thought, and still think, was a very important initiative. I sincerely believed that it was improper for Yeltsin to be the author of a bill that would stop the impeachment process and guarantee his immunity after the end of his constitutional term in office. I thought that my November conversation with Yeltsin gave me the authority to make such an initiative. But at the same time it gave the president an opportunity to correct the statement, since the letter stressed that upon approval of the suggested approach, it would be agreed to with Yeltsin.

I won't deny I was not overly eager to obtain preliminary approval of the text of the statement, since I knew that any discussion of the subject would have to consider the position of the Family, and that position was quite predictable. I did not attach any significance to the fact that when these letters were sent out, the president was in the Central Clinical Hospital. That was my mistake, and it was actively used against me.

Berezovsky was the first to react. In response to a question by the editor in chief of the newspaper *Kommersant,* he said, "Primakov's proposal is motivated not by a desire to stabilize the political situation but rather by a desire to show his importance. And this is dangerous. . . . In Primakov I see a man who first and foremost wants to become president and only then think about Russia." I interpreted this statement not only as a signal to Yeltsin but as a reflection of the point of view established in the Kremlin. And I proved to be right.

Before the beginning of my usual report, when the TV crew actually began shooting, Yeltsin said to me, frowning sullenly, "What are you up to behind my back?" Meeting my puzzled look, he clarified: "I mean your address to the State Duma."

"Boris Nikolaevich, I would like to talk to you without TV cameras aiming at us."

"All right, leave us alone," the president told the reporters.

"Don't you remember our conversation? We discussed the question of guarantees to the president after his retirement. We didn't mean you personally, but in general, the president of Russia. Naturally, I thought and still think that this question has to be resolved, and not separately, but rather in the context of other issues that together will result in the stabilization of society."

"Still, you should have cleared this initiative with me."

The media immediately quoted a "Kremlin source" to the effect that the conversation between the president and the prime minister was "difficult."

But the news was out, and reactions to the proposal came from all over. As a result, the administration had to come up with an initiative. The deputy head of the administration, Oleg Sysuev, very earnestly and professionally began preparing an alternative draft. I don't think Sysuev's action was welcomed by all of Yeltsin's close advisers. I also don't think (and I am sure of this) that they all liked the fact that the president assigned me to chair the meeting of the Security Council called to prepare the document. That was evidence of the fact that those who were plotting my dismissal could not yet turn the tide in their favor. Or perhaps this combination was meant to show the public that I had "changed my priorities"?

The meeting took place in the building that used to belong to the CPSU Politburo, on the Staraya Ploshchad (Old Square), on February 5, 1999. The alternative draft had certain shortcomings. Mutual obligations were now tied to the Duma election campaign; the presidential elections were not mentioned at all. Not a word was said about abandoning the impeachment effort, which made one think that somebody was intending to use the impeachment campaign as an excuse for a counterattack, accusing the government of "indirect complicity" in the attempt to remove the president. At the same time, the new version of the statement contained a number of useful provisions. Among them were refusal to permit proposals of amendments to the Constitution or calls for a vote of confidence in the government without prior consultations, and measures to be taken to improve the legislation on the State Duma elections to "prevent criminalization of the legislative and executive powers."

We supported the draft of the joint statement. In my closing remarks at the Security Council meeting I said: "Today we should all realize that the price for political ambitions may be the integrity of Russia and its democratic achievements. The citizens of Russia are tired of confrontation. They rightly demand that the government reach compromises and create normal living conditions. We need to extend our hand to all those working to bring people together and resolutely stop any action by those who create social tension or, even more important, violate the country's constitution. As we move toward improving the country's situation it is important to demonstrate firmness, to resolutely disassociate ourselves from populism and political games and focus on intense everyday work."

However, the idea of the joint statement, either mine or the alternative one, was never realized; it came to nothing.

In the meantime, the approval ratings of the government and its head continued to rise. But simultaneously a number of publications and television programs were subjecting the Cabinet to sharp and groundless criticism, rising in intensity with repeated predictions of its imminent replacement.

It reached its high point at a meeting devoted to preparations for the celebration of the third millennium. The president, after looking over all those seated around the massive round table in the Kremlin, made his "historic remark": "We've taken the wrong seats." By that time Sergei Stepashin had been appointed first deputy prime minister, and he was the one who had "taken the wrong seat." Instead of sitting next to the president, he sat a few chairs away from him.

And yet I thought that on the issue of dismissing me from the premiership, the positions of Yeltsin and his Family were not entirely identical. Even today I think they were not in agreement at the time. Could it be that I was mistaken back then, and am I mistaken now?

On March 15 I visited Boris Nikolaevich in the Central Clinical Hospital, and after lecturing me on how to behave with the journalists and advising me to meet with the chief editors and visit various TV channels (in fact I did follow those recommendations), Yeltsin addressed the TV reporters present there: "Some media are saying someone is trying to drive a wedge between me and the prime minister. Nature has not yet created a wedge that could split Yeltsin and Primakov."

Two years later I read a wonderful book titled *Memories,* by Grand Duke Aleksandr Mikhailovich, which had recently been published in Moscow. He recalled Sergei Witte's story about how Witte was dismissed as chairman of the Russian cabinet. "The Tsar is a man of the East, a typical Byzantine," Witte said of Nicholas II after his resignation in 1906. "We spoke for over two hours; he shook my hand; he hugged me. He wished me much happiness. I flew home on wings and the same day I got a decree on my resignation."[3]

Of course I don't compare myself with the brilliant Premier Witte in what I could and had time to do. And President Yeltsin can hardly be suspected of Byzantine refinement. Yet it's a pity I hadn't read the book when some media were poking fun at my imminent resignation while I was being guided or more correctly misguided by the president's public assurances to the contrary.

On April 9, at a meeting with the representatives of the heads of the republics in the Kremlin, Yeltsin once again said, "Don't believe the rumors that I want to dismiss Primakov, dissolve the government, and so on. It's all fantasies and rumors. It's not so and it won't happen."

It seemed that was it. But the president added, "I think at this time, at this stage, Primakov is useful, and then we shall see. But the government should be strengthened and that's a different matter. This question is on the agenda."

That alone could be regarded as an alarm signal. I decided to answer publicly. And not to forestall future developments. On the contrary, I realized that the Family would turn any public reply into a weapon to use against me: See how brave (or insolent) the premier has become, openly challenging the Kremlin? Didn't we tell you he has presidential ambitions? I knew perfectly well that this assessment would probably sink into the president's mind, but still I could not keep silent. Although I had a reputation for restraint, neither my character nor my emotions would permit the president to go unanswered. I disregarded the advice of many people around me.

My statement was recorded in the White House and broadcast by all television channels. I said, among other things:

> I would like to repeat my position, which I have held from
> the very beginning. Let no one distort it. Attempts to run the
> impeachment through the Duma are groundless and counter-
> productive. Such a political game is irresponsible and danger-
> ous. It may rock the society and provoke a very serious political
> crisis. . . .
>
> I also think that calls to dissolve the parties and the State
> Duma itself and to introduce a state of emergency present
> a serious danger. This is an audacious approach that threatens
> to explode the internal situation in the country. In other words,
> it is a road to nowhere.
>
> I regard those petty intrigues around the government and
> the recent campaign against its chairman as unworthy of this
> country and at odds with its interests.
>
> I take this opportunity to say once again, especially to those

who are engaged in these antigovernment intrigues, please calm down. I have no ambitions whatsoever or any desire to run in the presidential elections, and I am not clinging and holding on to the prime minister's chair, especially when a time limit is set for my term in office: today I am useful and we shall see about tomorrow.

I don't know whether what happened next was a reaction to my TV address, but on April 19, before awarding prizes and grants to journalists, the president called upon them not to set him against Primakov. "By provoking a clash between us," he said, "you create uncertainty. People begin to wonder, Who is right, the president or the premier? We treat each other with respect. We ask for each other's advice and meet on a regular basis." And then Yeltsin added: "The prime minister is still not used to criticism. Does the government work perfectly? No. Then why take offense?"

I sensed hesitation in Yeltsin's words and in his tone. Usually in such cases he shot from the hip. Or perhaps the time was still not ripe for that?

Meanwhile the Family continued to put pressure on the president and applied it now against his most sensitive spot. Perhaps for the first time there was a real problem with implementing not just his intention but his order. It turned out that removing Yury Skuratov from the post of prosecutor general was not an easy task. The Family decided to associate this problem with my name.

I had good relations with Skuratov. By coincidence, our two families twice spent summer vacations in Sochi at the same time. I met with him also on business when I was head of the Cabinet. I was upset when the videotape story came out.[4] On the eve of a conversation with Skuratov at the Central Clinical Hospital, Yeltsin called me and invited me to join them. The conversation took place early in the morning on March 18. Vladimir Putin was also present. I spoke in favor of a compromise, which was eventually found. Skuratov wrote a second time to the Federation Council, tendering his resignation. At the same time it was decided that he would continue to fulfill his duties as prosecutor general until the Federation Council met. When Skuratov gave an emotional explanation of his position, the president listened in silence, but it was obvious that he would be satisfied with nothing less than his resignation. In present-day Russia and probably in many other countries, this would prevent the prosecutor general from fully carrying out his duties.

Skuratov and I had a private conversation when we got outside. I tried to explain to him that under the circumstances, and in view of Yeltsin's attitude toward him, the decision that had been made looked optimal. It seemed that Yury Ilich believed me because he realized I had never been in his enemies' camp. I know that many of his friends and colleagues whose opinion Skuratov valued took a similar position.

At that time Aleksandr Voloshin, whom Yeltsin appointed to head the Presidential Administration, came to the fore. At first our working relations were normal. There is a direct telephone line in the prime minister's office that I used often to resolve issues with Voloshin. That is why what happened next and, more important, how it happened came as a surprise to me.

The Family instructed Voloshin to prepare for the second meeting of the Federation Council and to make sure that Skuratov's resignation was accepted. He stepped up to the podium and mumbled something incoherent. I think his speech to a large extent determined the result of the voting: for the second time the Federation Council rejected the resignation of the prosecutor general. That was a serious defeat of Skuratov's opponents, who had assured the president that this time the Federation Council would definitely accept the resignation.

Immediately after the voting, Voloshin gathered representatives of the leading mass media and told them, "Don't quote me directly, just refer to a 'high-ranking representative of the administration,' who told you that it was Primakov who was responsible for the Federation Council's decision on Skuratov. Primakov is playing his own game and cannot be the president's ally."

I am convinced Voloshin wouldn't have dared to step into the line of fire by himself, without the approval of someone like Berezovsky (he was considered to be Berezovsky's man, and not without reason). I also don't rule out the possibility that he wanted to protect himself against charges of responsibility for the failure of the operation in the Federation Council.

I learned the content of Voloshin's briefing not only from the ITAR-TASS transcription but also from a tape recording given to me by one of the journalists who was at the meeting with Voloshin. I was filled with indignation, principally because from the very beginning I had held the same position about Skuratov. I thought well of him, and thought that illegal and unconstitutional measures could not be used against the prosecutor general; but at the same time I told him he should leave his post. I said so at that meeting of the Federation Council.

But that wasn't the only problem. The head of the Presidential Administration struck a swinging blow against the prime minister in the open, in front of journalists. That was a direct challenge.

Soon after that I chaired a meeting of the Security Council. After going through the entire agenda, I asked the council members to stay a bit longer. They included the Speakers of both houses of the Federal Assembly and the ministers of foreign affairs, defense, and internal affairs, among others. Saying that he had to go to a scheduled meeting, Voloshin moved toward the door. I firmly asked him to stay. In front of everyone I asked Voloshin, "What right have you, the head of the Presidential Administration, to make inflammatory statements against me? Don't forget I am still chairman of the government. Who ordered you to rock our society?"

Many supported me, albeit in softer tones.

I decided not to stop there and went to see Yeltsin. After familiarizing himself with the verbatim report of Voloshin's statement to the journalists, he asked me whether the information was reliable. I replied, "You can ask Voloshin himself about it. I have the audio recording." The president resolutely pushed the button and called for Voloshin. When Voloshin came in, Yeltsin didn't even offer him a seat.

"Did you say all that?" asked Yeltsin, showing Voloshin the report I had given him.[5]

Voloshin said he did.

"What are you? You're just a bureaucrat. You're in my shadow. So far you have done nothing. How dare you set me against the chairman of the government?"

Turning to me, Boris Nikolaevich asked, "May I keep this document?"

To Voloshin he said, "I will put this in the safe. This will always hang over your head. Now get out."

When we were alone Yeltsin said, "Are you convinced it's not coming from me?"

The next day I learned that Voloshin had been invited to lunch with the president. And less than a month later I was fired.

REAL FEARS

The real attack against me began and my fate as prime minister was determined when it became clear that I seriously intended to fight against economic crimes and corruption.

The president's inner circle must have known that soon after my appointment as premier, I instructed the heads of various ministries and government organizations, including the law enforcement agencies, to submit personal reports on how they viewed the situation in respect to economic crime and corruption. The answers I received were quite revealing. I received firsthand testimony on the multitude of areas in which economic crime flourished and the depths it had penetrated. The reports demonstrated the writers' unquestionable knowledge of the channels through which corruption was flowing. At the same time the reports and the notes I received left no doubt that Yeltsin lacked the political will to put up a decisive fight against this most dangerous social phenomenon.

Here is an excerpt from the report of the chairman of the State Customs Committee (SCC):

> The SCC of Russia has repeatedly reported to the government about the situation concerning false exports and false transit. Russian and foreign firms conspire in this illegal activity— sellers, buyers, transporters, and intermediaries. They use false documents.
>
> An illegal deal by the joint Russian-British venture Quorum that took place between October 1997 and September 1998 is a typical example. It involved the use of a tax benefit granted for "export of products for processing." The joint venture Quorum signed a deal with two offshore companies, Total International Ltd. (Bermuda) and Quorum Enterprises (Great Britain), to process 3 million tons of fuel oil priced at $300 million at two refineries in France and one refinery in the Netherlands. The finished product was to be returned to the Russian Federation. The SCC licensed the deal. But additional investigation of the tankers' routes by Lloyd Shipping showed they were unloaded in Britain, Sweden, and Gibraltar. Under cover of the customs rule for "export of products for processing," regular commercial operations were conducted, including the import of gasoline purchased abroad, this time also by circumventing customs duties.

An excerpt from the document provided by the head of the Federal Service of Currency and Export Control (CEC):

The activity of companies and banks that are registered offshore boils down to taking currency out of the country and laundering it. Hundreds of millions of dollars are taken out of Russia that way.

In the Republic of Cyprus alone over 2,000 companies and fourteen branches of Russian banks are registered, engaged in getting uncontrolled profits and money laundering. According to data obtained by the CEC, during the financial crisis most of the foreign currency purchased in the internal hard currency market was designated for banks registered in the Baltic republics and the Republic of Nauru. A random analysis of five licensed banks showed that in August they purchased over $227 million for banks registered in the Republic of Nauru.

An excerpt from the report of the director of the Federal Security Service (FSS):

The inadequacy of legislation covering criminal activities, criminalization of the credit and finance system and of foreign economic activities, unlawful use and direct theft of budget funds, growth in the level of corruption, and increased activity of criminal groups contributes to the worsening of damaging developments taking place in the country. Economic crimes are becoming more and more daring and ingenious. Big opportunities are opening up for abuse by both officials of the executive branches of the government and representatives of commercial organizations. Cases of illegal appropriation of stock packages that are part of federal property have become more frequent, as have fraudulent activities by organized groups made up of Russian and foreign citizens. By signing fictitious deals to attract long-term investment under the guarantees of the state shares in enterprises, real estate, land, and natural resources, swindlers receive debt obligations and promissory notes guaranteed by the governments of the republics and the heads of administrations. Subsequently these debt obligations and promissory notes are deposited in foreign banks. They are used to obtain credits, and the money is then appropriated.

Many heads of banks create companies and firms naming

themselves, their relatives, or proxy agents as founders. These organizations are used to receive unaccounted profit by giving them credits at low interest rates that are then transferred abroad, which also allows the bank to evade taxation. Hard currency credits are being granted to nonresident banks. These credits are not returned and payments are constantly postponed.

An excerpt from the report of the prosecutor general of the Russian Federation:

The misuse and theft of budgetary funds result in the illegal enrichment of private individuals at the expense of the state, the proliferation of shadow financial and economic relations, and loss of opportunity for the government to control and manage enterprises that are potentially profitable.

The federal treasury bodies vested with control functions are themselves breaking many rules. Of 620 billion rubles (in 1997 rubles) due to be transferred to the federal budget, only 27.3 billion rubles, or 9.5%, was collected by the federal treasury in 1997. The Central Bank of the Russian Federation receives few requests for the withdrawal of licenses of banks that violate the regulations.

Analysis of the prosecutors' procedures suggests that the shadow economy actively finances corrupt connections between organized crime and state administration officials, whose decisions favor organizations controlled by criminals. According to various sources, criminal and commercial organizations spend between 20% and 50% of their profits to bribe representatives of the state administration.

Prosecutors' offices throughout the country ignore the legislative requirement that persons who hold federal or municipal positions cannot engage in business or parliamentary activity. At the same time, regional legislators, in violation of federal law, routinely grant immunity to members of legislative bodies who continue to be actively engaged in business.

And finally, these excerpts from the notes of the minister of internal affairs summarize many problems of the criminalization of the economy:

The scope of the theft of state resources and property has reached unprecedented heights, bringing the country close to catastrophe.

According to Russian Central Bank estimates, the volume of foreign currency leaving the country amounts to $1.5–2 billion monthly. The main channels for the outflow of illegal capital are:

Transfers for future deliveries, which often never take place.

Transfers of hard currency to the accounts of foreign firms as payment for fictitious services.

Overstatement of the contract prices of imports and understatement of the contract prices of exports.

Smuggling of capital by private individuals. Before the crisis hard currency was often carried abroad in bags by company couriers and shuttle traders. That currency was recorded in customs documents but the origins of these funds were not traced.

Inside Russia the most profitable sectors of the economy were divided among various financial-industrial organizations that were closely linked with criminal groups. All that was taking place, and still is, against a background of escalating corruption of the state apparatus and organs of local administrations. A considerable part of the law enforcement system has been drawn into the corruption orbit.

Thus officials responsible for privatization received bribes for conducting auctions and tenders in a way that would bring victory to the interested bidder. Fixed and working capital is deliberately undervalued. Enterprises arrange to go through bankruptcy and then are privatized at low prices. Characteristically, during the crisis many commercial banks intentionally engineered their own bankruptcy, transferred the capital abroad, and earned large sums by playing on currency fluctuations.

Today the corruption of customs organizations has become quite open. For instance, the rate for fraudulent clearance of a container of household appliances through customs has been set at between $7,000 and $12,000. A considerable number of importers pay it. In view of the volume of imports, the monthly sum that accumulates in the pockets of corrupt officials amounts to tens of millions of U.S. dollars. A similar situation prevails in the delivery of white sugar identified as raw sugar.

The heads of many state and stock companies put the illegally obtained money in foreign bank accounts and use it to purchase real estate, cars, yachts, and so on.

Analysis of criminal cases, company documents, and other materials makes it possible to identify several typical means by which the criminal world amasses illegal profits. Foremost are the activities of natural monopolies: the extraction, processing, transportation, and selling of raw materials on the internal and external markets; and energy, transportation, and communications.

Theft of large deliveries of metals has become normal in the metallurgical and machine building industries. It suffices to say that some Baltic states that have no deposits of nonferrous metals have become their leading world exporters.

The extraction and processing of precious metals and gems have become one of the most attractive spheres for criminal organizations. The illegal mining and transportation of gold to the traditional destinations in the North Caucasus and across Russia's borders have become more frequent. Processing plants are used as channels to legitimize stolen gold.

The misuse of state investment funds and credits intended for developing and restructuring industries and enterprises has become widespread. Inspections of coal mining operations in Kemerovo, Chelyabinsk, and other regions, conducted when unpaid miners attempted to block some main rail lines, established that state funds allocated to these companies had been misappropriated, and the amount stolen often exceeded all the back pay owed to the miners.

Lawbreaking in the consumer market has become endemic— business is conducted without registration and payment of taxes, sales are made through surrogates, consumer goods are imported without payment of customs duties, and the increase in fraud is catastrophic. Illegal production and distribution of alcoholic beverages is especially dangerous. Statistics indicate that the actual volume of vodka and other hard liquor produced is almost twice the volume documented in sales and tax reports.

Russia's Ministry of Internal Affairs has proposed a commission, headed by the chairman of the government, to be responsible for developing and implementing a package of interministerial measures aimed at eliminating the causes and conditions that contribute to the criminalization of the country's economy.

Relevant excerpts from the reports given to me were sent to the ministries and departments responsible for the state of affairs in their respective areas, with instructions to inform the head of the government as soon as possible of the specific measures they were undertaking. We began preparations for a special meeting of the Ministry of Internal Affairs on the fight against economic crime.

We in the government decided not to make these reports public until concrete and tangible measures had been adopted. We were sure that the people whose hands were deep in the state's pockets already knew about my correspondence, but still we needed to give the public an appropriate signal. I did it at a meeting of the government to deal with the amnesty of individuals incarcerated for petty crimes and prisoners who were sick or elderly, a total of 90,000. I said perhaps it was good that as a result the prisons would have some space for those who might fill them under the law on economic crimes. I repeated that in Davos.

What a fuss it caused! Voloshin was the ideologist of the attack against me. In one of his interviews he said that during the transition to a market economy there could be no economic crimes. The initial accumulation of capital was under way, he explained, and then "everything would fall into place."[6]

Boris Berezovsky was more pragmatic. Distorting my statement by substituting "businessmen and entrepreneurs" for my "economic criminals," he maintained: "It was a signal to the system. And the system began to act using old KGB methods. I am sure that the signal was given by Primakov, and it will be he who will pay for it." Then followed falsehoods, juggling of facts, forgery, lies, disinformation, and spreading of various incredible rumors through journalists on Berezovsky's payroll.

I am in no mood to describe all that dirt and have no need to do so. But still I would like to mention one episode that is quite typical.

On December 17, 1998, Minister of Internal Affairs Stepashin came to the White House and put a note on my desk saying that the enormous sums of money that kept flowing illegally to foreign accounts could be returned to Russia only if criminal charges were brought. I responded to Stepashin's note (it mentioned several names, but not Berezovsky's) with the following message: "Please discuss the matter with the prosecutor general. Criminal investigations should be started without delay. The damage to the country is tremendous. How much can be returned?"

I believed then, as I do now, that this was the appropriate answer to the problem rightly raised by the minister of internal affairs.

I returned the note with my reply to Stepashin personally (without registering it in the office). Stepashin responded to my message with one of his own addressed to Vladimir Rushailo, head of the Security Council, and Igor Kozhevnikov, deputy minister of the interior: "Please continue to work with the prosecutor general's office to actively conduct a series of detective operations and investigative measures. Strengthen our position in the credit and financial organizations by ensuring timely exposure of abuse and breaches of law. Discuss with Interpol the possibility of returning the stolen funds. Send progress reports regularly. Next report to Ye. M. Primakov on 01.05.99."[7]

The document got into the hands of the well-informed Berezovsky and he took full advantage of it. There you are, we've caught Primakov red-handed! He has ordered a criminal case to be brought against me, and I'm not the only one. Isn't this an abuse of power by the chairman of the government? Where is the law? Where is justice? One could continue the list of the rhetorical questions of which Boris Abramovich was so fond.

To turn not only the president but also the broad public against me, the so-called Primakov list was devised. Allegedly I ordered law enforcement bodies to collect compromising materials on 150 people and received "appropriate materials." The subservient (and by no means disinterested) *Novye Izvestia* published this list, claiming to have documentary evidence. The list was composed skillfully. Along with those who could easily be suspected of being corrupt, it included the names of people known for their probity and honesty, as if to say, "Look who Primakov is pointing his finger at!"

I decided my only recourse was court action. Of course I won the suit against the slanderers. After making inquiries of the government, the prosecutor general's office, the MVD, and the FSB and becoming convinced of the crude falsehoods in the article published in the newspaper, which of course was unable to provide any documentation, the court fined *Novye Izves-*

tia 200,000 rubles. After considerable effort, the court managed to collect this sum and then I transferred it to Moscow Orphanage no. 5. I admit I was happy. Let the oligarchs' money serve the children.

Thus, by illegally obtaining a confidential MVD document and falsifying its contents, Berezovsky set out to convince everyone that I was after him—an "honest businessman." Without trying to justify myself—I have nothing to make excuses for—I must say that everything I know about the investigations of Fimako, Matebeks, and Aeroflot, with their blackout of documents and arrest warrants, I learned on TV. As head of the government I not only gave no such instructions but could not have given them. With the help of journalists loyal to Berezovsky, however, my "administrative" role in all that became a hot issue.

Everything was done to make people believe that the head of the government was about to take the country back to 1937. In fact, some paid media reports actually said so. Emphasis was put on the fact that in the past I had headed one of the secret services and therefore had also belonged to the KGB. The intention was to prepare the ground for my removal on the one hand and to blackmail me on the other. Blackmailing me happened to be impossible. We in the government kept stepping up measures against economic crimes, and did so in keeping with the law. That was precisely what those who headed the campaign against me feared the most. That was what really scared them.

A meeting at the Interior Ministry on January 15, 1999, added fuel to the fire when the heads of all the law enforcement agencies spoke in favor of resolute actions against corrupt officials and criminals.

WHO'S WHO

I was not familiar with Voloshin, either personally or indirectly, until January 1999, when during one of my regular visits to Yeltsin he began reading aloud some critical comments on the government's economic policy. We were blamed for using an inflation rate of 30 percent rather than 100–120 percent in our 1999 budget. I replied that the 100–120 percent inflation rate would imply total inertia on the part of the government and the Central Bank on monetary and credit policy, while at the same time raising expectations of further inflation and thus accelerating it.

There were assertions that the planned level of tax collection was totally unrealistic. I said the budget was based on actual revenues as of the end of

1998 and on a higher rate of tax collection because of increased turnover in economic activity.

Another criticism was that the draft budget did not include the full amount of funds needed to pay and service the foreign debt. I answered it could not be done; we could not possibly repay the entire $17.5 billion, which amounted to 80 percent of budget revenues.

I will not quote all the critical remarks—there were too many of them, and characteristically, they pursued one idea: the government allegedly opposed some provisions in the president's 1999 budget message to the Federal Assembly of the Russian Federation.

Yeltsin listened to my objections silently and went on reading the next items in the paper without comment.

"Boris Nikolaevich, the author of this criticism either doesn't know the real situation or has something against the government. I don't even want to know his name. Please give me that paper and I'll answer each criticism in writing."

"Yes, please do it in writing," said Yeltsin. "As for the author's name, there's no secret here. It's the deputy head of administration for economic policy, Voloshin."

The slander that reached the president's desk proved once again that someone was trying hard to convince him of the Cabinet's economic incompetence. I asked Mikhail Zadornov to prepare a detailed reply to be sent to Yeltsin. Yeltsin never mentioned the issue again.

Did the entire Presidential Administration get involved in the secret struggle against the government? Until December 7, 1998, the Presidential Administration was headed by Valentin Yumashev. I don't think he could be called an opponent of the government or of me personally. Perhaps he was going with the flow, and probably continued to do so after he lost his position as head of administration and became an adviser to the president. But immediately after my ouster I received a letter from Yumashev: "Thank you very much for your courage, patience, and understanding. You have managed to do something that no one, neither the parties nor the movements nor the president nor the Duma, was able to achieve—to calm the people and put hope in their hearts. I would like to confirm something you must have sensed yourself. As head of administration I tried to do my best to help you and drilled all my staff, the entire administration, so that we worked as a team."

He had tried. But did he succeed? That is the question.

Yumashev was replaced as head of the Presidential Administration by Nikolai Bordyuzha, an honest and decent man. His behavior toward me was impeccable. On December 24, while conducting his first meeting with regional representatives of the president in his new capacity, Bordyuzha said that "a rise in positive expectations in the population following the formation of the new government is to a large extent associated with Primakov, a pragmatist and a man of his word." This statement must have alarmed certain individuals around Yeltsin. After all, when Bordyuzha was appointed, the mass media reported that he was picked for the position as a "strong personality," allegedly to oppose me.

Possibly the Family had failed to pay sufficient attention to the fact that before Bordyuzha was transferred to the Kremlin, we had enjoyed friendly relations. It is also possible that they underestimated Bordyuzha's consistently strong character. Or perhaps his appointment was initiated by Yeltsin, who treated him well at that time and who in his active periods, when he was his old vigorous self, could sometimes push through decisions despite the Family's opposition. But unfortunately, those periods could be measured only in hours and the decisions were few. The ratio kept growing in favor of a group of individuals in his inner circle. In the end it resulted in Bordyuzha's dismissal only a few months after Yumashev's resignation.

After Bordyuzha learned that I was writing a book about my eight-month stint in the government, he gave me the notes he had taken of his last telephone conversation with the president, after Yeltsin had decided to make Voloshin head of administration, with permission to use them. Yeltsin had been at his Rus residence and Bordyuzha in the Central Clinical Hospital. Bordyuzha retained his position as secretary of the Security Council of Russia. This telephone conversation, which took place at three o'clock on March 19, 1999, says a lot.

YELTSIN: Hello, Nikolai Nikolaevich. How are you? I have decided to separate the positions of secretary of the Security Council and head of Presidential Administration, since I believe I made a mistake when I combined them. I'm thinking of appointing Voloshin to head my administration, and you will keep your position as secretary of the Security Council. What do you think about that?

BORDYUZHA: Thank you, Boris Nikolaevich, for your proposal, but I have to decline. If you don't mind, let me tell you why.

First, this decision isn't yours, it was forced on you by your daughter, Dyachenko, who followed the recommendations of a group of individuals. The reason is not that combining the two positions was a mistake, but that I initiated the removal of Berezovsky from the position of executive secretary of the CIS and refused to take part in the campaign to discredit Primakov and his government. This campaign was organized by Dyachenko, Abramovich, Yumashev, Voloshin, and Mamut, with Berezovsky's blessing.[8]

Second, to keep on working in the Kremlin would be to implement the decisions forced on you by Dyachenko, Yumashev, Abramovich, Berezovsky, and Voloshin, even though many of these decisions go against the state's interests. I want no part of that.

Third, I was a general in the war, I was in many hot spots, I risked my life and was away from my family for long periods. I've always been confident that I've served the interests of Russia and the Russian president. After working in the Kremlin I've come to realize that it's not the president but a small group of dishonest characters that are ruling the country on his behalf, and they're acting not in the state's interests but in their own. I can't and won't be a part of that company.

YELTSIN: But if I order you to do so, will you comply?

BORDYUZHA: I will, but I ask you not to give that order.

YELTSIN: I'd like you to work near me, you've been doing very well. I hadn't expected them to gain so much power. I'll fire them all! All right! I'm canceling my decision! You stay as head of my administration and we'll work together. What do you say to that?

BORDYUZHA: Boris Nikolaevich, I am ready, but I have one condition. Your daughter, Dyachenko, Yumashev, and Voloshin must leave the Kremlin today, and Abramovich, Mamut, and Berezovsky must be denied access to it. In that case I'll continue to work.

YELTSIN: All right, I'll think about it. We'll meet and talk everything over.

At eight o'clock that evening the president signed a decree dismissing Nikolai Bordyuzha from his positions as head of the Presidential Administration and secretary of the Security Council.

There were two Yeltsins. There was one Yeltsin before the 1996 elections, especially before he was disheartened by the need for runoff elections when he had firmly believed that he was in full control of the situation. He began to change when a group appeared on the scene, rather mixed but united by their determination to ensure Yeltsin's victory in the presidential elections.

But that was not their only purpose. They also aimed to separate the president from his close associates, such as Aleksandr Korzhakov, who had been with him in various capacities since 1985 and was now chief of his security service; Mikhail Barsukov, head of the Counterintelligence Service; and Oleg Soskovets, deputy prime minister for industry. Those three were doing their utmost to consolidate Yeltsin's undivided authority and at the same time to protect their own interests. They concealed his periodic failures and tried to safeguard him from obvious blunders. Informally they addressed him as "Tsar Boris," but they never aspired to the throne themselves.

The new presidential advisers differed from the old ones in quality. Striving not to allow the election of any leader outside their control, the new advisers were betting on Yeltsin to use the persons they designated to rule the country for their own continuous enrichment and, most important, with no danger to themselves. Yeltsin's illness helped them achieve that goal. He changed completely after his heart surgery. Being dependent on medications and unable to work more than a few hours a day, and not every day at that, he simply could not physically resist the pressure applied by his new inner circle. The Family took full advantage of his disability.

But on those occasions when Yeltsin could work, he often turned into the old Yeltsin, as seen in his telephone conversation with Bordyuzha and in the conversation with me when he complained that I was "surrounded by leftists." But once the active phase was over, the Family's rule began. And the Family hoped to maintain this situation, if not by circumventing the Constitution, then at least for the duration of Yeltsin's constitutional term in office.

Boris Nikolaevich Yeltsin is undoubtedly an interesting personality. In the first half of the 1990s he was unquestionably a strong, self-assured leader with keen intuition. If he did not know something, he learned it through experience and practice. It suffices to follow his progress in the international arena—from a poorly prepared man with little understanding of international affairs to a leader whose friendship or at least personal contact was sought by many experienced and world-famous politicians. And that was not simply a tribute to Russia, one of the main players in the international arena, nor was it the halo effect enjoyed by the leader of such a large country. The thing was in Yeltsin himself, who would often grab hold of the main issue and demonstrate a constructive approach, despite his seeming toughness.

Certainly he made mistakes and blunders, many of which were caused by his abuse of alcohol, but to me this great and tragic figure has entered History.

Boris Berezovsky was my most active opponent and he does not deny it. The nature and methods of the activities that led to his quick and fantastic enrichment are not the subject of this book, and there is no need to retell a story that has been published many times. But the fact remains: Berezovsky is probably the most outstanding figure among those who got very rich very quickly during Russia's transition to a market economy. At the same time he can be distinguished by the ambition to go so far as to rule the country. In pursuit of this goal (which differentiates him from, say, the media magnate Vladimir Gusinsky), Berezovsky has laid his hands on many mass media.

The oligarchs' mission to rule the nation, which he openly proclaimed, was one side of his ideology, closely connected to the other—his truly special attitude toward business. In this regard, an interview with Boris Berezovsky published in *Vedomosti* (March 24, 2000) is of interest. Among other things, he said:

"The key element of power that I have had and still have is mass media. Private property is another important element of power, but its nature is different."

When he was asked about the monopolization of the aluminum industry, he said, "I think monopolization is very good for Russia today."

"If it's a clean deal, why do it through offshore companies?" asked the reporter.

"It's just a mechanism to evade taxes and resolve other purely financial matters because of defects in the law," answered Berezovsky. "You don't need to be an altruist. Business does not presume altruism."

I won't even comment on these words.

In one of his interviews Berezovsky said that he and I could have ideal relations. But after I came to the government, he discerned in me a man with a KGB mentality. I don't think we could have ideal relations regardless of my way of thinking. Berezovsky's behavior has become a determining factor in those relations.

When I served as foreign minister he visited Smolenskaya Square several times and came to see me. At first these were "theoretical" conversations, during which Berezovsky confidently (he was nothing if not confident) discussed subjects he knew little or nothing about.

But those "theoretical" disagreements were followed by a collision. Before going to Georgia, Berezovsky asked me to brief him on the relations between Georgia and Abkhazia. I replied that that was a very delicate matter and that he ought not to bring it up during his visit (back then Berezovsky was not the secretary of the Executive Committee of the CIS, and that issue was beyond his responsibilities). When he learned that we had a draft of a document we wanted to offer to both sides in the conflict, Berezovsky asked me to let him read it and swore he would not quote from it. After skimming the first page, he turned to me with another request: he wanted me to give him a copy of the document, and he promised he would never show it to anyone or mention it anywhere. He said he needed it only to be adequately prepared for his talks in Tbilisi.

Imagine my surprise when Berezovsky began to shuttle between Tbilisi and Sukumi with this draft, naturally taking care of his own business. On his return to Moscow, he called me and asked for a meeting. My reply was rather brusque. Not at all embarrassed, he replied, "It was you who gave me that paper and allowed me to use it. I don't recall any restrictions."

From bad to worse. I have already mentioned lies, distortion of facts, and slander. Shall I respond to that dirt? Many people around me urged me to do that. I rejected advice to sue him over an interview in the French newspaper *Figaro,* in which Berezovsky stated that he had documents signed by Primakov containing instructions and direct orders to investigators on how they should proceed against him. I was 100 percent sure I would win the case, because of course Berezovsky did not and could not have such documents, since they did not exist.

Furthermore, when Berezovsky was appointed executive secretary of the CIS, I even helped him prepare a plan to restructure the executive secretariat. On November 27, 1998, all of us—Boris Pastukhov, minister of CIS Affairs; Berezovsky; his deputy, Ivan Korochenia; and I—sat in my office reading and amending documents for a forthcoming meeting of the Council of the Heads of CIS States. Incidentally, although I did not support Berezovsky's appointment to that post, I had nothing to do with his dismissal, and he knows it. It resulted from Yeltsin's conflict with some members of the Family. I don't think Yeltsin ever did have a high opinion of him.

Berezovsky is a gifted man. But how has he used his gift? Mainly in shady deals and unscrupulous methods employed to present himself openly as an éminence grise, the person who made all the decisions in Russia. In a number of cases such demonstrated omnipotence became possible because Berezovsky skillfully exploited the flaws in our society and its members, especially the officials. It also affected some journalists. How many of them received the gift of his "valuable" friendship, valuable literally and otherwise?

Berezovsky left Russia in 2000. He chose to emigrate rather than go to prison when criminal charges were brought against him.

The mass media campaign against me escalated after I was dismissed as prime minister and reached its peak during the election campaign for the State Duma. But even when I headed the Cabinet, Berezovsky's minion Sergei Dorenko regularly featured anti-Primakov stories in his television program on Channel 1, which was controlled by his boss.

The journal *Expert* published an interview with Gleb Pavlovsky, a well-known PR man and head of the Fund for Policy Effectiveness, in its issue of January 17, 2000. I was intrigued by the parts of the interview that dealt with my work as prime minister and the opportunities he said I wasted.

> Of course, Primakov was not supposed to be a successor, but rather a fireman. But he had to be taken care of because he had formed a perfectly correct view of the situation and was therefore dangerous.
>
> *What has he done?*
>
> He provided an idea. He became an alternative to the power behind the throne. And that was exactly what the masses are looking for. And the story of Yeltsin and that of [Aleksandr] Lebed prove that the masses will not accept a power behind the throne who is outside the court. They are looking for an alternative within the court itself. And that is precisely what Primakov provided. It was as if he built a system for the transfer of authority— the charisma of authority left Yeltsin and entered Primakov. He was gaining general popular support, showing his potential. And he demonstrated this support to the elites, yet showed he was not dangerous. But at the same time he made several mistakes, precisely at the level of elite politics.
>
> *Could he be more successful as a politician?*
>
> Yes, if he hadn't made a mistake with regard to a number of Yeltsin's elites who engineered Yeltsin's resignation and were looking for a successor. Primakov might have offered them a

solution, but instead he sacrificed them, probably thinking they were isolated. However, by rejecting them, Primakov enabled his opponents among Yeltsin's elites to rally against him. It's important, though, that he left behind a certain model.

There is no doubt that Pavlovsky is a clever man, but did he seriously believe that I could have made a deal with the Family or any of "Yeltsin's elites" in order to guarantee my political future? That was entirely out of the question. That was why I was attacked so relentlessly.

THE LAST DOT OVER THE *i*

On May 12, 1999, I went to the president's office at the appointed time to make my regular report. As usual, we greeted each other warmly. He asked me to take my usual seat at the large table used for meetings. As usual, he sat at the end of the table next to me.

I was a bit alarmed, but only a bit, when he irritably asked the press secretary, "Why are there no journalists?" When the representatives of TV channels and agencies accredited to the Kremlin entered the room, Yeltsin asked them, "Why aren't you asking questions about the government?" To the questions that followed he replied, "Yes, there will be changes." And then, looking at me, he added, "And significant ones."

The thought flashed through my mind: He's decided to fire my deputies as a way of forcing me to resign. But events developed according to a different scenario. As soon as the journalists left, the president said, "You've fulfilled your mission and now it seems you need to resign. Make this task easier by writing a request to resign, citing any reason."

"No, I won't do that. I don't want to make it any easier for anyone. You have the constitutional authority to sign an appropriate decree. But I'd like to tell you, Boris Nikolaevich, that you're making a big mistake. I don't mean myself, I'm talking about the Cabinet, which is working well. The country is out of the crisis caused by the decisions of August 17, the lowest point of economic decline has passed, and growth has begun. We're close to an agreement with the International Monetary Fund. People trust the government and its policies. To replace the Cabinet without a reason is a mistake."

After another request to submit my resignation and my repeated refusal, the president summoned Voloshin, who brought in a decree that of course had been prepared in advance.

"Do you have any transport?" Boris Nikolaevich asked suddenly.

What an unexpected question! I said it was no problem, I could take a taxi.

Yeltsin appeared to feel upset by what was going on. He looked uneasy. Wincing, he put his hand on the left side of his chest. Doctors entered the room immediately. I wanted to get up and leave but he signaled me to stay. After medication Yeltsin felt much better. He got up and said, "Let's stay friends," and hugged me.

I left Yeltsin's office and in the reception area I saw Vladimir Shevchenko and the secretaries, who already knew what had happened and seemed to be upset by it. My own emotions were mixed. On the one hand, I certainly felt offended; on the other, there was that marvelous feeling of freedom, or to be more exact, of liberation. I called home and told my wife, who reacted joyfully.

The same day the president spoke on television, using a prepared text that said I had done my duty by bringing the people together and achieving stability under difficult circumstances. But those were tactical issues, he said; the strategic task was to achieve an economic breakthrough, and for that a new leader was required. "I am confident," Yeltsin concluded, "that the new premier will be able to give the Cabinet the needed energy and dynamics." Sergei Vladimirovich Stepashin became the new chairman of the government. Two months later he suffered the same fate: Stepashin, too, was unexpectedly replaced.

I went to the White House and said good-bye to my colleagues at the government conference hall. I was very touched when they stood to welcome me and applauded when I left. I was very brief. I said that we had done our best and had nothing to be ashamed of. I thanked all the ministers and department heads, with many of whom I do maintain friendly relations.

In the evening I went to a soccer game. Some people thought that was a deliberate move to show everybody I was in high spirits. I just wanted to see my favorite team, that's all.

Thus ended my eight months of leading the government.

Do I regret that I allowed myself to be persuaded to take the office of prime minister in September 1998? I not only had to live through quite a few difficult days in office but also endure many shots in the back. But looking back, I must say no, I don't regret it, primarily because I am confident that those eight months were beneficial to the country and to the people.

I think they showed the limits of the pseudoliberal practices that drew the country into the abyss of permanent crisis. I am sure that even though Russia may face some pitfalls in the future, nobody will again be able to drive our economy onto a course so ruinous for Russia. And I do believe in something else. The economic course adopted by the government, the ideas promulgated in the area of state power construction, the actions initiated against economic crime and corruption will undoubtedly be continued. Even if not in every direction, even if sometimes inconsistently, on the whole they will continue.

I am profoundly and sincerely grateful to the thousands of people who wrote letters and sent telegrams from all corners of Russia and from abroad expressing their support and kind feelings toward me and the government.

My foes' expectations that I would be forgotten as soon as I left office were disappointed. Despite that assessment, which to a large extent was responsible for my dismissal, my reputation continued to grow. That was a great surprise to the Family. I have heard that after a little shock, some of its "technical experts" proposed to enhance my reputation so that later they could bring it crashing down. But that was when I headed the list of the Fatherland–All Russia movement during the elections for the State Duma.

Do I regret that my term as head of the Cabinet was artificially limited to eight months? Of course, we hadn't done as much as we wanted for lack of time. But I did not leave politics and I hope to continue to serve Russia to the best of my abilities.

Do I hold a grudge against Yeltsin and the Family? On the eve of the Independence Day celebration on July 12, 1999, exactly a month after I left office, one of the people close to Yeltsin probed my feelings about being awarded the country's highest honor. I replied I would not accept it. I felt hurt, but not angry.

Other methods of neutralizing me before the Duma elections were explored as well. In November I received an invitation from President Yeltsin, whom I had not seen since the day he asked me to resign and who had not called me once, even after I had successful surgery on my hip and was no longer in pain. I declined the invitation. It was not because of Boris Nikolaevich, for whom I felt no hostility. But the way I was invited, through a low-ranking official from the presidential protocol secretariat, made me think some negative PR scheme against me might be afoot. After declining the invitation, I declared to media representatives that I was not going to have anything to do with the president's inner circle because I knew how they really felt about me.

Since I left office I have never spoken in a derogatory tone about the president. I sent Yeltsin a warm cable on his birthday, February 1, 2000. Madeleine Albright happened to be in Moscow that day. While I was with her I got a note from Vladimir Shevchenko that said: "Boris Nikolaevich would like to see you today if you agree. Please call before seven P.M." There was still some time before seven. I tried to call the number he gave me, but without success. Nobody could find Shevchenko. At first my assistant's questions were answered evasively and vaguely, and then nobody would take the call. I few days later I ran into Shevchenko. I could see he felt uneasy when he caught sight of me. The Family must have interfered again.

When I left the post of prime minister, I did not make up my mind immediately to continue an active political life. My doubts left me only after the surgery, when I realized that my health would not be an impediment. Unfortunately, our country has known too many leaders and prominent political figures who have lacked the ability to assess their own powers. Buoyed up by the flattery being sung to them, they overlooked their physical limitations and sometimes even the resultant mental shortcomings. The population and the state paid for that.

Physical limitations are not the only ones. Perhaps it is the nature of human beings who have been subjected to unwarranted shocks to stay aloof from important events taking place around them without any input from them. If people think gold is worth dying for, let them die, and the devil take the hindmost. A whip can't stand up to an ax, they say. Fortunately, I am not one of those who lose heart in such situations and withdraw into their own little world.

I was thankful for an offer to return to the academic environment, but chose not to do so. Neither was I attracted by numerous offers to serve as consultant to various commercial organizations. I also rejected an offer to go abroad as a diplomat and declined invitations to join and even to head a number of parties. As I told Mayor Yury Luzhkov, the only option I could entertain was an opportunity to participate in the State Duma elections as a leader of a centrist or left-centrist movement uniting several organizations.

Soon such a movement was formed. It consisted of Fatherland, led by Mayor Luzhkov; All Russia, headed by Mintimer Shaimiev (president of Tatarstan), Vladimir Yakovlev (governor of St. Petersburg), and Ruslan Aushev (president of Ingushetia); the Agrarian Party, headed by Mikhail Lapshin and Gennady Kulik; and trade union and women's organizations.

I won't describe the unprecedented slander and dirt thrown at Luzhkov and me by the same individuals who faced us across the barricade during my work in the government; the only comparison is the propaganda spewed by Joseph Goebbels. The Presidential Administration, which directed the whole campaign, treated us as their principal opponents. There was no limit to their audacity. It reached its peak in a TV broadcast of a surgical operation performed in one of the Moscow hospitals; according to the report, it was similar to the one I had had to go through "more than once." Blood filled the TV screen to the accompaniment of the soft baritone of the anchor, Sergei Dorenko. Fixing his eyes on the TelePrompTer, he ad-libbed the suggestion that I was a masochist and was seeking the presidency because it would enable me to stay in the hospital as long as I wanted.

The increasing popularity of Fatherland–All Russia (Otechestvo–Vsya Rossiya, or OVR) and its leaders—clearly demonstrated not only by the ratings but also by our reception at numerous meetings with the electorate throughout Russia—was making our enemies very nervous. It was these fears that prompted the Presidential Administration, under the guidance of a small group of businessmen, to form a controlled political movement called Unity (Yedinstvo) a few months before the election and, by applying the pressure that only the Kremlin can apply, to gain at least the second place in the State Duma, after the CPRF. The Presidential Administration sent direct orders to the governors to do their best to see that Unity won.

Of course not all of them fell in line, but some governors who had been praising OVR and predicting its overwhelming triumph now looked aside when they met with our movement's representatives or spread their arms as if to say: Please understand, we depend on money from the Center. Others said nothing at all, but we could see they didn't want to quarrel with the law enforcement organs. They say that fraud was committed. For their part, some businessmen made enormous financial contributions to the hastily formed organization.

The strategy worked. OVR was pulled down to third place. The boys in the Kremlin were rubbing their hands. Berezovsky kept repeating that it was he who had thought up those brilliant ideas, and in the heat of discussion with the new president, Putin, he admitted that he had financed Unity's triumph. This claim to copyright had no consequences.

My work at the head of the Duma faction in those turbulent times convinced me that OVR was serving the interests of Russia.

I HAVE TRIED to throw light on those processes, events, and people that have been out of focus for foreign politicians and political scientists study-ing Russia. When the lens is out of focus, even a close-up view lacks the sharpness of detail necessary for a complete picture. More important, forecasts are flawed. In a word, Russia has been scrutinized but not fully comprehended.

Lack of full knowledge is a direct road to distortion in politics. And the future development of all major events in the international arena depends to a large extent on the course the United States steers toward Russia. U.S. foreign policy cannot simply be an extension of what has gone before, not only because the situation has changed but also because earlier administra-tions did not always understand Russian events, particularly in the 1990s, and as a result did not always find an optimal course.

After September 11, 2001, Vladimir Putin demonstrated his resolve to support the United States' efforts against terrorism. Despite the United States' unilateral decision to withdraw from the ABM treaty, which many U.S. citizens and others throughout the world consider a grave mistake, Putin found it possible to reach agreement with George W. Bush on reduction of strategic offensive weapons, despite a lack of enthusiasm for it at home. That agreement should not be regarded as a retreat from his position. Putin once again showed himself to be a realist, but I don't think we could have reached an agreement with the United States during President Bush's visit to Moscow in May 2002 if the American side hadn't abandoned its refusal to mention the agreement in a binding treaty.

Our bilateral relations have been tested by the war in Iraq. The problem is not that Russia supported Saddam Hussein's regime and defended it. Russia was one of the first to insist that Iraq should comply with all the disarmament resolutions of the U.N. Security Council. It resolutely demanded that Iraq do everything in its power to facilitate the work of the U.N.'s inspectors. Moscow was against the war because the United States, together with Great Britain, prepared and carried out military actions without the sanction of the Security Council and in disregard of the opinion of the overwhelming majority of member countries. It dealt a crushing blow to the world order that had supported relative stability after World War II and threatened to undermine the role of the United Nations. Should the U.N. be modernized or adapted to new conditions? Of course it should. But any revision of its operations should be carried out collectively rather than by the unilateral action of a single member and without throwing out the baby with the bath water, without introducing new rules that would permit any member country to decide for itself whether and when to take military action.

Russia opposed the war in Iraq also because peaceful means of resolving disarmament issues in that country were available, and because at the time U.S. forces struck Iraq, there was no evidence that it possessed weapons of mass destruction.

But in speaking out against the United States' use of force without U.N. approval, Russia has not taken an anti-American stance. Moreover, during Putin's contacts with the leaders of France and Germany he did his best to discourage anti-American sentiments in those countries as well. Moscow is well aware that no effort against the proliferation of nuclear and other weapons of mass destruction or against international terrorism can be effective except in cooperation with the United States. It is these two evils that are the most serous threats to the world community today. President Putin's message to President Bush was that the matters that unite us far outweigh those that divide us.

President Putin appreciates the priority of Russian-American relations for world stability. That recognition should not be construed as a retreat from an understanding that a multipolar world is the best option for Russia, as well as for many other countries, including the United States. But that world is possible only when coalition ties between various centers can reliably predict a lack of confrontation, and when Russia's own policy ensures its equidistant positioning with respect to all the other world poles. The multipolar pattern envisages an enhanced role for the United Nations and its Security Council—the only body that has the authority to sanction the use of force by one country against another.

The features of the twenty-first century are still indistinct. What will it be like?

Profound changes took place not only in Russia but throughout the world in the 1990s. There are no longer two systems of states confronting each other on ideological principles. There is no real threat of a global military conflict now. World wars, in which states formed coalitions to fight one another, are past history.

At the same time, the absence of the prospect of world wars is not identical to international security. It is only the nature and the scope of threats that have changed. The danger of international terrorism is growing. As the events of September 11 showed, terrorism has emerged in the most dangerous form of a self-sustaining autonomous network. The threat posed by the proliferation of weapons of mass destruction is exacerbated by the possibility that they may be acquired by terrorist organizations such as al-Qaeda. International conflicts have shed their political and ideological coloring but acquired strong ethnic and religious foundations. Efforts to resolve them are impeded by the fact that in most cases they spread far beyond the borders of the country where they develop, as in the case of Islamic extremism.

What structure of the future world order will be affected by all that? Paradoxical as it may seem, there are no superpowers in the world today. The Soviet Union no longer exists; the United States, the most powerful nation economically, financially, technologically, and militarily, has also ceased to be a superpower. "Superpower" is a Cold War category. Its distinguishing feature cannot be limited to superiority in the economic, military, or any other realm. In addition it must function to ensure the security of a number of countries, especially when they are confronted by a real and *common* threat. Naturally, the superpower assumes the role of group leader, dictates its will, and issues orders. Such was the Soviet Union. Such was also the United States. Now conditions have changed, and nobody can ignore those changes.

Two scenarios can be outlined for the first decade of the twenty-first century.

The first scenario: Supporters of the unilateral approach prevail in the

United States. Fundamental decisions are made without consultation with the U.N. and with disregard for the positions of the majority of nations and the opinion of the major part of the world population. Even now that Europe is more independent than before and many of the United States' Cold War allies disagree with its position, the United States launches its forces not only against terrorists but also against disobedient regimes and "disadvantageous" situations. The U.N. becomes only one international organization among many. Russia finds itself with no voice in the resolution of world problems. Inevitably its internal and foreign policies become tougher as it looks for partners in its efforts to break out of isolation and protect its interests. It finds those partners in China and India. The result is a new post–Cold War confrontation. It is not necessarily a global conflict, but its effects are felt throughout the world.

The second scenario: The movement toward a new world order is clearly defined. Its distinguishing characteristic is development of areas of mutual interest, such as struggle against international terrorism, settlement of regional conflicts, and development of measures to prevent the proliferation of weapons of mass destruction and to protect the global environment.

The unfolding of these processes eventually results in the establishment of regional power centers. These developments affect the structure of international relations, among them the globalization process, which is characterized by vigorous technical and technological progress, interdependence in the financial sphere, and the predominance of multinational forms of production. Globalization in this form helps to bring the world together. The differences in rates of economic development, obvious in the twentieth century, gain strength and affect interstate regional integration. These differences between demographic groups stimulate the movement of population groups from one country to another and even from one continent to another. These developments unfold without wars or armed conflicts. The main players in the international arena work out a common position that permits the world situation to stabilize.

In this scenario the integration of not only Russia but also China into the world economy proceeds smoothly, without artificial delays imposed by either inside or outside forces. China, Great Britain, and France join the U.S.-Russian process of strategic arms reduction. The U.N. gets its second wind. When necessary, force is used in the international arena after a resolution by the U.N. Security Council. Peacekeeping forces from many countries are organized. The indivisibility of the world permits a realistic beginning to be made toward resolving the problems of its poorest segment.

Despite the spread of anti-Islamic sentiments brought to life by September 11 and intensified by the war in Iraq, the world community will not allow a new division of the world between two civilizations, the Christian and the Muslim. The idea that one civilization incorporates all the highest human values while the other denies any value to human life is highly dangerous. All those who intend to carry on the struggle against terrorism are eager to have Muslims actively join this effort, as some Eastern countries are doing. There is no one East, just as there is no one West.

The barbaric terrorist strikes against New York and Washington on September 11 undermined the idea, widespread at the time, that the United States could ensure world stability and security without coordinating its efforts with other countries. But a full appreciation of this fact cannot come immediately. Time is needed to digest all that has happened, to analyze and understand it.

I hope that the Russian factor will play an important part in the historic choice between the scenarios of the development of international relations.

Madeleine Albright once told me that the doctoral thesis she defended several decades ago was devoted to lost opportunities in the development of Soviet-American relations. Of course, it is important to recognize the opportunities one has lost. But it is even more important not to have any lost opportunities to remember.

CHAPTER 1. FROM YELTSIN TO PUTIN

1. "Family," the popular term for Yeltsin's inner circle, was used in the sense associated with the Mafia, as a criminal conspiracy.

2. In Russia an "oligarch" is a wealthy person who goes into politics and maneuvers his way into the ruling elite in order to create conditions for enormous personal enrichment at society's expense, either by criminal means or by exploiting loopholes in Russia's legal system. Ownership of mass media and their use to manipulate public opinion is one of the hallmarks of the oligarchy.

CHAPTER 2. LOOKING BACK

1. Reserved for the Party elite.

2. According to Lord Moran, Winston Churchill's personal physician, his patient told him privately in 1946: "'We should not wait until Russia is ready. I presume it will take them eight years to develop these bombs. America knows that 52 percent of Russia's machine building is located in Moscow and can be destroyed with one bomb. It would probably cost three million human lives, but they couldn't care less, those Americans.' Churchill smiled. 'They will care more about possible damage to some historical buildings like the Kremlin'" (Baron Charles McMoran Wilson, *Churchill: The Struggle for Survival, 1940–1965* [London and Boston, 1966]).

3. The first Pugwash conference was held at the estate of the industrialist and philanthropist Cyrus Eaton in Pugwash, Nova Scotia, in 1957, at the urging of Albert Einstein, Frédéric Joliot-Curie, Bertrand Russell, and other scientists and intellectuals.

4. An embassy room specially equipped to prevent eavesdropping.

CHAPTER 3. THE WAR THAT MIGHT NOT HAVE BEEN

1. Michael R. Beschloss and Strobe Talbott, *At the Highest Levels: The Inside Story of the End of the Cold War* (Boston: Little, Brown, 1993).

CHAPTER 5. IN THE INTELLIGENCE SERVICE

1. Perhaps one of the most colorful figures among "applicants" was A. I. Kulak, a colonel-engineer and an officer in the First Main Directorate (PGU). He was not just a World War II veteran but a Hero of the Soviet Union, a title bestowed on him during the war. While he was on a business trip to the United States in 1962 he offered to cooperate with the FBI. There was no trace of dissatisfaction with the Soviet system in Kulak's treachery, as the Americans were well aware. It was his status in the system that displeased him; it seemed to him he deserved a much higher position than deputy chief of a PGU department. His dissatisfaction was constantly fueled by unrestrained use of alcohol.

   It was only after Kulak retired that an intelligence source informed us of his treachery. Judging by the Center's reaction (according to Kulak's dossier in the archives), at first it did not believe the report. Then came a completely independent signal corroborating it. When Kulak died in 1984, "Fyodora's" treachery was an established fact. Nevertheless, he was buried with military honors for fear of exposing our sources. He was stripped of his state decorations posthumously.

2. One of the names on that list was Cecil Desmond Hughes. He attracted our special attention because throughout his term of service in British intelligence he specialized on Soviet and later Russian citizens. After Hughes quit the intelligence service (this may be only a legend) the Russian side found it possible to issue him a visa for entry to Russia, which he used on many occasions. That decision was taken in the hope that the USSR's helpfulness would be reciprocated, but it never was.

3. After his arrest, Ames was made briefly available to journalists. At one such meeting in jail he said he wanted to give an interview to Kolesnichenko. The request was published and Thomas applied to the U.S. embassy in Moscow for an entry visa, but was denied. As minister of foreign affairs I visited the United States in 1996. As was customary, I invited a group of journalists, including the representative of ITAR-TASS, Kolesnichenko, to accompany me. He said that "not to complicate matters" he would not interview Ames and would only cover my visit. Nevertheless, the U.S. visa that had been issued to Kolesnichenko was canceled on the eve of our departure, so he could not fly with us. Our ambassador to the United States, Yuly M. Vorontsov, told me that the Russian diplomats who were meeting us at the airport were informed that no one would be permitted to leave my plane until it was ascertained that Kolesnichenko was not aboard. Only a firm statement by our side that in that case the visit of the Russian minister would be canceled disrupted this unprecedented operation.

   The same day I told Madeleine Albright what had happened, confirming that Kolesnichenko had no intention of approaching anybody in any way about an interview with Ames. I added that I could guarantee that Kolesnichenko had never worked for special services. Two days later, during our negotiations, Madeleine gave me a note saying that a visa would be issued to my friend so that he could come to the United States to cover my visit. Although he did not feel well (perhaps because of the stress) and only two days remained till the end of our visit, Kolesnichenko did come over for a day, out of principle.

4. Yasenevo is the Moscow suburb where the Russian Intelligence Service is located.

CHAPTER 6. IN THE MINISTRY OF FOREIGN AFFAIRS

1. Court hearings held in 1996 found no grounds for putting Wolf behind bars. His rights were restored, including the right to travel abroad.
2. *International Affairs*, November–December 1997, pp. 16–17.
3. *New York Times*, January 15, 1996, p. A17.
4. The OSCE summit in Lisbon, December 1996.
5. The familiar Russian word "troika" is often used in the West to designate any three-member governing body. In Russia "troika" is associated with the three-member NKVD tribunals set up outside the judicial system in the 1930s and 1940s, which sentenced hundreds of thousands of innocent people to death.
6. Presidents Vladimir Putin and George W. Bush signed a strategic arms reduction treaty in Moscow on May 24, 2002. As a result of difficult preliminary work, a formula acceptable to both parties was found. Yet I believe a better outcome could have been had if Russia and the United States had extended to the new situation the agreements reached in Helsinki in 1998 and signed in New York City, because they blocked the militarization of outer space while at the same time protecting the ABM treaty. Unfortunately, those protocols were not ratified by the U.S. Congress, so the new Bush administration was able to ignore them.

CHAPTER 7. FORCE OR OTHER METHODS

1. We had met earlier in Kuala Lumpur, at a meeting of the heads of states and governments of the Asia-Pacific Economic Cooperation (APEC). After long and painful diplomatic efforts, Russia was inducted into that organization. Both Gore and I were substituting for our presidents. Gore made a good impression on me then.
2. At first the U.S. State Department considered the Kosovo Liberation Army (KLA) a terrorist organization.
3. When Milosevic was elected president of Yugoslavia, he transferred all power to that new post. Milutinovic replaced him as president of Serbia.

CHAPTER 8. MIDDLE EAST SETTLEMENT

1. I. P. Beliaev and E. M. Primakov, *Egipet: Vremia prezidenta Nasera* [Egypt in the time of President Nasser] (Moscow, 1974).
2. With the exception of Sharansky, Begin was the only one who spoke Russian.

He spent about two years in exile in the north of our country and later wrote a book about it. He was freed and served in the Polish army of General Wladislaw Anders during World War II.

3. Henry Kissinger, *Years of Upheaval* (Boston: Little, Brown, 1982), 460.

4. At that time I was head of the Foreign Intelligence Service. We were made aware of what was going on by our own sources, but not by the Palestinians, who did not inform us about their secret negotiations. Some of my colleagues became indignant. But I tried to calm them down, stressing that the important thing was the end result. And it was undoubtedly positive, since for the first time Israel and the PLO were engaging in direct dialogue at a high level and on such vital issues as the withdrawal of Israeli troops.

5. In this same plain-looking building in Kolpachny Pereulok I had lunch with Zbigniew Brzezinski. On another occasion I met there with my old friend Peter Jennings, the ABC news anchor, who at that time was going through a divorce from charming Kathy, a gifted journalist and writer who later married Richard Holbrooke. Truly, the world is small. As for Senator Smith, who was gathering information about American POWs in the Vietnam War, I received him at another place, in Yasenevo. This tall and friendly man was very surprised to be invited to the Russian Langley. "Am I the first American to visit this house?" he asked. "The first one who is not an agent," I clarified.

6. Once when I gave an interview to the Russian newspaper *Argumenty i facty* I was asked, "How can you explain why Boris Berezovsky, who is not a majority stockholder in the ORT TV station, has unlimited control over it?" I answered with a true story: "I have a three-year-old granddaughter. Once my wife asked her, 'Why is your nose running?' She spread her little hands and said, 'That's life!'" Those words headed the interview.

CHAPTER 9. CHAIRMAN OF THE GOVERNMENT

1. Before the collapse of the USSR Maslyukov served as first deputy chairman of the Soviet of Ministers. In 1995 he was elected to the State Duma as a member of a faction of the Communist Party of the Russian Federation.

2. On August 17, 1999, the ruble was devalued. When the government imposed restrictions on foreign exchange operations, the ruble went into free fall and a large part of Russia's fledgling banking sector was destroyed.

3. When I worked in the government, I discovered that privatization continued to be viewed as a means to pour revenue into the state budget. In fact, between 1992 and 1998 the budget received only about 1 percent of GDP from the massive and "global" privatization. The rest was appropriated by a small group of individuals.

4. Georgii Soros, "Berezovskii, Putin i Zapad," *Moskovskye Novosti*, August 22, 2000, no. 7, 15.

5. Chechnya separated from this "autonomous" republic within the USSR.

6. Salambek Hadzhiev was head of the government established by the Temporary Council of Chechnya.

7. According to these agreements, a decision on the status of Chechnya was delayed for five years. An article about the preservation of Russia's territorial integrity was removed; an article about the right of self-determination remained.

8. Khasbulatov, then chairman of the Federation Council of the Russian Federation, opposed the president's decree stripping the Parliament of its power and refused to obey it. He was among those who stayed in the White House before it was captured by forces loyal to the president on October 4, 1993. He was amnestied the same year.

9. The Russian mass media published a transcription of a telephone conversation between Berezovsky and Udugov, which proves a financial connection between them. The conversation took place after the Chechens invaded Dagestan. Udugov berated Berezovsky for not keeping his promise about planes, which according to him should not have been used against the Chechens. I have not heard of any denials from Berezovsky or charges of falsehood. In his book *Open Society: Reforming Global Capitalism* (New York, 2000), George Soros writes: "During the flight from Sochi to Moscow, Berezovsky bragged about how he bribed the field commanders in Chechnya and Abkhazia. That is why, when Shamil Basaev invaded Dagestan, this story seemed suspicious to me." In an interview published in *Komsomolskaya Pravda* on March 16, 1999, Maskhadov made the following comment while talking about the kidnapping of General Gennady Shpigun in Chechnya: "Everything that is happening in Moscow, all these trips by Berezovsky with suitcases filled with money, all this flirting with criminals, bandits, and my political opponents, will not be beneficial. I don't accuse Basaev or anyone else personally for the kidnapping of Shpigun. It's all tied together."

10. In Russia the so-called power structures are directly subordinate to the president.

11. After I left the government I had a meeting with Stephen Sestanovich, the special adviser to the U.S. secretary of state for the newly independent states, who was accompanied by Ambassador James Collins. Sestanovich admitted that between the agreement to let our troops through in the evening and the refusal to do so in the morning, Shevardnadze asked for his advice. According to Sestanovich, Shevardnadze told him that Russia was planning to shut down the border by stationing troops on Georgian territory. But from what I know, that was not Russia's intention; Russia was requesting permission to move our troops from their bases in Georgia to Chechnya—in other words, to the Russian Federation. It is possible that Shevardnadze feared resistance from the Kistin Chechens, who were in the majority in the Akhmeta district of Georgia. But was it better for Georgia when the Pankisi gorge was infiltrated by militants from Chechnya and Tbilisi actually lost control over that part of Georgian territory?

12. The export duty on gas was not abolished, the gas industry continued to be taxed, and export duties on oil were not rejected. Those duties naturally depended on fluctuations in world prices.

13. That meeting took place at the request of Camdessus, who said he was

extremely impressed by it. I took part in the discussion and I, too, was impressed when I saw how intelligently and purposefully but never presumptuously the patriarch tried to explain to the IMF director the need to understand the Russian reality. This was something new: the state and the church were acting together and on the same wavelength.

14. European currency units.

15. *Tribuna*, no. 83, May 11, 2000.

16. Talbott was probably referring to the election campaign, during which the Republicans skillfully used the Russia theme to proclaim the failure of the Clinton-Gore policy.

17. Special Drawing Rights, a conventional unit used by international financial institutions.

18. At this time a meeting of the contact group was winding up in Paris. We explained to Belgrade that it would be expedient to sign the political agreement drawn up in Rambouillet. Earlier I had worked hard to make it acceptable to Belgrade.

19. The *Frankfurter Rundshau*, March 31, 1999, reported the following polling data: 49 percent of Germans rejected military operations as a means to achieve humanitarian goals, with 41 percent justifying the use of force "against an authoritarian regime with the aim of preventing genocide." Characteristically, 55 percent of East Germans were against NATO strikes against Yugoslavia. In general, 58 percent of German respondents expressed the fear that air strikes against Yugoslavia could lead to a new Cold War.

20. After his appointment Chernomyrdin offered to attend the daily meetings that I held, but I told him he ought to call meetings with the power ministers himself. Unfortunately, those meetings ended, although they were undoubtedly very useful.

CHAPTER 10. THE FAMILY, THE PRESIDENT, AND I

1. Major General A. L. Kuznetsov was Yeltsin's aide-de-camp. Ordinarily Kuznetsov was constantly at his side.

2. Discussions at such meetings are off the record, but a lot of information usually leaks out.

3. Grand Duke Aleksandr Mikhailovich, *Memories* (Moscow, 1999), 174.

4. The state television channel broadcast a tape of pornographic material that featured either Skuratov or an individual who looked very much like him.

5. This was the only written "compromising material" that the prime minister gave the president. The ghost writers of Yeltsin's memoirs went out of their way to describe how I sat with my "old Soviet" black folder on my knees, picking out anonymous documents that I had received from the Secret Service. They must have forgotten that the heads of the Secret Service agencies reported to the president directly, not through me.

6. The same thesis was still being preached later on, albeit in modified form. "Under the existing conditions, everyone was breaking the law," said Berezovsky.

7. Quoted from a photocopied document passed to me by an indignant Berezovsky; also published in *Novye Izvestia,* October 15, 1999.

8. Roman Abramovich is a young oligarch who made a fortune in oil and aluminum. Aleksandr Mamut, with stakes in several banks, was said to be the Family's treasurer.

INDEX